BRITISH
MORALISTS

BRITISH MORALISTS

being selections from writers principally of the eighteenth century

edited with an introduction and analytical index by

L. A. Selby-Bigge, M. A.

in two volumes

volume I

Dover Publications, Inc., New York

This Dover edition, first published in 1965, is an unabridged and unaltered republication of the work first published by the Clarendon Press, Oxford, in 1897.

Library of Congress Catalog Card Number: 64-18370

Manufactured in the United States of America

Dover Publications, Inc.
180 Varick Street
New York, N. Y. 10014

PREFACE

———◦———

A BOOK of selections is never quite satisfactory, and
suggests apology on several grounds. Even if it is
wanted, its execution may easily be found fault with.
When all is irrevocably in print, one feels how much
better it might have been done—how niggardly one
has been to one author, how stupidly indulgent to
another, how badly proportioned is the whole, and how
awkwardly arranged. In the present case it may be
pleaded that no particular principle has been violated,
for I soon came to the conclusion that to adopt one
or even two principles only as the basis of such a
selection was impossible, and would not be very profitable. I abandoned myself therefore to the guidance of
the principle of utility in its vaguest form, and simply
tried to make a book which would be useful, and fairly
representative of the British moral philosophy of the
eighteenth century. In making it the limits of space

have been more troublesome than those of time. At the outset I found it necessary to exclude the deistical and free will controversies (with an exception in favour of Locke), though an interesting volume might be made out of those alone. I have had also to exclude many interesting and important passages in authors admitted to the selection, and it certainly would not be fair to pronounce judgement on the authors without regard to what has been left out. In some cases diffuseness, the bane of an easy style, was the disqualification; in others they did not bear closely enough upon the questions principally discussed in my period, though they had plenty of interest in themselves. In the first volume are printed in large type the three principal texts of the sentimental school—Shaftesbury, Hutcheson, and Butler, followed by Adam Smith and Bentham. In the Appendix, in smaller type, are given additional extracts from Hutcheson's other writings. In the second volume are printed at length S. Clarke, Balguy, and Price, with extracts from Cudworth and Wollaston, and additional extracts from Balguy in the Appendix, as representatives of the intellectual school. In the Appendix to this volume appear also extracts from the 'theological utilitarians,' Brown, J. Clarke, and Paley. Kames and Gay are included as more or less independent critics. Of Mandeville I have only given a specimen. Hobbes and Locke have really no business in the book except for convenience of reference. Cudworth belongs to the period because his ethical work was not published till 1731.

In the second volume I print a bibliographical note, from which those who take pleasure in making lists of 'the best books' may easily compile a rival selection. The Index is on the same plan as the Indices to the Clarendon Press edition of Hume's *Treatise* and *Inquiries*, to which edition reference is always made in the Introduction. The Introduction only pretends to be what it is called.

L. A. S.-B.

CONTENTS OF VOL. I

—◆◆—

INTRODUCTION.

§§

SHAFTESBURY.—Inquiry concerning Virtue or Merit . . . 1–67

HUTCHESON.—Inquiry concerning the original of our Ideas of
              Virtue or Moral Good 68–187

BUTLER.—Sermons 188–243
          Dissertation II.—Of the Nature of Virtue . . . 244–250

ADAM SMITH.—Theory of the Moral Sentiments . . . 251–357

BENTHAM.—Introduction to the Principles of Morals and Legis-
              lation 358–430

APPENDIX.

HUTCHESON.—Essay on the Nature and Conduct of the Passions 431–446
          Illustrations upon the Moral Sense . . . 447–470
          System of Moral Philosophy 471–481

INTRODUCTION

1. *Satire and moral philosophy.*

THE moralist and the satirist are not always suited to understand each other. The moralist seems to the satirist to discourse of a state of things which is not and never was, and to assume the prevalence of motives which never entirely determine and do not considerably influence the actions of ordinary men. When the moralist says that men ought to regulate their conduct on certain principles and ought to cultivate certain motives in preference to others, the satirist tests the possibility of these principles, by asking whether in fact men do usually or ever act on them: he does not ask how far men recognize them as ideals or standards of conduct. It is enough for the satirist that men do not practise what they preach, and the significance of the preaching itself does not concern him. Satire stops short of philosophy, even of sceptical philosophy.

On the other hand, the moralist is apt to regard the satirist less as scourging the unworthy than as denying the existence of worth altogether and dissolving morality into nothing at all, or replacing it by something which is positively immoral. In reality, the whole force of satire, as distinguished from cynicism, is the force of contrast—between profession and practice, between reality and sham ; and the denunciation of the sham is by implication the recognition of the reality. The temper of the satirist is very different from that of the sceptic and generally distinguishable from that of the cynic. He is content to show that what men flatter themselves is moral conduct, is generally immoral conduct when judged by the standard which those men profess. He does not discuss the origin or meaning of that standard itself, the recognition of which is implied in his exposure of the counterfeit. ' Nos vertus ne sont le plus souvent que des vices déguisés,' and ' private vices public benefits ' are phrases which, on the face of them, testify to the possible or ideal existence of morality, and the assertion of general immorality, offensive and inconvenient as it may be to the moralist in some respects, is not half so dangerous to his position as the reduction of the moral to the non-moral, which is the way of the sceptic.

2. *The ' selfish' theories of satire and scepticism.*

Much of the moral philosophy of the eighteenth century, even when it is hedonistic, may be regarded as a revolt against the selfish theory. It is therefore of some importance to distinguish between the selfish theory of the satirist, which claims to be nothing more than the product of an empirical study of human nature and social institutions as they exist at the present time, and the selfish theory of the sceptical philosopher, which rests upon an analysis of the primitive constituents of human nature and society, or a theory of the ultimate nature of desire or volition. It is indeed not always easy to distinguish the satirist from the cynic, or the cynic from the sceptic. The satirist sometimes drops the whip and throws mud, or allows his contempt for the actual to blind him to the ideal from which he started, and so degenerates into the cynic who is absorbed in a gloomy disgust of things as they are, missing both the serenity of the negative sceptic and the intellectual interest of the scientific sceptic, who finds it pleasant to note the sequence of appearances and register the shadows on the wall of his cave. Philosophers also sometimes take an unphilosophic pleasure in emphasizing the mean beginnings of things, and the respectable man, intolerant of the libels on human nature which are the common result of very different principles, classes all the libellers together, and so makes an ineffective reply.

Against the satirist and the cynic, whether of the court, the coffee house, or the tavern, it is legitimate to appeal to the plain man's experience of disinterested benevolent affections, which to him feel quite different from the products of calculating selfishness and are distinguished from such in his judgements of others. It is also very legitimate to urge that a fair interpretation of social institutions reveals elements in human nature which are not, proximately at all events, derivable from the individual's desire of private pleasure. It is further proper to point out that such an assertion as that moral virtue is 'the political offspring which flattery begot upon pride' may be true of some men and some virtue, but if asserted of all men and all virtue becomes literally preposterous; and, lastly, it is more profitable to take with the satirist than with the sceptic the 'short way' of pointing out that in his very denial he asserts or assumes what he denies.

But against the selfish theory of the empirical sceptic it is vain to allege a counter-experience of unselfishness. For on the one hand the sceptic does not deny the universality of the illusion of unselfishness or cavil at the genuineness of the plain man's testimony to his own feelings; he does not pretend that a superficial reflection on human nature is sufficient to expose its secret springs; but, on the other hand, he professes to trace the illusion itself to its origin in the operation of forces which are entirely selfish.

3. *The satiric criticism of morals.*

It is hard therefore to be fair to the 'benevolent' theory which figures so largely in this period unless we appreciate the irritation and alarm caused to sober moralists by the cynicism of Hobbes and the satire of Rochefoucauld, Mandeville, and the tribe of dull imitators, such as James Esprit, and Sir Richard Blackmore. It must be remembered that the first half of the eighteenth century was a period when the authority of the Church was weak, when the wantonness of the Restoration had given place to a dull lewdness in high places; when the materializing influences of prosperity and wealth were strong, and spiritual ideals were smothered under respectability. In such an age, and from a practical point of view, the satirist and his wit, especially when it takes the form of paradox, are sometimes more dangerous to morality than the sceptic and his malice. The respectable person finds that when his cloak of smug pretence is stripped off he is no more naked than the statesman or divine, and sees no reason why he should be better clothed than such good company, while the disreputable person takes credit to himself for his superior frankness. The moralist therefore who takes more than a speculative interest in good conduct, may well be excused if he does not penetrate the disguise which conceals from him the blessings of a Mandeville.

Mandeville is certainly not an innocent writer, but he has been considerably misunderstood both by his contemporaries and by modern critics. His business is the exposure of humbug and hypocrisy, and he does his work consistently and thoroughly, though he dips his pen in a very nasty mixture and carefully poses as a very disreputable person. His taste is as abominable as his style is effective. The essentially satirical character of his work is however concealed by his constant indulgence in paradox, a method which enables him to give a maximum of offence, while keeping in the background a few unexceptionable principles to which he can appeal in case of need. It does not need much penetration to see that when he is maintaining the odious thesis of 'private vices public benefits,' he is really concerned to argue the converse, viz. that persons lauded as public benefactors often show small regard for the Christian code of morals which they profess, and no regard at all for the public interest for the promotion of which they take credit ; that material progress by no means implies equivalent spiritual advance. So the panegyric of prodigality is a vehicle for an assault upon the complacent cant which sees in the accumulation of private wealth the height of social virtue. But these are perpetual topics of the pulpit, and we may apply to this case a remark made long ago, and say that it is a mark of ἀπαιδευσία to require speculative validity and completeness as well as practical value in such exercises as sermons or satires. From the practical point of view it may have been desirable that William Law should undertake a serious refutation of Mande‐ ville's paradoxes, but in truth if any one takes them seriously and literally nothing but a stick will do him much good [1].

[1] See *The True Meaning of the Fable of the Bees*, Lond. 1726, 8vo, and *Essays towards a Critical Method*, by J. M. Robertson, Lond. 1889.

Regarding Mandeville as a satirist, I see no reason to suppose, as some have supposed, that his introduction of ' self-sacrifice' as the touchstone of merit was meant by him as a backhanded attack upon ascetic and theological ethics. It is so essential to his theory and is introduced with such aptitude that I do not think he meant or indeed could afford to play a double game with it. The private character of the satirist may lead us to suppose that his real regard for the principle was small, but it is no argument of theoretical insincerity in its use. His treatment of luxury does not stand on this footing but is evidently ironical, and finds a close parallel in the second book of Plato's Republic.

4. *Mandeville's political theory of virtue.*

The name of Mandeville is particularly associated with the ' political' theory of the virtues, as originating in the ' artifice of politicians,' which represents Hobbism in its most artificial and least important form. It has however its place in the scheme of his satire proper. For many of us morals are little else than ' manners,' and, whatever their meaning for the race, for the individual they are only too often conventional and artificial, and the satirist is quite within his right in letting us know it. But as a general theory of virtue it is only an impertinence, though it has been treated by minor moralists as the most important and dangerous part of his work. Hume's few words of dismissal are quite effectual (*Treatise*, pp. 500, 578), and it is certainly not worth while setting up against it a theory of ' eternal fitnesses,' which can in no way be represented as the necessary alternative to the political theory. If a more detailed refutation be thought necessary, William Law has taken the right way with it, when he points out that you may as well ascribe man's erect position to the cunning flattery of politicians as his virtue;

the action of the politician being limited in both cases to emphasizing pre-existent tendencies, and coming in as a modifying influence only at a very late stage. It is also worth considering whether much which is attributed to the operation of flattery on pride is not implied in their very existence. The fallacy of the preposterous has a wide range, but nowhere can a better instance of it be found than in the artificial theory of society.

5. *General character of British moral philosophy.*

I have dwelt at some length on the position of the satirist in morals because it is connected essentially as well as accidentally with what I believe to be the chief characteristic of the British school of moralists. I have already said that satire so far as it is an exposure of the sham rests upon and assumes a reality of some kind or other in virtue. The British moralists, whether sceptical or otherwise, ask, what is this reality? what is the meaning of the right and wrong, good and evil, to which the evil-liver pays the tribute of hypocrisy, that is, what does the ordinary man mean by them? The level of the plain man, and even the 'honest farmer,' is in the first instance adopted, not that of the saint in his cell nor that of the philosopher in his closet, and his experience is treated as supplying the material for further examination. Just as the satirist appeals to the intelligence of the plain man and is refuted by an appeal to his experience, so the moralists of this period start from the plain man and the common sense of plain men (afterwards to be elevated into the principle of a system) in their inquiry into the reality of virtue. They concentrate their attention on the phenomena of the normal moral consciousness in a cool and impartial manner which reminds us of Aristotle, and had not notably been exhibited since Aristotle. It is generally said that British ethics are psychological, and though that epithet is to be avoided on account of the controversies with which it is associated, it may fairly be said that the chief achievements of the eighteenth-century moralists were in the psychology of ethics. They thought seriously about the content (assuming that 'content' is a possible object of psychology) of plain men's moral judgements and their natural and legitimate implications, and there is perhaps no body of ethical writing which within its own sphere can compare for originality and sincerity with the work of this period. It was a work in which any one could take a hand, and though there is much in it which is trivial, tedious, and commonplace, there is singularly little which is merely technical or formal. There is always an effort, even on the part of the intellectualists, to bring a formula to the test of a concrete and homely instance[1], and a determination to write so as to be understood by anybody. Philosophy is no longer ' a self-centred speculation, an oracle of wisdom': it is ' brought down from inaccessible heights, and compelled to be intelligible,' and the public is umpire[2]. The ease with which many of their fallacies are detected, and the simplicity of the confusions on which they rest, may tempt a casual reader to despise their intelligence. Experience of philosophy teaches, however, that it is the simplest confusions of thought which are the least suspected and which remain the longest undetected; that the expression of philosophic formulae in plain words is one of the most difficult things in the world, though never impossible, and that one of the most splendid qualities of

[1] Such as the boundaries of the Kingdom of Bohemia, or the incident of the keyhole in *Tristram Shandy*.

[2] M. Pattison, *Essays*, ii. 69, 73.

the philosopher is to write so as to be easily found out if he is wrong. It is not a small thing that philosophy should be written in the vulgar tongue and should use the words of ordinary men.

6. *The unmetaphysical character of the period.*

That the moral philosophy of the eighteenth century should be somewhat narrow in scope is the natural consequence of its starting-point, the common moral consciousness, and its method. It is essentially inductive ; it collects the facts and then looks for a theory to explain them, and the collection of the facts is the chief thing. It has therefore little inclination to exhibit the theory of ethics as part of a general system of philosophy or as an appendix to a theory of knowledge. Even the question on which it came most nearly into contact with the theory of knowledge, the question whether moral perceptions originate in sense or in reason, was commonly treated with reference to little beyond its strictly ethical issues, and there are none of those attempts, which are characteristic of modern idealism, to argue backwards from practical to speculative principles. The horizon of Cudworth and Price is indeed wider, but Cudworth belonged to the seventeenth century, when the appeal was still to authority and philosophy was still a matter of large erudition, and Price was his disciple. It is true that Hume combined in his principal work a discussion of the foundations of science and morality, and that the fundamental hypothesis of the supremacy of sensation runs through both. But one cannot also help remarking how little support his moral theory receives from his speculative. It illustrates the same assumption, but it stands in all essentials on its own legs. It is very psychological and very little metaphysical. And if we compare the treatment of 'self' in the practical and speculative portions of Hume's work, we shall see that the two theories do not tally, a point in which, as in others, Hume was the forerunner of Kant. In Locke's essay, moral theory comes in at intervals in order to round off the discussion, and though it certainly contains a great deal which is of great importance for the metaphysic of morals, it is distinctly episodical in character. Bishop Berkeley was a most metaphysical person with very interesting views on the relation of human and divine reason, which at once suggest to us consequences of the most vital importance for morals, but the ethical portions of his writings might, to all appearance, have been written by Paley. Whether anything of wider interest can be read into them by a careful student is another question [1]. And Butler, the most typical of British moralists, will have nothing whatever to do with the metaphysics of his subject—whether the moral faculty be regarded as a 'sentiment' of the understanding or a 'perception of the heart,' or both, is for him a matter of small importance (§ 244, cf. 188).

7. *Distinction of the moral from the legal and theological provinces.*

The moral philosophy of the period is therefore distinctly provincial, and 'home-made.' But there are compensations in its provinciality. That morals have a peculiar interest for the lawyer, the politician, and the divine needs no saying. In the development of the immense doctrine of the law of nature, the influence of the civilian and the statesman had

---

[1] *Mind*, vol. xv. no. 60. The following passages contain most of Berkeley's moral theory—*Principles*, § 100; *Passive Obedience*, §§ 4–15, 28–34, 41, 42, 53; *Alciphron*, Dial. iii. §§ 10, 11. The references are to Fraser's edition.

been supreme. In its lengthy history the legal and political view of morals had been fairly exhausted. For the rest ethics had been in the hands of theologians, and though in dealing with ethics the spiritual elements of theology, even in its most spiritual periods, had a way of evaporating, leaving little more than a legal code tempered with reminiscences of Aristotle, still the theological point of view dominated everything except the recalcitrant law of nature.

It is usual to trace the moralizing tendency of the eighteenth century to the decay of theology and the lessened authority of religious sanctions, and to represent the moral philosophy of that period as an attempt to find a substitute for religion as a basis of society and a guide of conduct [1]. It was perhaps rather the emptiness and insufficiency of theological ethics in which sanctions were the chief interest, which set serious people upon original moral inquiries, rather than contempt for theology altogether. Theologians themselves showed no unreadiness to accept the position, and from this point of view the moralizing character of theology itself is inevitable rather than contemptible, and the period may more properly be regarded as a necessary stage in the evolution of theology than as one of degradation. It is not my purpose to enter into the question of the relations of religion and morality. But it is hardly necessary to point out the great gain both to theology and ethics which was likely to result, and has in fact resulted, from the independent investigation of moral phenomena from the specifically moral point of view. It has been said that 'those periods in which morals have been represented as the proper study of man and his only business, have been periods of spiritual abasement and poverty [2].' But it would not be too

[1] Leslie Stephen, *English Thought in the Eighteenth Century*, ii. 2.
[2] M. Pattison, *Essays*, ii. 82.

much to say that the theological or religious revival of the present day, which is certainly not unspiritual, owes much of its richness and fullness to the labours of what is commonly stigmatized as a most unspiritual age. Whether in the last resort religion and morality merge, is a question which is not in any way prejudged when we congratulate our moralists on their emancipation from the theological tradition of their time. Their very narrowness certainly enabled them to do their work better, and in the result they produced for the use of future philosophers a mass of purely moral data which would have been both smaller and less pure if they had had the capacity or the inclination to consider their bearings on more general problems. The deduction of a moral category is an imposing undertaking, but whether that be possible or not, it is quite impossible to deduce the necessity of such a category from any consideration of the nature of things : for that we must go to experience, and it is because the philosophers of this period went there that the restoration of moral philosophy in the wider sense became possible for Kant and for us. And it is certainly impossible for us to understand Kant without some knowledge of his British predecessors.

8. *The will of God as the source of moral distinctions.*

I will not attempt to trace the various ways in which our writers attempted to regulate their position towards religion : this belongs mainly to the history of the deistical controversy, and partly also to that of the free-will controversy. But both the intellectual and sentimental schools were agreed that it was not the mere will of God which constituted the distinction between right and wrong, nor his power which constituted the obligation to goodness. The legislative theory ot God's relation to moral law was decidedly rejected. To the intellectual school represented by Cudworth, S. Clarke, Price, and Balguy the eternal relations of things, dependent on their essences, to which 'moral relations' were traced, were at all events not merely an expression of God's will. Moral duties were deducible apart from revelation, though their revelation as God's will was a great assistance to weak man, and though secondarily, but not primarily, we may treat opposition to the natures of things as self-will or rebellion against God's will (§§ 525, 1032, 1053). To help themselves out of the theological difficulty caused by asserting the independence of morality on God, they employed the distinction between essence and existence, between the formal and efficient cause, between the will of God and his wisdom and goodness(§§ 813–14, 507, 828–29), and the 'wisdom' of God is of course a meeting-point of the metaphysics of religion and knowledge.

The sentimental school, on the other hand, represents our amiable, that is our moral affections, as analogous to God's, and our conscience, whether regarded as supplying an additional motive or constituting the obligation of virtue, as the voice of God within. That this explanation is not a final one is easily seen by the intellectual school, and they ask what then constitutes the goodness of God's own benevolence. The will to make man happy is in the last resort the essence of God's goodness for both schools (§§ 524, 112, 186–87, 243, cf. 376, 802, 864), though the intellectualist stands out for the antecedent 'fitness' of making the world happy (§§ 483, 528–29, 734). Happiness even for Butler is ultimately the only thing worth having (§§ 239, 240 , and though it is foolish to think too much about happiness (§ 231), and illegitimate to make the thought of future happiness the motive of our action, it is concluded, as Kant afterwards concluded, that the final coincidence between virtue and happiness can only be brought about by God's dispensation of rewards in a future life, and this coincidence is essential to their scheme of the universe, which without it would be immoral.

We may however notice the utilitarian objection to the 'divine legislator' theory of morals—that the will of God can only be ascertained by reference to happiness, which is the ultimate criterion (§ 864), and what is more, by reference to happiness as we conceive it (§ 376 *n*) We may also notice Cudworth's theory of the participation of created minds in the divine mind (§ 838), which figures so largely in recent speculation, and which is peculiarly serviceable in correlating the practical and speculative [1].

9. *Positive law and moral distinctions.*

What was denied to the divine was not likely to be allowed to the human legislator. The political or legal theory may have something to say for itself as an explanation of obligation, but as an explanation of the distinction between right and wrong, between just and unjust, it is clearly preposterous ; and even if the position is shifted from positive law to a compact antecedent to law, the necessity of moral distinctions antecedent to the compact is the same. Hume, who rejects the theory of an explicit social contract or promise, rests social institutions on an unspoken convention like that of the rowers in a boat to combine their efforts for a common end, or like that by which language is established. The obligation to justice is thus like the obligation of the members of a boat's crew to keep time (*Treatise*, p. 490). The question thus will be—does the inarticulate sense of common interest on

---

[1] Green, *Prolegomena to Ethics*, §§ 66–73, 173.

which this convention rests imply anything more in man than can be derived from his accumulated experience of pleasure [1] ?

The theory of Hobbes is effectively criticized, especially by the intellectualists (§§ 486, 514, 587, 672, 816), and they do not fail to point out his arbitrary and illegitimate use of the laws of nature (§ 515). It is possible, however, to take Hobbes's moral theory too seriously and literally, and it is impossible to do him justice unless we make allowances for his object, which was far more political than philosophical. Adam Smith's remark (§ 341) was not unnecessary, that Hobbes's intention was 'to subject the consciences of men immediately to the civil and not to the ecclesiastical powers, whose turbulence and ambition he had been taught by the example of his own times to regard as the principal source of the disorders of society.' There is much in Hobbes which is more dangerous to morality than his political theory, but this for the most part escaped the notice of his critics, who leave the foundation while they demolish the superstructure. There is on the other hand an obscurity in Hobbes's first principles, due largely to confusion of expression if not of thought, which renders him a bad starting-point. Much of the obscurity of Hume's treatment of justice seems due to a desire to follow Hobbes in asserting its artificiality, although he had rejected the ideas of the state of nature and social compact which alone made it plausible. (Hume, *Treatise*, p. 484, cf. *Inquiry*, p. 258.)

As to the acknowledged obligatoriness of civil laws, the sentimental school is willing to rest it either upon their object—the promotion of general happiness, in which we are all interested, or upon their sanctions, but Hutcheson and his followers do

[1] Green, *Proleg.* §§ 219, 282-83.

not lay much stress on obligation in any connexion. For the intellectualists, on the other hand, the obligatoriness of civil laws is the same as that of the moral law from which it is derived. In his distinctions between the will of the commander and the intellectual nature of him that is commanded (§ 817), and between the formality and materiality of an act of obedience (§ 820), Cudworth emphasized ideas of the greatest importance in the subsequent history of idealistic philosophy.

As to the nature and meaning of sanctions themselves, little is said by the sentimental school: they were thoroughly discredited as motives, and were not suspected of any other import than their obvious utility. Butler, however, with his keen sense of the significance of concrete social institutions, endeavoured to recover in his treatment of punishment that absolute distinction between the right and the useful, the authoritative and the merely persuasive, which he had lost in his co-ordination of conscience and cool self-love, on this point coming into agreement with the intellectualists (§§ 246, 658), and with Adam Smith in his anti-utilitarian mood (§§ 293, 302–4).

10. *The law of nature.*

The moralists of our period are not anxious to exhibit the laws of morals in relation to the 'law of nature' as explained by Grotius, Puffendorff, and Cumberland. That law is the law of sociality, the law which primarily binds man to man in a society, and secondarily binds one society to another. Its commentators indeed did not confine themselves, as Hobbes did, to considerations of the intolerable nature of unsocial life; they dwelt upon the kindly social tendencies of human nature—'naturalis iuris mater est ipsa humana natura, quae nos, etiamsi re nulla indigeremus, ad societatem mutuam appetendam ferret[1].' But in two respects it was disagreeable to the age—it rested to some extent upon authority, and that by no means the authority of the 'honest farmer,' and in its treatment of benevolence and the obligation to benevolence appealed frankly to self-interest. 'The endeavour to the utmost of our power of promoting the common good of the whole system of rational agents, conduces as far as in us lies to the good of every part, in which our own happiness, as that of a part, is contained,' and 'the greatest benevolence of every rational agent towards all, forms the happiest state of every and of all the benevolent[2],' are phrases which would appear likely to be acceptable enough to Shaftesbury and Hutcheson, the latter of whom in fact has to fall back on them for his explanation of 'obligation.' They are capable however of a use obnoxious to the 'disinterested' theory, and also to the theory of spontaneous and immediate approbation (§§ 79, 107, 186). As a fact we find Cumberland's translator, John Maxwell[3], submitting him to a severe criticism from the point of view of Shaftesbury as well as from the point of view of 'absolute' morality. There is in some ways more temptation for the intellectualists to adopt the 'law of nature,' in order to give content to the eternal, immutable, and necessary law to which they are committed, and of which it is so difficult to find concrete instances. Thus S. Clarke, as well as Hutcheson, accepts the tendency of benevolence to produce happiness as an illustration of a necessary law arising from the natures or reasons of things (§§ 502, 506–7, cf. 466), and Locke might have pointed to this kind of law

---

[1] Grotius, *de Iure Belli*, prol. § 16.

[2] Cumberland, *Laws of Nature*, Introd. § ix., c. i. § 4, ed. Maxwell, 1727.

[3] *Dissertation on the Law of Nature*, cap. i. ; published as Appendix to the translation of Cumberland. London, 1727.

when he declared that morality was capable of demonstration. This law may be stated indeed as a 'law of nature' in the ordinary physical sense, and as such is capable of support by empirical evidence, and if proved is as necessary as any other empirical law; but it is evident that in this sense it cannot be a law of morals in Clarke's own sense, and that its necessity is not what he means by necessity. His adoption of it however is quite consistent with the utilitarian tendency of the intellectual school which is so conspicuous in Wollaston (§§ 1066–7). Gay, who was by no means a supporter of 'absolute fitnesses,' put forward the relations of things as the criterion of happiness in very much the way in which Clarke had attempted to use them.

11. *Virtue declared to be real and 'natural.'*

I have already several times spoken of the 'intellectual' and 'sentimental' schools as representing two principal lines of thought in this period, but have not thought it necessary to define or even describe them. They are primarily distinguished by their adoption of reason and feeling respectively as the faculty which perceives moral distinctions, a faculty declared in each case to be peculiar and not identifiable with ordinary reason or ordinary feeling. When they draw inferences from the faculty to the criterion, the subject-matter, the motive and the obligation of morality, the issues become confused, and there is much ground for Bentham's assertion that both schools, as soon as they come to particulars, are equally utilitarian. The fact is that, whatever the particular form or topic of discussion, they have one common object — to show that virtue is real and is worth pursuing in itself; that virtue and the motive to it are irreducible to a merely animal experience of pleasure and pain. The dispute between them is as to the most effective way of attaining this object, and it may fairly be said that they are much stronger in their criticisms of each other than in their own solutions of the problem. They see clearly enough the difficulty of maintaining the specific character of morality ; the tendency of the moral to dissipate itself into the non-moral, whether on the side of experience or on the side of mathematical abstract truth opposite to experience. The fact is that they both start from an uncritical view of experience itself, from the abstract view of their common opponents the sensationalists, and so whether they appeal to or revolt from experience they rest their theories on an equally insecure foundation. Their dispute however is on its own plane very instructive, and in the following pages some of its principal turns and issues are followed out.

That virtue is 'natural' and 'according to nature' is indeed an article of faith with both schools, though they are not unaware of that ambiguity of the term on which Hume remarks (*Treatise*, p. 474). The sense of 'nature' adopted by Hobbes is of course rejected by both, and both are inclined to minimize rather unduly the artificial element in morality. For the intellectual school virtue is natural primarily because it conforms to the 'intelligible nature and essence of things,' or the relations arising from them (§§ 825, 491, 550, 1053 , secondarily because it recognizes the actual nature, i. e. the constitution of man (§§ 550, 1007). For the sentimental school, on the other hand, virtue is natural because it conforms to and is the normal expression of uncorrupted human nature. When it is asked however what is human nature, some difference of opinion arises : for Shaftesbury and Hutcheson the kindly or benevolent affections regulated by regard to the whole 'system of rationals' made up the

real nature of man, though they sometimes put in a saving
word for other affections : for Butler conscience speaks with
the voice of the whole man, and the real nature of man
is that constitution (not entirely benevolent) which conscience (and cool self-love) approves of (§§ 216–17) : for
Hume that conduct is natural which we ordinarily expect,
and for Adam Smith that conduct with which the impartial
spectator is able to sympathize.   There is a vagueness in these
conceptions which renders welcome the further definition
contributed by Kames : the common and proper nature of man
is that constitution which best enables the species to maintain
itself in relation to the external circumstances, now called the
environment [1], in which it is placed (§ 911).

12. *Moral laws and natural relations.*

The attempt of one section at least of the intellectual school
to deduce moral laws from the 'nature of things' requires
closer scrutiny.   Everything is said to have a permanent
nature, essence, or character which determines its relations to
other things.   Since the essences are eternal and immutable,
so also are the relations.   A thing which is once equal to
another is always so, as long as they both remain the same,
and the propositions which arise from or are made about
their relations are eternally and immutably true.   This
reminds us of the 'permanent system of relations' on which
the modern idealist dwells in his theory of knowledge,
but the moralists of our period were bolder in its use than
we should be.   Most of the instances of their natural
relations and truths are taken from mathematics, and it is
asserted that to deny a moral proposition, such as 'gratitude
is due to benefactors,' is as *formally* absurd as to deny the

[1] Herbert Spencer, *Data of Ethics*, c. 6.

mathematical truth that 'two straight lines cannot enclose
a space,' or that 'things which are equal to the same thing
are equal to each other' (§§ 490–91). Conduct suitable to
a certain person in certain circumstances might by a stretch
of language be described as proportionate to the person's
relations, i.e. his character and circumstances (§ 483), and
advantage is taken of the word proportion to suggest the
identity of moral and mathematical relations. The same
jugglery is practised with equity and equality, and it is
declared that 'the reason which obliges every man in
practice so to deal always with another as he would . . .
expect that others should . . . deal with him, is the *very
same* as that which forces him in speculation to affirm,
that if one line or number be equal to another, that other
is reciprocally equal to it' (§ 500). It is candidly admitted
(§ 491) that it is not in our power to withhold assent from a
plain speculative truth, whereas we can refuse to act up to
a plain moral truth, but this admission is not followed up
to its proper conclusion that 'practical truth' is a metaphorical
phrase and that the 'practical absurdity' of refusing to perform
the act indicated cannot be a 'formal absurdity.'

It is of course possible to contend that immoral action is
absurd in another sense—i. e. of defeating its own end, but
this is material absurdity, like that of refusing to act on
a known physical law. This idea of material absurdity as
a test of vice, has a long and not undistinguished history.
It figures in Hobbes as an argument for the obligation of
justice (injustice being as if a man should deny in the end
what he had declared in the beginning) (§ 903), and it figures
in Kant [1], and again in Prof. Green, who ultimately condemns
the hedonist as seeking satisfaction in pursuits which cannot

---

[1] *Metaphysic of Morals*, Transl. Abbott, § 2, p. 39, ed. 3.

afford it [1]. In the writers of the intellectual school it appears as the absurdity of treating things as other than they are—the absurdity of treating men as brutes and brutes as stones—of ignoring the eternal natures of things, but it soon appears that it is not the absurdity which makes such action wrong, but the self-will (§§ 491, 525, 1032, 1053) and wantonness and waste of opportunity which it implies, which are not necessarily absurd at all. This line of argument moreover leads easily into utilitarianism, for to treat men as they are is to treat them primarily as capable of and desiring happiness (§§ 1066–67, 665, cf. 241).

13. *Morality and ' truth.'*

In the same way as the ' absurdity ' relied on by the intellectualists turns out to be self-will, so the violation of truth, of which Wollaston makes so much, turns out to be ' untruthfulness,' which can certainly be practised without absurdity (though it cannot be imagined a universal practice without some absurdity; lying would cease to be profitable to the liar if no one spoke the truth or expected others to speak the truth). His system, as Balguy points out (§ 550), rests on a confusion between ' objective and subjective truth,' and as Price argues (§ 693), it is hard to regard the evil of cruelty or ingratitude as being the same as that of telling a lie. The attempt, however, made by Balguy and Price themselves to exhibit virtue as ' truth,' breaks down almost as easily. Truth is of propositions, and is about things. The object of science is to attain truth about things, but it is not the object of morals to attain truth about actions. You can make as many true propositions about a bad action as about a good one, as Hutcheson points out (§§ 448, 454), and moral laws are a good deal more than such truths, at all events to anybody who is not a philosopher.

[1] *Prolegomena*, §§ 176–77.

They can of course be cast into the form of a proposition, and 'thou shalt not steal' may be rendered 'it is wrong to steal,' but the form in which they naturally appeal to the unsophisticated man is that of the imperative, whether it be hypothetical or categorical. It seems that in the last resort the insistence displayed by Balguy and Price (§§ 551, 626) in describing a right action as a 'true' one, is due to their conviction that moral distinctions are a function of reason and are also objective, and that if so they must be in some way or other an expression of 'truth,' 'practical reason' not yet being invented, or not yet applied to the solution of this difficulty. It is perhaps noticeable that there is a tendency to couple 'order and truth' (§§ 719, 730), and it may be admitted that the idea of a moral 'order' is much more suitable for the purpose of these writers, than that of truth, but in their minds it is at least partly a theological idea.

14. *The fitness of actions.*

As for 'relations,' Balguy is easily driven to admit that mathematical relations can only be used figuratively in morals, and that moral perceptions, e.g. of moral agreement and fitness, are different in kind from mathematical perceptions (§§ 714–19), though they are still perceptions of reason and not of sense. A great deal of the intellectualist argument turns upon merely verbal ambiguity, which Price is obliged to admit (§§ 670, 694); relation, agreement, congruity, suitableness, fitness, form a series which lead, conveniently but loosely, from the non-moral to the moral. But to serve the purpose of the intellectualist, with his demand for absolute virtue, it must be absolute fitness (§ 483), and absolute fitness is a contradiction in terms. Moral fitness must mean either fitness to an end, e.g. happiness, or fitness to gratify a desire

(§§ 807, 1014), or that conformity to a certain standard of character, otherwise determined, which is more usually called propriety or decency. Suitableness to human nature, whether that of the ideal man or the ordinary man (§§ 220, 262), is a quite intelligible phrase, but it recognizes a standard which the intellectualists could not accept. That a virtuous act must not violate the physical laws of the universe, and in this sense must be suitable to the nature of things, is quite true, but that is only a negative condition of virtue, and such violation would constitute folly rather than vice, and an action which was calculated with most exact reference to physical conditions might yet be a very bad one. Abstract fitness is certainly not sufficient to constitute virtue (§§ 739, 747 *n*), and it is impossible to give a definition of virtuous fitness without including in the definition the idea of virtue. 'These expressions,' says Price, referring to congruity, suitability, &c., 'are of no use and have little meaning if considered as intended to define virtue; for they evidently presuppose it' (§ 697). Hume's remark on the writers of this school, that 'they thought it sufficient if they could bring the word relation into the argument without troubling themselves whether it was to the purpose or not' (*Treatise*, p. 464 *n*), is much to the point, as indeed is his whole criticism of the theory which places virtue and vice in relations (*ib.* pp. 463–470). If you say that the virtue of an act is a relation, he replies that all the four relations discoverable by reason are perceptible between inanimate objects or animals just as much as between persons: there is no actual relation in parricide which does not exist between the ivy and the oak, nor in incest which does not occur between animals. If it be replied that the moral relation is a new relation different from any of the four recognized relations, he says, show it me!

That is precisely what the intellectualists are inclined to do, and they name it 'fitness' or 'rectitude.' Fitness we have already dealt with, and shown that it carries us beyond itself to some standard which is already moral or else not founded in the 'nature of things'; of 'Rectitude' we may say with Price that it is only another name for 'oughtness' (§§ 671, 686 *n*). And if 'oughtness' is a relation it is at all events a different kind of relation from the other relations, and thus far there is no ground for ascribing its perception to the same kind of reason as perceives them, nor is there any ground for deducing this new relation from others which are entirely different from it (Hume, *Treatise*, p. 469).

15. *Are there acts which are virtuous in all relations?*

Hume properly points out (loc. cit.) that no conclusion can be drawn as to the nature of virtue or the faculty which perceives it from the assertion that 'we perceive an act in certain relations to be virtuous or vicious.' It may also be pointed out that it warrants no conclusion as to the immutable nature of morality. It may be granted that the same act in the same relations is always virtuous or vicious, if 'relations' be taken in the widest possible sense, but that is a perfectly barren proposition. What the intellectualists want to assert is something very different, viz. that there are certain acts, or classes of acts, which are virtuous or vicious in all relations and all circumstances. They instance 'keeping faith and performing equitable covenants and equity' (§§ 487, 498), 'making a virtuous agent happy' (§ 654 f.), and gratitude (§ 717). But as soon as they come to define that gratitude which is always virtuous they are obliged to limit their statement to the state of mind or will, 'the ultimate principle of conduct or the deter-

mination of a reasonable being' (§ 622), as distinguished from
the overt act, for we clearly cannot say that any particular act is
always virtuous or vicious in all circumstances.   But can we say
any more of any state of mind that it is always and in all circumstances virtuous? Is there not a proper and an improper gratitude, as Adam Smith suggests (§§ 290, 294–6)? and is it possible
to advance a single step in the definition of the gratitude or
other state of mind which is proper, without including in the
definition the idea of virtue itself? Can we ever say more
than that 'the gratitude which is virtuous is always virtuous,'
which again is. a perfectly barren proposition? We are thus
driven practically to reduce immutable morality to the one
empty proposition of Kant: there is nothing good but a good
will, the goodness of which consists in formality alone.   His
efforts to get materiality into his moral law led him to recur
to those considerations of material absurdity which we have
already examined.   It may be repeated, in this connexion, that
Kant would be a good deal better understood if he were read in
connexion with the British Moralists, with whom he was well
acquainted.   There is little in him that is not in them, though
his general attitude towards ethics is a different and more
distinguished one.   It is perhaps worth noting that the theory
of the absolute fitness of certain kinds of action sometimes
takes the form of asserting that one kind of action is '*fitter*'
in itself than another, generally its opposite (§§ 483, 619).
This suggests the modification, lately revived by Dr. Mar-
tineau, of an absolute code of duties into an absolute *scale*
of duties, in which each class of act or motive appears not as
'good' or 'bad' but as better or worse than those below or
above it [1].

---

[1] *Types of Ethical Theory*, part ii. c. 1. § 2, vol. ii. p. 40 f.

16. *Reason as the moral faculty.*

Let us pass from the consideration of the attempt to deduce morality from the 'nature of things' to exhibit it as part of that order of nature with which science is concerned, and to apply the formal tests of truth and falsehood to virtue and vice, and consider the meaning of the attempt to exhibit morality as a function of Reason.   And first let us take it in its weakest aspect, in which it appears as a positive rather than a negative theory.   We have here to deal with bold intuitionists.   Price quite rightly points out that the sensationalist argument that reason gives rise to no new ideas is framed with reference primarily to deductive reason (to which we may add inductive reason, if there is any essential difference), the function of which in morals can only be ancillary.   This reason, which 'is and only ought to be the slave of the passions' (Hume, *Treatise*, p. 415), is not the only form of reason, and it is asserted that intuitive reason does give rise to new ideas.   Price (§§ 589–604) goes through the stock arguments (borrowed from Plato and Cudworth) for the activity of reason in the formation of general and abstract ideas, in the criticism and correction of sensation; he also instances the ideas of solidity, power, and causation. He then boldly asserts that right and wrong are simple ideas arising from 'some power of immediate perception in the human mind' (§ 605), i. e. from 'our intuition of the nature of things' (§ 612).   He means presumably that as soon as the idea of gratitude or truthfulness is brought before us we also form the idea of 'right,' and that this perception of right, being simple, is ultimate and undefinable (§§ 670, 682). This statement may be true, and yet not warrant any conclusion such as he has drawn.   We touch, of course, here upon the general Idealist argument that the activity of reason

is necessary for the constitution of the world of knowledge, and even for the constitution of 'objects' of sense.
The argument is mainly negative and rests, even in the speculative sphere, upon the alleged insufficiency of sense, but in
the practical sphere it is still more negative. The modern form
of the idealist argument deals in the speculative sphere chiefly
with the manufacture of relations, which are felt to furnish
the most satisfactory instances of the activity of reason : and
there is no lack of such instances, whether we take time and
space, or causation, or the mathematical relations. But in
the practical sphere it is no longer possible to deal with relations, and it is very hard to give any definite instances at all
of the products of reason, especially if it be desired to exhibit
those products as 'universal and necessary.' The whole force
of the argument lies therefore in the negative criticism of sense,
and it is peculiarly hard in the practical region to force on an
opponent the alternative, 'either sense or reason,' which, in
fact, Adam Smith refuses to accept (§ 343). He is always
able to reply, ' The sense which you declare to be insufficient
is not the sense which I mean : I mean by sense a good deal
more than Hume meant, and I quite agree with you that such
a sense as Hume referred everything to is a mere fiction.' The
same reply, of course, can be and is made in the speculative
sphere, but it is easier to make and more difficult to meet in
morals. I am not going to enter into the general Idealist
controversy. It may be noted, however, that the argument
that, as reason is necessary to constitute objects of knowledge,
so it is necessary to constitute any motives or objects of desire [1],
does not appear in the writings of this period, though the
analysis of desire plays a very important part in them.
Whether that argument strengthens the Idealist position is

[1] Green, *Prol.* §§ 88 f., 120.

another question. It may also be noted that the attribution of self-determination to reason, and the vindication of freedom in morals by reference to that self-determination, do not distinctly appear [1] (§§ 597, 701): how far that self-determination which characterizes speculative as well as practical reason is a sufficient foundation for responsibility is again another question [2]. Price indeed asserts that, though reason implies liberty, yet liberty does not imply reason, true liberty being possessed by animals (§ 703).

17. Can reason move to action?

Hume's principal argument against reason is that it excites to no action, is 'perfectly inert,' and 'can never be the source of so active a principle as conscience or a sense of morals' (*Treatise*, §§ 413–18, 457). Reason can indicate the means to an end, or can show us the existence of a desired end, but it cannot itself recommend an end (§§ 449 f., 450). This argument primarily applies to discursive, not to intuitive reason, and it may be said that the hard distinction drawn by Hume (as previously by Aristotle) between means and end does not prevail in morals: we do not as a matter of fact when judging of an action always or often regard it as a means or as distinct from its end (cf. §§ 572, 304, 881–5). When we judge morally of an act, we more often regard it as the part of a whole, a system of conduct than as the means to an end. But when we do consider our actions as means to an end it is not easy to say in what sense the end can be called 'reasonable.' Whether there are ultimate ends, and whether virtue is an ultimate end, or whether pleasure is the only ultimate

[1] Cf. Cudworth, *Of Freewill*, p. 71. Ed. Allen, 1838.
[2] Green, *Prol.* §§ 76–7, 86–9, 108.

end, are further questions ; I am now only concerned with the attempt made to exhibit reason as constituting 'ends' which are capable of moving us to action, and for this purpose something more is required than that function of reason by which it makes an end or anything else an object of knowledge. The modern argument which attributes to reason an important part in the constitution of the ideas of 'self' and 'self-satisfaction,' and so in the constitution of all motives, is curiously reversed by Balguy (§§ 724–5). Balguy's own arguments are perhaps less convincing on this point than on any other, especially when he rings the changes on 'reason' and 'reasons.' It is useless in this connexion to reiterate, as Price does (§ 706), that the 'perception of right and wrong does excite to action'; this is not only admitted by Hume, but urged by him to show that the perception cannot be a function of Reason. In the same way it is no good urging that the moral law moves to action by its inherent worth (by exciting 'respect' as Kant would say) unless you can prove that the perception of 'worth' is peculiar to reason, the difficulty of which I have suggested in the last paragraph. Balguy identifies 'Reason and moral good' (§§ 563, 720) and says that in pursuing reason or moral good a reasonable creature is acting according to his nature, i. e. reasonably. It is as absurd therefore to ask why a reasonable creature should act reasonably as to ask why a sensible creature should pursue happiness (§ 732), an argument which still has considerable vitality. The difficulty is to give any particular meaning to acting 'reasonably' which does not contradict the argument. Kant gave some meaning to 'reasonably' when he interpreted it as 'universally,' but the difficulty then arose of distinguishing 'universal' action from action that was not 'universal.' Of course both schools recognize that 'reasonable' action in the sense of considerate and careful action is generally best : rational is thus contrasted with instinctive benevolence, rational or cool self-love with passion. Hume indeed traces the fallacy of the intellectual school to the universal acknowledgement of the superiority of the calm passions (*Treatise*, pp. 417, 437).

18. *The sentimental theory of human nature.*

Let us now turn to the sentimentalists and examine their attempt to show that virtue is real and natural by relating it, not to the ' nature of things,' but to ' human nature.' There are two points on which they have to defend themselves against the sceptic : they have to show that moral ideas are not resolvable into non-moral by any of the great solvents, sympathy, or habit, or association of ideas : they have also to show that, though they are ultimate, yet they are inherently attractive and influential and do not owe their power to anything which is non-moral. At the same time they have to defend themselves against the intellectualists who urge that no sense or sentiment whatever can yield moral ideas possessing either the qualities required by the controversy with scepticism, or the quality of obligatoriness required by the intellectualist. For the sentimentalist, therefore, it is a ' war with two fronts,' and when he faces one enemy he generally exposes his flank to the other. When he has vindicated against the sceptic the distinction between moral and natural good, the intellectualist meets him with the objection that his moral good imposes only a natural obligation, and is therefore no more acceptable as a basis of morality than pleasure pure and simple. When he has succeeded to his own satisfaction in showing that the feeling of approbation is quite different from the feeling of the anticipation of pleasure, that it is differently regarded by all men and leads to a different course of action, he is met by the intellectualist with the objection that a subjective feeling is never the same as an objective quality, and that in point of subjectivity, i.e. arbitrariness, variability, particularity, the feeling of approbation is not at all superior to the feeling of pleasure. On one point, however, the two schools are in fact more or less agreed—and that is on the possibility of disinterested desire. This has not much effect in bringing them together, though Price refers to Butler's theory with approval (§ 651 ff.).

19. *The 'reflex sense' in human nature.*

Virtue is natural, urges the sentimentalist, because it is an expression of the uncorrupted nature of man, of his nature regarded in all its relations and as part of a system, of his nature as distinguished by self-consciousness and reflection and 'affection towards affections' from that of animals, of his whole nature as comprising a peculiar moral sense, of his nature as an organic whole organized under two authoritative and reflective principles, conscience and self-love : it is an expression of the real and entire nature of man as distinguished from those partial and distorted aspects of human nature to which the enemies of virtue appeal.

In Shaftesbury's theory there is no strong contrast between the moral and non-moral, except that for morality a further complication of animal nature is required, viz. reflection on affection ('reflected sense') and consequent affection towards affection (§§ 11, 25). It might, of course, be urged that this difference is one of degree only, not of kind, and it is pointed out afterwards by Kames (§ 931), with reference to Butler's stronger doctrine, that mere 'reflection' does not constitute the authority of conscience. In the modern Idealist controversy indeed great stress is laid upon self-consciousness, and the evidence it gives of the activity of reason [1], but Shaftesbury's theory can hardly be regarded as an adumbration of that theory. As against the satirists, indeed, his picture of the natural benevolence (with which he generally identifies virtue) of man has some force, and against the individualists his picture of the essential relation in which man stands to the social system has also force, though it is weakened rather than strengthened by his reference to universal nature (§ 4). At this point Shaftesbury's theory comes in appearance close to that of the intellectualist. By giving free play to his kindly affections man plays his part not only in the limited system or society of which he is primarily a member, but in the wider 'system of all rationals, and ultimately in that great systematic scheme of all things with reference to which alone things can be called absolutely good or ill. But in this scheme there is no room for the essential difference of moral and natural, and the theory easily admits of a naturalistic or biological interpretation. Also his theory has no power of resistance in the face of 'universalistic hedonism,' nor indeed against 'individualistic hedonism' except in its rawest form.

Hutcheson is not contented with a mere 'reflex sense': he considers that man has in him a peculiar sense giving rise to a peculiar and disinterested feeling of approbation, distinguishable from all other feelings and more particularly from the anticipation of pleasure immediate or remote, consequential or concomitant. Virtue, which he also generally identifies with benevolence, is the object of this sense, and man is incited to its pursuit by this sense and the love which springs from it. This theory has some force against the theory

---

[1] Green, *Prol.* § 88.

of conscious calculating selfishness, but not much against the more refined forms of hedonism. Its assertion of the essential difference between moral and natural good (§§ 68, 472) is verbally an advance on Shaftesbury, but it is exposed to very rough criticism by the intellectualists.

It is in Butler that the sentimental school really reaches its climax. He is indeed careful not to commit himself to any decision between the claims of reason and sense (§§ 188, 244), but it is impossible not to treat his theory as intimately related to the speculation of Hutcheson, who indeed in his last work (§§ 472–4) evidently has taken a good deal from Butler. Man as an organic whole consists not only of parts, but of parts interrelated under a reflective faculty, which is endued not only with power or attractiveness but with authority. It is not merely the source of an additional feeling, distinguishable from other feelings : its deliverances stand on a different level from those of the other faculties, they are superior and imperative. To act according to human nature is to fall in with the system imposed by this authority, which has regard to all the capacities of human nature and by no means confines its interest to benevolence.

20. *Sense as a source of obligation.*

But, urges the intellectualist, how does your system secure the obligatoriness of virtue ? Even if it be true that the view of benevolent acts or affections does not leave us indifferent, even if a 'reflex sense' on consideration of them yields a peculiar and exquisite pleasure or gives rise to a new feeling which we call approbation, does this impose on me any obligation to perform such acts or gratify such affections ? It may move or attract me, as a matter of fact, more than anything else, but does it oblige me ? And, supposing that at any time it fails to move or attract a man, or supposing a man to be naturally weak or altogether deficient in it, is that to excuse him partially or wholly for his vicious acts? Balguy urges the distinction between the natural obligation of pleasure and pain, viewed as the sanctions or consequences of acts, which appeals to us as sensible creatures, and moral obligation, which cannot be derived from our sensible natures (§§ 720–2). Price urges that 'the attraction or excitement which the mind feels upon perceiving right and wrong . . . is the effect of obligation perceived rather than obligation itself' (§ 682)[1]. As a matter of fact Shaftesbury and Hutcheson have very little to say about obligation, and they do not claim as against the hedonist that the obligation of moral laws is other than that of pleasure. When Shaftesbury sets out to show the obligations to virtue he only attempts to show that to have that balance of affections which he calls virtue 'is to have the chief means and power of self-enjoyment' (§§ 26, 37). This really is nothing more than a discussion of the motive to virtue, and, though Hutcheson objects to the inclusion of the 'concomitant pleasure' of benevolence in such motive, he does not really advance upon Shaftesbury's position as to the nature of obligation. He has indeed no liking for the topic. With some justification perhaps he denounces 'ought' as a 'confused word,' and obligation as 'a term both complex and ambiguous' (§§ 460, 481). When he is dealing with the theory that all obligation proceeds from laws, he asks (§ 172), How can we then say that God ought to make the innocent happy? This question might have suggested to him that there is a sense of obligation other than those which he enumerates elsewhere (§§ 166–7),

---

[1] Kant, *Analytic of Pure Practical Reason*, transl. Abbott, ed. 3, p. 128.

unless he is prepared to accept J. Clarke's hedonistic theory of God's action (§ 802). But when he deals with obligation it is always in accordance with his own pronouncement that 'the principal business of the moral philosopher' is to show from solid reasons 'that universal benevolence tends to the happiness of the benevolent.' In the whole of the controversy, indeed, the ideas of 'obligation' and 'motive' are so mixed up by the Intellectual (the confusion is pointed out by Price, § 682) as well as by the Sentimental school that nothing very useful emerges, except with regard to the definition of 'duty' (§ 688 f.) and the relation of obligation and 'constraint' (§ 174).

21. *Butler's theory of obligation and punishment.*

Whether from incapacity to do otherwise or for some better reason, the Intellectualists really confine themselves to declaring that obligation is part of the notion of virtue : to ask what obliges us to virtue is to ask why we are obliged to do what we are obliged to do (§ 679). This is also Butler's position : his assertion of the authority and supremacy of conscience is only another way of asserting that the moral law has the aspect of an imperative, obedience to which is obligatory as obedience to a rightly constituted civil authority is obligatory. In this connexion Butler, like Shaftesbury and Hutcheson, lays great stress upon the superiority of a reflective faculty to a simple propension or appetite. In Butler's case it looks almost like a sop to the intellectualists (cf. § 687). But, besides being open to Kames' criticism, referred to above, it lands him in serious difficulties with self-love, which is also a reflective principle, and as such seems to have a co-ordinate authority with conscience (§§ 217, 226). Conscience, however, and self-love look on pleasure and pain with different eyes—to self-love they are natural consequences of actions, to conscience they always appear as punishment or reward. This point of view is at least partly theological, and conscience is not only that which enables a man to be a law to himself, but it also speaks as the voice of God. This throws the whole stress of the obligatoriness of the moral law on the theory of punishment, which is certainly one of the most important parts of Butler's speculation [1]. The introduction of punishment has indeed the advantage of once more assimilating the moral to the legal notion of obligation and relieving moral obligation from the charge of being something merely in the clouds to which no intelligible meaning could be attached—a mere name. But this theory of punishment is not only open to the utilitarian criticism, but is also liable to be treated from the naturalistic point of view as based on a non-moral principle of retaliation (cf. §§ 293, 302). It also, as above suggested, lets in the theological point of view, though of course in the eyes of one to whom the whole world is but 'the ante-room of heaven and hell,' this would be no disadvantage.

We may also notice again the hint in Cudworth of the peculiar 'formality' of moral obligation (§ 820, cf. § 492).

22. *The sentimental theory supplies no criterion.*

The point on which sentimentalist morals are chiefly attacked by the intellectualist is their subjectivity and consequent lack of universality : and this attack takes two directions. The sentimentalist is first accused of substituting a faculty for a criterion, the subjective act of approbation for an objective quality, and, secondly, of identifying the moral faculty, from which approbation proceeds, with a sense. These two criticisms are as a fact seldom distinguished by their authors, nor is the idea of a criterion very distinctly conceived by any of the chief

[1] Cf. Bradley, *Ethical Studies*, p. 25 f.

parties to the controversy. Wollaston, who has most to say about it (§§ 1023, 1044 f.), is not the most successful in dealing with it, and some of the absurdity of his theory is due to his preoccupation with it. But the intellectualists are quite clear in general that to say that 'good' means and is nothing more than what we approve is preposterous (§§ 536, 685). Both parties are agreed, as against the hedonist, that no reason can be given for our approbation, which is necessary and ultimate (§§ 585, 608, 559, cf. §§ 369–371) ; but so long as the intellectualist is unable to do more than name the quality which is approved the controversy is rather barren. The effort to give material content to 'rectitude' is a failure, and he has not yet resigned himself to merely formal content. The sentimentalist, on the other hand, boldly produces 'benevolence' as the quality approved, and the controversy shifts its ground and becomes an inquiry into the sufficiency of benevolence to constitute moral good. Two questions therefore are mainly discussed : if the approving faculty is of the nature of a sense, and if the approved quality is of the nature of an instinct, can anything but an arbitrary morality be constructed upon such a basis?

23. *Is a moral sense 'arbitrary'?*

Against the identification of the approving faculty with any kind of sense or anything like a sense it is urged that the constitution of our senses is arbitrary and might have been different. Might not God have given us a sense to which malicious instead of benevolent acts were agreeable, and which would approve of ingratitude and perfidy (§§ 186, 538)? If so, then virtue is made dependent on the arbitrary will of God, and the question arises which we have already discussed. Hutcheson suggests two answers: first, that the present constitution of our moral sense is good, because it tends on the whole to the happiness of creation, which must be a matter of concern to a benevolent God (§§ 186, 457). He does not lay much stress on this argument, because it seems to make moral dependent on natural good, but rather urges that God's approval of the present constitution of our moral sense proceeds from some principle in him analogous to man's moral sense (§ 459). This explanation, of course, only puts the difficulty one step further back, as Balguy points out (§ 528). Besides the arbitrariness of virtue alleged to follow from this theory there is its variability; you cannot expect uniformity in the senses of different men, or of the same man at different times; 'to make the rectitude of moral actions, . . . in proportion to the warmth and strength of the moral sense, rise and fall like spirits in a thermometer is depreciating the most sacred thing in the world and almost exposing it to ridicule' (§ 539)—and certainly rendering morality 'incapable of demonstration' (§ 728), besides ascribing to it a low origin and impairing its dignity (§ 540). If Hutcheson urges that as a matter of fact 'it is highly probable that the senses of all men are pretty uniform' (§ 463), Balguy replies that 'this universality does not remove the imputation we are speaking of. Hunger and thirst are universal instincts, but, however suitable they may be to our present condition, they are never reckoned honourable to human nature' (§ 731). It is clear that to Balguy, whose arguments are more than slightly rhetorical, 'the hunger and thirst after righteousness' could not be an acceptable phrase.

24. *Moral sense as furnishing a criterion and motive.*

But a greater difficulty lies behind. All senses stand in need of correction, and it was a principle of ancient idealism that the faculty which judges of and corrects the senses cannot be itself sense. It is admitted that moral sense at times requires correction, and can be improved by education and training. What sets the standard of this correction and improvement? Hutcheson (§§ 465–7) boldly faces this question, and it strains his theory almost to the breaking point. He says that reason undoubtedly corrects our opinions—(a) as to the tendencies of certain actions to happiness (Bentham thinks this is the only possible form of correction, § 366), (b) as to the affections by which an agent is actually influenced, and in these ways rather corrects the data upon which our moral sense pronounces judgement than regulates our moral sense itself. He admits that our organs of sense may be disordered or may mislead us, and that we correct their deliverances by the standard of a normal sense. He expresses a doubt whether in fact our moral sense itself ever is disordered as the organs of sight or hearing are disordered (Adam Smith has no doubts as to this, § 350), but if it were so disordered he says that reason could do nothing to correct it except by 'suggesting to its remembrance its former approbations and representing the general sense of mankind,' and from this, he declares, we cannot infer that reason antecedently to sensation has ideas of virtue and vice. It must of course be admitted that the inference drawn by the intellectualist is not justifiable, but, on the other hand, Hutcheson's subjective empiricism, if followed up, lands him in difficulties. The doctrine of the moral sense is a sensationalist, individualist doctrine, through which Locke's metaphysical assumptions can easily be seen. His morality is a 'protestant' morality of private judgement, and there is no hint of a 'national conscience,' or of that organic conception of the good, evolved in and through society alone, on which Green laid so much stress, and which corresponds to the organic conception of a κόσμος of inter-related phenomena which serves as the basis of science [1]. Hutcheson therefore would, if he pursued the subject, find that the correction of the individual's moral sense by the general sense is peculiarly difficult for him. In speculative matters we are all accustomed to correct our opinions by those of others or by the verified laws of science : but are we entitled to correct our own moral judgements by those of others in a matter of right as distinguished from a matter of fact ? How far is the appeal to the 'general sense' either attractive to the unreflective or valid for the reflective ? Respectability has many merits, but it does not often raise enthusiasm. On a really social and 'catholic' theory, such as Aristotle's was, the σπουδαῖος takes a rank as standard and motive which on a 'protestant' theory he cannot have. Speaking generally, the idealist contention has much truth, that sense (as regarded by sensationalists themselves) is not a bond of union or a basis of common action, and that the conception of a common good is a cause rather than an effect of sympathy.

But the real fact is that the moral sense theory is a theory of motive rather than of criterion. It is not put forward with a view to assisting us to distinguish right from wrong (§ 136) : for this purpose to refer us to a faculty would be a good deal more futile than to refer us to the σπουδαῖος. Nor is it really framed with much reference to the intellectualist school ; except in so far as Hutcheson's metaphysics convince him that sense is the only sure basis of any experience. It is really a counter-theory to the selfish theory, which is essentially a theory of motives. Virtue is real and natural, says the sentimentalist, because there is in every man a sufficient motive to it. We all of us have some benevolence, but purely natural benevolence is apt to be weak or partial. It is strengthened and corrected by the moral sense, which adds a novel and exquisite pleasure

[1] Green, *Prol.* § 232 ; *Pol. Obligation,* §§ 138-9.

to that which accompanies the gratification of any natural impulse.   When benevolence is wide and impartial this accessory
pleasure derived from the moral sense reaches its highest pitch.

25. *Is moral sense itself an element in virtue?*

This is very well urged by Hutcheson against the crude
form of the selfish theory.   Virtue or benevolence is made our
greatest happiness, apart from any external consequences, by
the action of moral sense.   But some confusion results
as regards the nature of virtue.   Does the virtue of an act
consist in the strong benevolence it shows, or in the keen moral
sense which regulates the benevolence?   He says (§ 473) that
we do not call an acute moral sense itself virtuous, but we
'approve it above all other abilities,' nor will he (§ 474, but cf.
§ 349) identify virtue with the 'love of moral excellence or love
of complacency' which is the direct expression of the moral
sense.   To some extent the distinction between benevolence
and complacency corresponds to that between instinctive and
rational benevolence, which he admits (§ 442), inasmuch as 'calm
universal benevolence' can only be the effect of long operation
of the moral sense.   Balguy is quite justified in identifying
universal benevolence and complacency (§ 557) and in making
this rational complacency rather than benevolence the basis of
virtue.

Hutcheson was no doubt wise in his generation in refusing
to identify virtue with anything so recondite as love of moral
excellence, though he was obliged to recognize its existence.
It would be difficult for him to assert against the selfish
school that such a love was universal among common men.
He wanted something which he could plausibly ascribe to the
mass of men, for he certainly wanted to make most men out
to be virtuous if he could.   But in reality, though the moral

sense theory reinforces his theory of benevolence, it embarrasses his theory of virtue, and it does so all the more because he does not avail himself of the ' will ' as the seat of virtue. He seems once on the point of doing so (§ 442, *note*), but he was probably unwilling to involve his theory in the free-will controversy, and we for our part may be thankful that he did not. Since Kant the will has been freely referred to as the ultimate residence of virtue, but not always with profit.

26. *Is a moral sense necessary ?*

In the moral sense theory the questions of the nature and subject-matter and motives of virtue are so mixed up that it is almost impossible to separate them, as Price would have us do (§ 586). It is therefore difficult, and would after all be rather artificial, to develop one's criticism of the theory in any very logical or consecutive way. But before coming to the discussion of desire, which is in some ways the most interesting part of the writings of this period, we may mention some miscellaneous criticisms of the moral sense theory.

The intellectualists of course denounce the moral sense theory not only as offensive but as gratuitous (§§ 538, 607). Butler does not commit himself (§ 244), but Adam Smith denounces it as contrary to the economy of nature (§ 347), and Gay says that it is at the best based on an argument *ad ignorantiam,* by which we should be as justified in asserting a ' pecuniary sense' as a moral sense (§§ 855, 883). As a matter of fact, Hutcheson displays a most alarming readiness to multiply senses (§§ 441-3), which finds its proper caricature in Kames' 'sense of property' (§ 948 f.). The real sting however of these criticisms lies in their counter-assertions of sympathy or asso-ciation of ideas as explanations of the admitted phemomenon of 'immediate approbation.' To these we shall recur.

There is also certainly some ground for J. Clarke's assertion that what the theory gives with one hand it takes away with the other : that it invents a sense to make virtue pleasant, and then says we must not pursue that pleasure (§ 806). Hutcheson, who had criticized Shaftesbury for allowing the virtuous man to have regard to the concomitant pleasure of benevolence (§ 470), is most careful to impress on us that our benevolence must be entirely disinterested if it is to be virtuous : the concomitant pleasure of benevolence must not and indeed cannot be the motive to benevolence. But he is not so clear about the pleasure of the moral sense. He of course asserts that approbation is itself disinterested and is not excited by desire to obtain the concomitant pleasure of approbation, but he does admit (§ 460) that 'the prospect of the pleasure of self-approbation is often a motive to choose one action rather than another,' and he would presumably regard it as a proper motive in 'choosing to continue in the agreeable state' of benevolence (§ 131). In general, however, he runs a risk with his theory of disinterested desire of proving too much—viz. that all desire is disinterested, in which case disinterestedness is no longer the mark of virtuous desire ; or that no thought of the pleasure of moral sense must enter into the mind of the virtuous person, in which case the moral sense is not very useful to virtue, but on the contrary frequently imperils its existence. It may also be noted that Hutcheson's limitation of the function of moral sense to the production of a peculiar pleasure opens the way to such an assimilation of this pleasure to other pleasure as Hume carried out through the medium of sympathy. His theory comes perilously near to saying that virtue is 'that which pleases us after a particular manner' (Hume, *Treatise*, p. 470).

27. *Virtue as benevolence.*

As for benevolence itself, the sentimentalists are quite sure that disinterested benevolence is the foundation and summary of virtue. The rigour of their altruism is, however, qualified by the admission that in considering the good of 'the system of rationals' a man is allowed to regard himself as a member of that system, and if the good resulting to others from a given act is not so great as the evil resulting to himself he may properly abstain from it for that reason (§§ 117–118, cf. §§ 133, 180). Benevolence itself, or regard for the good of a system, requires a man to be solicitous about himself, and to have special regard to his relations and friends.

It is quite clear here that something else is considered than the amount of benevolence implied in an act. It may perhaps be said that regard to the good of a wide system requires more benevolence than regard to the good of a narrow system, but when we are instructed to prefer the good of the higher to that of the lower system the appeal is evidently to other considerations than those of benevolence : the difficulty is, in fact, the same as arises for the hedonist over 'higher' and 'lower' pleasures (§ 479, cf. § 476).

The theory of benevolence, moreover, was founded on the assumption of what Butler calls 'the natural principle of attraction between man and man' (§ 207), or a benevolence, as Hutcheson says, 'in some degree extended to all mankind' (§ 108). Hume had attacked the 'benevolent' theory by declaring that ' there was no such passion in human minds as the love of mankind merely as such, independent of personal qualities, of genius, or of relation to oneself ' (*Treatise*, pp. 481–2), or, as Kames puts it, ' there is no such principle of general fondness of man to man by nature as there is in dogs towards man' (§ 937). Such general benevolence as is displayed is said to be due to 'sympathy,' on the theory of which a good deal of the controversy turns. The benevolent theory was also attacked by the intellectualists as basing virtue upon instincts the operation of which is necessary and so devoid of merit (§§ 532–5). As against the selfish school and their instinct of self-love, Hutcheson is prepared to defend a 'bene-volent universal instinct' (§ 131), but as a rule he prefers to emphasize against both criticisms the distinction between 'calm universal benevolence,' the product of reflection, and the particular benevolent affections (§ 442). This reflection upon 'all mankind or the system of rationals' turns out, however, to be only the reflection that by regard to them 'we may gratify either our self-love or kind affections in the fullest manner.' The good of the species appears to be hardly a possible object of affection, and the reflective love seems hardly disinterested (§§ 452–3). Thus the idea of the 'universal natural good of mankind' or 'the system of rationals' which in his earlier writings is distinctly 'constitutive' (§ 112) becomes attenuated into a very regulative principle in his later writings. And if we appeal to the moral sense we find that it often approves and disapproves without any regard to the good of any system (§ 480), and it turns out (probably under the influence of Butler) that 'the righteousness or good-ness of actions is not the same notion with their tendency to universal happiness or flowing from the desire of it.'

Butler's treatment of benevolence is indeed of great im-portance in the history of moral philosophy : benevolence is disinterested indeed, but it is no more disinterested than any of the particular affections, every one of which 'rests in its object as an end' (§ 207). The love of our neighbour is as interested or disinterested as the love of anything else ; there is no peculiar contrariety between benevolence and self-love (§§ 233–4); disinterestedness is not the distinguishing mark of virtue, and 'benevolence and the want of it, simply considered, are in no sort the whole of virtue and vice' (§ 249, cf. § 532), though most of the common virtues and vices may be traced up to benevolence or the want of it (§ 242). Benevolence is for some purposes placed by Butler on the same level as the particular affections, though it is not therefore a blind propension, but is to be regarded as naturally allied with calculative reason (§ 240), but on a lower level than the two great reflective principles, self-love and conscience. Both of these combine to encourage benevolence to the greatest extent, though conscience certainly is influenced by other considerations than the amount of happiness produced, and more particularly by that of 'desert' (§ 244). The way is thus opened for a more liberal view of human nature and its 'perfection,' a conception which had been almost stifled by the weight of benevolence, and for other aspects of morality besides its hedonistic, though he is not afraid to admit that 'nothing can be of consequence to mankind or any other creature but happiness' (§ 241). Butler's theory is by no means free from confusion, but he gets rid of the confusions which grew so thick round the 'calm universal benevolence' of the sentimentalists, and also of that narrowness which is so apt to make the 'disinterested' theory merely uninteresting.

28. *Sympathy.*

Before we consider the significance of Butler's theory of desire it may be convenient to notice the two great principles which have been used to explain the admitted immediacy of moral approbation and the alleged disinterestedness of both

approbation and benevolence—sympathy and association of
ideas. Hume's theory of sympathy is primarily designed to
explain how an individual whose experience is absolutely
confined to his own feelings can yet acquire such an interest in
the feelings of other individuals as to form a society in which
his own feelings are subordinated to those of others. Hume's
psychology of sympathy has a metaphysical interest beyond
that of an explanation of a disputed moral phenomenon, and
effective criticism of it involves metaphysical considerations
on which it is neither possible nor desirable to dwell here,
because they belong to a totally different level of thought from
that adopted by the other moralists of the period. Let us,
therefore, take his metaphysics and his psychological machinery
(*Treatise*, p. 317 f.) for granted, and assume that it is possible
for a man to enter into the feelings of another man by
sympathy. This assumption he uses to explain the inconsistency between the theory that the virtue of an act is nothing
but the pleasure it gives us and the admitted fact that we
often approve (i. e. feel pleasure at the sight of) actions which
are decidedly hurtful to us and advantageous to our enemies.
We sympathize, he says, with the supposed pleasure which a
quality or character gives the possessor, as we do with the
supposed pleasure of the owner of a useful article, and that
transferred pleasure is sufficient to overcome the pleasure we
feel in surveying qualities useful to ourselves, and to raise in
us a disapproval of our own unjust though profitable actions.
He repudiates the idea that we sympathize with others by
imagining ourselves in their place, but yet he is obliged to
admit that we often sympathize with a purely imaginary pleasure
which no one feels. He also has to admit that sympathy itself
is partial and varies with the proximity and relationship of the
other persons whose supposed pleasure causes ours, whereas

our moral esteem is impartial and does not vary. To get over these difficulties Hume has to call in the assistance of 'general rules' by reference to which we correct the natural variations and deficiencies of our sympathy (§§ 581–6). But the whole difficulty which the theory of sympathy is invoked to solve is the difficulty of explaining how such a 'creature of feeling' as Hume supposes man to be can form or subject himself to general rules of judgement. It is difficult to acquit Hume here of a '*suppositio probandi*' of a very flagrant kind. Somewhat on the lines of this criticism the idealist sets up a theory of sympathy which reverses the relation between sympathy, other than merely animal sympathy, and the conception of a common good, and condemns Hume's theory as preposterous. It is only, he urges, through the conception of a common good that we get that close relation between ourselves and other persons' selves which is required for the working of sympathy. It is because we love and identify ourselves with our neighbour that we are able to sympathize with him. A curious hint of this criticism crops up in Hutcheson (§ 106, cf. § 811), though he arrives at it in a very different way, and the same point is raised by Plato's theory of simultaneous feeling in the fifth book of the *Republic*[1].

Adam Smith is mainly concerned with the psychology of sympathy, but incidentally he makes considerable contributions to the metaphysics of the subject. He starts with an assertion of the individualism of sense, and therefore at once establishes sympathy on a basis of thought. He rejects the 'transfusion' and communicated vivacity of feelings as the foundation of sympathy, and dispenses with all Hume's elaborate machinery for transferring into ourselves the pleasure of another person in things useful to him. He bases moral

---

[1] *Rep.* v. 462; cf. Green, *Proleg.* §§ 200–1; *Introd. to Hume*, ii. § 40.

approval neither on direct nor indirect utilitarianism. We
approve of another's passions when we observe that we entirely
sympathize with them (§ 262) ; we approve of our own passions
when we are able to think that an impartial spectator can sympathize with them (§ 306), and the effect of this sympathy is
that every member of society tries to lower or raise his passions
to that pitch at which the ordinary spectator can sympathize
with them (§§ 273–4, 276–7). At first sight this looks merely
like Hume's standard of morality over again—'the ordinary
course of our passions and actions,' 'the natural and usual force
of our passions' (*Treatise*, pp. 483–8, 532)—and seems to be
only a glorified respectability : indeed it is put forward under the
not very inspiring title of an account of 'propriety.' On examination, however, it reveals a view of the organic unity of social
feeling based on common circumstances and conditions of life
and well-being, which is a great advance on anything which
had fallen from his benevolent or utilitarian predecessors.
Neither party to the controversy had fully recognized the significance of society, nor the really essential relation of morality
to it : the utilitarian had assumed that in society there was
very little to explain, and the sentimentalist accepted this
assumption and offered an explanation which was altogether
insufficient. It was an age of facile individualism, and men
started from a conception of society as built up of individuals
equipped each with a complete moral faculty. The idea of the
individual conscience as only emerging from the social conscience (§§ 307–10), the idea of society as the whole from which
the individual disentangles himself, and in which alone he can
find himself, which is the central idea of Adam Smith's system,
was a notable return to a more concrete method of thought.
As has already been said, the most serious moralists of the time
were preoccupied with the content of the individual moral

consciousness, and their method was mainly introspective. They did their work well, but their method was not one which would lead them to exhaust the meaning of society. Adam Smith was one of the least metaphysical persons that ever wrote, but in some respects he anticipated a theory which some people would regard as metaphysical in the highest degree, that of the 'social self,' and it is a social self which enables us to effect not only an imaginary change of situation with the persons chiefly concerned, but a complete identification of our own person and character with that of another person (§ 339). Yet he does not ignore the influence of common interest, and, if sympathy with the motives of the agent is the source of our idea of propriety, sympathy with the gratitude of the person acted on is the source of our idea of merit: but the latter sympathy does not arise unless there be, first, propriety in the motives of the agent. He is thus enabled to recognize the undeniable element of utility in moral institutions, to which the selfish school had confined its view, and also to preserve those other elements which distinguish moral approval from the approval which we bestow on a well-contrived machine (§ 357). His deliverance of moral approbation from the dead level imposed on it by the selfish and benevolent schools alike, and his restoration of variety and elasticity to that function, would alone be a considerable achievement (§ 353). His theory of sympathy is rather a preservative than a solvent. His system, however, is a 'closed system,' and he refused to recognize the existence of any question which necessarily leads beyond it, and, however useful for practical purposes, as a theory of the moral criterion it is insufficient. He insists, as against Hutcheson, that we do approve, if not of the faculty of approbation, at all events of acts of approbation, and regard them as morally good or bad :

but we can only do this if the basis of approbation is the coincidence of approbations (§ 354). In the same way the 'general rules' which, like Hume, he uses for the correction of our sympathies can only arise from experience of what in particular cases we approve or disapprove of : 'We do not originally approve or condemn particular actions because upon examination they appear to be agreeable or inconsistent with a certain general rule. The general rule, on the contrary, is formed by finding from experience that all actions of a certain kind or circumstanced in a certain manner are approved or disapproved of' (§ 315). The difficulty which we found in allowing Hume to claim the assistance of general rules does not arise here, at all events in the same form. Hume's theory of general rules is preposterous, in the literal sense of the term ; Adam Smith's is rather circular, but the essence of his system is that it is a closed circle of reciprocal sympathy, and as such it deserves more attention than it has recently received from the sociologist, the psychologist, and the moralist.

29. *Association of ideas.*

Association of ideas does not figure as largely in the controversies of this period as one would expect. Hartley, whose *Observations on Man* were published in 1748, states that he was 'put upon considering the power of association' by hearing that 'the Rev. Mr. Gay asserted the possibility of deducing all our intellectual pleasures and pains from association.' Gay asserts that ultimately all affections arise from a desire of private happiness, and that all approbation of acts arises from the consideration of this tendency to private happiness : but the admitted fact that we approve acts and desire objects without considering or being able to see this tendency is due to association of ideas, such approval and affection being properly called habits (§ 855). Under the influence of association we come to look on acts, which originally were only valued as means to pleasure, as ends in themselves, and the origin of these habits is still further concealed from us by the fact that we ' do not always (and perhaps not for the most part) make this association for ourselves, but learn it from others—by imitation, inheritance, or education ' (§§ 881–7). Hartley's work is of the first importance, but it stands on such a different level, and is carried out in such a different spirit from that of the ordinary moral philosophy of the period, that it is omitted from consideration here as well as from the selections.

30. *Desire and pleasure.*

And now we come at last to the fundamental principle of the ' selfish ' system—that in the last resort a man does and can desire nothing but his own pleasure, a fact concealed from himself and others by the thousand complications introduced by social life. Locke makes an important contribution to the psychology of this theory when he asserts that the thought of future pleasure is not sufficient alone to move us to action : it is only when its absence causes us uneasiness that we are stirred to change our situation (§§ 977–980). Locke's theory certainly has the appearance of eliminating conscious thought altogether from desire, of treating desire as a mere sensation, and of reducing to a minimum that contemplation of an object upon which modern Idealism lays so much stress. Whether it really has that effect or is conceived with the malice sometimes attributed to it is doubtful. His theory seems to be not so much that desire is uneasiness, as that desire is never effectual until it reaches the pitch of an uneasiness.

Hutcheson in his earlier book is chiefly concerned to assert the existence in man of a direct desire for another person's good, and he finds evidence of its existence in the fact that it is the object of moral approbation. He is especially careful to show that what we approve is not the subordinate desire of another person's good as a means to our own. Afterwards he enters more seriously into the nature of desire, and asserts as against Locke that desire is ' as distinct from any sensation as the will is from the understanding or senses' (§§ 441, 443), though he admits that perhaps 'we are never conscious of any desire absolutely free from all uneasiness.' The ultimate question, however, is not so much whether desire at its ordinary level is a sensation, as whether it is a natural product of sensation, and further of our own sensation of our own pleasure. This question is concealed behind a crowd of other questions in the decision of which it is not vitally interested. It is not suggested by the sensationalists and hedonists that the immediate conscious object of all desire is pleasure, but it is suggested that we desire other things (e.g. wealth, friendship) for the sake of the pleasures resulting as consequences from their possession or for the sake of the pleasure of successful activity, or for the sake of the pleasure of satisfying a desire and so removing a cause of uneasiness, or for the sake of the concomitant pleasure of self-approval, e.g. in benevolence : that is, that we have had antecedent experience of these pleasures, and the remembrance of them incites us to desire the actions by which they were obtained.

Now with regard to some of these pleasures it is not difficult to show that the selfish theory is preposterous. If it be true that what our moral sense approves in benevolence is only the direct desire of other persons' good, it is clear that we must have had the desire before we could experience the pleasure of approving it. Also we must have had the desire before we could experience the pleasure of feeling that its uneasiness is removed, or what is more commonly called the pleasure of the gratification or satisfaction of the desire. Perhaps also it might be said that the pleasure of success only comes to the man who has entertained a desire for the activity. But with regard to the pleasure which results from an activity as its consequence it must be remembered that the selfish school is entitled to all the benefit of the theory of association of ideas (until that theory is shown to be fallacious or inapplicable) whereby actions, which have in the course of undesigned experience been associated with pleasure, first become regarded as means to pleasure, and afterwards become regarded as ends in themselves. It does not seem, therefore, to be a sufficient answer to the selfish theory to say with Butler that at the present stage of man's existence his desires 'rest in their objects' as ends. You will have to show from an analysis of the idea of desire itself that there is something more in it than can be accounted for by a reminiscence of pleasure as modified by association. But he, it is true, ingeniously defines pleasure, or rather happiness, in such a way as to support his theory of ultimate desires, when he says (§ 231) that 'happiness ... consists only in the enjoyment of those objects which are by nature suited to our several particular appetites, passions, and affections': if this be meant not merely as a description of the present psychological conditions of happiness for man, but as a statement of the nature of happiness, it does indeed imply that appetites, &c., are necessarily antecedent to the experience of happiness. But it may obviously be accepted in the other sense as the judgement of a reflective person on the present position of mankind, of the same kind and entitled to the same respect as his declaration that 'disengagement is absolutely necessary to enjoyme'nt.' In other words, it forms part of his argument that we are not moved to all our actions by a reflective and conscious self-love, and that we are not nearly so engrossed with ourselves as some people tell us. It is noticeable that Butler lumps together for this purpose 'appetites, passions, and affections,' though one would have thought it necessary to distinguish, in an account of desire, between hunger and the desire of esteem or benevolence. Price concurs with Butler and Hutcheson in their criticisms of the selfish theory (§§ 651-3), and he definitely asserts the foundation of ultimate desires in the 'nature of things' (§§ 644, 648). Grave considerations of 'economy' have to be reckoned with here, and, though we may admit that against the crude theory of conscious selfishness Butler and Hutcheson make a fair defence, we have to ask, Is their theory valid against a further analysis ? We may also admit that at a certain level, the level of the adult civilized man, their analysis is fairly good, but to offer as final a theory of desire which is based on such an analysis is obviously impossible. It may be true that in the desire of a social human being there is some element which is not present in animal desire, but it is clear that a theory of desire which ignores its physiological and biological aspects is even more impossible at the present day than it was when Plato discoursed about ἔρως, the continuous principle alike of animal reproduction and of philosophic absorption in reality ; and when we are considering the relation of desire to pleasure those aspects become especially prominent. The empirical hedonistic explanation of desire such as is given by J. Clarke (§§ 778-782) accepts the alternative offered it by Price (§ 652) and assumes that our first activities are unmotived gropings and our first experiences of pleasure accidental so far as the individual is concerned, though for the scientific observer they have a great significance [1] (§§ 808, 941). The experience of pleasure in an act or resulting from an act tends to make us repeat the act, until we come consciously to perform the act for the sake of obtaining the pleasure attached to it. The love of our neighbour is as much interested as the love of oysters, though the theory requires the first oyster to have been eaten by accident. The 'mind is conscious of a pleasure arising from the observed union of virtue and happiness, and of uneasiness from their separation, and this without the mixture of any selfish views; but then the disposition of the mind to actions of civility and kindness in favour of the eminently virtuous arises from the reflection upon the said pleasure and pain, and the performance of those actions is visibly intended in order to avoid the pain and procure the pleasure' (§ 782).

It is worth noting that the argument used by Balguy (§ 725) to depreciate pleasure—viz. that in desiring pleasure the ultimate end of the agent is not pleasure but self, the idea of which is perpetually uppermost—has been reversed and used to show the presence in all human desire of an element attributable to reason alone [2].

31. *The greatest happiness of the greatest number.*

There is very little discussion of the 'summum bonum' in our writers. It is generally assumed to be happiness, though there is a visible tendency to modify it into 'deserved happiness,' and though the intellectualists assert the distinction between moral and natural good.

It was not reserved for Bentham to formulate 'the greatest happiness of the greatest number' principle, though he may fairly claim the credit of 'one man to count for one and no

[1] Cf. Herbert Spencer, *Data of Ethics*, c. 6. § 33 f.
[2] Green, *Proleg.* §§ 129–130, 222–3.

more than one,' a principle which alone makes the calculation of 'lots of happiness' theoretically possible and morally useless. The moralists of our period were indeed very well aware of the difficulties of the greatest happiness formula. Hutcheson points out truly enough (§ 452) that the conception of 'the greatest possible aggregate or sum of happiness,' like the conception of 'all mankind or the system of rationals,' is not a working conception, used by us in deciding on particular actions. 'These conceptions only serve to suggest greater ends than would occur to us without reflection,' 'that so we may gratify our self-love or kind affections in the fullest manner as far as our power extends, and may not content ourselves with smaller degrees either of public or private good while greater are in our power.' On the other hand, Kames (§ 939) justly points out the notable effect of general terms upon our imagination ; 'nothing is more wonderful than that a general term to which a very faint, if any, idea is affixed should be the foundation of a more intense affection than is bestowed, for the most part, upon particular objects, how attractive soever '; and so we do for ' our country, our religion, our government,' what we would not do for our friends, and give up to mankind, like Mrs. Jellyby in *Bleak House*, what were more properly bestowed upon our families.

Hutcheson also (§ 453) emphatically blocks the direct road between 'individualistic' and 'universalistic' hedonism. Unless we have public affections, he says, 'this truth "that a hundred felicities is a greater sum than one felicity" will no more excite to study the happiness of the hundred than this truth, "an hundred stones are greater than one," will excite a man who has no desire of heaps to cast them together.' The distinction between the quality and quantity of pleasure, and the selection of the experienced man, who can only be the good man, as arbitrator in the question of the superiority of pleasures, of which Mill[1] makes such use, both appear in Hutcheson (§ 478).

32. *Conclusion.*

To carry the examination of the moral philosophy of this period further would lead me beyond the limits of space and method suitable to an introduction. From the topics, however, upon which I have been able to touch, it is evident that modern moral speculation has developed principally on lines which took a fresh start even if they did not originate in the eighteenth century. Kant, whose principal moral writings were published between 1785 and 1788, adopts an attitude towards experience which is essentially that of the intellectualists. He goes indeed far beyond them, in that he offers his theory of morals in connexion with a systematic theory of experience, speculative and practical; but he starts as they do, and as Professor Green does, by accepting the assumption of the sensationalist, that sense alone is blank, chaotic, and incapable of organization into such a cosmos of experience as we all claim to possess. The depreciation of sense is willingly accepted in order to magnify the function of reason, and though later English adherents of the school repudiate the doctrine that sensation apart from reason is anything but a name, they continue to take full advantage of the antithesis which is admitted to be false, instead of beginning over again with a more concrete conception of sense. So far, however, as Kant is concerned, no criticism of his moral theory (apart from the doctrine of the 'practical reason') is more useful than that which proceeds on the sober, rather unimaginative lines of the British moralist,

[1] *Utilitarianism*, c. 2.

and demands the justification of each argument before the bar of the common moral consciousness.

The sentimentalists may seem to have contributed comparatively little to living moral theory, but we owe a good deal to their method of holding fast to the content of experience and resisting all attempts to explain it away. If, as appears probable, the recent developments of scientific psychology are destined to modify very considerably our views as to the capacity of sensible experience, it may be that the sentimentalists will be found not to have been stranded so far from the main stream of speculation as once was thought. In spite of the development of sociology, social psychology has received very little attention. Utilitarianism and scientific hedonism have proceeded mainly on an individualistic basis, for which the atomism of the sensationalist theory on which they rest is at least partly responsible. There has, it is true, been of recent years quite an Aristotelian reaction in our Universities against atomism in political and social theory, but the development of this tendency into a re-examination of the psychological data has so far been rather disappointing. We have been so much engrossed with tracing the historical evolution of institutions from the primitive to the civilized, that we have been rather neglectful of their interpretation, the key to which, even more conspicuously in the theory of practice than in the theory of knowledge, lies in psychological analysis.

Feb. 1, 1897.

BRITISH MORALISTS

SHAFTESBURY

AN INQUIRY CONCERNING VIRTUE OR MERIT

[First printed, 1699. Reprinted in ' Characteristics of Men, Manners, Opinions, and Times,' vol. ii. 1711. Reprinted here from the fifth edition of the 'Characteristics,' 1732.]

SHAFTESBURY

An Inquiry concerning Virtue

———◆———

BOOK I. PART II.

Sect. I.

1 WHEN we reflect on any ordinary Frame or Constitution either of Art or Nature; and consider how hard it is to give the least account of a particular *Part*, without a competent Knowledg of *the Whole* : we need not wonder to find our-selves at a loss in many things relating to the Constitution and Frame of *Nature* her-self. For to what End in Nature many things, even whole Species of Creatures, refer; or to what purpose they serve; will be hard for any-one justly to determine: But to what End the many Proportions and various Shapes of Parts in many Creatures actually serve; we are able, by the help of Study and Observation, to demonstrate, with great exactness.

We know that every Creature has a private Good and Interest of his own; which Nature has compel'd him to seek, by all the Advantages afforded him, within the compass of his Make. We know that there is in reality a right and a wrong State of every Creature; and that his right-one is by Nature forwarded, and by himself affectionately sought. There being therefore in every Creature a certain *Interest or Good*; there

must be also a certain END, to which every thing in his Constitution must *naturally* refer.   To this END, if any thing, either
in his Appetites, Passions, or Affections, be not conducing, but
the contrary; we must of necessity own it *ill* to him.   And in
this manner he is *ill, with respect to himself*; as he certainly
is, *with respect to others of his kind*, when any such Appetites
or Passions make him any-way injurious to them.   Now, if by
the natural Constitution of any rational Creature, the same
Irregularitys of Appetite which make him ill *to Others*, make
him ill also *to Himself*; and if the same Regularity of Affections, which causes him to be good in *one* sense, causes
him to be good also in *the other*; then is that Goodness by
which he is thus useful to others, a real Good and Advantage
to himself.   And thus *Virtue* and *Interest* may be found at
last to agree.

Of this we shall consider particularly in the latter part of
our *Inquiry*.   Our first Design is, to see if we can clearly
determine what that Quality is to which we give the Name of
Goodness, or VIRTUE.

2 Shou'd a Historian or Traveller describe to us a certain
Creature of a more solitary Disposition than ever was yet heard
of ; one who had neither Mate nor Fellow of any kind ; nothing
of his own Likeness, towards which he stood well-affected or
inclin'd ; nor any thing without, or beyond himself, for which
he had the least Passion or Concern : we might be apt to
say perhaps, without much hesitation, ' That this was doubtless
a very melancholy Creature, and that in this unsociable and
sullen State he was like to have a very disconsolate kind of
Life.'   But if we were assur'd, that notwithstanding all Appearances, the Creature enjoy'd himself extremely, had a great
relish of Life, and was in nothing wanting to his own Good ;
we might acknowledg perhaps, ' That the Creature was no
Monster, nor absurdly constituted *as to himself*.'   But we
shou'd hardly, after all, be induc'd to say of him, ' That he
was *a good Creature*.'   However, shou'd it be urg'd against

us, 'That such as he was, the Creature was still *perfect in himself*, and therefore to be esteem'd good : *For what had he to do with others ?*' In this sense, indeed, we might be forc'd to acknowledg, 'That he was *a good Creature*; if he cou'd be understood to be absolute and compleat in himself ; without any real relation to any thing in the Universe besides.' For shou'd there be any where in Nature *a System*, of which this living Creature was to be consider'd as *a Part*; then cou'd he no-wise be allow'd *good* ; whilst he plainly appear'd to be such *a Part*, as made rather to the harm than good of that System or *Whole* in which he was included.

3   If therefore in the Structure of this or any other Animal, there be any thing which points beyond himself, and by which he is plainly discover'd to have relation to some other Being or Nature besides his own ; then will this Animal undoubtedly be esteem'd *a Part* of some other System.   For instance, if an Animal has the Proportions of a Male, it shews he has relation to a Female.   And the respective Proportions both of the Male and Female will be allow'd, doubtless, to have a joint-relation to another Existence and Order of things beyond themselves.   So that the Creatures are both of 'em to be con-sider'd as Parts of *another System :* which is that of a particular Race or Species of living Creatures, who have some one *common Nature*, or are provided for, by some one *Order* or *Constitution* of things subsisting together, and co-operating towards their Conservation, and Support.

In the same manner, if a whole Species of Animals con-tribute to the Existence or Well-being of some other ; then is that whole Species, in general, *a Part* only of some other System.

For instance ; To the Existence of the Spider, that of the Fly is absolutely necessary.   The heedless Flight, weak Frame, and tender Body of this latter Insect, fit and determine him as much *a Prey*, as the rough Make, Watchfulness, and Cunning of the former, fit him for Rapine, and the ensnaring part.   The

Web and Wing are suted to each other. And in the Structure
of each of these Animals, there is as apparent and perfect
a relation to the other, as in our own Bodys there is a relation
of Limbs and Organs; or, as in the Branches or Leaves of
a Tree, we see a relation of each to the other, and all, in
common, to *one* Root and Trunk.

In the same manner are Flies also necessary to the Existence
of other Creatures, both Fowls and Fish. And thus are other
Species or Kinds subservient to one another; as being *Parts*
of *a certain System*, and included in one and the same *Order*
of Beings.

So that there is a System of all Animals; an *Animal-Order*
or *Œconomy*, according to which the animal Affairs are
regulated and dispos'd.

Now, if the whole System of Animals, together with that of
Vegetables, and all other things in this inferior World, be
properly comprehended in *one System* of a Globe or Earth:
And if, again, this *Globe* or *Earth* it-self appears to have a real
Dependence on something still beyond; as, for example, either
on its Sun, the Galaxy, or its Fellow-Planets; then is it in
reality a PART only of some other System. And if it be
allow'd, that there is in like manner a SYSTEM *of all Things,
and a Universal Nature*; there can be no particular Being or
System which is not either good or ill in that *general one* of
the *Universe*: For if it be insignificant and of no use, it is
a Fault or Imperfection, and consequently ill in the general
System.

4   Therefore if any Being be *wholly* and *really* ILL, it must
be ill with respect to the Universal System; and then the
System of the Universe is ill, or imperfect. But if the Ill of
one private System be the Good of others; if it makes still to
the Good of the general System, (as when one Creature lives
by the Destruction of another; one thing is generated from
the Corruption of another; or one planetary System or *Vortex*
may swallow up another) then is the Ill of that private System

no real Ill in it-self; any more than the pain of breeding
Teeth is ill, in a System or Body which is so constituted,
that without this occasion of Pain, it wou'd suffer worse, by
being defective.

So that we cannot say of any Being, that it is *wholly* and
absolutely ill, unless we can positively shew and ascertain, that
what we call ILL is no where GOOD besides, in any other
System, or with respect to any other Order or Œconomy
whatsoever.

But were there in the World any intire Species of Animals
destructive to every other, it may be justly call'd an *ill* Species;
as being ill in the *Animal-System*. And if in any Species of
Animals (as in *Men*, for example) one Man is of a nature
pernicious to the rest, he is in this respect justly styl'd *an ill Man*.

5   We do not however say of any-one, that he is an *ill Man*
because he has the Plague-Spots upon him, or because he has
convulsive Fits which make him strike and wound such as
approach him. Nor do we say on the other side, that he is
a good Man, when having his Hands ty'd up, he is hinder'd
from doing the Mischief he designs; or (which is in a manner
the same) when he abstains from executing his ill purpose, thro'
a fear of some impending Punishment, or thro' the allurement
of some exterior Reward.

So that in a sensible Creature, that which is not done thro'
any Affection at all, makes neither Good nor Ill in the nature
of that Creature; who then only is suppos'd *Good*, when the
Good or Ill of the System to which he has relation, is the
immediate Object of some Passion or Affection moving him.

Since it is therefore by Affection merely that a Creature is
esteem'd good or ill, *natural* or *unnatural*; our business will
be, to examine which are the *good* and *natural*, and which the
ill and *unnatural* Affections.

Sect. II.

6   In the first place then, it may be observ'd, that if there be
an Affection towards any Subject consider'd as private Good,

which is[1] not really such, but imaginary; this Affection, as being superfluous, and detracting from the Force of other requisite and good Affections, is in it-self vitious and ill, even in respect of the private Interest or Happiness of the Creature.

If there can possibly be suppos'd in a Creature such an Affection towards Self-Good, as is actually, in its natural degree, conducing to his private Interest, and at the same time inconsistent with the publick Good; this may indeed be call'd still a vitious Affection : And on this Supposition a Creature[1] cannot really be good and natural in respect of his Society or Publick, without being ill and unnatural toward himself. But if the Affection be then only injurious to the Society, when it is immoderate, and not so when it is moderate, duly temper'd, and allay'd; then is *the immoderate* degree of the Affection truly vitious, but not *the moderate.* And thus, if there be found in any Creature a more than ordinary Self-concernment, or Regard to private Good, which is inconsistent with the Interest of the Species or Publick; this must in every respect be esteem'd an ill and vitious Affection. And this is what we commonly call[1] SELFISHNESS, and disapprove so much, in whatever Creature we happen to discover it.

7   On the other side, if the Affection towards private or Self-good, however *selfish* it may be esteem'd, is in reality not only consistent with publick Good, but in some measure contributing to it; if it be such, perhaps, as for the good of the Species in general, every Individual ought to share ; 'tis so far from being ill, or blameable in any sense, that it must be acknowledg'd absolutely necessary to constitute a Creature *Good.* For if the want of such an Affection as that towards Self-preservation, be injurious to the Species; a Creature is ill and unnatural as well thro' this Defect, as thro' the want of any other natural Affection. And this no-one wou'd doubt to pronounce, if he saw a Man who minded not any Precipices which lay in his way, nor made any distinction of Food, Diet, Clothing, or

[1] *Infra,* § 27, 60, &c.

whatever else related to his Health and Being. The same wou'd be aver'd of one who had a Disposition which render'd him averse to any Commerce with Womankind, and of consequence unfitted him thro' *Illness of Temper* (and not merely thro' *a Defect of Constitution*) for the propagation of his Species or Kind.

8   Thus the Affection towards Self-good, may be a good Affection, or an ill-one. For if this private Affection be too strong, (as when the *excessive Love of Life* unfits a Creature for any generous Act) then is it undoubtedly vitious ; and if vitious, the Creature who is mov'd by it, is vitiously mov'd, and can never be otherwise than vitious in some degree, when mov'd by that Affection. Therefore if thro' such an earnest and passionate *Love of Life*, a Creature be accidentally induc'd to do Good, (as he might be upon the same terms induc'd to do ILL) he is no more a good Creature for this Good he executes, than a Man is the more an honest or good Man either for pleading a just Cause, or fighting in a good one, for the sake merely of his Fee or Stipend.

9   Whatsoever therefore is done which happens to be advan·tageous to the Species, thro' an Affection merely towards Self-good, does not imply any more Goodness in the Creature than as the Affection it-self is good. Let him, in any particular, act ever so well ; if at the bottom, it be that selfish Affection alone which moves him ; he is in himself still vitious. Nor can any Creature be consider'd otherwise, when the Passion towards Self-good, tho ever so moderate, is his real motive in the doing that, to which a natural Affection for his Kind ought by right to have inclin'd him.

And indeed whatever exterior Helps or Succours an ill-dispos'd Creature may find, to push him on towards the performance of any one good Action ; there can no Goodness arise in him, till his *Temper* be so far chang'd, that in the issue he comes in earnest to be led by some immediate Affection, *directly*, and not *accidentally*, to Good, and against Ill.

For instance ; if one of those Creatures suppos'd to be by Nature tame, gentle, and favourable to Mankind, be, contrary to his natural Constitution, fierce and savage; we instantly remark the Breach of *Temper*, and own the Creature to be unnatural and corrupt. If at any time afterwards, the same Creature, by good Fortune or right Management, comes to lose his Fierceness, and is made tame, gentle, and treatable, like other Creatures of his Kind; 'tis acknowledg'd that the Creature thus restor'd becomes good and natural. Suppose, now, that the Creature has indeed a tame and gentle Carriage ; but that it proceeds only from *the fear of his Keeper* ; which if set aside, his predominant Passion instantly breaks out : then is his Gentleness not his real Temper ; but, his true and genuine *Nature* or *natural Temper* remaining just as it was, the Creature is still as *ill* as ever.

10   Nothing therefore being properly either Goodness or Illness in a Creature, except what is from *natural Temper*; 'A good Creature is such a one as by the natural Temper or Bent of his Affections is carry'd *primarily and immediately*, and not *secondarily and accidentally*, to Good, and against Ill : ' And an *ill Creature* is just the contrary ; *viz.* 'One who is wanting in right Affections, of force enough to carry him *directly* towards Good, and bear him out against Ill ; or who is carry'd by other Affections directly to Ill, and against Good.'

When in general, all the Affections or Passions are suted to the publick Good, or good of the Species, as above-mention'd ; then is the *natural Temper* intirely good. If, on the contrary, any requisite Passion be wanting ; or if there be any one super-numerary, or weak, or any-wise disserviceable, or contrary to that main End ; then is the natural Temper, and consequently the Creature himself, in some measure corrupt and *ill*.

There is no need of mentioning either *Envy, Malice, Frowardness*, or other such hateful Passions ; to shew in what manner they are ill, and constitute an *ill* Creature. But it may be necessary perhaps to remark, that even as to *Kindness* and *Love* of the most natural sort, (such as that of any Creature for its Offspring) if it be immoderate and beyond a certain degree, it is undoubtedly vitious.   For thus over-great *Tenderness* destroys the Effect of Love, and excessive *Pity* renders us uncapable of giving succour.   Hence the Excess of motherly Love is own'd to be a *vitious Fondness*; over-great Pity, *Effeminacy and Weakness*; over-great Concern for Self-preservation, *Meanness and Cowardice*; too little, *Rashness*; and none at all, or that which is contrary, (*viz.* a Passion leading to Self-destruction) a *mad* and *desperate Depravity*.

Sect. III.

11   But to proceed from what is esteem'd mere *Goodness*, and lies within the reach and capacity of all *sensible Creatures*, to that which is call'd Virtue or Merit, and is allow'd to *Man* only.

In a Creature capable of forming general Notions of Things, not only the outward Beings which offer themselves to the Sense, are the Objects of the Affection ; but the very *Actions* themselves, and the *Affections* of Pity, Kindness, Gratitude, and their Contrarys, being brought into the Mind by Reflection, become Objects.   So that, by means of this reflected Sense, there arises another kind of Affection towards those very Affections themselves, which have been already felt, and are now become the Subject of a new Liking or Dislike.

12   The Case is the same in *mental* or *moral* Subjects, as in ordinary *Bodys*, or the common Subjects of *Sense*.   The Shapes, Motions, Colours, and Proportions of these latter being presented to our Eye ; there necessarily results a [1] Beauty or Deformity, according to the different Measure, Arrangement and Disposition of their several Parts.   So in *Behaviour* and *Actions*, when presented to our Understanding, there must be found, of necessity, an apparent Difference, according to the Regularity or Irregularity of the Subjects.

[1] *Infra,* § 67.

The Mind, which is Spectator or Auditor of *other Minds*, cannot be without its *Eye* and *Ear* ; so as to discern Proportion, distinguish Sound, and scan each Sentiment or Thought which comes before it.   It can let nothing escape its Censure.   It feels the Soft and Harsh, the Agreeable and Disagreeable, in the Affections ; and finds a *Foul* and *Fair*, a *Harmonious* and a *Dissonant*, as really and truly here, as in any musical Numbers, or in the outward Forms or Representations of sensible Things.   Nor can it[1] with-hold its *Admiration* and *Extasy*, its *Aversion* and *Scorn*, any more in what relates to one than to the other of these Subjects.   So that to deny the common and natural Sense of a SUBLIME and BEAUTIFUL in Things, will appear an Affectation merely, to any-one who considers duly of this Affair.

Now as in the *sensible* kind of Objects, the Species or Images of Bodys, Colours, and Sounds, are perpetually moving before our Eyes, and acting on our Senses, even when we sleep ; so in the *moral* and *intellectual* kind, the Forms and Images of Things are no less active and incumbent on the Mind, at all Seasons, and even when the real Objects themselves are absent.

In these vagrant Characters or Pictures of *Manners*, which the Mind of necessity figures to it-self, and carrys still about with it, the Heart cannot possibly remain neutral ; but constantly takes part one way or other.   However false or corrupt it be within it-self, it finds the difference, as to Beauty and Comeliness, between one *Heart* and another, one *Turn of Affection*, one *Behaviour*, one *Sentiment* and another ; and accordingly, in all disinterested Cases, must approve in some measure of what is natural and honest, and disapprove what is dishonest and corrupt.

Thus the several Motions, Inclinations, Passions, Dispositions, and consequent Carriage and Behaviour of Creatures in the various Parts of Life, being in several Views or Per-

[1] *Infra*, § 67.

spectives represented to the Mind, which readily discerns the Good and Ill towards the Species or Publick; there arises a new Trial or Exercise of the Heart: which must either rightly and soundly affect what is just and right, and disaffect what is contrary; or, corruptly affect what is ill, and disaffect what is worthy and good.

13   And in this Case alone it is we call any Creature *worthy* or *virtuous*, when it can have the Notion of a publick Interest, and can attain the Speculation or Science of what is morally good or ill, admirable or blameable, right or wrong. For tho we may vulgarly call an ill Horse *vitious*, yet we never say of a good one, nor of any mere Beast, Idiot, or Changeling, tho ever so good-natur'd, that he is *worthy* or *virtuous*.

So that if a Creature be generous, kind, constant, compassionate; yet if he cannot reflect on what he himself does, or sees others do, so as to take notice of what is *worthy* or *honest*; and make that Notice or Conception of *Worth* and *Honesty* to be an Object of his Affection; he has not the Character of being *virtuous*: for thus, and not otherwise, he is capable of having *a Sense of Right or Wrong*; a Sentiment or Judgment of what is done, thro' just, equal, and good Affection, or the contrary.

Whatsoever is done thro' any unequal Affection, is *iniquous*, *wicked*, and *wrong*. If the Affection be equal, sound, and good, and the Subject of the Affection such as may with advantage to Society be ever in the same manner prosecuted, or affected; this must necessarily constitute what we call *Equity* and *Right* in any Action. For, WRONG is not such Action as is barely the Cause of Harm, (since at this rate a dutiful Son aiming at an Enemy, but by mistake or ill chance happening to kill his Father, wou'd do *a Wrong*) but when any thing is done thro' insufficient or unequal Affection, (as when a Son shews no Concern for the Safety of a Father; or, where there is need of Succour, prefers an indifferent Person to him, this is the nature of *Wrong*).

14   Neither can any Weakness or Imperfection in the Senses
be the occasion of *Iniquity* or *Wrong*; if the Object of the
Mind it-self be not at any time absurdly fram'd, nor any way
improper, but sutable, just, and worthy of the Opinion and
Affection apply'd to it.   For if we will suppose a Man, who
being sound and intire both in his Reason and Affection, has
nevertheless so deprav'd a Constitution or Frame of Body,
that the natural Objects are, thro' his Organs of Sense, as thro'
ill Glasses, falsly convey'd and misrepresented ; 'twill be soon
observ'd, in such a Person's case, that since his Failure is not
in his principal or leading Part; he cannot in himself be
esteem'd *iniquous*, or unjust.

15   'Tis otherwise in what relates to *Opinion*, Belief, or Speculation.   For as the Extravagance of Judgment or Belief is such,
that in some Countrys even Monkeys, Cats, Crocodiles, and
other vile or destructive Animals, have been esteem'd *holy*,
and worshipp'd even as *Deitys*; shou'd it appear to any-one of
the Religion or Belief of those Countrys, that to save such
a Creature as a Cat, preferably to a Parent, was *Right*; and
that other Men, who had not the same religious Opinion, were
to be treated as Enemys, till converted ; this wou'd be certainly
Wrong, and wicked in the Believer : and every Action,
grounded on this Belief, wou'd be an *iniquous*, wicked, and
vitious Action.

And thus whatsoever causes a Misconception or Misapprehension of the Worth or Value of any Object, so as to
diminish a due, or raise any undue, irregular, or unsocial
Affection, must necessarily be the occasion of *Wrong*.   Thus
he who affects or loves a Man for the sake of something which
is reputed honourable, but which is in reality vitious, is himself
vitious and ill.   The beginnings of this Corruption may be
noted in many Occurrences : As when an ambitious Man, by
the Fame of his high Attempts, a Conqueror or a Pirate by
his boasted Enterprizes, raises in another Person an Esteem
and Admiration of that immoral and inhuman Character,

which deserves Abhorrence : 'tis then that the Hearer becomes corrupt, when he secretly approves the Ill he hears. But on the other side, the Man who loves and esteems another, as believing him to have that Virtue which he has not, but only counterfeits, is not on this account either vitious or corrupt.

16   A Mistake therefore *in Fact* being no Cause or Sign of ill Affection, can be no Cause of Vice. But a Mistake *of Right* being the Cause of unequal Affection, must of necessity be the Cause of vitious Action, in every intelligent or rational Being.

But as there are many Occasions where the matter of *Right* may even to the most discerning part of Mankind appear difficult, and of doubtful Decision, 'tis not a slight Mistake of this kind which can destroy the Character of *a virtuous or worthy Man.* But when, either thro' Superstition or ill Custom, there come to be very gross Mistakes in the assign-ment or application of the Affection ; when the Mistakes are either in their nature so gross, or so complicated and frequent, that a Creature cannot well live in a natural State; nor with due Affections, compatible with human Society and civil Life ; then is the Character of VIRTUE fofeited.

17   And thus we find how far WORTH and VIRTUE depend on a knowledg of *Right* and *Wrong,* and on a use of Reason, sufficient to secure a right application of the Affections ; that nothing horrid or unnatural, nothing unexemplary, nothing destructive of that natural Affection by which the Species or Society is upheld, may, on any account, or thro' any Principle or Notion of Honour or Religion, be at any time affected or prosecuted as a good and proper object of Esteem. For such a Principle as this must be wholly vitious : and whatsoever is acted upon it, can be no other than Vice and Immorality. And thus if there be any thing which teaches Men either Treachery, Ingratitude, or Cruelty, by divine Warrant; or under colour and pretence of any present or future Good to Mankind : if there be any thing which teaches Men to per-

secute their Friends thro' Love ; or to torment Captives of
War in sport ; or to offer human Sacrifice ; or to torment,
macerate, or mangle themselves, in a religious Zeal, before
their God ; or to commit any sort of Barbarity, or Brutality, as
amiable or becoming : be it Custom which gives Applause, or
Religion which gives a Sanction ; this is not, nor ever can be
Virtue, of any kind, or in any sense ; but must remain still
horrid Depravity, notwithstanding any Fashion, Law, Custom,
or Religion ; which may be ill and vitious *it-self*, but can
never alter the *eternal Measures*, and immutable independent
Nature of *Worth* and VIRTUE.

Sect. IV.

18   Upon the whole. As to those Creatures which are only
capable of being mov'd by *sensible Objects* ; they are accordingly
good or *vitious*, as the sensible Affections stand with them.
'Tis otherwise in Creatures capable of framing *rational
Objects* of moral Good. For in one of this kind, shou'd the
sensible Affections stand ever so much amiss ; yet if they prevail
not, because of those other *rational Affections* spoken of ; 'tis
evident, the Temper still holds good in the main ; and the
Person is with justice esteem'd virtuous by all Men.

19   More than this. If by Temper any one is passionate,
angry, fearful, amorous ; yet resists these Passions, and notwithstanding the force of their Impression, adheres to *Virtue* ;
we say commonly in this case, *that the Virtue is the greater :*
and we say well. Tho if that which restrains the Person, and
holds him to a virtuous-like Behaviour, be no Affection
towards Goodness or Virtue it-self, but towards private Good
merely, he is not in reality the more virtuous ; as has been
shewn before. But this still is evident, that if voluntarily, and
without foreign Constraint, an angry Temper bears, or an
amorous one refrains, so that neither any cruel or immodest
Action can be forc'd from such a Person, tho ever so strongly
tempted by his Constitution ; we applaud his Virtue above
what we shou'd naturally do, if he were free of this Temptation,

and these Propensitys. At the same time, there is no body will say that a Propensity to Vice can be an Ingredient in Virtue, or any way necessary to compleat a virtuous Character.

There seems therefore to be some kind of difficulty in the Case : but it amounts only to this. If there be any part of the Temper in which ill Passions or Affections are seated, whilst in another part the Affections towards moral Good are such as absolutely to master those Attempts of their Antagonists; this is the greatest *Proof* imaginable, that a strong Principle of Virtue lies at the bottom, and has possess'd it-self of the natural Temper. Whereas if there be no ill Passions stirring, a Person may be indeed more *cheaply virtuous* ; that is to say, he may conform himself to the known Rules of Virtue, without sharing so much of a virtuous Principle as another. Yet if that other Person, who has the Principle of Virtue so strongly implanted, comes at last to lose those contrary Impediments suppos'd in him, he certainly loses nothing in Virtue; but on the contrary, losing only what is vitious in his Temper, is left more intire to Virtue, and possesses it in a higher degree.

20   Thus is *Virtue* shar'd in different degrees by rational Creatures; such at least as are call'd *rational* ; but who come short of that sound and well-establish'd Reason, which alone can constitute a *just Affection*, a uniform and steddy *Will* and *Resolution*. And thus Vice and Virtue are found variously mix'd, and alternately prevalent in the several Characters of Mankind. For it seems evident from our *Inquiry*, that how ill soever the Temper or Passions may stand with respect either to the sensible or the moral Objects ; however passionate, furious, lustful, or cruel any Creature may become ; however vitious the Mind be, or whatever ill Rules or Principles it goes by ; yet if there be any Flexibleness or favourable Inclination towards the least moral Object, the least appearance of moral Good, (as if there be any such thing as *Kindness*, *Gratitude*, *Bounty*, or *Compassion*) there is still something of *Virtue* left ; and the Creature is not wholly vitious and unnatural.

Thus a Ruffian, who out of a sense of Fidelity and Honour of any kind, refuses to discover his Associates ; and rather than betray them, is content to endure Torments and Death ; has certainly some Principle of Virtue, however he may mis-apply it. 'Twas the same Case with that Malefactor, who rather than do the Office of Executioner to his Companions, chose to keep 'em company in their Execution.

In short : As it seems hard to pronounce of any Man, ' That he is *absolutely an Atheist* ; ' so it appears altogether as hard to pronounce of any Man, ' That he is *absolutely corrupt or vitious* ; ' there being few, even of the horridest Villains, who have not something of *Virtue* in this imperfect sense. Nothing is more just than a known saying, ' *That it is as hard to find a Man wholly Ill, as wholly Good* : ' because wherever there is any good Affection left, there is certainly some *Goodness* or *Virtue* still in being.

And, having consider'd thus of VIRTUE, *What it is in it-self ;* we may now consider how it stands *with respect to the Opinions concerning a* DEITY, as above-mention'd.

BOOK I. PART III.

Sect. I.

21   The Nature of VIRTUE consisting (as has been explain'd) *in a certain just Disposition, or proportionable Affection of a rational Creature towards the moral Objects of Right and Wrong* ; nothing can possibly in such a Creature exclude a Principle of Virtue, or render it ineffectual, except what,

1. Either takes away the *natural* and *just* Sense of Right and Wrong :

2. Or creates *a wrong* Sense of it :

3. Or causes the right Sense to be oppos'd, by *contrary* Affections.

On the other side, nothing can assist, or advance the Principle of Virtue, except what *either* in some manner nourishes and promotes a Sense of Right and Wrong ; *or* preserves it genuine and uncorrupt ; *or* causes it, when such, to be obey'd, by subduing and subjecting the other Affections to it.

We are to consider, therefore, how any of the above-mention'd Opinions on the Subject of a DEITY, may influence in these Cases, or produce either of these *three* Effects.

I. As to *the first Case* ; THE TAKING AWAY THE NATURAL SENSE OF RIGHT AND WRONG.

It will not surely be understood, that by this is meant *the taking away the Nation of what is* good *or* ill *in the Species, or Society*. For of the Reality of such a *Good* and *Ill*, no rational Creature can possibly be insensible. Every one discerns and owns a publick Interest, and is conscious of what affects his Fellowship or Community. When we say therefore of a Creature, ' That he has wholly lost the Sense of Right and Wrong ; ' we suppose that being able to discern the *Good* and *Ill* of his Species, he has at the same time no Concern for either, nor any Sense of Excellency or Baseness in any moral Action, relating to one or the other. So that except merely with respect to a private and narrowly confin'd Self-good, 'tis suppos'd there is in such a Creature no *Liking* or *Dislike* of Manners ; no Admiration, or Love of any thing as morally good ; nor Hatred of any thing as morally ill, be it ever so unnatural or deform'd.

There is in reality no rational Creature whatsoever, who knows not that when he voluntarily offends or does harm to anyone, he cannot fail to create an Apprehension and Fear of like harm, and consequently a Resentment and Animosity in every Creature who observes him. So that the Offender must needs be conscious of being liable to such Treatment from every-one, as if he had in some degree offended All.

Thus Offence and Injury are always known as punishable by every-one ; and equal Behaviour, which is therefore call'd MERIT, as rewardable and well-deserving from every-one. Of this even the wickedest Creature living must have a *Sense*. So

that if there be any further meaning in this *Sense* of Right and
Wrong; if in reality there be any *Sense* of this kind which an
absolute wicked Creature has not; it must consist in a real
Antipathy or Aversion to *Injustice* or *Wrong*, and in a real
Affection or Love towards *Equity* and *Right*, for its own sake,
and on the account of its own natural Beauty and Worth.

22   'Tis impossible to suppose a mere sensible Creature originally so ill-constituted, and unnatural, as that from the moment
he comes to be try'd by sensible Objects, he shou'd have no
one good Passion towards his Kind, no foundation either of
Pity, Love, Kindness, or social Affection.   'Tis full as impossible to conceive, that a rational Creature coming first to be
try'd by rational Objects, and receiving into his Mind the
Images or Representations of Justice, Generosity, Gratitude, or
other Virtue, shou'd have no *Liking* of these, or *Dislike* of
their contrarys; but be found absolutely indifferent towards
whatsoever is presented to him of this sort.   A Soul, indeed,
may as well be without *Sense*, as without Admiration in the
Things of which it has any knowledg.   Coming therefore to
a Capacity of seeing and admiring in this new way, it must
needs find a Beauty and a Deformity as well in Actions, Minds,
and Tempers, as in Figures, Sounds, or Colours.   If there be
no *real* Amiableness or Deformity in moral Acts, there is at
least *an imaginary one* of full force.   Tho perhaps the Thing
itself shou'd not be allow'd in Nature, the Imagination or
Fancy of it must be allow'd to be from Nature alone.   Nor
can any thing besides Art and strong Endeavour, with long
Practice and Meditation, overcome such a *natural Prevention*,
or *Prepossession* of the Mind, in favour of this moral Distinction.

23   Sense of Right and Wrong therefore being as natural to us
as *natural Affection* itself, and being a first Principle in our
Constitution and Make; there is no speculative Opinion,
Persuasion or Belief, which is capable *immediately* or *directly*
to exclude or destroy it.   That which is of original and pure
Nature, nothing beside contrary Habit and Custom (a second

Nature) is able to displace. And this Affection being *an original one* of earliest rise in the Soul or affectionate Part; nothing beside contrary Affection, by frequent check and controul, can operate upon it, so as either to diminish it in part, or destroy it in the whole.

'Tis evident in what relates to the Frame and Order of our *Bodys*; that no particular odd Mein or Gesture, which is either natural to us, and consequent to our Make, or accidental and by Habit acquir'd, can possibly be overcome by our immediate Disapprobation, or the contrary Bent of our Will, ever so strongly set against it. Such a Change cannot be effected without extraordinary Means, and the intervention of Art and Method, a strict Attention, and repeated Check. And even thus, Nature, we find, is hardly master'd; but lies sullen, and ready to revolt, on the first occasion. Much more is this *the Mind's* Case in respect of that natural Affection and anticipating Fancy, which makes the sense of Right and Wrong. 'Tis impossible that this can instantly, or without much Force and Violence, be effac'd, or struck out of the natural Temper, even by means of the most extravagant Belief or Opinion in the World.

Neither *Theism* therefore, nor *Atheism*, nor *Dæmonism*, nor any religious or irreligious Belief of any kind, being able to operate immediately or directly in this Case, but indirectly, by the intervention of opposite or of favourable Affections casually excited by any such Belief; we may consider of this Effect in our last Case, where we come to examine the Agreement or Disagreement of other Affections with this natural and moral one which relates to Right and Wrong.

Sect. II.

24   II. As to the second Case, *viz.* THE WRONG SENSE OR FALSE IMAGINATION OF RIGHT AND WRONG.

This can proceed only from the Force of Custom and Education in opposition to Nature; as may be noted in those Countrys where, according to Custom or politick Institution,

certain Actions naturally foul and odious are repeatedly view'd
with Applause, and Honour ascrib'd to them. For thus 'tis
possible that a Man, forcing himself, may eat the Flesh of his
Enemys, not only against his Stomach, but against his Nature ;
and think it nevertheless both right and honourable ; as
supposing it to be of considerable service to his Community,
and capable of advancing the Name, and spreading the Terror
of his Nation.

But to speak of the Opinions relating to a DEITY ; and
what effect they may have in this place. As to *Atheism*, it
does not seem that it can directly have any effect at all towards
the setting up a false Species of Right or Wrong. For notwithstanding a Man may thro' Custom, or by licentiousness of
Practice, favour'd by Atheism, come in time to lose much of
his natural *moral Sense* ; yet it does not seem that Atheism
shou'd *of it-self* be the cause of any estimation or valuing of
any thing as fair, noble, and deserving, which was the contrary.
It can never, for instance, make it be thought that the being able
to eat Man's Flesh, or commit Bestiality, *is good and excellent
in it-self.* But this is certain, that by means of *corrupt Religion*, or SUPERSTITION, many things the most horridly
unnatural and inhuman, come to be receiv'd as excellent, good,
and laudable in *themselves.*

*   *   *   *   *   *   *

As to this second Case therefore ; RELIGION (according as
the kind may prove) is capable of doing great Good, or Harm ;
and ATHEISM nothing positive in either way. For however it
may be indirectly an occasion of Mens losing a good and
sufficient Sense of Right and Wrong ; it will not, *as Atheism
merely*, be the occasion of setting up a false Species of it ;
which only false Religion, or fantastical Opinion, deriv'd
commonly from Superstition and Credulity, is able to effect.

Sect. III.

25   Now as to the last Case, THE OPPOSITION MADE BY OTHER
AFFECTIONS TO THE NATURAL SENSE OF RIGHT AND WRONG.

'Tis evident, that a Creature having this sort of SENSE or *good Affection* in any degree, must necessarily act according to it ; if it happens not to be oppos'd, either by some settled sedate Affection towards a conceiv'd *private Good*, or by some sudden, strong and forcible Passion, as of *Lust* or *Anger* ; which may not only subdue the Sense of Right and Wrong, but the very Sense of private Good itself ; and overrule even the most familiar and receiv'd Opinion of what is conducing to Self-interest.

But it is not our business in this place to examine the several Means or Methods by which this Corruption is introduc'd or increas'd. We are to consider only how the Opinions concerning *a Deity* can influence one way or another.

That it is possible for a Creature capable of using Reflection, to have a Liking or Dislike of moral Actions, and consequently a Sense of Right and Wrong, before such time as he may have any settled Notion of A GOD, is what will hardly be question'd : it being a thing not expected, or any-way possible, that a Creature such as *Man*, arising from his Childhood, slowly and gradually, to several degrees of Reason and Reflection, shou'd, at the very first, be taken up with those Speculations, or more refin'd sort of Reflections, about the Subject of GOD's Existence.

Let us suppose a Creature, who wanting Reason, and being unable to reflect, has, notwithstanding, many good Qualitys and Affections ; as Love to his Kind, Courage, Gratitude, or Pity. 'Tis certain that if you give to this Creature a reflecting Faculty, it will at the same instant approve of Gratitude, Kindness, and Pity ; be taken with any shew or representation of the social Passion, and think nothing more amiable than this, or more odious than the contrary. And this is *to be capable of* VIRTUE, and *to have a Sense of* RIGHT *and* WRONG.

Before the time, therefore, that a Creature can have any plain or positive Notion one way or other, concerning the Subject of a GOD, he may be suppos'd to have an Apprehension or Sense of *Right* and *Wrong*, and be possess'd of *Virtue* and *Vice* in different degrees ; as we know by Experience of those, who having liv'd in such places, and in such a manner as never to have enter'd into any serious Thoughts of Religion, are nevertheless very different among themselves, as to their Characters of Honesty and Worth : some being naturally *modest, kind, friendly*, and consequently Lovers of *kind* and *friendly Actions* ; others *proud, harsh, cruel*, and consequently inclin'd to admire rather the Acts of *Violence* and mere *Power*.

*   *   *   *   *   *   *

BOOK II.   PART I.
Sect. I.

26   We have consider'd *what* VIRTUE *is*, and to whom the Character belongs.   It remains to inquire, *What Obligation* there is *to* VIRTUE ; or *what Reason* to embrace it.

We have found, that to deserve the name of *good* or *virtuous*, a Creature must have all his Inclinations and Affections, his Dispositions of Mind and Temper, sutable, and agreeing with the Good of his *Kind*, or of that *System* in which he is included, and of which he constitutes a PART.   To stand thus well affected, and to have one's Affections *right* and *intire*, not only in respect of one's self, but of Society and the Publick : This is *Rectitude, Integrity*, or VIRTUE.   And to be wanting in any of these, or to have their Contrarys, is *Depravity, Corruption*, and VICE.

It has been already shewn, that in the Passions and Affections of particular Creatures, there is a constant relation to the Interest of *a Species*, or *common Nature*.   This has been demonstrated in the case of *natural Affection*, parental Kindness, Zeal for Posterity, Concern for the Propagation and Nurture of the Young, Love of Fellowship and Company, Compassion, mutual Succour, and the rest of this kind.   Nor will any-one deny that this Affection of a Creature towards the Good of the Species or common Nature, is as *proper* and

natural to him, as it is to any Organ, Part or Member of
an Animal-Body, or mere Vegetable, to work in its known
Course, and regular way of Growth. 'Tis not more *natural*
for the Stomach to digest, the Lungs to breathe, the Glands
to separate Juices, or other Intrails to perform their several
Offices; however they may by particular Impediments be
sometimes disorder'd, or obstructed in their Operations.

27   There being allow'd therefore in a Creature such Affections
as these towards *the common Nature*, or *System of the Kind*,
together with those other which regard *the private Nature*, or
Self-system; it will appear that in following the *first* of these
Affections, the Creature must on many Occasions contradict
and go against *the latter*. How else shou'd the Species be
preserv'd? Or what wou'd signify that implanted *natural
Affection*, by which a Creature thro' so many Difficultys and
Hazards preserves its Offspring, and supports its Kind?

It may therefore be imagin'd, perhaps, that there is a plain
and absolute Opposition between these *two* Habits or Affections. It may be presum'd, that the pursuing the common
Interest or publick Good thro' the Affections of *one kind*, must
be a hindrance to the Attainment of private Good thro' the
Affections of *another*. For it being taken for granted, that
Hazards and Hardships, of whatever sort, are naturally the *Ill*
of the private State; and it being certainly the Nature of
those publick Affections to lead often to the greatest Hardships
and Hazards of every kind; 'tis presently infer'd, 'That 'tis
the Creature's Interest to be without any publick Affection
whatsoever.'

28   This we know for certain; That all social Love, Friendship,
Gratitude, or whatever else is of this generous kind, does by
its nature take place of the self-interesting Passions, draws
us out of ourselves, and makes us disregardful of our own
Convenience and Safety. So that according to a known way
of reasoning on *Self-interest*, that which is of a social kind in
us, shou'd of right be abolish'd. Thus Kindness of every sort,

Indulgence, Tenderness, Compassion, and in short, all natural
Affection shou'd be industriously suppress'd, and, as mere
Folly, and Weakness or Nature, be resisted and overcome;
that, by this means, there might be nothing remaining in us,
which was contrary to a direct *Self-end*; nothing which might
stand in opposition to a steddy and deliberate Pursuit of the
most narrowly confin'd *Self-interest*.

According to this extraordinary Hypothesis, it must be taken
for granted, 'That in the System of a Kind or Species,
the Interest of *the private Nature* is directly opposite to
that of *the common one*; the Interest of *Particulars* directly
opposite to that of *the Publick in general*.'—A strange Constitution! in which it must be confess'd there is much Disorder
and Untowardness; unlike to what we observe elsewhere in
Nature. As if in any vegetable or animal Body, the *Part* or
Member cou'd be suppos'd in a good and prosperous State *as
to it-self*, when under a contrary Disposition, and in an unnatural
Growth or Habit *as to its* WHOLE.

Now that this is in reality quite otherwise, we shall endeavour
to demonstrate; so as to make appear, 'That what Men
represent as an ill Order and Constitution in the Universe, by
making moral Rectitude appear *the Ill*, and Depravity *the
Good* or Advantage of a Creature, is in Nature just the contrary.
That to be well affected towards the *Publick Interest* and *one's
own*, is not only consistent, but inseparable; and that moral
Rectitude, or *Virtue*, must accordingly be the Advantage, and
Vice the Injury and Disadvantage of every Creature.'

Sect. II.

29　　There are few perhaps, who when they consider a Creature
void of natural Affection, and wholly destitute of a communi-
cative or social Principle, will suppose him, at the same time,
either tolerably happy in himself, or as he stands abroad, with
respect to his Fellow-Creatures or Kind. 'Tis generally
thought, that such a Creature as this, feels slender Joy in Life,
and finds little Satisfaction in the mere sensual Pleasures

which remain with him, after the Loss of social Enjoyment, and whatever can be call'd *Humanity* or *Good-nature.* We know that to such a Creature as this, 'tis not only *incident,* to be morose, rancorous and malignant; but that, *of necessity,* a Mind or Temper thus destitute of Mildness and Benignity, must turn to that which is contrary, and be wrought by Passions of a different kind. Such a Heart as this must be a continual Seat of perverse Inclinations and bitter Aversions, rais'd from a constant ill Humour, Sourness, and Disquiet. The Consciousness of such a Nature, so obnoxious to Mankind, and to all Beings which approach it, must overcloud the Mind with dark Suspicion and Jealousy, alarm it with Fears and Horror, and raise in it a continual Disturbance, even in the most seeming fair and secure State of Fortune, and in the highest degree of outward Prosperity.

This, as to the *compleat* immoral State, is what, of their own accord, Men readily remark. Where there is this *absolute* Degeneracy, this *total* Apostacy from all Candour, Equity, Trust, Sociableness, or Friendship; there are few who do not see and acknowledg the Misery which is consequent. Seldom is the Case misconstru'd, when *at worst.* The misfortune is, we look not on this Depravity, nor consider how it stands, *in less degrees.* The Calamity, we think, does not of necessity hold proportion with the Injustice or Iniquity. As if to be *absolutely* immoral and inhuman, were indeed the greatest misfortune and misery; but that to be so, in *a little degree,* shou'd be no misery nor harm at all! Which to allow, is just as reasonable as to own, that 'tis the greatest Ill of a Body to be in the utmost manner distorted and maim'd; but that to lose the use only of *one* Limb, or to be impair'd in some *one single* Organ or Member, is no Inconvenience or Ill worthy the least notice.

30   The Parts and Proportions of *the Mind,* their mutual Relation and Dependency, the Connexion and Frame of those Passions which constitute the Soul or Temper, may easily be understood

by any-one who thinks it worth his while to study this inward
Anatomy. 'Tis certain that the Order or Symmetry of this
inward Part is, in it-self, no less real and exact, than that of
the *Body.* However, 'tis apparent that few of us endeavour
to become *Anatomists* of this sort. Nor is any-one asham'd of
the deepest Ignorance in such a Subject. For tho the greatest
Misery and Ill is generally own'd to be from *Disposition,* and
Temper; tho 'tis allow'd that *Temper* may often change, and
that it actually varys on many occasions, much to our disadvantage ; yet how this Matter is brought about, we inquire
not. We never trouble our-selves to consider thorowly by
what means or methods our *inward Constitution* comes at any
time to be impair'd or injur'd. The *Solutio Continui,* which
bodily Surgeons talk of, is never apply'd in this case, by
Surgeons of another sort. The Notion of *a Whole* and *Parts*
is not apprehended in this Science. We know not what the
effect is, of straining any Affection, indulging any wrong Passion,
or relaxing any proper and natural Habit, or good Inclination.
Nor can we conceive how a particular Action shou'd have such
a sudden Influence on the whole Mind, as to make the Person
an immediate Sufferer. We suppose rather that a Man may
violate his Faith, commit any Wickedness unfamiliar to him
before, engage in any Vice or Villany, without the least prejudice
to *himself,* or any Misery *naturally* following from the ill Action.

'Tis thus we hear it often said, ' Such a Person has done ill
indeed : But what is he the worse for it ? ' Yet speaking of
any Nature thorowly savage, curst, and inveterate, we say
truly, 'Such a one is a plague and torment to himself : ' And
we allow, 'That thro' certain *Humours,* or *Passions,* and from
Temper merely, a Man may be compleatly miserable ; let his
outward *Circumstances* be ever so fortunate.' These different
Judgments sufficiently demonstrate that we are not accustom'd
to think with much coherency on these moral Subjects ; and
that our Notions, in this respect, are not a little confus'd, and
contradictory.

Now if the Fabrick of the Mind or Temper appear'd such to us as it really is; if we saw it impossible to remove hence any one good or orderly Affection, or introduce any ill or disorderly one, without drawing on, *in some degree*, that dissolute State, which *at its height* is confess'd to be so miserable: 'twou'd then undoubtedly be own'd, that since no ill, immoral, or unjust Action cou'd be committed without either a new inroad and breach on the Temper and Passions, or a farther advancing of that Execution already begun; whoever did ill, or acted in prejudice of his Integrity, Good-nature, or Worth, wou'd of necessity act with greater Cruelty towards himself, than he who scrupled not to swallow what was poisonous, or who with his own hands shou'd voluntarily mangle or wound his outward Form or Constitution, natural Limbs or Body.

Sect. III.

31　It has been shewn before, that no Animal can be said properly *to act*, otherwise than thro' Affections or Passions, such as are proper to an Animal. For in convulsive Fits, where a Creature strikes either himself or others, 'tis a simple Mechanism, an Engine, or Piece of Clock-work, which acts, and not the Animal.

Whatsoever therefore is done or acted by any Animal *as such*, is done only thro' some Affection or Passion, as of Fear, Love, or Hatred moving him.

32　And as it is impossible that a weaker Affection shou'd overcome a stronger, so it is impossible but that where the Affections or Passions are strongest in the main, and form in general the most considerable Party, either by their Force or Number; thither the Animal must incline: And according to this *Balance* he must be govern'd, and led to Action.

The Affections or Passions which must influence and govern the Animal, are either,

1. The *natural Affections*, which lead to the Good of THE PUBLICK.

2. Or the *Self-affections*, which lead only to the Good of THE PRIVATE.

3. Or such as are neither of these ; nor tending either to any Good of THE PUBLICK or PRIVATE ; but contrary-wise : and which may therefore be justly styl'd *unnatural Affections*.

So that according as these Affections stand, a Creature must be virtuous or vitious, good or ill.

The *latter* sort of these Affections, 'tis evident, are wholly vitious.   The *two former* may be vitious or virtuous, according to their degree.

33   It may seem strange, perhaps, to speak of natural Affections as *too strong*, or of Self-affections as *too weak*.   But to clear this Difficulty, we must call to mind what has been already explain'd, 'That *natural Affection* may, in particular Cases, be excessive, and in an unnatural degree : '   As when Pity is so overcoming as to destroy its own End, and prevent the Succour and Relief requir'd ; or as when Love to the Offspring proves such a Fondness as destroys the Parent, and consequently the Offspring it-self.   And notwithstanding it may seem harsh to call that *unnatural* and *vitious*, which is only an Extreme of some natural and kind Affection ; yet 'tis most certain, that where-ever any single good Affection of this sort is over-great, it must be injurious to the rest, and detract in some measure from their Force and natural Operation.   For a Creature possess'd with such an immoderate Degree of Passion, must of necessity allow too much to that *one*, and too little to *others* of the same Character, and equally natural and useful as to their End.   And this must necessarily be the occasion of Partiality and Injustice, whilst only *one Duty* or *natural Part* is earnestly follow'd ; and *other Parts* or *Dutys* neglected, which shou'd accompany it, and perhaps take place and be prefer'd.

*   *   *   *   *   *   *

34   Now as in particular Cases, *publick Affection*, on the one hand, may be *too high* ; so *private Affection* may, on the other hand, be *too weak*.   For if a Creature be self-neglectful, and insensible of Danger; or if he want such a degree of Passion in any kind, as is useful to preserve, sustain, or defend himself; this must certainly be esteem'd vitious, in regard of the Design and End of Nature.   She her-self discovers this in her known Method and stated Rule of Operation.   'Tis certain, that her provisionary Care and Concern for the whole Animal, must at least be equal to her Concern for a single Part or Member. Now to the several Parts she has given, we see proper Affections, sutable to their Interest and Security; so that even without our Consciousness, they act in their own Defense, and for their own Benefit and Preservation.   Thus *an Eye*, in its natural State, fails not to shut together, of its own accord, unknowingly to us, by a peculiar Caution and Timidity; which if it wanted, however we might intend the Preservation of our Eye, we shou'd not in effect be able to preserve it, by any Observation or Forecast of our own.   To be wanting therefore in those principal Affections, which respect the Good of the whole Constitution, must be a Vice and Imperfection, as great surely in the principal part, (the Soul or Temper) as it is in any of those inferior and subordinate parts, to want the self-preserving Affections which are proper to them.

And thus the Affections towards private Good become necessary and essential to Goodness.   For tho no Creature can be call'd good, or virtuous, merely for possessing these Affections; yet since it is impossible that the publick Good, or Good of the System, can be preserv'd without them; it follows that a Creature really wanting in them, is in reality wanting in some degree to Goodness and natural Rectitude; and may thus be esteem'd vitious and defective.

'Tis thus we say of a Creature, in a kind way of Reproof, that he is *too good*; when his Affection towards others is so warm and zealous, as to carry him even beyond his *Part*; or when he really acts beyond it, not thro' too warm a Passion of that sort, but thro' an over-cool one of another, or thro' want of some Self-passion to restrain him within due Bounds.

35   It may be objected here, that the having the natural Affections too strong, (where the Self-affections are over-much so) or the having the Self-affections defective or weak, (where the natural Affections are also weak) may prove upon occasion the only Cause of a Creature's acting honestly and in moral proportion. For, thus, one who is to a fault regardless of his Life, may with the smallest degree of natural Affection do all which can be expected from the highest Pitch of social Love, or zealous Friendship. And thus, on the other hand, a Creature excessively timorous may, by as exceeding a degree of natural Affection, perform whatever the perfectest Courage is able to inspire.

To this it is answer'd, That whenever we arraign any Passion as *too strong*, or complain of any as *too weak* ; we must speak with respect to a certain Constitution or *Œconomy* of a particular Creature, or Species. For if a Passion, leading to any right end, be only so much the more serviceable and effectual, for being strong; if we may be assur'd that the strength of it will not be the occasion of any disturbance within, nor of any disproportion between it self and other Affections ; then consequently the Passion, however strong, cannot be condemn'd as vitious. But if to have *all* the Passions in equal proportion with it, be what the Constitution of the Creature cannot bear ; so that only *some* Passions are rais'd to this height, whilst *others* are not, nor can possibly be wrought up to the same proportion ; then may those strong Passions, tho of the better kind, be call'd excessive. For being in unequal proportion to the others, and causing an *ill Balance* in the Affection at large, they must of course be the occasion of Inequality in the Conduct, and incline the Party to a wrong moral Practice.

  * * * * * * *

36   But having shewn what is meant by a Passion's being *in too high*, or *in too low* a degree ; and that, ' To have any natural Affection too high, or any Self-affection too low,' tho it be often approv'd as *Virtue*, is yet, strictly speaking, a *Vice* and *Imper-*

fection : we come now to the plainer and more essential part of
VICE, and which alone deserves to be consider'd *as such* : that
is to say,

1. 'When *either* the publick Affections are weak or deficient.

2. 'Or the private and Self-affections too strong.'

3. 'Or that such Affections arise as are neither of these, nor
in any degree tending to the Support either of the publick or
private System.'

Otherwise than *thus*, it is impossible any Creature can be
such as we call ILL or VITIOUS. So that if once we prove that
it is really not the Creature's Interest to be thus *vitiously*
affected, but contrariwise ; we shall then have prov'd, 'That it
is his Interest to be wholly GOOD and VIRTUOUS :' Since in a
wholesom and sound State of his Affections, such as we have
describ'd, he cannot possibly be other than sound, *good* and
virtuous, in his Action and Behaviour.

37   Our Business, therefore, will be, to prove ;

I. 'That *to have* THE NATURAL, KINDLY, *or* GENEROUS
AFFECTIONS *strong and powerful towards the Good of the Publick,
is to have the chief Means and Power of Self-enjoyment.'* And,
'*That to want them, is certain Misery and Ill.*'

II. 'That *to have* THE PRIVATE *or* SELF-AFFECTIONS *too
strong, or beyond their degree of Subordinacy to the kindly and
natural, is also miserable.*'

III. And, '*That to have* THE UNNATURAL AFFECTIONS (*viz.*
such as are neither founded on the Interest of the Kind, or
Publick ; nor of the *private* Person, or Creature himself) *is to be
miserable in the highest degree.*'

PART II.

Sect. I.

38   To begin therefore with this Proof, ' THAT TO HAVE THE
NATURAL AFFECTIONS (such as are founded in Love, Complacency, Good-will, and in a Sympathy with the Kind or

Species) IS TO HAVE THE CHIEF MEANS AND POWER OF SELF-
ENJOYMENT : *And* THAT TO WANT THEM IS CERTAIN MISERY
AND ILL.'

We may inquire, first, what those are, which we call *Pleasures*
or *Satisfactions*; from whence happiness is generally computed.
They are (according to the common distinction) Satisfactions
and Pleasures either *of the Body*, or *of the Mind*.

39   That *the latter of these Satisfactions are the greatest*, is allow'd
by most People, and may be prov'd by this : That whenever
the Mind, having conceiv'd a high Opinion of the Worth of
any Action or Behaviour, has receiv'd the strongest Impression
of this sort, and is wrought up to the highest pitch or degree
of Passion towards the Subject; at such time it sets itself
above all bodily Pain as well as Pleasure, and can be no-way
deverted from its purpose by Flattery or Terror of any kind.
Thus we see *Indians, Barbarians, Malefactors*, and even the
most execrable *Villains*, for the sake of a particular Gang or
Society, or thro' some cherish'd Notion or Principle of Honour
or Gallantry, Revenge, or Gratitude, embrace any manner of
Hardship, and defy Torments and Death.   Whereas, on the
other hand, a Person being plac'd in all the happy Circumstances of outward Enjoyment, surrounded with every
thing which can allure or charm the Sense, and being then actually in the very moment of such a pleasing Indulgence; yet no
sooner is there any thing amiss *within*, no sooner has he
conceiv'd any *internal Ail* or *Disorder*, any thing *inwardly*
vexatious or distemper'd, than instantly his Enjoyment ceases,
the pleasure of sense is at an end; and every means of that
sort becomes ineffectual, and is rejected as uneasy, and subject
to give Distaste.

The *Pleasures of the Mind* being allow'd, therefore, superior to
those of *the Body*; it follows, ' That whatever can create in
any intelligent Being a constant flowing Series or Train of
mental Enjoyment, or Pleasures of the Mind, is more considerable to his Happiness, than that which can create to him

a like constant Course or Train of sensual Enjoyments, or
Pleasures of the Body.'

40   Now the mental Enjoyments are either actually *the very
natural Affections themselves in their immediate Operation* : Or
they wholly in a manner *proceed from them,* and are no other
than *their Effects.*

If so ; it follows, that the natural Affections duly establish'd
in a rational Creature, being the only means which can procure
him a constant Series or Succession of the mental Enjoyments,
they are the only means which can procure him a certain and
solid *Happiness.*

41   Now, in the first place, to explain, ' How much *the natural
Affections are in themselves the highest Pleasures and Enjoyments* : ' There shou'd methinks be little need of proving this
to any-one of human Kind, who has ever known the Condition
of the Mind under a lively Affection of Love, Gratitude,
Bounty, Generosity, Pity, Succour, or whatever else is of a social
or friendly sort.   He who has ever so little Knowledg of human
Nature, is sensible what pleasure the Mind perceives when it
is touch'd in this generous way.   The difference we find between Solitude and Company, between a common Company
and that of Friends ; the reference of almost all our Pleasures
to mutual Converse, and the dependence they have on Society
either present or imagin'd ; all these are sufficient Proofs in
our behalf.

How much the social Pleasures are superior to any other,
may be known by visible Tokens and Effects. The very outward
Features, the Marks and Signs which attend this sort of Joy,
are expressive of a more intense, clear, and undisturb'd Pleasure,
than those which attend the Satisfaction of Thirst, Hunger,
and other ardent Appetites.   But more particularly still may
this Superiority be known, from the actual Prevalence and
Ascendency of this sort of Affection over all besides.   Where-
ever it presents it-self with any advantage, it silences and appeases
every other Motion of Pleasure.   No Joy, merely of Sense,

can be a Match for it. Whoever is Judg of *both* the Pleasures, will ever give the preference to *the former.* But to be able to judg of both, 'tis necessary to have a Sense of each. The honest Man indeed can judg of *sensual Pleasure*, and knows its utmost Force. For neither is his Taste, or Sense the duller ; but, on the contrary, the more intense and clear, on the account of his Temperance, and a moderate Use of Appetite. But the immoral and profligate Man can by no means be allow'd a good Judg of *social Pleasure*, to which he is so mere a Stranger by his Nature.

Nor is it any Objection here ; That in many Natures the good Affection, tho really present, is found to be of insufficient force. For where it is not *in its natural degree*, 'tis the same indeed as if it *were not* or had *never been.* The less there is of this good Affection in any untoward Creature, the greater the wonder is, that it shou'd *at any time* prevail ; as in the very worst of Creatures it sometimes will. And if it prevails but for *once*, in any *single* Instance ; it shews evidently, that if the Affection were thorowly experienc'd or known, it wou'd prevail *in all.*

Thus *the* CHARM of kind Affection is superior to all other Pleasure : since it has the power of drawing from every other Appetite or Inclination. And thus in the Case of Love to the Offspring, and a thousand other Instances, *the Charm* is found to operate so strongly on the Temper, as, in the midst of other Temptations, to render it susceptible of this Passion alone ; which remains as the *Master-Pleasure* and *Conqueror* of the rest.

42   There is no-one who, by the least progress in Science or Learning, has come to know barely the Principles of *Mathematicks*, but has found, that in the exercise of his Mind on the Discoverys he there makes, tho merely of speculative Truths, he receives a Pleasure and Delight superior to that of Sense. When we have thorowly search'd into the nature of this contemplative Delight, we shall find it of a kind which relates not

in the least to any private Interest of the Creature, nor has for its Object any Self-good or Advantage of the private System. The Admiration, Joy, or Love, turns wholly upon what is exterior, and foreign to our-selves. And tho the reflected Joy or Pleasure, which arises from the notice of this Pleasure once perceiv'd, may be interpreted *a Self-passion*, or *interested Regard* : yet the original Satisfaction can be no other than what results from the Love of Truth, Proportion, Order, and Symmetry, in the Things without. If this be the Case, the Passion ought in reality to be rank'd with *natural Affection*. For having no Object within the compass of the private System; it must either be esteem'd superfluous and *unnatural*, (as having no tendency towards the Advantage or Good of any thing in Nature) or it must be judg'd to be, what it truly is, ' A natural Joy in the Contemplation of those *Numbers*, that *Harmony*, *Proportion*, and *Concord*, which supports the universal Nature, and is essential in the Constitution and Form of every particular Species, or Order of Beings.'

But this speculative Pleasure, however considerable and valuable it may be, or however superior to any Motion of mere Sense ; must yet be far surpass'd by *virtuous Motion*, and *the Exercise of Benignity and Goodness* ; where, together with the most delightful Affection of the Soul, there is join'd a pleasing Assent and Approbation of the Mind to what is acted in this good Disposition and honest Bent. For where is there on Earth a fairer Matter of Speculation, a goodlier View or Contemplation, than that of a *beautiful*, *proportion'd*, and *becoming* Action ? Or what is there relating to us, of which the Consciousness and Memory is more solidly and lastingly entertaining ?

We may observe, that in the Passion of Love between the Sexes, where, together with the Affection of a *vulgar* sort, there is a mixture of the *kind and friendly*, the Sense or Feeling of this *latter* is in reality superior to the *former* ; since often thro' this Affection, and for the sake of the Person belov'd, the greatest Hardships in the World have been submitted to, and even Death it-self voluntarily imbrac'd, without any expected *Compensation*. For where shou'd the Ground of such an Expectation lie? Not *here*, in *this World* surely ; for Death puts an end to all. Nor yet *hereafter*, in *any other* : for who has ever thought of providing a Heaven or future Recompence for the suffering Virtue of Lovers?

We may observe, withal, in favour of the natural Affections, that it is not only when Joy and Sprightliness are mix'd with them, that they carry a real Enjoyment above that of the sensual kind. The very Disturbances which belong to natural Affection, tho they may be thought wholly contrary to Pleasure, yield still a Contentment and Satisfaction greater than the Pleasures of indulg'd Sense. And where a Series or continu'd Succession of the tender and kind Affections can be carry'd on, even thro' Fears, Horrors, Sorrows, Griefs ; the Emotion of the Soul is still agreeable. We continue pleas'd even with this melancholy Aspect or Sense of Virtue. Her Beauty supports it-self under a Cloud, and in the midst of surrounding Calamitys. For thus, when by mere Illusion, as in *a Tragedy*, the Passions of this kind are skilfully excited in us ; we prefer the Entertainment to any other of equal duration. We find by our-selves, that the moving our Passions in this mournful way, the engaging them in behalf of Merit and Worth, and the exerting whatever we have of social Affection, and human Sympathy, is of the highest Delight ; and affords a greater Enjoyment in the way of *Thought* and *Sentiment*, that any thing besides can do in a way of *Sense* and *common Appetite*. And after this manner it appears, ' How much *the mental Enjoyments are actually the very natural Affections themselves.*'

43   Now, in the next place, to explain, ' How they *proceed from them*, as their natural *Effects* ;' we may consider first, That the EFFECTS of Love or kind Affection, in a way of mental Pleasure, are, '*An Enjoyment of Good by Communication : A receiving it, as it were by Reflection, or by way of Participa-*

tion in the Good of others:' And '*A pleasing Consciousness of the actual Love, merited Esteem or Approbation of others.*'

How considerable a part of Happiness arises from the former of these *Effects*, will be easily apprehended by one who is not exceedingly ill natur'd. It will be consider'd how many the Pleasures are, of *sharing Contentment and Delight with others*; of receiving it in Fellowship and Company; and gathering it, in a manner, from the pleas'd and happy States of those around us, from accounts and relations of such Happinesses, from the very Countenances, Gestures, Voices and Sounds, even of Creatures foreign to our Kind, whose Signs of Joy and Contentment we can anyway discern. So insinuating are these Pleasures of Sympathy, and so widely diffus'd thro' our whole Lives, that there is hardly such a thing as Satisfaction or Contentment, of which they make not an essential part.

As for that other *Effect* of social Love, viz. *the Consciousness of merited Kindness or Esteem*; 'tis not difficult to perceive how much this avails in mental Pleasure, and constitutes the chief Enjoyment and Happiness of those who are, in the narrowest sense, *voluptuous*. How natural is it for the most selfish among us, to be continually drawing some sort of Satisfaction from a Character, and pleasing our-selves in the Fancy of deserv'd Admiration and Esteem? For tho it be mere Fancy, we endeavour still to believe it Truth; and flatter our-selves, all we can, with the Thought of *Merit* of some kind, and the Persuasion of our deserving well from some few at least, with whom we happen to have a more intimate and familiar Commerce.

What Tyrant is there, what Robber, or open Violater of the Laws of Society, who has not a Companion, or some particular Sect, either of his own Kindred, or such as he calls Friends; with whom he gladly shares his Good; in whose Welfare he delights; and whose Joy and Satisfaction he makes *his own*? What Person in the world is there, who receives not some Impressions from the Flattery or Kindness of such as are familiar with him? 'Tis to this soothing Hope and Expectation of Friendship, that almost all our Actions have some reference. 'Tis this which goes thro' our whole Lives, and mixes it-self even with most of our Vices. Of this, *Vanity*, *Ambition*, and *Luxury*, have a share; and many other Disorders of our Life partake. Even the unchastest *Love* borrows largely from this Source. So that were Pleasure to be computed in the same way as other things commonly are; it might properly be said, that out of these two Branches (viz. *Community or Participation in the Pleasures of others*, and *Belief of meriting well from others*) wou'd arise more than nine Tenths of whatever is enjoy'd in Life. And thus in the main Sum of Happiness, there is scarce a single Article, but what derives it-self from social Love, and depends immediately on the natural and kind Affections.

Now such as CAUSES are, such must be their EFFECTS. And therefore as *natural Affection* or *social Love* is perfect, or imperfect; so must be *the Content* and *Happiness* depending on it.

44   But lest any shou'd imagine with themselves that an *inferior* Degree of natural Affection, or an *imperfect partial* Regard of this sort, can supply the place of an *intire*, *sincere*, and *truly moral* one; lest a small Tincture of social Inclination shou'd be thought sufficient to answer the End of Pleasure in Society, and give us that Enjoyment of *Participation* and *Community* which is so essential to our Happiness; we may consider first, That PARTIAL AFFECTION, or social Love *in part*, without regard to a compleat Society or *Whole*, is in it-self an Inconsistency, and implies an absolute Contradiction. Whatever Affection we have towards any thing besides *our-selves*; if it be not of the *natural sort* towards the System, or Kind; it must be, of all other Affections, the most *dissociable*, and destructive of the Enjoyments of Society: If it be really of the natural sort, and apply'd only to some *one* Part of Society, or of a Species, but not to the Species or Society *it-self*; there can be no more account given of it, than of the most odd, capricious,

or humoursom Passion which may arise. The Person, therefore, who is conscious of this Affection, can be conscious of no
Merit or *Worth* on the account of it. Nor can the Persons on
whom this capricious Affection has chanc'd to fall, be in any
manner secure of its Continuance or Force. As it has no
Foundation or Establishment *in Reason*; so it must be easily
removable, and subject to alteration, *without Reason*. Now
the Variableness of such sort of Passion, which depends solely
on Capriciousness and Humour, and undergoes the frequent
Successions of alternate Hatred and Love, Aversion and Inclination, must of necessity create continual Disturbance
and Disgust, give an allay to what is immediately enjoy'd in
the way of Friendship and Society, and in the end extinguish,
in a manner, the very Inclination towards Friendship and
human Commerce. Whereas, on the other hand, INTIRE
AFFECTION (from whence *Integrity* has its name) as it is
answerable to it-self, proportionable, and rational; so it is ir-
refragable, solid, and durable. And as in the case of *Partiality*,
or vitious Friendship, which has no rule or order, every Reflection of the Mind necessarily makes to its disadvantage, and
lessens the Enjoyment; so in the case of *Integrity*, the Consciousness of just Behaviour towards Mankind in general,
casts a good reflection on each friendly Affection in particular,
and raises the Enjoyment of Friendship still the higher, in the
way of *Community* or *Participation* above-mention'd.

And in the next place, as PARTIAL AFFECTION is fitted only
to a short and slender Enjoyment of those Pleasures of
Sympathy or *Participation with others*; so neither is it able
to derive any considerable Enjoyment from that other
principal Branch of human Happiness, *viz. Consciousness of the
actual or merited Esteem of others.* From whence shou'd this
Esteem arise? The *Merit*, surely, must in it-self be mean
whilst the Affection is so precarious and uncertain. What Trust
can there be to a mere *casual Inclination* or *capricious Liking*?
Who can depend on such a Friendship as is founded on no

moral Rule, but fantastically assign'd to some single Person, or small *Part* of Mankind, exclusive of Society, and *the Whole?*

It may be consider'd, withal, as a thing impossible; that they who esteem or love by any other Rule than that of *Virtue*, shou'd place their Affection on such Subjects as they can long esteem or love. 'Twill be hard for them, in the number of their so belov'd Friends, to find any, in whom they can heartily rejoice; or whose reciprocal Love or Esteem they can sincerely prize and enjoy. Nor can those Pleasures be sound or lasting, which are gather'd from a Self-flattery, and false Persuasion of the Esteem and Love of others, who are incapable of any sound Esteem or Love. It appears therefore how much the Men of narrow or *partial* Affection must be Losers in this sense, and of necessity fall short in this second principal part of mental Enjoyment.

45   Mean while *intire Affection* has all the opposite advantages. It is equal, constant, accountable to it-self, ever satisfactory, and pleasing. It gains Applause and Love from the *best*; and in all disinterested cases, from the very *worst* of Men. We may say of it, with justice, that it carry with it a Consciousness of merited Love and Approbation from all Society, from all intelligent Creatures, and from whatever is original to all other Intelligence. And if there be in Nature any such *Original*; we may add, that the Satisfaction which attends *intire Affection*, is full and noble, in proportion to its *final Object*, which contains all Perfection; according to the Sense of *Theism* above-noted. For this, as has been shewn, is the result of *Virtue*. And to have this INTIRE AFFECTION or INTEGRITY of Mind, is *to live according to Nature*, and the Dictates and Rules of *supreme Wisdom*. This is Morality, Justice, Piety, and natural Religion.

46   But lest this Argument shou'd appear perhaps too *scholastically* stated, and in Terms and Phrases, which are not of familiar use; we may try whether possibly we can set it yet in a plainer light.

Let any-one, then, consider well those Pleasures which he

receives either in private Retirement, Contemplation, Study
and Converse *with himself*; or in Mirth, Jollity, and Entertainment with *others*; and he will find, That they are wholly
founded in *An easy Temper, free of Harshness, Bitterness, or
Distaste*; and in *A Mind or Reason well compos'd, quiet, easy
within itself, and such as can freely bear its own Inspection and
Review.* Now such A MIND, and such A TEMPER, which fit
and qualify for the Enjoyment of the Pleasures mention'd,
must of necessity be owing to the *natural* and *good Affections.*

47 As to what relates to TEMPER, it may be consider'd thus.
There is no State of outward Prosperity, or flowing Fortune,
where *Inclination* and *Desire* are always satisfy'd, *Fancy* and
Humour pleas'd. There are almost hourly some Impediments
or Crosses to the Appetite ; some Accidents or another *from
without*; or something *from within*, to check the licentious
Course of the indulg'd Affections. They are not always to be
satisfy'd by mere Indulgence. And when a Life is guided by
Fancy only, there is sufficient ground of Contrariety and
Disturbance. The very ordinary Lassitudes, Uneasinesses,
and Defects of Disposition in the soundest Body ; the interrupted Course of the Humours, or Spirits, in the healthiest
People ; and the accidental Disorders common to every Constitution, are sufficient, we know, on many occasions, to breed
Uneasiness and Distaste. And this, in time, must grow into
a Habit; where there is nothing to oppose its progress, and
hinder its prevailing on the Temper. Now the only sound
Opposite to ILL HUMOUR, is *natural* and *kind Affection.* For
we may observe, that when the Mind, upon reflection, resolves
at any time to suppress this Disturbance already risen in the
Temper, and sets about this reforming Work with heartiness,
and in good earnest ; it can no otherwise accomplish the Undertaking, than by introducing into the affectionate Part some
gentle Feeling of the social and friendly kind ; some enlivening
Motion of Kindness, Fellowship, Complacency, or Love, to allay
and convert that contrary Motion of Impatience and Discontent.

If it be said perhaps, that in the case before us, *Religious Affection* or *Devotion* is a sufficient and proper Remedy ; we answer, That 'tis according as the Kind may happily prove. For if it be of the pleasant and chearful sort, 'tis of the very kind of *natural Affection* it-self : if it be of the dismal or fearful sort ; if it brings along with it any Affection opposite to Man-hood, Generosity, Courage, or Free-thought ; there will be nothing gain'd by this Application ; and the *Remedy* will, in the issue, be undoubtedly found *worse than the Disease.* The severest Reflections on our *Duty*, and the Consideration merely of what is *by Authority* and *under Penaltys* enjoin'd, will not by any means serve to calm us on this occasion. The more dismal our Thoughts are on such a Subject, the worse our Temper will be, and the readier to discover it-self in Harshness, and Austerity. If, perhaps, by Compulsion, or thro' any Necessity or Fear incumbent, a different Carriage be at any time effected, or different Maxims own'd ; the Practice at the bottom will be still the same. If *the Countenance* be compos'd ; *the Heart*, however, will not be chang'd. The ill Passion may for the time be with-held from breaking into Action ; but will not be subdu'd, or in the least debilitated against the next occasion. So that in such a Breast as this, whatever *Devotion* there may be ; 'tis likely there will in time be little of *an easy Spirit*, or *good Temper* remaining ; and consequently few and slender Enjoyments of a *mental kind*.

If it be objected, on the other hand, that tho in melancholy Circumstances ill Humour may prevail, yet in a Course of outward Prosperity, and in the height of Fortune, there can nothing probably occur which shou'd thus sour *the Temper*, and give it such disrelish as is suggested ; we may consider, that the most humour'd and indulg'd State is apt to receive the most disturbance from every Disappointment or smallest Ail. And if Provocations are easiest rais'd, and the Passions of Anger, Offence, and Enmity, are found the highest in the most indulg'd State of Will and Humour ; there is still the greater need of a Supply from *social Affection,* to preserve *the Temper* from running into Savageness and Inhumanity.   And this, the Case of Tyrants, and most unlimited Potentates, may sufficiently verify and demonstrate.

48   Now as to the other part of our Consideration, which relates to a MIND *or Reason well compos'd and easy within it-self;* upon whaL account this Happiness may be thought owing to *natural Affection,* we may possibly resolve our-selves, after this manner.   It will be acknowledg'd that a Creature, such as Man, who from several degrees of Reflection has risen to that Capacity which we call Reason and Understanding ; must in the very use of this his reasoning Faculty, be forc'd to receive Reflections back into his Mind of what passes in itself, as well as in the Affections, or Will ; in short, of whatsoever relates to his Character, Conduct, or Behaviour amidst his Fellow-Creatures, and in Society.   Or shou'd he be of himself unapt ; there are others ready to remind him, and refresh his Memory, in this way of Criticism.   We have all of us Remembrancers enow to help us in this work.   Nor are the greatest Favourites of Fortune exempted from this Task of Self-inspection.   Even Flattery itself, by making the View agreeable, renders us more attentive this way, and insnares us in the Habit.   The vainer any Person is, the more he has his Eye inwardly fix'd upon himself ; and is, after a certain manner, employ'd in this home-Survey.   And when a true Regard to our-selves cannot oblige us to this Inspection, a false Regard to others, and a Fondness for Reputation raises a watchful Jealousy, and furnishes us sufficiently with Acts of Reflection on our own Character and Conduct.

In whatever manner we consider of this, we shall find still that every reasoning or reflecting Creature is, by his Nature, forc'd to endure the *Review* of his own Mind, and Actions ; and to have Representations of himself, and his inward Affairs, constantly passing before him, obvious to him, and revolving in his Mind.   Now as nothing can be more grievous than this

is, to one who has thrown off *natural Affection* ; so nothing can
be more delightful to one who has preserv'd it with sincerity.

49   There are TWO Things, which to a rational Creature must
be horridly offensive and grievous ; *viz.* ' To have the
Reflection in his Mind of any *unjust* Action or Behaviour,
which he knows to be naturally *odious* and *ill-deserving* : Or,
of any foolish Action or Behaviour, which he knows to be
prejudicial to his own *Interest* or *Happiness.*'

The former of these is alone properly call'd CONSCIENCE ;
whether in a moral, or religious Sense.   For to have Awe and
Terror of the Deity, does not, of itself, imply Conscience.
No one is esteem'd the more conscientious for the fear of evil
Spirits, Conjurations, Enchantments, or whatever may proceed
from any unjust, capricious, or devilish Nature.   Now to fear
GOD any otherwise than as in consequence of some justly
blameable and imputable Act, is to fear *a devilish* Nature, not
a divine one.   Nor does the Fear of Hell, or a thousand
Terrors of *the* DEITY, imply Conscience ; unless where there
is an Apprehension of what is *wrong, odious, morally deform'd*
and *ill-deserving.*   And where this is the Case, there *Conscience*
must have effect, and Punishment of necessity be apprehended ;
even tho it be not expressly threaten'd.

And thus *religious Conscience* supposes *moral* or *natural
Conscience.*   And tho the former be understood to carry with it
the Fear of divine Punishment ; it has its force however from
the apprehended moral Deformity and Odiousness of any
Act, with respect purely to the Divine Presence, and the
natural Veneration due to such a suppos'd Being.   For in such
a Presence, the Shame of Villany or Vice must have its force,
independently on that farther Apprehension of the magisterial
Capacity of such a Being, and his Dispensation of particular
Rewards or Punishments in a future State.

It has been already said, that no Creature can maliciously
and intentionally *do ill*, without being sensible, at the same
time, that he *deserves ill*.   And in this respect, every sensible

Creature may be said to have *Conscience*. For with all Mankind, and all intelligent Creatures this must ever hold, 'That
what they know they deserve from every-one, *that* they
necessarily must fear and expect from all.' And thus Suspicions and ill Apprehensions must arise, with Terror both of
Men and of *the* DEITY. But besides this, there must in every
rational Creature, be yet farther *Conscience* ; *viz.* from Sense
of *Deformity in what is thus ill-deserving and unnatural*: and
from *a consequent Shame or Regret of incurring what is odious,
and moves Aversion.*

50   There scarcely is, or can be any Creature, whom Consciousness of Villany, *as such merely*, does not at all offend ;
nor any thing opprobrious or heniously imputable, move, or
affect. If there be such a one ; 'tis evident he must be
absolutely indifferent towards moral Good or Ill. If this
indeed be his Case ; 'twill be allow'd he can be no-way capable
of natural Affection : If not of that, then neither of any social
Pleasure, or mental Enjoyment, as shewn above ; but on the
contrary, he must be subject to all manner of horrid, unnatural,
and ill Affection. So that to want CONSCIENCE, or *natural
Sense of the Odiousness of Crime and Injustice*, is to be most
of all miserable in Life : but where *Conscience*, or *Sense* of this
sort, remains ; there, consequently, whatever is committed
against it, must of necessity, by means of Reflection, as we
have shewn, be continually shameful, grievous and offensive.

A man who in a Passion happens to kill his Companion,
relents immediately on the sight of what he has done. His
Revenge is chang'd into Pity, and his Hatred turn'd against
himself. And this merely by the Power of the Object. On
this account he suffers Agonys ; the Subject of this continually occurs to him ; and of this he has a constant ill
Remembrance and displeasing Consciousness. If on the
other side, we suppose him *not* to relent or suffer any real
Concern or Shame ; then, either he has no Sense of the
Deformity of the Crime and Injustice, no natural Affection, and

consequently no Happiness or Peace within : or if he has
any Sense of moral Worth or Goodness, it must be of a perplex'd, and contradictory kind. He must pursue an inconsistent Notion, idolize some *false Species* of Virtue ; and affect
as noble, gallant, or worthy, that which is irrational and absurd.
And how tormenting this must be to him, is easy to conceive.
For never can such *a Phantom* as this be reduc'd to any
certain Form. Never can this PROTEUS of *Honour* be held
steddy, to one Shape. The Pursuit of it can only be vexatious
and distracting. There is nothing beside real Virtue, as has
been shewn, which can possibly hold any proportion to Esteem,
Approbation, or good Conscience. And he who, being led
by false Religion or prevailing Custom, has learnt to esteem or
admire any thing as Virtue which is not really such ; must
either thro' the Inconsistency of such an Esteem, and the
perpetual Immoralitys occasion'd by it, come at last to lose all
Conscience ; and so be miserable in the worst way : or, if
he retains any Conscience at all, it must be of a kind never
satisfactory, or able to bestow Content. For 'tis impossible
that a cruel Enthusiast, or *Bigot*, a Persecutor, a Murderer,
a *Bravo*, a Pirate, or any Villain of less degree, who is false to
the Society of Mankind in general, and contradicts natural
Affection ; shou'd have any fix'd Principle at all, any real
Standard or Measure by which he can regulate his Esteem, or
any solid Reason by which to form his Approbation of *any one*
moral Act. And thus the more he sets up *Honour*, or
advances *Zeal* ; the worse he renders his Nature, and the more
detestable his Character. The more he engages in the Love
or Admiration of any Action or Practice, as great and glorious,
which is in it-self morally ill and vitious ; the more Contradiction and Self-disapprobation he must incur. For there
being nothing more certain than this, ' That no natural
Affection can be contradicted, nor any unnatural one advanc'd,
without a prejudice in some degree to all natural Affection in
general : ' it must follow, ' That inward Deformity growing

greater, by the Incouragement of unnatural Affection; there must be so much the more Subject for dissatisfactory Reflection, the more any false Principle of Honour, any false Religion, or Superstition prevails.'

So that whatever Notions of this kind are cherish'd; or whatever Character affected, which is contrary to moral Equity, and leads to Inhumanity, thro' *a false Conscience*, or *wrong Sense of Honour*, serves only to bring a Man the more under the lash of *real* and *just Conscience*, Shame, and Self-reproach. Nor can any one, who, by any pretended Authority, commits one single Immorality, be able to satisfy himself with any Reason, why he shou'd not at another time be carry'd further into all manner of Villany; such perhaps as he even abhors to think of. And this is a Reproach which a Mind must of necessity make to it-self upon the least Violation of natural Conscience; in doing what is *morally deform'd, and ill-deserving*; tho warranted by any Example or Precedent amongst Men, or by any suppos'd Injunction or Command of higher Powers.

51   Now as for that other part of Conscience, *viz.* the remembrance of *what was at any time unreasonably and foolishly done, in prejudice of one's real Interest or Happiness*: This dissatisfactory Reflection must follow still and have effect, wheresoever there is a Sense of moral Deformity, contracted by Crime, and Injustice. For even where there is no Sense of moral Deformity, as *such merely*; there must be still a Sense of the ill Merit of it with respect to God and Man. Or tho there were a possibility of excluding for ever all Thoughts or Suspicions of any superior Powers, yet considering that this Insensibility towards moral Good or Ill implies a total Defect in natural Affection, and that this Defect can by no Dissimulation be conceal'd; 'tis evident that a Man of this unhappy Character must suffer a very sensible Loss in the Friendship, Trust, and Confidence of other Men; and consequently must suffer in his Interest and outward Happiness. Nor can the Sense of this Disadvantage fail to occur to

him; when he sees, with Regret, and Envy, the better
and more grateful Terms of Friendship, and Esteem, on
which better People live with the rest of Mankind. Even
therefore where natural Affection is wanting; 'tis certain still,
that by Immorality, necessarily happening thro' want of such
Affection, there must be disturbance from Conscience of this
sort, *viz.* from *Sense of what is committed imprudently, and
contrary to real Interest and Advantage.*

52   From all this we may easily conclude, how much our
Happiness depends on *natural and good Affection.* For if the
chief Happiness be from the MENTAL PLEASURES ; and the
chief *mental Pleasures* are such as we have describ'd, and are
founded in *natural Affection* ; it follows, ' That *to have
the natural Affections, is to have the chief Means and Power of
Self-enjoyment, the highest Possession and Happiness of Life.'*

53   Now as to the *Pleasures of* THE BODY, and the Satisfactions
belonging to *mere* SENSE ; 'tis evident, they cannot possibly
have their Effect, or afford any valuable Enjoyment, otherwise
than by the means of *social and natural Affection.*

To *live well,* has no other meaning with some People, than
to *eat* and *drink well.* And methinks 'tis an unwary Concession
we make in favour of these pretended *good Livers,* when we
join with 'em, in honouring their way of Life with the Title
of *living fast.* As if they liv'd the fastest who took the greatest
pains to enjoy least of Life : For if our Account of Happiness
be right ; the greatest Enjoyments in Life are such as these
Men pass over in their haste, and have scarce ever allow'd
themselves the liberty of tasting.

But as considerable a Part of Voluptuousness as is founded
in *the Palat* ; and as notable as the Science is, which depends
on it ; one may justly presume that the Ostentation of Elegance,
and a certain Emulation and Study how to excel in this
sumptuous Art of Living, goes very far in the raising such
a high Idea of it, as is observ'd among the Men of Pleasure.
For were the Circumstances of a Table and Company,

Equipages, Services, and the rest of the Management with-drawn; there wou'd be hardly left any Pleasure worth acceptance, even in the Opinion of the most debauch'd themselves.

The very Notion of *a Debauch* (which is a Sally into what-ever can be imagin'd of Pleasure and Voluptuousness) carrys with it a plain reference to Society, or Fellowship. It may be call'd a *Surfeit*, or *Excess of Eating and Drinking*, but hardly a *Debauch* of that kind, when the Excess is committed separately, out of all Society, or Fellowship. And one who abuses himself in this way, is often call'd a *Sot* but never a *Debauchee*. The Courtizans, and even the commonest of Women, who live by Prostitution, know very well how necessary it is, that every-one whom they entertain with their Beauty, shou'd believe there are Satisfactions reciprocal; and that Pleasures are no less *given* than *receiv'd*. And were this Imagination to be wholly taken away, there wou'd be hardly any of the grosser sort of Mankind, who wou'd not perceive their remaining Pleasure to be of slender Estimation.

*   *   *   *   *   *   *

Thus, therefore, not only the *Pleasures of the Mind*, but even those of *the Body*, depend on natural Affection : insomuch that where this is wanting, they not only lose their Force, but are in a manner converted into Uneasiness and Disgust. The Sensations which shou'd naturally afford Contentment and Delight, produce rather Discontent and Sourness, and breed a Wearisomness and Restlesness in the Disposition. This we may perceive by the perpetual Inconstancy, and Love of Change, so remarkable in those who have nothing communi-cative or friendly in their Pleasures. *Good Fellowship*, in its abus'd Sense, seems indeed to have something more constant and determining. The Company supports the Humour. 'Tis the same in *Love*. A certain Tenderness and Generosity of Affection supports the Passion, which otherwise wou'd instantly be chang'd. The perfectest Beauty cannot, of it-self, retain, or fix it. And that Love which has no other Foundation, but relies on this exterior kind, is soon turn'd into Aversion. Satiety, perpetual Disgust, and Feverishness of Desire, attend those who passionately study Pleasure. They best enjoy it, who study to regulate their Passions. And by this they will come to know how absolute an Incapacity there is in any thing sensual to please, or give contentment, where it depends not on something friendly or social, something conjoin'd, and in affinity with *kind* or *natural Affection.*

54   But ere we conclude this Article of *social* or *natural Affection*, we may take a general View of it, and bring it, once for all, into the Scale ; to prove what kind of BALANCE it helps to make *within ;* and what the Consequence may be, of its *Deficiency*, or *light Weight.*

There is no-one of ever so little Understanding in what belongs to a human Constitution, who knows not that without Action, Motion, and Employment, *the Body* languishes, and is oppress'd ; its Nourishment turns to Disease ; the Spirits, unimploy'd abroad, help to consume the Parts within ; and Nature, as it were, preys upon her-self. In the same manner, the sensible and living Part, *the Soul* or *Mind*, wanting its proper and natural Exercise, is burden'd and diseas'd. Its Thoughts and Passions being unnaturally with-held from their due Objects, turn against itself, and create the highest Impatience and Ill-humour.

*   *   *   *   *   *   *

It happens with *Mankind*, that whilst some are by necessity confin'd to Labour, others are provided with abundance of all things, by the Pains and Labour of Inferiors. Now, if among the superior and easy sort, there be not something of fit and proper Imployment rais'd in the room of what is wanting in common Labour and Toil; if instead of an Application to any sort of Work, such as has a good and honest End in Society, (as Letters, Sciences, Arts, Husbandry, publick Affairs, Œconomy, or the like) there be a thorow

Neglect of all Duty or Imployment; a settled Idleness, Supineness, and Inactivity : this of necessity must occasion a most relax'd and dissolute State ; It must produce a total Disorder of the Passions, and break out in the strangest Irregularity imaginable.

We see the enormous Growth of Luxury in capital Citys, such as have been long the Seat of Empire. We see what Improvements are made in Vice of every kind, where numbers of Men are maintain'd in lazy Opulence, and wanton Plenty. 'Tis otherwise with those who are taken up in honest and due Imployment, and have been well inur'd to it from their Youth. This we may observe in the hardy remote Provincials, the Inhabitants of smaller Towns, and the industrious sort of common People ; where 'tis rare to meet with any Instances of those Irregularitys, which are known in Courts and Palaces, and in the rich Foundations of easy and pamper'd Priests.

Now if what we have advanc'd concerning an *inward Constitution* be real and just ; if it be true that Nature works by a just Order and Regulation as well in the Passions and Affections, as in the Limbs and Organs which she forms ; if it appears withal, that she has so constituted this *inward Part*, that nothing is so essential to it as *Exercise* ; and no Exercise so essential as that of *social* or *natural Affection* : it follows, that where this is remov'd or weaken'd, the *inward Part* must necessarily suffer and be impair'd. Let Indolence, Indifference or Insensibility, be study'd as an Art, or cultivated with the utmost Care ; the Passions thus restrain'd will force their Prison, and in one way or other procure their Liberty, and find full Employment. They will be sure to create to themselves *unusual* and *unnatural* Exercise, where they are cut off from such as is *natural* and *good*. And thus in the room of orderly and natural Affection, new and unnatural must be rais'd, and all *inward Order* and *Œconomy* destroy'd.

     *   *   *   *   *   *   *

55   Thus it may appear, how much NATURAL AFFECTION is predominant; how it is inwardly join'd to us, and implanted in
our Natures; how interwoven with our other Passions; and how
essential to that regular Motion and Course of our Affections,
on which our Happiness and Self-enjoyment so immediately
depend.

And thus we have demonstrated, That as, *on one side*, TO
HAVE THE NATURAL AND GOOD AFFECTIONS, IS TO HAVE THE
CHIEF MEANS AND POWER OF SELF-ENJOYMENT: SO, *on the
other side*, TO WANT THEM, IS CERTAIN MISERY, AND ILL.

Sect. II.

56   We are now to prove, That BY HAVING THE SELF-PASSIONS
TOO INTENSE OR STRONG, A CREATURE BECOMES MISERABLE.

In order to this, we must, according to Method, enumerate
those Home-affections which relate to the private Interest or
separate Œconomy of the Creature: such as *Love of Life;—
Resentment of Injury;—Pleasure, or Appetite towards Nourishment, and the Means of Generation;—Interest, or Desire* of
those *Conveniences*, by which we are all well *provided for*, and
maintain'd;—Emulation, or *Love of Praise and Honour;—
Indolence*, or *Love of Ease and Rest.*—These are the Affections
which relate to the private System, and constitute whatever
we call *Interestedness* or *Self-love*.

Now these Affections, if they are moderate, and within
certain bounds, are neither injurious to social Life, nor
a hindrance to Virtue: but being in an extreme degree,
they become *Cowardice,—Revengefulness,—Luxury,—Avarice,
—Vanity* and *Ambition,—Sloth*;—and, as such, are own'd
vitious and ill, with respect to human Society.   How they are
ill also with respect to the private Person, and are to his
own disadvantage as well as that of the Publick, we may
consider, as we severally examine them.

57   If there were any of these Self-passions which for the
Good and Happiness of the Creature might be oppos'd to
Natural Affection, and allow'd to over-balance it; THE DESIRE

AND LOVE OF LIFE wou'd have the best Pretence. But it will be found perhaps, that there is no Passion which, by having much allow'd to it, is the occasion of more Disorder and Misery.

There is nothing more certain, or more universally agreed than this; 'That *Life* may sometimes be even a Misfortune and Misery.' To inforce the continuance of it in Creatures reduc'd to such Extremity, is esteem'd the greatest Cruelty. And tho Religion forbids that any-one shou'd be his own Reliever; yet if by some fortunate accident, Death offers *of it-self,* it is embrac'd as highly welcome. And on this account the nearest Friends and Relations often rejoice at the Release of one intirely belov'd ; even tho he himself may have been so weak as earnestly to decline Death, and endeavour the utmost Prolongment of his own un-eligible State.

Since *Life,* therefore, may frequently prove a Misfortune and Misery ; and since it naturally becomes so, by being only prolong'd to the Infirmitys of old Age ; since there is nothing, withal, more common than to see Life over-valu'd, and purchas'd at such a Cost as it can never justly be thought worth : it follows evidently, that the Passion itself (viz. *the Love of Life,* and *Abhorrence or Dread of Death*) if beyond a certain degree, and over-balancing in the Temper of any Creature, must lead him directly against his own Interest ; make him, upon occasion, become the greatest Enemy to himself ; and necessitate him to act as such.

But tho it were allow'd the Interest and Good of a Creature, by all Courses and Means whatsoever, in any Circumstances, or at any rate, to preserve *Life* ; yet wou'd it be against his Interest still to have this Passion in a high degree. For it wou'd by this means prove ineffectual, and no-way conducing to its End. Various Instances need not be given. For what is there better known, than that at all times an excessive *Fear* betrays to danger, instead of saving from it ? 'Tis impossible for any-one to act sensibly, and with Presence of Mind, even in his own Preservation and Defense, when he is strongly press'd by such a Passion. On all extraordinary Emergences, 'tis *Courage* and *Resolution* saves; whilst *Cowardice* robs us of the means of Safety, and not only deprives us of our defensive Facultys, but even runs us to the brink of Ruin, and makes us meet that Evil which of it-self wou'd never have invaded us.

But were the *Consequences* of this Passion less injurious than we have represented; it must be allow'd still that *in it-self* it can be no other than miserable; if it be Misery to feel Cowardice, and be haunted by those Specters and Horrors, which are proper to the Character of one who has a thorow Dread of Death. For 'tis not only when Dangers happen, and Hazards are incurr'd, that this sort of *Fear* oppresses and distracts. If it in the least prevails, it gives no quarter, so much as at the safest stillest hour of Retreat and Quiet. Every Object suggests Thought enough to employ it. It operates when it is least observ'd by others; and enters at all times into the pleasantest parts of Life; so as to corrupt and poison all Enjoyment, and Content. One may safely aver, that by reason of this Passion alone, many a Life, if inwardly and closely view'd, wou'd be found to be thorowly miserable, tho attended with all other Circumstances which in appearance render it happy. But when we add to this, the Meannesses, and base Condescensions, occasion'd by such a passionate Concern for living; when we consider how by means of it we are driven to Actions we can never view without Dislike, and forc'd by degrees from our natural Conduct, into still greater Crookednesses and Perplexity; there is no-one, surely, so disingenuous as not to allow, that *Life*, in this case, becomes a sorry Purchase, and is pass'd with little Freedom or Satisfaction. For how can this be otherwise, whilst every thing which is generous and worthy, even the chief *Relish*, *Happiness*, and *Good* of Life, is *for Life's sake* abandon'd and renounc'd.

And thus it seems evident, 'That to have this Affection of DESIRE and LOVE OF LIFE, too intense, or beyond a moderate degree, is against the Interest of a Creature, and contrary to his *Happiness* and *Good.*'

58   There is another Passion very different from that of *Fear*, and which in a certain degree is equally preservative to us, and conducing to our Safety.   As *that* is serviceable, in prompting us to shun Danger; so is *this*, in fortifying us against it, and enabling us to repel Injury, and resist Violence when offer'd. 'Tis true, that according to strict Virtue, and a just Regulation of the Affections in a wise and virtuous Man, such Efforts towards Action amount not to what is justly styl'd *Passion* or *Commotion*.   A Man of Courage may be cautious without real *Fear*.   And a Man of Temper may resist or punish without *Anger*.   But in ordinary Characters there must necessarily be some Mixture of the real Passions themselves; which however, in the main, are able to allay and temper one another.   And thus ANGER in a manner becomes necessary.   'Tis by this Passion that one Creature offering Violence to another, is deter'd from the Execution; whilst he observes how the Attempt affects his Fellow; and knows by the very Signs which accompany this rising Motion, that if the Injury be carry'd further, it will not pass easily or with impunity. * * * As to this Affection therefore, notwithstanding its immediate Aim be indeed *the Ill* or Punishment *of another*, yet it is plainly of the sort of those which tend to the Advantage and Interest of the Self-system, *the Animal himself*; and is withal in other respects contributing to the Good and Interest of the Species.

*   *   *   *   *   *   *

Now as to that Passion which is esteem'd peculiarly *interesting*; as having for its Aim the Possession of Wealth, and what we call a *Settlement* or *Fortune* in the World: If the Regard towards this kind be moderate, and in a reasonable degree; if it occasions no passionate Pursuit, nor raises any ardent Desire or Appetite; there is nothing in this Case which is not compatible with Virtue, and even sutable and beneficial to Society.   The publick as well as private System is advanc'd

by the Industry, which this Affection excites. But if it grows
at length into a real *Passion*; the Injury and Mischief it does
the Publick, is not greater than that which it creates to the
Person himself. Such a one is in reality a Self-oppressor, and
lies heavier on himself than he can ever do on Mankind.

*   *   *   *   *   *   *

59 Thus have we consider'd the *Self-passions*; and what the
Consequence is of their rising beyond a moderate degree.
These Affections, as self-interesting as they are, can often, we
see, become contrary to our real Interest. They betray us
into most Misfortunes, and into the greatest of Unhappinesses,
that of a profligate and abject Character. As they grow im-
perious and high, they are the occasion that a Creature in
proportion becomes mean and low. They are original to that
which we call *Selfishness*, and give rise to that sordid Disposition
of which we have already spoken. It appears there can be
nothing so miserable in it-self, or so wretched in its Consequence, as to be thus impotent in Temper, thus master'd by
Passion, and by means of it, brought under the most servile
Subjection to the World.

'Tis evident withal, that as this *Selfishness* increases in us, so
must a certain *Subtlety*, and *feignedness* of Carriage, which
naturally accompanys it. And thus the Candour and Ingenuity
of our Natures, the Ease and Freedom of our Minds must be
forfeited; all *Trust and Confidence*, in a manner lost; and
Suspicions, *Jealousys*, and *Envys* multiply'd. A *separate End*
and *Interest* must be every day more strongly form'd in us;
generous Views and *Motives* laid aside: And the more we are
thus sensibly disjoin'd every day from Society and our Fellows;
the worse Opinion we shall have of those uniting Passions,
which bind us in strict Alliance and Amity with others. Upon
these Terms we must of course endeavour to silence and
suppress our natural and good Affections: since they are such
as wou'd carry us to the good of Society, against what we fondly
conceive to be our private Good and Interest; as has been shewn.

Now if these SELFISH PASSIONS, besides what other Ill they are the occasion of, are withal the certain means of losing us our *natural Affections* ; then (by what has been prov'd before) 'tis evident, ' That they must be the certain means of losing us the chief Enjoyment of Life, and raising in us those horrid and *unnatural Passions*, and that Savageness of Temper, which makes THE GREATEST OF MISERYS, and the most wretched State of Life : ' as remains for us to explain.

Sect. III.

60   The Passions therefore, which, in the last place, we are to examine, are those which lead neither to *a publick* nor *a private* Good ; and are neither of any advantage to the Species in general, or the Creature in particular.   These, in opposition to the *social and natural*, we call the UNNATURAL AFFECTIONS.

Of this kind is that UNNATURAL *and* INHUMAN DELIGHT *in beholding Torments*, and in viewing Distress, Calamity, Blood, Massacre and Destruction, with a peculiar Joy and Pleasure. This has been the reigning Passion of many Tyrants, and barbarous Nations ; and belongs, in some degree, to such Tempers as have thrown off that Courteousness of Behaviour, which retains in us a just Reverence of Mankind, and prevents the Growth of Harshness and Brutality.   This Passion enters not where Civility or affable Manners have the least place. Such is the Nature of what we call *good Breeding*, that in the midst of many other Corruptions, it admits not of INHUMANITY, or *savage Pleasure*.   To see the Sufferance of an Enemy with cruel Delight, may proceed from the height of Anger, Revenge, Fear, and other extended Self-passions : But to delight in the Torture and Pain of other Creatures indifferently, Natives or Foreigners, of our own or of another Species, Kindred or no Kindred, known or unknown ; to feed, as it were, on Death, and be entertain'd with dying Agonys ; this has nothing in it accountable in the way of Self-interest or private Good abovemention'd, but is wholly and absolutely unnatural, as it is horrid and miserable.

*   *   *   *   *   *   *

There is also among these, a sort of HATRED OF MANKIND AND SOCIETY ; a Passion which has been known perfectly reigning in some Men, and has had a peculiar Name given to it. A large share of this belongs to those who have long indulg'd themselves in a habitual *Moroseness,* or who by force of ill Nature, and ill Breeding, have contracted such a Reverse of Affability, and civil Manners, that to see or meet a Stranger is offensive. The very Aspect of Mankind is a disturbance to 'em, and they are sure always to hate at first sight. The Distemper of this kind is sometimes found to be in a manner *National* ; but peculiar to the more savage Nations, and a plain *Characteristick* of unciviliz'd Manners, and Barbarity. This is the immediate Opposite to that noble Affection, which in antient Language, was term'd *Hospitality, viz.* extensive Love of Mankind, and Relief of Strangers.

*   *   *   *   *   *   *

TREACHERY and INGRATITUDE are in strictness mere negative Vices ; and, in themselves, no real Passions ; having neither Aversion or Inclination belonging to them ; but are deriv'd from the Defect, Unsoundness, of Corruption of the Affections in general. But when these Vices become remarkable in a Character, and arise in a manner from Inclination and Choice ; when they are so forward and active, as to appear of their own accord, without any pressing occasion ; 'tis apparent they borrow something of the mere *unnatural* Passions, and are deriv'd from *Malice, Envy,* and *Inveteracy* ; as explain'd above.

61   It may be objected here, that these Passions, *unnatural* as they are, carry still a sort of *Pleasure* with them ; and that however barbarous a Pleasure it be, yet still it is a Pleasure and *Satisfaction* which is found in Pride, or Tyranny, Revenge, Malice, or Cruelty exerted. Now if it be possible in Nature, that any-one can feel a barbarous or malicious Joy, otherwise than in consequence of mere Anguish and Torment, then may we perhaps allow this kind of Satisfaction to be call'd *Pleasure*

or *Delight.* But the Case is evidently contrary. To love, and
to be kind ; to have social or natural Affection, Complacency
and Good-will, is to feel immediate Satisfaction and genuine
Content. 'Tis in it-self *original Joy*, depending on no preceding
Pain or Uneasiness ; and producing nothing beside Satisfaction
merely. On the other side, Animosity, Hatred, and Bitterness,
is *original Misery* and *Torment,* producing no other Pleasure
or Satisfaction, than as the unnatural Desire is for the instant
satisfy'd by something which appeases it. How strong soever
this Pleasure, therefore, may appear ; it only the more implies
the Misery of that State which produces it. For as the cruel-
lest bodily Pains do by intervals of Assuagement, produce (as
has been shewn) the highest bodily Pleasure ; so the fiercest
and most raging Torments of the Mind, do, by certain
Moments of Relief, afford the greatest of mental Enjoyments
to those who know little of the truer kind.

62   The Men of gentlest Dispositions, and best of Tempers,
have at some time or other been sufficiently acquainted with
those Disturbances, which, at ill hours, even small occasions
are apt to raise. From these slender Experiences of Harshness
and Ill-humour, they fully know and will confess the ill
Moments which are pass'd, when the Temper is ever so little
gall'd or fretted. How must it fare, therefore, with those who
hardly know any better hours in Life ; and who, for the greatest
part of it, are agitated by a thorow active Spleen, a close and
settled Malignity, and Rancour ? How lively must be the Sense
of every thwarting and controuling Accident ? How great
must be the Shocks of Disappointment, the Stings of Affront,
and the Agonys of a working Antipathy, against the multiply'd
Objects of Offence ; Nor can it be wonder'd at, if to Persons
thus agitated and oppress'd, it seems a high Delight to appease
and allay for the while those furious and rough Motions, by an
Indulgence of their Passion in Mischief and Revenge.

Now as to the Consequences of this *unnatural State*, in
respect of Interest, and the common Circumstances of Life ;

upon what Terms a Person who has in this manner lost all
which we call *Nature,* can be suppos'd to stand, in respect of
the Society of Mankind ; how he feels himself in it ; what
Sense he has of his own Disposition towards others, and of the
mutual Disposition of others towards himself; this is easily
conceiv'd.

What Injoyment or Rest is there for one, who is not
conscious of the merited Affection or Love, but, on the contrary
of the Ill-will and Hatred of every human Soul ? What ground
must this afford for Horror and Despair ? What foundation of
Fear, and continual Apprehension from Mankind, and from
superior Powers ? How thorow and deep must be that
Melancholy, which being once mov'd, has nothing soft or
pleasing from the side of Friendship, to allay or divert it?
Wherever such a Creature turns himself ; whichever way he casts
his Eye ; every thing around must appear ghastly and horrid ;
every thing hostile, and, as it were, *bent* against a private and
single Being, who is thus divided from every thing, and at
defiance and war with the rest of Nature.

'Tis thus, at last, that A MIND becomes *a Wilderness* ;
where all is laid waste, every thing *fair* and *goodly* remov'd,
and nothing extant beside what is savage and deform'd.   Now
if Banishment from one's Country, Removal to a foreign Place,
or any thing which looks like Solitude or Desertion, be so heavy
to endure ; what must it be to feel this *inward Banishment,*
this real *Estrangement* from human Commerce ; and to be
after this manner in a Desart, and in the horridest of Solitudes,
even when in the midst of Society ?   What must it be to live
in this *Disagreement,* with everything, this *Irreconcilableness*
and *Opposition* to the Order and Government of the Universe ?

Hence it appears, That the greatest of Miserys accompanys
that State which is consequent to the Loss of natural Affection ;
and That TO HAVE THOSE HORRID, MONSTROUS, AND UN-
NATURAL AFFECTIONS, IS TO BE MISERABLE IN THE HIGHEST
DEGREE.

Conclusion.

63   Thus have we endeavour'd to prove what was propos'd in the beginning. And since in the common and known Sense of *Vice* and *Illness*, no-one can be vitious or ill except either,

1. By the Deficiency or Weakness of *natural Affections*;

Or, 2. by the Violence of *the selfish*;

Or, 3. by such as are plainly *unnatural*:

It must follow, that if each of these are pernicious and destructive to the Creature, insomuch that his compleatest State of Misery is made from hence; To be wicked or vitious, is to be miserable and unhappy.

And since every vitious Action must in proportion, more or less, help towards this Mischief, and *Self-ill*; it must follow, That every vitious action must be self-injurious and ill.

64   On the other side; *the Happiness* and *Good* of Virtue has been prov'd from the contrary Effect of other Affections, such as are according to *Nature*, and the Œconomy of the Species or Kind. We have cast up all those Particulars, from whence (as by way of Addition and Subtraction) the main *Sum* or general Account of Happiness, is either augmented or diminish'd. And if there be no Article exceptionable in this Scheme of *Moral Arithmetick*; the Subject treated may be said to have an Evidence as great as that which is found in Numbers, or Mathematicks. For let us carry *Scepticism* ever so far, let us doubt, if we can, of every thing about us; we cannot doubt of what passes *within ourselves*. Our Passions and Affections are known to us. *They* are certain, whatever the *Objects* may be, on which they are employ'd. Nor is it of any concern to our Argument, how these exterior Objects stand; whether they are Realitys, or mere Illusions; whether we wake or dream. For *ill Dreams* will be equally disturbing. And a good *Dream*, if Life be nothing else, will be easily and happily pass'd. In this Dream of Life, therefore, our Demonstrations have the same force; our *Balance* and *Œconomy* hold good, and our Obligation to Virtue is in every respect the same.

65   Upon the whole : There is not, I presume, the least degree of Certainty wanting in what has been said concerning the Preferableness of *the mental Pleasures to the sensual*; and even *of the sensual, accompany'd with Good Affection, and under a temperate and right use*, to those which are *no ways restrain'd, nor supported by any thing social or affectionate*.

Nor is there less Evidence in what has been said, of *the united Structure and Fabrick of the Mind,* and of those Passions which constitute *the Temper*, or Soul ; and on which its Happiness or Misery so immediately depend.   It has been shewn, That in *this Constitution*, the impairing of any one Part must instantly tend to the disorder and ruin of other Parts and of the Whole it-self ; thro' the necessary *Connexion* and *Balance* of the Affections : That those very Passions thro' which Men are vitious, are of themselves a Torment and Disease ; and that whatsoever is done which is knowingly *ill,* must be of *ill Consciousness* ; and in proportion, as the Act is ill, must impair and corrupt social Enjoyment, and destroy both *the Capacity and kind Affection, and the Consciousness of meriting any such.*   So that neither can we *participate* thus in Joy or Happiness with others, or receive Satisfaction *from the mutual Kindness or imagin'd Love of others* : on which, however, the greatest of all our Pleasures are founded.

If this be the Case of moral Delinquency ; and if the State which is consequent to this *Defection* from nature, be of all other the most horrid, oppressive, and miserable ; 'twill appear, ' *That to yield or consent to any thing ill or immoral, is a Breach of Interest, and leads to the greatest Ills* :' and, 'That on the other side, *Every thing which is an Improvement of Virtue, or an Establishment of right Affection and Integrity, is an Advancement of Interest, and leads to the greatest and most solid Happiness and Enjoyment.*'

66   Thus the Wisdom of what rules, and is FIRST and CHIEF *in Nature*, has made it to be according to the *private Interest* and *Good* of every-one, to work towards the *general Good* ; which

if a Creature ceases to promote, he is actually so far wanting to himself, and ceases to promote his own Happiness and Welfare. He is, on this account, directly his own Enemy : Nor can he any otherwise be good or useful to himself, than as he continues good to Society, and to that *Whole* of which he is himself *a Part.* So that VIRTUE, which of all Excellencys and Beautys is the chief, and most amiable ; *that* which is the Prop and Ornament of human Affairs ; which upholds Communitys, maintains Union, Friendship, and Correspondence amongst Men ; *that* by which Countrys, as well as private Familys, flourish and are happy ; and for want of which, everything comely, conspicuous, great and worthy, must perish, and go to ruin ; *that single Quality*, thus beneficial to all Society, and to Mankind *in general*, is found equally a Happiness and Good to each Creature *in particular* ; and is *that* by which alone Man can be happy, and without which he must be miserable.

And, thus VIRTUE is *the Good*, and VICE *the Ill* of everyone.

[EXTRACT FROM 'THE MORALISTS, A RHAPSODY.'

PART III. Sect. II.

67   Is there then, said he, a natural Beauty of *Figures?* and is there not as natural a one of ACTIONS [1] ? No sooner the Eye opens upon *Figures*, the Ear to *Sounds*, than straight *the Beautiful* results, and *Grace* and *Harmony* are known and acknowledg'd. No sooner are ACTIONS view'd, no sooner the *human Affections* and *Passions* discern'd (and they are most of 'em as soon discern'd as felt), than straight *an inward* EYE distinguishes, and sees *the Fair* and *Shapely, the Amiable* and *Admirable*, apart from *the Deform'd, the Foul, the Odious*, or *the Despicable.* How is it possible therefore not to own, ' That as these *Distinctions* have their Foundation *in Nature*, the Discernment it-self is *natural*, and from NATURE *alone?* '

[1] *Supra,* § 12.

If this, I told him, were as he represented it; there cou'd never, I thought, be any Disagreement among Men concerning Actions and Behaviour: as which was *Base*, which *Worthy*; which *Handsom*, and which *Deform'd*. But now we find perpetual Variance among Mankind; whose Differences were chiefly founded on this Disagreement in Opinion; 'The one *affirming* the other *denying* that this, or ' that, was *fit* or *decent*.'

Even by this then, reply'd he, it appears there is Fitness and Decency in Actions; since *the Fit* and *Decent* is in this Controversy ever pre-suppos'd: And whilst Men are at odds about the Subjects, the Thing it-self is universally agreed. For neither is there agreement in Judgments about other *Beautys*. 'Tis controverted ' Which is the finest *Pile*, the loveliest *Shape*, or *Face*:' But without controversy, 'tis allow'd ' There is a BEAUTY of *each* kind.' This no-one goes about to *teach*: nor is it *learnt* by any; but *confess'd* by All. *All* own the *Standard*, *Rule*, and *Measure*: But in applying it to Things, Disorder arises, Ignorance prevails, Interest and Passion breed Disturbance. Nor can it otherwise happen in the Affairs of Life, whilst that which interests and engages Men as *Good*, is thought different from that which they admire and praise as *Honest*.— But with us, PHILOCLES! 'tis better settled; since for our parts, we have already decreed, ' That *Beauty* and *Good* are still the same.']

HUTCHESON

AN INQUIRY CONCERNING THE
ORIGINAL OF OUR IDEAS OF
VIRTUE OR MORAL GOOD

[First edition 1725.   Reprinted here from the second edition, London 1726, omitting the author's italics.]

HUTCHESON

An Inquiry concerning Moral Good and Evil

———•———

INTRODUCTION.

68   THE Word MORAL GOODNESS, in this Treatise, denotes our
Idea of some Quality apprehended in Actions, which procures
Approbation, and Love toward the Actor, from those who
receive no Advantage by the Action.   MORAL EVIL, denotes
our Idea of a contrary Quality, which excites Aversion, and
Dislike toward the Actor, even from Persons unconcern'd in
its natural Tendency.   We must be contented with these imperfect Descriptions, until we discover whether we really have
such Ideas, and what general Foundation there is in Nature
for this Difference of Actions, as morally Good or Evil.

These Descriptions seem to contain an universally acknowledg'd Difference of Moral Good and Evil, from Natural.
All Men who speak of moral Good, acknowledge that it
procures Love toward those we apprehend possess'd of it ;
whereas natural Good does not.   In this matter Men must
consult their own Breasts.   How differently are they affected
toward those they suppose possess'd of Honesty, Faith,
Generosity, Kindness, even when they expect no Benefit from
these admir'd Qualitys ; and those who are possess'd of the

natural Goods, such as Houses, Lands, Gardens, Vineyards, Health, Strength, Sagacity? We shall find that we necessarily love and approve the Possessors of the former; but the Possession of the latter procures no Love at all toward the Possessor, but often contrary Affections of Envy and Hatred. In the same manner, whatever Quality we apprehend to be morally Evil, raises our Hatred toward the Person in whom we observe it, such as Treachery, Cruelty, Ingratitude, even when they are no way hurtful to our selves; whereas we heartily love, esteem, and pity many who are expos'd to natural Evils, such as Pain, Poverty, Hunger, Sickness, Death, even when we our selves suffer Inconveniencies, by these natural Evils of others.

69 Now the first Question on this Subject is, ' Whence arise these different Ideas of Actions.'

Because we shall afterwards frequently use the Words Interest, Advantage, natural Good, it is necessary here to fix their Ideas. The Pleasure in our sensible Perceptions of any kind, gives us our first Idea of natural Good, or Happiness; and then all Objects which are apt to excite this Pleasure are call'd immediately Good. Those Objects which may procure others immediately pleasant, are call'd Advantageous : and we pursue both Kinds from a View of Interest, or from Self-Love.

Our Sense of Pleasure is antecedent to Advantage or Interest, and is the Foundation of it. We do not perceive Pleasure in Objects, because it is our Interest to do so; but Objects or Actions are Advantageous, and are pursu'd or undertaken from Interest, because we receive Pleasure from them. Our Perception of Pleasure is necessary, and nothing is Advantageous or naturally Good to us, but what is apt to raise Pleasure mediately, or immediately. Such Objects as we know, either from Experience of Sense, or Reason, to be immediately, or mediately Advantageous, or apt to minister Pleasure, we are said to pursue from Self-Interest,

when our Intention is only to enjoy this Pleasure, which
they have the Power of exciting. Thus Meats, Drink,
Harmony, fine Prospects, Painting, Statues, are perceiv'd by
our Senses to be immediately Good; and our Reason shews
Riches and Power to be mediately so, that is, apt to furnish
us with Objects of immediate Pleasure: and both Kinds
of these natural Goods are pursu'd from Interest, or Self-Love.

70   Now the greatest part of our latter Moralists establish
it as undeniable, 'That all moral Qualitys have necessarily
some Relation to the Law of a Superior, of sufficient Power
to make us Happy or Miserable;' and since all Laws operate
only by Sanctions of Rewards, or Punishments, which
determine us to Obedience by Motives of Self-Interest, they
suppose, 'that it is thus that Laws do constitute some Actions
mediately Good, or Advantageous, and others the same way
Disadvantageous.' They say indeed, 'That a benevolent Legislator constitutes no Actions Advantageous to the Agent by
Law, but such as in their own Nature tend to the natural
Good of the Whole, or, at least, are not inconsistent with it;
and that therefore we approve the Virtue of others, because
it has some small Tendency to our Happiness, either from
its own Nature, or from this general Consideration, That
Obedience to a benevolent Legislator, is in general Advantageous to the Whole, and to us in particular; and that for the
contrary Reasons alone, we disapprove the Vice of others,
that is, the prohibited Action, as tending to our particular
Detriment in some degree.' But then they maintain, 'That
we are determin'd to Obedience to Laws, or deterr'd from
Disobedience, merely by Motives of Self-Interest, to obtain
either the natural Good arising from the commanded Action,
or the Rewards promised by the Sanction; or to avoid the
natural evil Consequences of Disobedience, or at least the
Penaltys of the Law.'

71   Some other Moralists suppose 'an immediate natural Good
in the Actions call'd Virtuous; that is, That we are determin'd

to perceive some Beauty in the Actions of others, and to
love the Agent, even without reflecting upon any Advantage
which can any way redound to us from the Action ; that
we have also a secret Sense of Pleasure accompanying such
of our own Actions as we call Virtuous, even when we expect
no other Advantage from them.' But they alledge at the
same time, 'That we are excited to perform these Actions,
even as we pursue, or purchase Pictures, Statues, Landskips,
from Self-Interest, to obtain this Pleasure which accompanys
the very Action, and which we necessarily enjoy in doing it.'
The Design of the following Sections is to enquire into this
matter ; and perhaps the Reasons to be offer'd may prove,

72 I. 'That some Actions have to Men an immediate Goodness ;
or, that by a superior Sense, which I call a Moral one, we
perceive Pleasure in the Contemplation of such Actions
in others, and are determin'd to love the Agent, (and much
more do we perceive Pleasure in being conscious of having
done such Actions our selves) without any View of further
natural Advantage from them.'

II. It may perhaps also appear, 'That what excites us to
these Actions which we call Virtuous, is not an Intention
to obtain even this sensible Pleasure ; much less the future
Rewards from Sanctions of Laws, or any other natural Good,
which may be the Consequence of the virtuous Action ; but
an entirely different Principle of Action from Interest or
Self-Love.'

Sect. I.

OF THE MORAL SENSE BY WHICH WE PERCEIVE VIRTUE AND VICE, AND APPROVE OR DISAPPROVE THEM IN OTHERS.

73 I. That the Perceptions of moral Good and Evil, are
perfectly different from those of natural Good, or Advantage
every one must convince himself, by reflecting upon the
different Manner in which he finds himself affected when

these Objects occur to him. Had we no Sense of Good
distinct from the Advantage or Interest arising from the
external Senses, and the Perceptions of Beauty and Harmony;
our Admiration and Love toward a fruitful Field, or commodious
Habitation, would be much the same with what we have
toward a generous Friend, or any noble Character; for both
are, or may be advantageous to us: And we should no more
admire any Action, or love any Person in a distant Country,
or Age, whose Influence could not extend to us, than we love
the Mountains of PERU, while we are unconcern'd in the
Spanish Trade. We should have the same Sentiments and
Affections toward inanimate Beings, which we have toward
rational Agents; which yet every one knows to be false.
Upon Comparison, we say, 'Why should we admire or love
with Esteem inanimate Beings? They have no Intention
of Good to us; their Nature makes them fit for our Uses,
which they neither know nor study to serve. But it is not
so with rational Agents: they study our Interest, and delight
in our Happiness, and are Benevolent toward us.'

74 We are all then conscious of the Difference between that
Love and Esteem, or Perception of moral Excellence, which
Benevolence excites toward the Person in whom we observe
it, and that Opinion of natural Goodness, which only raises
Desire of Possession toward the good Object. Now 'what
should make this Difference, if all Approbation, or Sense
of Good be from Prospect of Advantage? Do not inanimate
Objects promote our Advantage, as well as Benevolent Persons
who do us Offices of Kindness, and Friendship? Should we
not then have the same endearing Sentiments of both? or
only the same cold Opinion of Advantage in both?' The
Reason why it is not so, must be this, 'That we have
a distinct Perception of Beauty, or Excellence in the kind
Affections of rational Agents; whence we are determin'd
to admire and love such Characters and Persons.'

Suppose we reap the same Advantage from two Men, one of

whom serves us from Delight in our Happiness, and Love toward us; the other from Views of Self-Interest, or by Constraint: both are in this Case equally beneficial or advantageous to us, and yet we shall have quite different Sentiments of them. We must then certainly have other Perceptions of moral Actions than those of Advantage: And that Power of receiving these Perceptions may be call'd a MORAL SENSE, since the Definition agrees to it, *viz.* a Determination of the Mind, to receive any Idea from the Presence of an Object which occurs to us, independent on our Will.

75   This perhaps will be equally evident from our Ideas of Evil, done to us designedly by a rational Agent. Our Senses of natural Good and Evil would make us receive, with equal Serenity and Composure, an Assault, a Buffet, an Affront from a Neighbour, a Cheat from a Partner, or Trustee, as we would an equal Damage from the Fall of a Beam, a Tile, or a Tempest; and we should have the same Affections and Sentiments of both. Villany, Treachery, Cruelty, would be as meekly resented as a Blast, or Mildew, or an overflowing Stream. But I fancy every one is very differently affected on these Occasions, tho there may be equal natural Evil in both. Nay, Actions no way detrimental, may occasion the strongest Anger, and Indignation, if they evidence only impotent Hatred, or Contempt. And, on the other hand, the Intervention of moral Ideas may prevent our Hatred of the Agent, or bad moral Apprehension of that Action, which causes to us the greatest natural Evil. Thus the Opinion of Justice in any Sentence, will prevent all Ideas of moral Evil in the Execution, or Hatred toward the Magistrate, who is the immediate Cause of our greatest Sufferings.

76   II. In our Sentiments of Actions which affect our selves, there is indeed a Mixture of the Ideas of natural and moral Good, which require some Attention to separate them. But when we reflect upon the Actions which affect other Persons only, we may observe the moral Ideas unmix'd with those of natural

Good, or Evil.   For let it be here observ'd, that those Senses
by which we perceive Pleasure in natural Objects, whence they
are constituted Advantageous, could never raise in us any
Desire of publick Good, but only of what was good to our
selves in particular.   Nor could they ever make us approve an
Action because of its promoting the Happiness of others.
And yet as soon as any Action is represented to us as flowing
from Love, Humanity, Gratitude, Compassion, a Study of the
good of others, and a Delight in their Happiness, altho it
were in the most distant Part of the World, or in some past
Age, we feel Joy within us, admire the lovely Action, and
praise its Author.   And on the contrary, every Action represented as flowing from Hatred, Delight in the Misery of
others, or Ingratitude, raises Abhorrence and Aversion.

77   It is true indeed, that the Actions we approve in others, are
generally imagin'd to tend to the natural Good of Mankind, or
of some Parts of it.   But whence this secret Chain between
each Person and Mankind?   How is my Interest connected
with the most distant Parts of it?   And yet I must admire
Actions which are beneficial to them, and love the Author.
Whence this Love, Compassion, Indignation and Hatred toward
even feign'd Characters, in the most distant Ages, and Nations,
according as they appear Kind, Faithful, Compassionate, or of
the opposite Dispositions, toward their imaginary Contemporaries?   If there is no moral Sense, which makes rational
Actions appear Beautiful, or Deform'd; if all Approbation be
from the Interest of the Approver,

What's HECUBA to us, or we to HECUBA [1]?

78   III. Some refin'd Explainers of Self-Love may tell us,
' That we hate, or love Characters, according as we apprehend
we should have been supported, or injur'd by them, had we
liv'd in their Days.'   But how obvious is the Answer, if we
only observe, that had we no Sense of moral Good in Humanity,

[1] Tragedy of Hamlet.

Mercy, Faithfulness, why should not Self-Love, and our Sense of natural Good engage us always to the victorious Side, and make us admire and love the successful Tyrant, or Traitor? Why do not we love SINON, or PYRRHUS, in the Æneid? for had we been GREEKS, these two would have been very advantageous Characters. Why are we affected with the Fortunes of PRIAMUS, POLITES, CHORŒBUS or ÆNEAS? It is plain we have some secret Sense which determines our Approbation without regard to Self-Interest; otherwise we should always favour the fortunate Side without regard to Virtue, and suppose our selves engaged with that Party.

Suppose any great Destruction occasion'd by mere Accident, without any Design, or Negligence of the Person who casually was the Author of it: This Action might have been as disadvantageous to us as design'd Cruelty, or Malice; but who will say he has the same Idea of both Actions, or Sentiments of the Agents? 'Whence then this Difference?'

And further, Let us make a Supposition, which perhaps is not far from Matter of Fact, to try if we cannot approve even disadvantageous Actions, and perceive moral Good in them. A few ingenious Artisans, persecuted in their own Country, flee to ours for Protection; they instruct us in Manufactures which support Millions of Poor, increase the Wealth of almost every Person in the State, and make us formidable to our Neighbours. In a Nation not far distant from us, some resolute Burgomasters, full of Love to their Country, and Compassion toward their Fellow-Citizens, opprest in Body and Soul by a Tyrant, and Inquisition, with indefatigable Diligence, public Spirit, and Courage, support a tedious perilous War against the Tyrant, and form an industrious Republick, which rivals us in Trade, and almost in Power. All the World sees whether the former or the latter have been more advantageous to us: and yet let every Man consult his own Breast, which of the two Characters he has the most agreeable Idea of? whether of the useful Refugee, or the public-spirited

Burgomaster, by whose Love to his own Country, we have
often suffer'd in our Interests? and I am confident he will
find some other Foundation of Esteem than Advantage, and
will see a just Reason, why the Memory of our Artisans is so
obscure among us, and yet that of our Rivals is immortal.

79   IV. Some Moralists, who will rather twist Self-Love into
a thousand Shapes, than allow any other Principle of Approbation than Interest, may tell us, 'That whatever profits
one Part without detriment to another, profits the Whole, and
then some small Share will redound to each Individual ; that
those Actions which tend to the Good of *the* Whole, if
universally perform'd, would most effectually secure to each
Individual his own Happiness; and that consequently, we
may approve such Actions, from the Opinion of their tending
ultimately to our own Advantage.

We need not trouble these Gentlemen to shew by their nice
Train of Consequences, and Influences of Actions by way of
Precedent in particular Instances, that we in this Age reap any
Advantage from ORESTES's killing the treacherous ÆGYSTHUS,
or from the Actions of CODRUS or DECIUS. Allow their
Reasonings to be perfectly good, they only prove, that after
long Reflection, and Reasoning, we may find out some ground,
even from Views of Interest, to approve the same Actions which
every Man admires as soon as he hears of them ; and that too
under a quite different Conception.

Should any of our Travellers find some old Grecian Treasure
the Miser who hid it, certainly perform'd an Action more to
the Traveller's Advantage than CODRUS or ORESTES ; for he
must have but a small Share of Benefit from their Actions,
whose Influence is so dispers'd, and lost in various Ages, and
Nations : Surely then this Miser must appear to the Traveller
a prodigious Hero in Virtue ! For Self-Interest will make us
only esteem Men according to the Good they do to our Selves,
and not give us high Ideas of public Good, but in proportion
to our Share of it. But must a Man have the Reflection of

CUMBERLAND, or PUFFENDORF, to admire Generosity, Faith,
Humanity, Gratitude? Or reason so nicely to apprehend the
Evil in Cruelty, Treachery, Ingratitude? Do not the former
excite our Admiration, and Love, and Study of Imitation,
wherever we see them, almost at first View, without any such
Reflection; and the latter, our Hatred, Contempt, and Ab-
horrence? Unhappy would it be for Mankind, if a Sense of
Virtue was of as narrow an Extent, as a Capacity for such
Metaphysicks.

80   V. This moral Sense, either of our own Actions, or of those
of others, has this in common with our other Senses, that however our Desire of Virtue may be counterballanc'd by Interest,
our Sentiment *or* Perception of its Beauty cannot; as it
certainly might be, if the only Ground of our Approbation
were Views of Advantage. Let us consider this both as to our
own Actions and those of others.

A Covetous Man shall dislike any Branch of Trade, how
useful soever it may be to the Publick, if there is no Gain for
himself in it; here is an Aversion from Interest. Propose
a sufficient Premium, and he shall be the first who sets about
it, with full Satisfaction in his own Conduct. Now is it the
same way with our Sense of moral Actions? Should any one
advise us to wrong a Minor, or Orphan, or to do an ungrateful Action toward a Benefactor; we at first View abhor
it: Assure us that it will be very advantageous to us, propose
even a Reward; our Sense of the Action is not alter'd. It is
true, these Motives may make us undertake it; but they have
no more Influence upon us to make us approve it, than
a Physician's Advice has to make a nauseous Potion pleasant
to the Taste, when we perhaps force our selves to take it for
the Recovery of Health.

81   Had we no Notion of Actions, beside our Opinion of their
Advantage, or Disadvantage, could we ever chuse an Action
as Advantageous, which we are conscious is still Evil? as it
too often happens in human Affairs. Where would be the

need of such high Bribes to prevail with Men to abandon the
Interests of a ruin'd Party, or of Tortures to force out the
Secrets of their Friends? Is it so hard to convince Mens
Understandings, if that be the only Faculty we have to do
with, that it is probably more advantageous to secure present
Gain, and avoid present Evils, by joining with the prevalent
Party, then to wait for the remote Possibility of future Good,
upon a Revolution often improbable, and sometimes unexpected? And when Men are overpersuaded by Advantage, do
they always prove their own Conduct? Nay, how often is
their remaining Life odious, and shameful, in their own sense of
it, as well as in that of others, to whom the base Action was
profitable?

If any one becomes satisfy'd with his own Conduct in such
a Case, upon what Ground is it? How does he please himself,
or vindicate his Actions to others? Never by reflecting upon his
private Advantage, or alledging this to others as a Vindication ;
but by gradually warping into the moral Principles of his new
Party ; for no Party is without them. And thus Men become
pleas'd with their Actions under some Appearance of moral
Good, distinct from Advantage.

82   It may perhaps be alledg'd, ' That in those Actions of our
own which we call Good, there is this constant Advantage,
superior to all others, which is the Ground of our Approbation,
and the Motive to them from Self-love, *viz.* That we suppose,
the DEITY will reward them.' This will be more fully
consider'd [1] afterwards : At present it is enough to observe,
that many have high Notions of Honour, Faith, Generosity,
Justice, who have scarce any Opinions about the DEITY, or any
Thoughts of future Rewards ; and abhor any thing which is
Treacherous, Cruel, or Unjust, without any regard to future
Punishments.

But further, tho these Rewards, and Punishments, may
make my own Actions appear advantageous to me, and make

---

[1] See *Sect.* ii. *Art.* 7.

me approve them from Self-Love, yet they would never make me approve, and love another Person for the like Actions, whose Merit would not be imputed to me. Those Actions are advantageous indeed to the Agent ; but his Advantage is not my Advantage : and Self-Love could never influence me to approve Actions as advantageous to others, or to love the Authors of them on that account.

83   This is the second thing to be consider'd, 'Whether our Sense of the moral Good or Evil, in the Actions of others, can be over-ballanc'd, or brib'd by Views of Interest.' Now I may indeed easily be capable of wishing, that another would do an Action I abhor as morally Evil, if it were very Advantageous to me : Interest in that Case may overballance my Desire of Virtue in another. But no Interest to my self will make me approve an Action as morally Good, which, without that Interest to my self, would have appear'd morally Evil ; if, upon computing its whole Effects, it appears to produce as great a moment of Good in the Whole, when it is not beneficial to me, as it did before when it was. In our Sense of moral Good or Evil, our own private Advantage of Loss is of no more moment, than the Advantage or Loss of a third Person, to make an Action appear Good or Evil. This Sense therefore cannot be over-ballanc'd by Interest. How ridiculous an Attempt wou'd it be, to engage a Man by Rewards, or to threaten him into a good Opinion of an Action, which was contrary to his moral Notions ? We may procure Dissimulation by such means, and that is all.

84   VI. A late witty Author [1] says, 'That the Leaders of Mankind do not really admire such Actions as those of REGULUS, or DECIUS, but only observe, that Men of such Dispositions are very useful for the Defence of any State ; and therefore by Panegyricks, and Statues, they encourage such Tempers in others, as the most tractable, and useful.' Here first let us consider, If a Traitor, who would sell his own Country to us,

---

[1] See the Fable of the Bees, *pages* 34, 36, *3rd Ed.*

may not often be as advantageous to us, as a Hero who defends us : And yet we can love the Treason, and hate the Traitor. We can at the same time praise a gallant Enemy, who is very pernicious to us.   Is there nothing in all this but an Opinion of Advantage ?

Again, upon this Scheme what could a Statue or Panegyrick effect ?—Men love Praise—They will do the Actions which they observe to be praised.—Praise, with Men who have no other Idea of Good but Self-Interest, is the Opinion which a Nation or Party have of a Man as useful to them—REGULUS, or CATO, or DECIUS, had no Advantage by the Actions which profited their Country, and therefore they themselves could not admire them, however the Persons who reap'd the Advantage might praise such Actions.—REGULUS or CATO could not possibly praise or love another Hero for a virtuous Action ; for this would not gain them the Advantage of Honour ; and their own Actions they must have look'd upon as the hard Terms on which Honour was to be purchas'd, without any thing amiable in them,· which they could contemplate or reflect upon with Pleasure.—Now how unlike is this to what the least Observation would teach a Man concerning such Characters ?

But says he [1], 'These wondrous cunning Governours made Men believe, by their Statues and Panegyricks, that there was publick Spirit, and that this was in it self Excellent ; and hence Men are led to admire it in others, and to imitate it in themselves, forgetting the Pursuit of their own Advantage.' So easy a matter it seems to him, to quit judging of others by what we feel in our selves !—for a Person who is wholly selfish, to imagine others to be publick-spirited !—for one who has no Ideas of Good but in his own Advantage, to be led, by the Persuasions of others, into a Conception of Goodness in what is avowedly detrimental to himself, and profitable to others ; nay so entirely, as not to approve the Action thorowly, but so

---

[1] See the same Author in the same Place.

far as he was conscious that it proceeded from a disinterested Study of the Good of others !—Yet this it seems Statues and Panegyricks can accomplish !

Nil intra est oleam, nil extra est in nuce duri[1]*!*

85   It is an easy matter for Men to assert any thing in Words ; but our own Hearts must decide the Matter, ' Whether some moral Actions do not at first View appear amiable, even to those who are unconcern'd in their Influence ? Whether we do not sincerely love a generous kind Friend, or Patriot, whose Actions procure Honour to him only, without any Advantage to our selves ? ' It is true, that the Actions which we approve, are useful to Mankind ; but not always to the Approver.   It would perhaps be useful to the Whole, that all Men agreed in performing such Actions ; and then every one would have his Share of the Advantage : But this only proves, that Reason and calm Reflection may recommend to us, from Self-Interest, those Actions, which at first View our moral Sense determines us to admire, without considering this Interest.   Nay, our Sense shall operate even where the Advantage to our selves does not hold. We can approve the Justice of a Sentence against our selves : A condemn'd Traitor may approve the Vigilance of a CICERO in discovering Conspiracies, tho it had been for the Traitor's Advantage, that there never had been in the World any Men of such Sagacity.   To say that he may still approve such Conduct as tending to the publick Good, is a Jest from one whose only Idea of Good is Self-Interest.   Such a Person has no Desire of publick Good further than it tends to his own Advantage, which it does not at all in the present Case.

86   VII. If what is said makes it appear, that we have some other amiable Idea of Actions than that of Advantageous to our selves, we may conclude, ' That this Perception of moral Good is not deriv'd from Custom, Education, Example, or Study.' These give us no new Ideas : They might make us see

---

[1] Hor. *Ep.* 1. *Lib.* 2. *v.* 31.

Advantage to our selves in Actions whose Usefulness did not at first appear; or give us Opinions of some Tendency of Actions to our Detriment, by some nice Deductions of Reason, or by a rash Prejudice, when upon the first View of the Action we should have observ'd no such thing : but they never could have made us apprehend Actions as amiable or odious, without any Consideration of our own Advantage.

87   VIII. It remains then, 'That as the AUTHOR of Nature has determin'd us to receive, by our external Senses, pleasant or disagreeable Ideas of Objects, according as they are useful or hurtful to our Bodys ; and to receive from uniform Objects the Pleasures of Beauty and Harmony, to excite us to the Pursuit of Knowledge, and to reward us for it ; or to be an Argument to us of his Goodness, as the Uniformity it self proves his Existence, whether we had a Sense of Beauty in Uniformity or not : in the same manner he has given us a MORAL SENSE, to direct our Actions, and to give us still nobler Pleasures ; so that while we are only intending the Good of others, we 'undesignedly promote our own greatest private Good.'

88   We are not to imagine, that this moral Sense, more than the other Senses, supposes any innate Ideas, Knowledge, or practical Proposition : We mean by it only a Determination of our Minds to receive amiable or disagreeable Ideas of Actions, when they occur to our Observation, antecedent to any Opinions of Advantage or Loss to redound to our selves from them ; even as we are pleas'd with a regular Form, or an harmonious Composition, without having any Knowledge of Mathematicks, or seeing any Advantage in that Form, or Composition, different from the immediate Pleasure.

Sect. II.

CONCERNING THE IMMEDIATE MOTIVE TO VIRTUOUS ACTIONS.

89   The Motives of human Actions, or their immediate Causes, would be best understood after considering the Passions and

Affections ; but here we shall only consider the Springs of the Actions which we call virtuous, as far as it is necessary to settle the general Foundation of the Moral Sense.

I. Every Action, which we apprehend as either morally good or evil, is always suppos'd to flow from some Affection toward rational Agents ; and whatever we call Virtue or Vice, is either some such Affection, or some Action consequent upon it. Or it may perhaps be enough to make an Action, or Omission, appear vitious, if it argues the Want of such Affection toward rational Agents, as we expect in Characters counted morally good. All the Actions counted religious in any Country, are suppos'd, by those who count them so, to flow from some Affections toward the DEITY ; and whatever we call social Virtue, we still suppose to flow from Affections toward our Fellow-Creatures : for in this all seem to agree, 'That external Motions, when accompany'd with no Affections toward GOD or Man, or evidencing no Want of the expected Affections toward either, can have no moral Good or Evil in them.'

Ask, for instance, the most abstemious Hermit, if Temperance of it self would be morally good, supposing it shew'd no Obedience toward the DEITY, made us no fitter for Devotion, or the Service of Mankind, or the Search after Truth, than Luxury ; and he will easily grant, that it would be no moral Good, tho still it might be naturally good or advantageous to Health : And mere Courage, or Contempt of Danger, if we conceive it to have no regard to the Defence of the Innocent, or repairing of Wrongs, or Self-Interest, wou'd only entitle its Possessor to Bedlam. When such sort of Courage is sometimes admir'd, it is upon some secret Appehension of a good Intention in the use of it, or as a natural Ability capable of an useful Application. Prudence, if it was only employ'd in promoting private Interest, is never imagined to be a Virtue : and Justice, or observing a strict Equality, if it has no regard to the Good of Mankind, the Preservation of Rights, and securing Peace, is a Quality properer for its ordinary Gestamen, a Beam and Scales, than for a rational Agent. So that these four Qualitys, commonly call'd Cardinal Virtues, obtain that Name, because they are Dispositions universally necessary to promote publick Good, and denote Affections toward rational Agents; otherwise there would appear no Virtue in them.

90 II. Now if it can be made appear, that none of these Affections which we call virtuous, spring from Self-love, or Desire of private Interest; since all Virtue is either some such Affections, or Actions consequent upon them; it must necessarily follow, 'That Virtue is not pursued from the Interest or Self-love of the Pursuer, or any Motives of his own Advantage.'

The Affections which are of most Importance in Morals, are LOVE and HATRED : All the rest seem but different Modifications of these two original Affections. Now in discoursing of Love toward rational Agents, we need not be caution'd not to include that Love between the Sexes, which, when no other Affections accompany it, is only Desire of Pleasure, and is never counted a Virtue. Love toward rational Agents, is subdivided into Love of Complacence or Esteem, and Love of Benevolence : And Hatred is subdivided into Hatred of Displicence or Contempt, and Hatred of Malice. Concerning each of these separately we shall consider, 'Whether they can be influenc'd by Motives of Self-Interest.'

91 Love of Complacence, Esteem, or Good-liking, at first view appears to be disinterested, and so the Hatred of Displicence or Dislike; and are entirely excited by some moral Qualitys, Good or Evil, apprehended to be in the Objects; which Qualitys the very Frame of our Nature determines us to love or hate, to approve or disapprove, according to the moral Sense above explain'd . Propose to a Man all the Rewards in the World, or threaten all the Punishments, to engage him to love with Esteem and Complacence, a third Person entirely unknown, or if known, apprehended to be cruel, treacherous, ungrateful ; you may procure external Obsequiousness, or good Offices, or

---

¹ See *Sect.* i.

Dissimulation of Love; but real Love of Esteem no Price can purchase. And the same is obvious as to Hatred of Contempt, which no Motive of Advantage can prevent. On the contrary, represent a Character as generous, kind, faithful, humane, tho in the most distant Parts of the World, and we cannot avoid loving it with Esteem, and Complacence. A Bribe may make us attempt to ruin such a Man, or some strong Motive of Advantage may excite us to oppose his Interest; but it can never make us hate him, while we apprehend him as morally excellent. Nay, when we consult our own Hearts, we shall find, that we can scarce ever persuade our selves to attempt any Mischief against such Persons, from any Motive of Advantage, nor execute it, without the strongest Reluctance, and Remorse, until we have blinded our selves into a bad Opinion of the Person in a moral Sense.

92   III. As to the Love of Benevolence, the very Name excludes Self-Interest. We never call that Man benevolent, who is in fact useful to others, but at the same time only intends his own Interest, without any desire of, or delight in, the Good of others. If there be any Benevolence at all, it must be dis-interested; for the most useful Action imaginable, loses all appearance of Benevolence, as soon as we discern that it only flowed from Self-Love or Interest. Thus, never were any human Actions more advantageous, than the Inventions of Fire, and Iron; but if these were casual, or if the Inventor only intended his own Interest in them, there is nothing which can be call'd Benevolent in them. Wherever then Benevolence is suppos'd, there it is imagin'd disinterested, and design'd for the Good of others.

93   But it must be here observ'd, That as all Men have Self-Love, as well as Benevolence, these two Principles may jointly excite a Man to the same Action; and then they are to be consider'd as two Forces impelling the same Body to Motion; sometimes they conspire, sometimes are indifferent to each other, and sometimes are in some degree opposite. Thus, if a Man have such strong Benevolence, as would have produc'd an Action without any Views of Self-Interest ; that such a Man has also in View private Advantage, along with publick Good, as the Effect of his Action, does no way diminish the Benevolence of the Action. When he would not have produc'd so much publick Good, had it not been for Prospect of Self-Interest, then the Effect of Self-Love is to be deducted, and his Benevolence is proportion'd to the remainder of Good, which pure Benevolence would have produc'd. When a Man's Benevolence is hurtful to himself, then Self-Love is opposite to Benevolence, and the Benevolence is proportion'd to the Sum of the Good produc'd, added to the Resistance of Self-Love surmounted by it. In most Cases it is impossible for Men to know how far their Fellows are influenc'd by the one or other of these Principles ; but yet the general Truth is sufficiently certain, That this is the way in which the Benevolence of Actions is to be computed. Since then, no Love to rational Agents can proceed from Self-Interest, every Action must be disinterested, as far as it flows from Love to rational Agents.

94 If any enquire, ' Whence arises this Love of Esteem, or Benevolence, to good Men, or to Mankind in general, if not from some nice Views of Self-Interest ? Or, how we can be mov'd to desire the Happiness of others, without any View to our own ? ' It may be answer'd, ' That the same Cause which determines us to pursue Happiness for our selves, determines us both to Esteem and Benevolence on their proper Occasions ; even the very Frame of our Nature, or a generous Instinct. which shall be afterwards explain'd.

95 IV. Here we may observe, That as Love of Esteem and Complacence is always join'd with Benevolence, where there is no strong Opposition of Interest ; so Benevolence seems to presuppose some small degree of Esteem, not indeed of actual good Qualitys ; for there may be strong Benevolence, where there is the Hatred of Contempt for actual Vices ; as a Parent may have great Benevolence to a most abandon'd Child, whose

Manners he hates with the greatest Displicence: but Benevolence
supposes a Being capable of Virtue. We judge of other rational
Agents by our selves. The human Nature is a lovely Form ;
we are all conscious of some morally good Qualitys and Inclinations in our selves, how partial and imperfect soever they
may be ; we presume the same of every thing in human Form,
nay almost of every living Creature : so that by this suppos'd
remote Capacity of Virtue, there may be some small degree of
Esteem along with our Benevolence, even when they incur our
greatest Displeasure by their Conduct.

96   As to Malice, Human Nature seems scarce capable of
malicious disinterested Hatred, or a sedate Delight in the
Misery of others, when we imagine them no way pernicious
to us, or opposite to our Interest : And for that Hatred
which makes us oppose those whose Interests are opposite
to ours, it is only the effect of Self-Love, and not of disinterested
Malice. A sudden Passion may give us wrong Representations
of our Fellow-Creatures, and for a little time represent them
as absolutely Evil ; and during this Imagination perhaps we
may give some Evidences of disinterested Malice : but as
soon as we reflect upon human Nature, and form just Conceptions, this unnatural Passion is allay'd, and only Self-Love
remains, which may make us, from Self-Interest, oppose our
Adversarys.

*   *   *   *   *   *   *

97   V. Having offer'd what may perhaps prove, That our Love
either of Esteem, or Benevolence, is not founded on Self-Love,
or views of Interest ; let us see 'if some other Affections,
in which Virtue may be plac'd, do arise from Self-Love ;'
such as Fear, or Reverence, arising from an Apprehension
of Goodness, Power, and Justice. For no body apprehends
any Virtue in base Dread and Servitude toward a powerful
Evil Being : This is indeed the meanest Selfishness. Now
the same Arguments which prove Love of Esteem to be
disinterested, will prove this honourable Reverence to be so

too; for it plainly arises from an Apprehension of amiable
Qualitys in the Person, and Love toward him, which raises an
Abhorrence of offending him.   Could we reverence a Being
because it was our Interest to do so, a third Person might
bribe us into Reverence toward a Being neither Good, nor
Powerful, which every one sees to be a Jest.   And this we
might shew to be common to all other Passions, which have
rational Agents for their Objects.

98   VI. There is one Objection against disinterested Love, which
occurs from considering, 'That nothing so effectually excites
our Love toward rational Agents, as their Beneficence to us ;
whence we are led to imagine, that our Love of Persons,
as well as irrational Objects, flows intirely from Self-Interest.'
But let us here examine our selves more narrowly.   Do we
only love the Beneficent, because it is our Interest to love
them ? Or do we chuse to love them, because our Love
is the means of procuring their Bounty ? If it be so, then
we could indifferently love any Character, even to obtain
the Bounty of a third Person ; or we could be brib'd by
a third Person to love the greatest Villain heartily, as we
may be brib'd to external Offices : Now this is plainly
impossible.

99   But further, is not our Love always the Consequent of
Bounty, and not the Means of procuring it ? External Shew,
Obsequiousness, and Dissimulation may precede an Opinion
of Beneficence ; but real Love always presupposes it, and shall
necessarily arise even when we expect no more, from consideration of past Benefits.   Or can any one say he only
loves the Beneficent, as he does a Field or Garden, because
of its Advantage ? His Love then must cease toward one
who has ruin'd himself in kind Offices to him, when he can
do him no more ; as we cease to love an inanimate Object
which ceases to be useful, unless a Poetical Prosopopœia
animate it, and raise an imaginary Gratitude, which is indeed
pretty common.   And then again, our Love would be the

same towards the worst Characters that 'tis towards the best,
if they were equally bountiful to us, which is also false.
Beneficence then must raise our Love as it is an amiable moral
Quality : and hence we love even those who are beneficent to
others.

100   It may be further alledg'd, 'That Bounty toward our selves
is a stronger Incitement to Love, than equal Bounty toward
others.' This is true for a Reason to be offer'd below[1] :
but it does not prove, that in this Case our Love of Persons
is from Views of Interest ; since this Love is not prior to
the Bounty, as the means to procure it, but subsequent upon
it, even when we expect no more. In the Benefits which
we receive our selves, we are more fully sensible of their
Value, and of the Circumstances of the Action which are
Evidences of a generous Temper in the Donor ; and from
the good Opinion we have of our selves, we are apt to look
upon the Kindness as better employ'd, than when it is
bestow'd on others, of whom perhaps we have less favourable
Sentiments. It is however sufficient to remove the Objection,
that Bounty from a Donor apprehended as morally Evil,
or extorted by Force, or conferr'd with some View of Self-
Interest, will not procure real Love ; nay, it may raise Indignation, if we suspect Dissimulation of Love, or a Design to
allure us into any thing Dishonourable : whereas wisely
employ'd Bounty is always approv'd, and gains love to the
Author from all who hear of it.

   If then no Love toward Persons be influenc'd by Self-
Love, or Views of Interest, and all Virtue flows from Love
toward Persons, or some other Affection equally disinterested ;
it remains, 'That there must be some other Motive than
Self-Love, or Interest, which excites us to the Actions we call
Virtuous.'

101   VII. There may perhaps still remain another Suspicion
of Self-Interest in our Prosecution of Virtue arising from

---

[1] See *Sect.* v. *Art.* 2.

this, 'That the whole Race of Mankind seems persuaded of the Existence of an Almighty Being, who will certainly secure Happiness either now, or hereafter, to those who are Virtuous, according to their several Notions of Virtue in various Places : and upon this Persuasion, Virtue may in all Cases be pursu'd from Views of Interest [1].'   Here again we might appeal to all Mankind, whether there be no Benevolence but what flows from a View of Reward from the DEITY? Nay, do we not see a great deal of it among those who entertain few if any Thoughts of Devotion at all? Not to say that this Benevolence scarce deserves the Name, when we desire not, nor delight in the Good of others, further than it serves our own Ends.

But if we have no other Idea of Good, than Advantage to our selves, we must imagine that every rational Being acts only for its own Advantage ; and however we may call a beneficent Being, a good Being, because it acts for our Advantage, yet upon this Scheme we should not be apt to think there is any beneficent Being in Nature, or a Being who acts for the Good of others.   Particularly, if there is no Sense of Excellence in publick Love, and promoting the Happiness of others, whence should this Persuasion arise, 'That the DEITY will make the Virtuous happy?' Can we prove that it is for the Advantage of the DEITY to do so? This I fancy will be look'd upon as very absurd, unless we suppose some beneficent Dispositions essential to the DEITY, which determine him to consult the publick Good of his Creatures, and reward such as cooperate with his kind Intention.   And if there be such Dispositions in the DEITY, where is the impossibility of some small degree of this publick Love in his Creatures? And why must they be suppos'd incapable of acting but from Self-Love?

102   In short, without acknowledging some other Principle of Action in rational Agents than Self-Love, I see no Foundation to expect Beneficence, or Rewards from God, or Man, further

[1] See above *Sect.* i. *Art.* 5. *Par.* 5.

than it is the Interest of the Benefactor; and all Expectation of Benefits from a Being whose Interests are independent on us, must be perfectly ridiculous. What should engage the DEITY to reward Virtue? Virtue is commonly suppos'd, upon this Scheme, to be only a consulting our own Happiness in the most artful way, consistently with the Good of the Whole; and in Vice the same thing is foolishly pursu'd, in a manner which will not so probably succeed, and which is contrary to the Good of the Whole. But how is the DEITY concern'd in this Whole, if every Agent always acts from Self-Love? And what Ground have we, from the Idea of a God it self, to believe the DEITY is good in the Christian Sense, that is, studious of the Good of his Creatures? Perhaps the Misery of his Creatures may give him as much Pleasure, as their Happiness: And who can find fault, or blame such a Being to study their Misery; for what else should we expect? A Manichean Evil God, is a Notion which Men would as readily run into, as that of a Good one, if there is no Excellence in disinterested Love, and no Being acts but for its own Advantage; unless we prov'd that the Happiness of Creatures was advantageous to the DEITY.

103   VIII. The last, and only remaining Objection against what has been said, is this, 'That Virtue perhaps is pursu'd because of the concomitant Pleasure.' To which we may answer, first, by observing, that this plainly supposes a Sense of Virtue antecedent to Ideas of Advantage, upon which this Advantage is founded; and that from the very Frame of our Nature we are determin'd to perceive Pleasure in the practice of Virtue, and to approve it when practis'd by our selves, or others.

104   But further, may we not justly question, whether all Virtue is pleasant? Or, whether we are not determin'd to some amiable Actions in which we find no Pleasure? 'Tis true, all the Passions, and Affections justify themselves; or, we approve our being affected in a certain manner on certain Occasions, and condemn

a Person who is otherwise affected.   So the Sorrowful, the
Angry, the Jealous, the Compassionate, think it reasonable they
should be so upon the several Occasions which move these
Passions; but we should not therefore say that Sorrow, Anger,
Jealousy, or Pity are pleasant, and that we chuse to be in
these Passions because of the concomitant Pleasure.   The
matter is plainly this.   The Frame of our Nature, on such
Occasions as move these Passions, determines us to be thus
affected, and to approve our being so: Nay, we dislike any
Person who is not thus affected upon such occasions, notwithstanding the uneasiness of these Passions.   This uneasiness
determines us to endeavour an Alteration in the state of the
Object ; but not otherwise to remove the painful Affection,
while the occasion is unalter'd : which shews that these
Affections are neither chosen for their concomitant Pleasure,
nor voluntarily brought upon our selves with a view to private
Good.   The Actions which these Passions move us to, tend
generally to remove the uneasy Passion by altering the state of
the Object ; but the Removal of our Pain is seldom directly
intended in the uneasy Benevolent Passions : nor is the
Alteration intended in the State of the Objects by such Passions,
imagin'd to be a private Good to the Agent, as it always is in
the selfish Passions.   If our sole Intention, in Compassion or
Pity, was the Removal of our Pain, we should run away,
shut our Eyes, divert our Thoughts from the miserable Object,
to avoid the Pain of Compassion, which we seldom do : nay,
we croud about such Objects, and voluntarily expose our selves
to Pain, unless Reason, and Reflection upon our Inability to
relieve the Miserable, countermand our Inclination ; or some
selfish Affection, as fear of Danger, overballances it.

Now there are several morally amiable Actions, which flow
from these Passions which are so uneasy ; such as Attempts of
relieving the Distress'd, of defending the Injur'd, of repairing of
Wrongs done by ourselves.   These Actions are often accompany'd with no Pleasure in the mean time, nor have they any

subsequent Pleasure, except as they are successful ; unless it be that which may arise from calm Reflection, when the Passion is over, upon our having been in a Disposition, which to our moral Sense appears lovely and good: but this Pleasure is never intended in the Heat of Action, nor is it any Motive exciting to it.

105   Besides, In the pleasant Passions, we do not love, because it is pleasant to love ; we do not chuse this State, because it is an advantageous, or pleasant State : This Passion necessarily arises from seeing its proper Object, a morally good Character. And if we could love, whenever we see it would be our Interest to love, Love could be brib'd by a third Person ; and we could never love Persons in Distress, for then our Love gives us Pain.   The same Observation may be extended to all the other Affections from which Virtue is suppos'd to flow : And from the whole we may conclude, 'That the virtuous Agent is never apprehended by us as acting only from Views of his own Interest, but as principally influenc'd by some other Motive.'

106   IX. Having remov'd these false Springs of virtuous Actions, let us next establish the true one, *viz.* some Determination of our Nature to study the Good of others ; or some Instinct, antecedent to all Reason from Interest, which influences us to the Love of others; even as the moral Sense above explain'd [1], determines us to approve the Actions which flow from this Love in our selves or others.   This disinterested Affection, may appear strange to Men impress'd with Notions of Self-Love, as the sole Motive of Action, from the Pulpit, the Schools, the Systems, and Conversations regulated by them : but let us consider it in its strongest, and simplest Kinds ; and when we see the Possibility of it in these Instances, we may easily discover its universal Extent.

An honest Farmer will tell you, that he studies the Preservation and Happiness of his Children, and loves them without any design of Good to himself.   But say some of our Philosophers, ' The Happiness of their Children give Parents

[1] See *Sect.* i.

Pleasure, and their Misery gives them Pain ; and therefore to
obtain the former, and avoid the latter, they study, from Self-
Love, the Good of their Children.' Suppose several Merchants
join'd in Partnership of their whole Effects ; one of them is
employ'd abroad in managing the Stock of the Company ; his
Prosperity occasions Gain to all, and his Losses give them Pain
from their Share in the Loss : is this then the same Kind of
Affection with that of Parents to their Children ? Is there the
same tender, personal Regard ? I fancy no Parent will say so.
In this Case of Merchants there is a plain Conjunction of
Interest ; but whence the Conjunction of Interest between the
Parent and Child ? Do the Child's Sensations give Pleasure or
Pain to the Parent ? Is the Parent hungry, thirsty, sick, when
the Child is so ? ' No, but his Love to the Child makes him
affected with his Pleasures or Pains.' This Love then is
antecedent to the Conjunction of Interest, and the Cause of it,
not the Effect : this Love then must be disinterested. ' No, says
another Sophist, Children are Parts of our selves, and in loving
them we but love our selves in them.' A very good Answer !
Let us carry it as far as it will go. How are they Parts of our
selves ? Not as a Leg or an Arm : We are not conscious of
their Sensations. ' But their Bodys were form'd from Parts of
ours.' So is a Fly, or a Maggot which may breed in any
discharg'd Blood or Humour : Very dear Insects surely ! There
must be something else then which makes Children Parts of
our selves and what is this but that Affection which NATURE
determines us to have towards them ? This Love makes them
Parts of our selves, and therefore does not flow from their
being so before. This is indeed a good Metaphor ; and
wherever we find a Determination among several rational
Agents to mutual Love, let each Individual be look'd upon as
a Part of a great Whole, or System, and concern himself in the
publick Good of it.

107   But a later Author observes [1], ' That natural Affection in

---

[1] See the Fable of the Bees, *page* 68. 3rd *Ed.*

Parents is weak, till the Children begin to give Evidences of Knowledge and Affections.' Mothers say they feel it strong from the very first : and yet I could wish for the Destruction of his Hypothesis, that what he alledges was true ; as I fancy it is in some measure, tho we may find in some Parents an Affection towards Idiots. The observing of Understanding and Affections in Children, which make them appear moral Agents, can increase Love toward them without prospect of Interest; for I hope this Increase of Love, is not from Prospect of Advantage from the Knowledge or Affections of Children, for whom Parents are still toiling, and never intend to be refunded their Expences, or recompens'd for their Labour, but in Cases of extreme Necessity. If then the observing a moral Capacity can be the occasion of increasing Love without Self-Interest even from the Frame of our Nature ; pray, may not this be a Foundation of weaker degrees of Love where there is no preceding tie of Parentage, and extend it to all Mankind ?

108　X. And that this is so in fact, will appear by considering some more distant Attachments. If we observe any Neighbours, from whom perhaps we have receiv'd no good Offices, form'd into Friendships, Familys, Partnerships, and with Honesty and Kindness assisting each other ; pray ask any Mortal if he would not be better pleas'd with their Prosperity, when their Interests are no way inconsistent with his own, than with their Misery, and Ruin ; and you shall find a Bond of Benevolence further extended than a Family and Children, altho the Ties are not so strong. Again, suppose a Person, for Trade, had left his native Country, and with all his Kindred had settled his Fortunes abroad, without any view of returning ; and only imagine he had receiv'd no Injurys from his Country : ask such a Man, would it give him no Pleasure to hear of the Prosperity of his Country ? Or could he, now that his Interests are separated from that of his Nation, as gladly hear that it was laid waste by Tyranny or a foreign Power ? I fancy his Answer would show us a Benevolence extended beyond Neighbourhoods or Acquaintances. Let a Man of a compos'd Temper, out of the hurry of private Affairs, only read of the Constitution of a foreign Country, even in the most distant parts of the Earth, and observe Art, Design, and a Study of publick Good in the Laws of this Association ; and he shall find his Mind mov'd in their favour ; he shall be contriving Rectifications and Amendments in their Constitution, and regret any unlucky part of it which may be pernicious to their Interest ; he shall bewail any Disaster which befalls them, and accompany all their Fortunes with the Affections of a Friend.   Now this proves Benevolence to be in some degree extended to all mankind, where there is no interfering Interest, which from Self-Love may obstruct it. And had we any Notions of rational Agents, capable of moral Affections, in the most distant Planets, our good Wishes would still attend them, and we should delight in their Happiness.

109   XI. Here we may transiently remark the Foundation of what we call national Love, or LOVE of one's native Country. Whatever place we have liv'd in for any considerable time, there we have most distinctly remark'd the various Affections of human Nature ; we have known many lovely Characters ; we remember the Associations, Friendships, Familys, natural Affections, and other human Sentiments : our moral Sense determines us to approve these lovely Dispositions where we have most distinctly observ'd them ; and our Benevolence concerns us in the Interests of the Persons possess'd of them. When we come to observe the like as distinctly in another Country, we begin to acquire a national Love toward it also ; nor has our own Country any other preference in our Idea, unless it be by an Association of the pleasant Ideas of our Youth, with the Buildings, Fields, and Woods where we receiv'd them.   This may let us see, how Tyranny, Faction, a Neglect of Justice, a Corruption of Manners, or any thing which occasions the Misery of the Subjects, destroys this national Love, and the dear Idea of a COUNTRY.

We ought here to observe, That the only Reason of that

apparent want of natural Affection among collateral Relations, is, that these natural Inclinations, in many Cases, are over-power'd by Self-Love, where there happens any Opposition of Interests; but where this does not happen, we shall find all Mankind under its Influence, tho with different degrées of Strength, according to the nearer or more remote Relations they stand in to each other; and according as the natural Affection of Benevolence is join'd with and strengthen'd by Esteem, Gratitude, Compassion, or other kind Affections; or on the contrary, weaken'd by Displicence, Anger, or Envy.

Sect. III.

THE SENSE OF VIRTUE, AND THE VARIOUS OPINIONS ABOUT IT, REDUCIBLE TO ONE GENERAL FOUNDATION. THE MANNER OF COMPUTING THE MORALITY OF ACTIONS.

110   I. If we examine all the Actions which are counted amiable any where, and enquire into the Grounds upon which they are approv'd, we shall find, that in the Opinion of the Person who approves them, they always appear as BENEVOLENT, or flowing from Love of others, and a Study of their Happiness, whether the Approver be one of the Persons belov'd, or profited, or not; so that all those kind Affections which incline us to make others happy, and all Actions suppos'd to flow from such Affections, appear morally Good, if while they are benevolent toward some Persons, they be not pernicious to others. Nor shall we find any thing amiable in any Action whatsoever, where there is no Benevolence imagin'd; nor in any Disposition, or Capacity, which is not suppos'd applicable to, and design'd for benevolent Purposes. Nay, as we before observ'd[1], the Actions which in fact are exceedingly useful, shall appear void of moral Beauty, if we know they proceeded from no kind Intentions toward others; and yet an unsuccessful Attempt of Kindness, or of promoting publick Good,

[1] See *Sect.* ii. Art. 3. *Par.* i. (§ 92); *Art.* 6. *Par.* 3. (§ 100).

shall appear as amiable as the most successful, if it flow'd from
as strong Benevolence.

111   II. Hence those Affections which would lead us to do good
to our Benefactor, shall appear amiable, and the contrary
Affections odious, even when our Actions cannot possibly
be of any advantage or hurt to him.   Thus a sincere Love
and Gratitude toward our Benefactor, a chearful Readiness
to do whatever he shall require, how burdensom soever,
a hearty Inclination to comply with his Intentions, and
Contentment with the State he has plac'd us in, are the
strongest Evidences of Benevolence we can shew to such
a Person ; and therefore they must appear exceedingly amiable.
And under these is included all the rational Devotion, or
Religion toward a DEITY apprehended as Good, which we can
possibly perform.

*   *   *   *   *   *   *

112   III. Again, that we may see how Love, or Benevolence, is
the Foundation of all apprehended Excellence in social Virtues,
let us only observe, That amidst the diversity of Sentiments
on this Head among various Sects, this is still allow'd to
be the way of deciding the Controversy about any disputed
Practice, *viz.* to enquire whether this Conduct, or the contrary,
will most effectually promote the publick Good.   The Morality
is immediately adjusted, when the natural Tendency, or
Influence of the Action upon the universal natural Good
of Mankind is agreed upon.   That which produces more
Good than Evil in the Whole, is acknowledg'd Good; and
what does not, is counted Evil.   In this Case, we no other
way regard the good of the Actor, or that of those who are
thus enquiring, than as they make a Part of the great System.

In our late Debates about Passive Obedience, and the Right
of Resistance in Defence of Privileges, the Point disputed
among Men of Sense was, 'whether universal Submission
would probably be attended with greater natural Evils, than
temporary Insurrections, when Privileges are invaded ; and

not, whether what tended in the Whole to the publick natural Good, was also morally Good?' And if a divine Command was alledg'd in favour of the Doctrine of Passive Obedience, this would, no doubt, by its eternal Sanctions cast the ballance of natural Good to its own side, and determine our Election from Interest; and yet our Sense of the moral Good in Passive Obedience, would still be founded upon some Species of Benevolence, such as Gratitude toward the DEITY, and Submission to his Will to whom we are so much oblig'd.   But I fancy those, who believe the DEITY to be Good, would not rashly alledge such a Command, unless they also asserted, that the thing commanded did tend more to the universal Good, than the contrary, either by preventing the external Evils of Civil War, or by enuring Men to Patience, or some other Quality which they apprehended necessary to their everlasting Happiness.   And were it not so, Passive Obedience might be recommended as an inglorious Method of escaping a greater Mischief, but could never have any thing morally amiable in it.

113   But let us quit the Disputes of the Learned, on whom, it may be alledg'd, Custom and Education have a powerful Influence; and consider upon what Grounds, in common Life, Actions are approv'd or condemn'd, vindicated or excus'd. We are universally asham'd to say an Action is Just, because it tends to my Advantage, or to the Advantage of the Actor: And we as seldom condemn a beneficent kind Action, because it is not advantageous to us, or to the Actor.   Blame, and Censure, are founded on a Tendency to publick Evil, or a Principle of private Malice in the Agent, or Neglect at least of the Good of others; on Inhumanity of Temper, or at least such strong Selfishness as makes the Agent careless of the Sufferings of others: and thus we blame and censure when the Action no way affects our selves.   All the moving and persuasive Vindications of Actions, which may, from some partial evil Tendency, appear evil, are taken from this, that they were necessary to some greater Good which counterballanc'd the Evil : 'Severity toward a few, is Compassion toward multitudes.—Transitory Punishments are necessary for avoiding more durable Evils.—Did not some suffer on such Occasions, there would be no living for honest Men.'— and such like. And even when an Action cannot be entirely justify'd, yet how greatly is the Guilt extenuated, if we can alledge ; 'That it was only the Effect of Inadvertence without Malice, or of partial good Nature, Friendship, Compassion, natural Affection, or Love of a Party?' All these Considerations shew what is the universal Foundation of our Sense of moral Good, or Evil, *viz.* Benevolence toward others on one hand, and Malice, or even Indolence, and Unconcernedness about the apparent publick Evil on the other. And let it be here observ'd, that we are so far from imagining all Men to act only from Self-Love, that we universally expect in others a Regard for the Publick ; and do not look upon the want of this, as barely the absence of moral Good, or Virtue, but even as positively evil and hateful.

114   IV. Contrarys may illustrate each other ; let us therefore observe the general Foundation of our Sense of moral Evil more particularly. Disinterested Malice, or Delight in the Misery of others, is the highest pitch of what we count vitious ; and every Action appears evil, which is imagin'd to flow from any degree of this Affection. Perhaps a violent Passion may hurry Men into it for a few Moments, and our rash angry Sentiments of our Enemys, may represent them as having such odious Dispositions ; but it is very probable, from the Reasons offer'd above[1], that there is no such degree of Wickedness in human Nature, as, in cold blood, to be pleas'd with the Misery of others, when it is conceiv'd no way useful to our Interests.

The Story of NERO and PÆTUS may be alledg'd against this, but perhaps unjustly, even allowing the Fact to be true. NERO was conscious he was hated by those whom the World

[1] See *Sect.* ii. *Art.* 4. (§ 95).

call'd good Men, and that they were dangerous to him; he fancy'd his best Security lay in being terrible, and appearing such on all Occasions, by making others miserable when he pleas'd, to let his Enemys see, that they should have no Security from that Compassion which a NERO would imagine argu'd Weakness. This unfortunate Gentleman's Happiness might by some foolish Courtier be so related, as to carry a Reproof of the Tyrant's unnatural Pursuits, whereby his Passion might be excited to cut off the Person admir'd, and prefer'd before him. Any of these Motives of apparent Interest seem more probably to have influenc'd him, than that we should in him, and a few others, suppose a Principle of calm Malice without Interest, of which the rest of Mankind seem entirely incapable.

The Temper of a Tyrant seems probably to be a continu'd state of Anger, Hatred, and Fear. To form our Judgment then of his Motives of Action, and those of Men of like Tempers in lower Stations, let us reflect upon the Apprehensions we form of Mankind, when we are under any of those Passions which to the Tyrant are habitual. When we are under the fresh Impressions of an Injury, we plainly find, that our Minds are wholly fill'd with Apprehensions of the Person who injur'd us, as if he was absolutely Evil, and delighted in doing Mischief: We overlook the Virtues, which, when calm, we could have observ'd in him: we forget that perhaps only Self-Love, and not Malice, was his Motive; or it may be some generous or kind Intention toward others. These, probably, are the Opinions which a Tyrant constantly forms concerning Mankind; and having very much weaken'd all kind Affections in himself, however he may pretend to them, he judges of the Tempers of others by his own. And were Men really such as he apprehends them, his Treatment of them would not be very unreasonable. We shall generally find our Passions arising suitably to the Apprehensions we form of others: if these be rashly form'd upon some sudden slight Views, it is no wonder if we find Dispositions following upon them, very little suited to the real State of human Nature.

115   The ordinary Springs of Vice then among Men, must be a mistaken Self-Love, made so violent as to overcome Benevolence; or Affections arising from false, and rashly form'd Opinions of Mankind, which we run into thro the weakness of our Benevolence. When Men, who had good Opinions of each other, happen to have contrary Interests, they are apt to have their good Opinions of each other abated, by imagining a design'd Opposition from Malice; without this, they can scarcely hate one another. Thus two Candidates for the same Office wish each other dead, because that is an ordinary way by which Men make room for each other; but if there remains any Reflection on each other's Virtue, as there sometimes may in benevolent Tempers, then their Opposition may be without Hatred; and if another better Post, where there is no Competition, were bestow'd on one of them, the other shall rejoice at it.

116   V. The Actions which flow solely from Self-Love, and yet evidence no Want of Benevolence, having no hurtful Effects upon others, seem perfectly indifferent in a moral Sense, and neither raise the Love or Hatred of the Observer. Our Reason can indeed discover certain Bounds, within which we may not only act from Self-Love, consistently with the Good of the Whole, but every Mortal's acting thus within these Bounds for his own Good, is absolutely necessary for the Good of the Whole; and the Want of such Self-Love would be universally pernicious. Hence, he who pursues his own private Good, with an Intention also to concur with that Constitution which tends to the Good of the Whole; and much more he who promotes his own Good, with a direct View of making himself more capable of serving GOD, or doing good to Mankind; acts not only innocently, but also honourably, and virtuously; for in both these Cases, a Motive

of Benevolence concurs with Self-Love to excite him to the
Action. And thus a Neglect of our own Good, may be
morally evil, and argue a Want of Benevolence toward the
Whole. But when Self-Love breaks over the Bounds above-
mention'd, and leads us into Actions detrimental to others,
and to the whole; or makes us insensible of the generous
kind Affections; then it appears vitious, and is disapprov'd.
So also, when upon any small Injurys, or sudden Resentment,
or any weak superstitious Suggestions, our Benevolence becomes
so faint, as to let us entertain odious Conceptions of Men,
or any Part of them, without just Ground, as if they were
wholly Evil, or Malicious, or as if they were a worse Sort of
Beings than they really are; these Conceptions must lead
us into malevolent Affections, or at least weaken our good ones,
and make us really Vitious.

117   VI. Here we must also observe, that every moral Agent
justly considers himself as a Part of this rational System,
which may be useful to the Whole; so that he may be,
in part, an Object of his own Benevolence. Nay further,
as we hinted above, he may see, that the Preservation of the
System requires every one to be innocently sollicitous about
himself. Hence he may conclude, that an Action which
brings greater Evil to the Agent, than Good to others, however
it may evidence strong Benevolence or a virtuous Disposition
in the Agent, yet it must be founded upon a mistaken Opinion
of its Tendency to publick Good, when it has no such
Tendency: so that a Man who reason'd justly, and consider'd
the Whole, would not be led into it, were his Benevolence
ever so strong; nor would he recommend it to the Practice
of others; however he might acknowledge, that the Detriment
arising to the Agent from a kind Action, did evidence a strong
Disposition to Virtue. Nay further, if any Good was propos'd
to the Pursuit of an Agent, and he had a Competitor in every
respect only equal to himself; the highest Benevolence possible
would not lead a wise Man to prefer another to himself,

were there no Ties of Gratitude, or some other external Circumstance to move him to yield to his Competitor. A Man surely of the strongest Benevolence, may just treat himself as he would do a third Person, who was a Competitor of equal Merit with the other; and as his preferring one to another, in such a Case, would argue no Weakness of Benevolence; so, no more would he evidence it by preferring himself to a Man of only equal Abilitys.

118   Wherever a Regard to my self, tends as much to the good of the Whole, as Regard to another; or where the Evil to my self, is equal to the Good obtain'd for another; tho by acting, in such Cases, for the good of another, I really shew a very amiable Disposition; yet by acting in the contrary manner, from Regard to my self, I evidence no evil Disposition, nor any want of the most extensive Benevolence; since the Moment of good to the Whole is, in both Cases, exactly equal. And let it be here observ'd, that this does not supersede the necessity of Liberality, and gratuitous Gifts, altho in such Actions the Giver loses as much as the other receives; since the Moment of Good to any Person, in any given Case, is in a compound Ratio of the Quantity of the Good it self, and the Indigence of the Person. Hence it appears, that a Gift may make a much greater Addition to the happiness of the Receiver, than the Diminution it occasions in the happiness of the Giver: And that the most useful and important Gifts are those from the Wealthy to the Indigent. Gifts from Equals are not useless neither, since they often increase the Happiness of both, as they are strong Evidences of mutual Love: but Gifts from the Poor to the Wealthy are really foolish, unless they be only little Expressions of Gratitude, which are also fruitful of Joy on both Sides: for these Expressions of Gratitude are really delightful and acceptable to the Wealthy, if they have any Humanity; and their Acceptance of them is matter of Joy to the poor Giver.

119   In like manner, when an Action does more Harm to the Agent, than Good to the Publick; the doing it evidences an amiable and truly virtuous Disposition in the Agent, tho 'tis plain he acts upon a mistaken View of his Duty.   But if the private Evil to the Agent be so great, as to make him incapable at another time, of promoting a publick Good of greater moment than what is attain'd by this Action; the Action may really be Evil, so far as it evidences a prior Neglect of a greater attainable publick Good for a smaller one; tho at present this Action also flows from a virtuous Disposition.

120   VII. The moral Beauty, or Deformity of Actions, is not alter'd by the moral Qualitys of the Objects, any further than the Qualitys of the Objects increase or diminish the Benevolence of the Action, or the publick Good intended by it.   Thus Benevolence toward the worst Characters, or the Study of their Good, may be as amiable as any whatsoever; yea often more so than that toward the Good, since it argues such a strong Degree of Benevolence as can surmount the greatest Obstacle, the moral Evil in the Object.   Hence the Love of unjust Enemys, is counted among the highest Virtues.   Yet when our Benevolence to the Evil, encourages them in their bad Intentions, or makes them more capable of Mischief; this diminishes or destroys the Beauty of the Action, or even makes it evil, as it betrays a Neglect of the Good of others more valuable; Beneficence toward whom, would have tended more to the publick Good, than that toward our Favourites: But Benevolence toward evil Characters, which neither encourages them, nor enables them to do Mischief, nor diverts our Benevolence from Persons more useful, has as much moral Beauty as any whatsoever.

121   VIII. In comparing the moral Qualitys of Actions, in order to regulate our Election among various Actions propos'd, or to find which of them has the greatest moral Excellency, we are led by our moral Sense of Virtue to judge thus; that in equal Degrees of Happiness, expected to proceed from the Action, the Virtue is in proportion to the Number of Persons to whom the Happiness shall extend; (and here the Dignity, or moral Importance of Persons, may compensate Numbers) and in equal Numbers, the Virtue is as the Quantity of the Happiness, or natural Good; or that the Virtue is in a compound Ratio of the Quantity of Good, and Number of Enjoyers. In the same manner, the moral Evil, or Vice, is as the Degree of Misery, and Number of Sufferers; so that, that Action is best, which procures the greatest Happiness for the greatest Numbers; and that, worst, which, in like manner, occasions Misery.

122 IX. Again, when the Consequences of Actions are of a mix'd Nature, partly Advantageous, and partly Pernicious; that Action is good, whose good Effects preponderate the evil, by being useful to many, and pernicious to few; and that, evil, which is otherwise. Here also the moral Importance of Characters, or Dignity of Persons may compensate Numbers; as may also the Degrees of Happiness or Misery: for to procure an inconsiderable Good to many, but an immense Evil to few, may be Evil; and an immense Good to few, may preponderate a small Evil to many.

But the Consequences which affect the Morality of Actions, are not only the direct and natural Effects of the Actions themselves; but also all those Events which otherwise would not have happen'd. For many Actions which have no immediate or natural evil Effects, nay, which actually produce good Effects, may be evil; if a man foresees that the evil Consequences, which will probably flow from the Folly of others, upon his doing of such Actions, are so great as to overballance all the Good produc'd by those Actions, or all the Evils which would flow from the Omission of them: And in such Cases the Probability is to be computed on both sides. Thus if an Action of mine will probably, thro the Mistakes or Corruption of others, be made a Precedent in unlike Cases, to very evil Actions; or when my Action, tho good in it self, will probably provoke Men to very evil Actions, upon some mistaken Notion of their Right; any of these Considerations foreseen by me, may make such an Action of mine evil, whenever the Evils which will probably be occasion'd by the Action, are greater than the Evils occasion'd by the Omission.

And this is the Reason that many Laws prohibit Actions in general, even when some particular Instances of those Actions would be very useful; because an universal Allowance of them, considering the Mistakes Men would probably fall into, would be more pernicious than an universal Prohibition; nor could there be any more special Boundarys fix'd between the right and wrong Cases. In such Cases, it is the Duty of Persons to comply with the generally useful Constitution; or if in some very important Instances, the Violation of the Law would be of less evil Consequence than Obedience to it, they must patiently resolve to undergo those Penalties, which the State has, for valuable Ends to the Whole, appointed : and this Disobedience will have nothing criminal in it.

123 X. From the two last Observations, we may see what Actions our moral Sense would most recommend to our Election, as the most perfectly Virtuous : *viz.* such as appear to have the most universal unlimited Tendency to the greatest and most extensive Happiness of all the rational Agents, to whom our Influence can reach. All Benevolence, even toward a Part, is amiable, when not inconsistent with the Good of the Whole : But this is a smaller Degree of Virtue, unless our Beneficence be restrain'd by want of Power, and not want of Love to the Whole. All strict Attachments to Partys, Sects, Factions, have but an imperfect Species of Beauty, unless when the Good of the Whole requires a stricter Attachment to a Part, as in natural Affection, or virtuous Friendships; or when some Parts are so eminently useful to the Whole, that even universal Benevolence would determine us with special Care and Affection to study their Interests. Thus universal Benevolence would incline us to a more strong Concern for the Interests of great and generous Characters in a high Station, or make us more earnestly study the Interests of any generous Society, whose whole Constitution was contriv'd to promote universal Good. Thus a good fancy in Architecture, would lead a Man, who was not able to bear the Expence of a compleatly regular Building, to chuse such a Degree of Ornament as he could keep uniformly thro the Whole, and not move him to make a vain unfinished Attempt in one Part, of what he foresaw he could not succeed in as to the Whole. And the most perfect Rules of Architecture condemn an excessive Profusion of Ornament on one Part, above the Proportion of the Whole, unless that Part be some eminent Place of the Edifice, such as the chief Front, or publick Entrance; the adorning of which, would beautify the Whole more than an equal Expence of Ornament on any other Part.

124 This Increase of the moral Beauty of Actions, or Dispositions, according to the Number of Persons to whom the good Effects of them extend, may shew us the Reason why Actions which flow from the nearer Attachments of Nature, such as that between the Sexes, and the Love of our Offspring, are not so amiable, nor do they appear so virtuous as Actions of equal Moment of Good towards Persons less attach'd to us. The Reason is plainly this. These strong Instincts are by Nature limited to small Numbers of Mankind, such as our Wives or Children; whereas a Disposition, which would produce a like Moment of Good to others, upon no special Attachment, if it was accompany'd with natural Power to accomplish its Intention, would be incredibly more fruitful of great and good Effects to the Whole.

125 From this primary Idea of moral Good in Actions, arises the Idea of Good in those Dispositions, whether natural or acquir'd,

which enable us to do good to others ; or which are presum'd
to be design'd, and acquir'd or cultivated for that purpose.
And hence those Abilitys, while nothing appears contrary to
our Presumption, may increase our Love to the Possessor of
them ; but when they are imagin'd to be intended for publick
Mischief, they make us hate him the more : Such are a pene-
trating Judgment or tenacious Memory, a quick Invention ;
Patience of Labour, Pain, Hunger, Watching ; a Contempt of
Wealth, Rumour, Death. These may be rather call'd natural
Abilitys, than moral Qualitys. Now, a Veneration for these
Qualitys, any further than they are employ'd for the publick
Good, is foolish, and flows from our moral Sense, grounded
upon a false Opinion ; for if we plainly see them maliciously
employ'd, they make the Agent more detestable.

126 XI. To find a universal Canon to compute the Morality of
any Actions, with all their Circumstances, when we judge of
the Actions done by our selves, or by others, we must observe
the following Propositions or Axioms.

1. The moral Importance of any Agent, or the Quantity of
publick Good produc'd by him, is in a compound Ratio of his
Benevolence and Abilitys : or (by substituting the initial Letters
for the Words, as $M = $ Moment of Good, and $u = $ Moment of
Evil) $M = B \times A$.

2. In like manner, the Moment of private Good, or Interest
produc'd by any Person to himself, is in a compound Ratio of
his Self-Love, and Abilitys : or (substituting the initial Letters)
$I = S \times A$.

3. When in comparing the Virtue of two Actions, the Abilitys
of the Agents are equal ; the Moment of publick Good produc'd
by them in like Circumstances, is as the Benevolence : or $M = $
$B \times 1$.

4. When Benevolence in two Agents is equal, and other
Circumstances alike ; the Moment of publick Good is as the
Abilitys : or $M = A \times 1$.

5. The Virtue then of Agents, or their Benevolence, is always

directly as the Moment of Good produc'd in like Circumstances, and inversly as their Abilitys : or $B = \dfrac{M}{A}$.

6. But as the natural Consequences of our Actions are various, some good to our selves, and evil to the Publick ; and others evil to our selves, and good to the Publick ; or either useful both to our selves and others, or pernicious to both ; the entire Motive to good Actions is not always Benevolence alone ; or Motive to Evil, Malice alone ; (nay, this last is seldom any Motive at all) but in most Actions we must look upon Self-Love as another Force, sometimes conspiring with Benevolence, and assisting it, when we are excited by Views of private Interest, as well as publick Good ; and sometimes opposing Benevolence, when the good Action is any way difficult or painful in the Performance, or detrimental in its Consequences to the Agent. In the former Case, $M = \overline{B + S} \times A = BA + SA$; and therefore $BA = M - SA = M - I$, and $B = \dfrac{M - I}{A}$. In the latter Case, $M = \overline{B - S} \times A = BA - SA$; therefore $BA = M + SA = M + I$, and $B = \dfrac{M + I}{A}$.

These selfish Motives shall be [1] hereafter more fully explain'd ; here we may in general denote them by the Word Interest : which when it concurs with Benevolence, in any Action capable of Increase, or Diminution, must produce a greater Quantity of Good, than Benevolence` alone in the same Abilitys ; and therefore when the Moment of Good, in an Action partly intended for the Good of the Agent, is but equal to the Moment of Good in the Action of another Agent, influenc'd only by Benevolence, the former is less virtuous : and in this Case the Interest must be deducted to find the true Effect to the Benevolence, or Virtue. In the same manner, when Interest is opposite to Benevolence, and yet is surmounted by it ; this Interest must be added to the Moment, to increase the Virtue of the Action, or the Strength of the Benevolence : Or thus, in advantageous

[1] Vide *Sect.* v.

Virtue, $B = \frac{M-I}{A}$. And in laborious, painful, dangerous or expensive Virtue, $B = \frac{M+I}{A}$. By Interest, in this last Case, is understood all the Advantage which the Agent might have obtain'd by omitting the Action, which is a negative Motive to it; and this, when subtracted, becomes positive.

But here we must observe, that no Advantage, not intended, altho casually, or naturally redounding to us from the Action, does at all affect its Morality to make it less amiable; nor does any Difficulty or Evil unforeseen, or not resolved upon, make a kind Action more virtuous; since in such Cases Self-Love neither assists nor opposes Benevolence. Nay, Self-Interest then only diminishes the Benevolence, when without this View of Interest the Action would not have been undertaken, or so much Good would not have been produc'd by the Agent; and it extenuates the Vice of an evil Action, only when without this Interest the Action would not have been pleasing to the Agent, or so much Evil have been produc'd by him.

The sixth Axiom only explains the external Marks by which Men must judge, who do not see into each others Hearts; for it may really happen in many Cases, that Men may have Benevolence sufficient to surmount any Difficulty, and yet they may meet with none at all: And in that Case, it is certain there is as much Virtue in the Agent, tho he does not give such Proof of it to his Fellow-Creatures, as if he had surmounted Difficultys in his kind Actions. And this too must be the Case with the DEITY, to whom nothing is difficult.

Since then Benevolence, or Virtue in any Agent, is as $\frac{M}{A}$, or as $\frac{M \pm I}{A}$, and no Being can act above his natural Ability; that must be the Perfection of Virtue where $M = A$, or when the Being acts to the utmost of his Power for the publick Good; and hence the Perfection of Virtue in this Case, or $\frac{M}{A}$, is as

Unity. And this may shew us the only Foundation for the boasting of the Stoicks, 'That a Creature suppos'd Innocent by pursuing Virtue with his utmost Power, may in Virtue equal the Gods.' For in their Case, if [A] or the Ability be Infinite, unless [M] or the Good to be produc'd in the whole, be so too, the Virtue is not absolutely perfect ; and the Quotient can never surmount Unity.

127   XII. The same Axioms may be apply'd to compute the moral Evil in Actions ; that is, calling the Disposition which leads us to Evil, Hatred, tho it is oftner only Self-Love, with Inadvertence to its Consequences : then,

1st. The Moment of Evil produc'd by any Agent, is as the Product of his Hatred into his Ability, or $\mu = H \times A$. And,

2dly. In equal Abilitys, $\mu = H \times I$.

3dly. When Hatred is equal ; $\mu = A \times 1$: And,

4thly. The Degree of moral Evil, or Vice, which is equal to the Hatred or Neglect of publick Good, is thus express'd, $H = \frac{\mu}{A}$.

5thly. The Motives of Interest may co-operate with Hatred, or oppose it the same way as with Benevolence ; and then according as Self-Interest may partly excite to the Action, and so diminish the Evil ; or dissuade from it, and so increase it, the Malice which surmounts it, or $H = \frac{\mu \pm I}{A}$, in like manner as in the Case of moral Good.

But we must observe, that not only Innocence is expected from all Mortals, but they are presum'd from their Nature, in some measure inclin'd to publick Good ; so that a bare Absence of this Desire is enough to make an Agent be reputed Evil : Nor is a direct Intention of publick Evil necessary to make an Action evil, it is enough that it flows from Self-Love, with a plain Neglect of the Good of others, or an Insensibility of their Misery, which we either actually foresee, or have a probable Presumption of.

It is true indeed, that that publick Evil which I neither

ccrtainly foresee, nor have actual Presumptions of, as the Consequence of my Action, does not make my present Action Criminal, or Odious; even altho I might have foreseen this Evil by a serious Examination of my own Actions; because such Actions do not, at present, evidence either Malice, or want of Benevolence. But then it is also certain, that my prior Negligence, in not examining the Tendency of my Actions, is a plain Evidence of the want of that Degree of good Affections which is necessary to a virtuous Character; and consequently the Guilt properly lies in this Neglect, rather than in an Action which really flows from a good Intention. Human Laws however, which cannot examine the Intentions, or secret Knowledge of the Agent, must judge in gross of the Action itself; presupposing all that Knowledge as actually attain'd, which we are oblig'd to attain.

In like manner, no good Effect which I did not actually foresee and intend, makes my Action morally Good; however Human Laws or Governours, who cannot search into Men's Intentions, or know their secret Designs, justly reward Actions which tend to the publick Good, altho the Agent was engag'd to those Actions only by selfish Views; and consequently had no virtuous Disposition influencing him to them.

The difference in degree of Guilt between Crimes of Ignorance when the Ignorance is Vincible, and Faulty, as to the natural Tendency of the Action; and Crimes of Malice, or direct evil Intention, consists in this; that the former, by a prior Neglect, argues a want of the due degree of Benevolence, or right Affections; the latter, evidences direct evil Affections, which are vastly more odious.

128   XIII. From Axiom the 5th, we may form almost a demonstrative Conclusion, 'that we have a Sense of Goodness and moral Beauty in Actions, distinct from Advantage;' for had we no other Foundation of Approbation of Actions, but the Advantage which might arise to us from them, if they were done toward our selves, we should make no Account of the

Abilitys of the Agent, but would barely esteem them according
to their Moment.   The Abilitys come in only to shew the
Degree of Benevolence, which supposes Benevolence necessarily
amiable.   Who was ever the better pleas'd with a barren rocky
Farm, or an inconvenient House, by being told that the poor
Farm gave as great Increase as it could ; or that the House
accommodated its Possessor as well as it could ?   And yet in
our Sentiments of Actions, whose Moment is very inconsiderable, it shall wonderfully increase the Beauty to alledge, 'That
it was all the poor Agent could do for the Publick, or his Friend.'

129   XIV. The moral Beauty of Characters arises from their
Actions, or sincere Intentions of the publick Good, according to
their Power.   We form our Judgment of them according to
what appears to be their fix'd Disposition, and not according
to any particular Sallys of unkind Passions ; altho these abate
the Beauty of good Characters, as the Motions of the kind
Affections diminish the Deformity of the bad ones.   What then
properly constitutes a virtuous Character, is not some few
accidental Motions of Compassion, natural Affection, or
Gratitude ; but such a fix'd Humanity, or Desire of the
publick Good of all, to whom our Influence can extend, as
uniformly excites us to all Acts of Beneficence, according to our
utmost Prudence and Knowledge of the Interests of others :
and a strong Benevolence will not fail to make us careful of
informing our selves right, concerning the truest Methods of
serving the Interests of Mankind.   Every Motion indeed of
the kind Affections appears in some degree amiable ; but we
denominate the Character from the prevailing Principle.

130   XV. I Know not for what Reason some will not allow that to
be Virtue, which flows from Instincts, or Passions ; but how do
they help themselves ?   They say, 'Virtue arises from Reason.'
What is Reason but that Sagacity we have in prosecuting any
End ?   The ultimate End propos'd by the common Moralists
is the Happiness of the Agent himself, and this certainly he is
determin'd to pursue from Instinct.   Now may not another

Instinct toward the Publick, or the Good of others, be as proper a Principle of Virtue, as the Instinct toward private Happiness? And is there not the same Occasion for the Exercise of our Reason in pursuing the former, as the latter? This is certain, that whereas we behold the selfish Actions of others, with Indifference at best, we see something amiable in every Action which flows from kind Affections or Passions toward others; if they be conducted by Prudence, so as any way to attain their End. Our passionate Actions, as we shew'd[1] above, are not always Self-interested; since our Intention is not to free our selves from the Uneasiness of the Passion, but to alter the State of the Object.

131   If it be said, 'That Actions from Instinct, are not the Effect of Prudence and Choice;' this Objection holds full as strongly against the Actions which flow from Self-Love; since the use of our Reason is as requisite, to find the proper Means of promoting publick Good, as private Good. And as it must be an Instinct, or a Determination previous to Reason, which makes us pursue private Good, as well as publick Good, as our End; there is the same occasion for Prudence and Choice, in the Election of proper Means for promoting of either. I see no harm in supposing, 'that Men are naturally dispos'd to Virtue, and not left merely indifferent, to be ingag'd in Actions only as they appear to tend to their own private Good.' Surely, the Supposition of a benevolent universal Instinct, would recommend human Nature, and its AUTHOR, more to the Love of a good Man, and leave room enough for the Exercise of our Reason, in contriving and settling Rights, Laws, Constitutions; in inventing Arts, and practising them so as to gratify, in the most effectual manner, that generous Inclination. And if we must bring in Self-Love to make Virtue Rational, a little Reflection will discover, as shall appear hereafter, that this Benevolence is our greatest Happiness; and thence we may resolve to cultivate, as much as possible, this sweet Disposition,

[1] See *Sect.* ii. *Art.* 8 (§ 104).

and to despise every opposite Interest. Not that we can be truly Virtuous , if we intend only to obtain the Pleasure which accompanies Beneficence, without the Love of others : Nay, this very Pleasure is founded on our being conscious of disinterested Love to others, as the Spring of our Actions. But Self-Interest may be our Motive, in chusing to continue in this agreeable State, tho it cannot be the sole, or principal Motive of any Action, which to our moral Sense appears Virtuous.

132 The applying a mathematical Calculation to moral Subjects, will appear perhaps at first extravagant and wild ; but some Corollarys, which are easily and certainly deduc'd below [1], may shew the Conveniency of this Attempt, if it could be further pursu'd. At present, we shall only draw this one, which seems the most joyful imaginable, even to the lowest rank of Mankind, *viz.* ' That no external Circumstances of Fortune, no involuntary Disadvantages, can exclude any Mortal from the most heroick Virtue.' For how small soever the Moment of publick Good be, which any one can accomplish, yet if his Abilitys are proportionably small, the Quotient, which expresses the Degree of Virtue, may be as great as any whatsoever. Thus, not only the Prince, the Statesman, the General, are capable of true Heroism, tho these are the chief Characters, whose Fame is diffus'd thro various Nations and Ages ; but when we find in an honest Trader, the kind Friend, the faithful prudent Adviser, the charitable and hospitable Neighbour, the tender Husband and affectionate Parent, the sedate yet chearful Companion, the generous Assistant of Merit, the cautious Allayer of Contention and Debate, the Promoter of Love and good Understanding among Acquaintances ; if we consider, that these were all the good Offices which his Station in the World gave him an Opportunity of performing to Mankind, we must judge this Character really as amiable, as those, whose external Splendor dazzles an injudicious World into an Opinion, ' that they are the only Heroes in Virtue.'

[1] See *Sect.* vii. *Art.* 8, 9 (§§ 180, 181).

Sect. IV.

ALL MANKIND AGREE IN THIS GENERAL FOUNDATION OF THEIR
APPROBATION OF MORAL ACTIONS. THE GROUNDS OF THE
DIFFERENT OPINIONS ABOUT MORALS.

133   I. To shew how far Mankind agree in that which we have
made the universal Foundation of this moral Sense, *viz.*
BENEVOLENCE, we have observ'd already[1], that when we are
ask'd the Reason of our Approbation of any Action, we
perpetually alledge its Usefulness to the Publick, and not to the
Actor himself.   If we are vindicating a censur'd Action, and
maintaining it lawful, we always make this one Article of our
Defence, 'That it injur'd no body, or did more Good than
Harm.'   On the other hand, when we blame any piece of
Conduct, we shew it to be prejudicial to others, besides the
Actor ; or to evidence at least a Neglect of their Interest, when
it was in our power to serve them ; or when Gratitude, natural
Affection, or some other disinterested Tye should have rais'd in
us a Study of their Interest.   If we sometimes blame foolish
Conduct in others, without any reflection upon its Tendency
to publick Evil, it is still occasion'd by our Benevolence, which
makes us concern'd for the Evils befalling the Agent, whom we
must always look upon as a part of the System.   We all know
how great an Extenuation of Crimes it is, to alledge, 'That the
poor Man does harm to no body but himself ; ' and how often
this turns Hatred into Pity.   And yet if we examine the
Matter well, we shall find, that the greatest part of the Actions
which are immediately prejudicial to our selves, and are often
look'd upon as innocent toward others, do really tend to the
publick Detriment, by making us incapable of performing the
good Offices we could otherwise have done, and perhaps would
have been inclin'd to do.   This is the Case of Intemperance
and extravagant Luxury.

134   II. And further, we may observe, that no Action of any
other Person was ever approv'd by us, but upon some Appre-

[1] See above *Sect.* iii. *Art.* 3. *Par.* 3 (§ 113).

hension, well or ill grounded, of some really good moral
Quality.   If we observe the Sentiments of Men concerning
Actions, we shall find, that it is always some really amiable and
benevolent Appearance which engages their Approbation.   We
may perhaps commit Mistakes, in judging that Actions tend
to the publick Good, which do not; or be so stupidly inadvertent, that while our Attention is fix'd on some partial good
Effects, we may quite over-look many evil Consequences which
counter-ballance the Good.   Our Reason may be very deficient
in its Office, by giving us partial Representations of the
tendency of Actions; but it is still some apparent Species of
Benevolence which commands our Approbation.   And this
Sense, like our other Senses, tho counter-acted from Motives of
external Advantage, which are stronger than it, ceases not to
operate, but has Strength enough to make us uneasy and
dissatisfy'd with our selves ; even as the Sense of Tasting makes
us loath, and dislike the nauseous Potion which we may force
our selves, from Interest, to swallow.

135   It is therefore to no purpose to alledge here, ' That many
Actions are really done, and approv'd, which tend to the
universal Detriment.'   For the same way, Actions are often
perform'd, and in the mean time approv'd, which tend to the
Hurt of the Actor.   But as we do not from the latter, infer the
Actor to be void of Self-Love, or a Sense of Interest ; no more
should we infer from the former, that such Men are void of a
Sense of Morals, or a desire of publick Good.   The matter is
plainly this.   Men are often mistaken in the Tendency of
Actions either to publick, or private Good : Nay, sometimes
violent Passions, while they last, will make them approve very
bad Actions in a moral Sense, or very pernicious ones to the
Agent, as advantageous : But this proves only, ' That some
times there may be some more violent Motive to Action, than
a Sense of moral Good ; or that Men, by Passion, may become
blind even to their own Interest.'

But to prove that Men are void of a moral Sense, we should

find some Instances of cruel, malicious Actions, done, and approv'd in others, when there is no Motive of Interest, real or apparent, save gratifying that very Desire of Mischief to others : We must find a Country where Murder in cold blood, Tortures, and every thing malicious, without any Advantage, is, if not approv'd, at least look'd upon with indifference, and raises no Adversion toward the Actors in the unconcern'd Spectators : We must find Men with whom the Treacherous, Ungrateful, Cruel, are in the same account with the Generous, Friendly, Faithful, and Humane ; and who approve the latter, no more than the former, in all Cases where they are not affected by the Influence of these Dispositions, or when the natural Good or Evil befals other Persons.   And it may be question'd, whether the Universe,tho large enough, and stor'd with no inconsiderable variety of Characters, will yield us any Instance, not only of a Nation, but even of a Club, or a single Person, who will think all Actions indifferent, but those which regard his own Concerns.

136   III. From what has been said, we may easily account for the vast Diversity of moral Principles, in various Nations, and Ages ; which is indeed a good Argument against innate Ideas, or Principles, but will not evidence Mankind to be void of a moral Sense to perceive Virtue or Vice in Actions, when they occur to their Observation.

The Grounds of this Diversity are principally these :

1st. Different Opinions of Happiness, or natural Good, and of the most effectual Means to advance it.   Thus in one Country, where there prevails a courageous Disposition, where Liberty is counted a great Good, and War an inconsiderable Evil, all Insurrections in Defence of Privileges, will have the Appearance of moral Good to our Sense, because of their appearing benevolent ; and yet the same Sense of moral Good in Benevolence, shall in another Country, where the Spirits of Men are more abject and timorous, where Civil War appears the greatest natural Evil, and Liberty no great Purchase, make the same Actions appear odious.   So in SPARTA, where, thro'

Contempt of Wealth, the Security of Possessions was not much regarded, but the thing chiefly desir'd, as naturally good to the State, was to abound in a hardy shifting Youth ; Theft, if dexterously perform'd, was so little odious, that it receiv'd the Countenance of a Law to give it Impunity.

But in these, and all other Instances of the like nature, the Approbation is founded on Benevolence because of some real, or apparent Tendency to the publick Good.   For we are not to imagine, that this Sense should give us, without Observation, Ideas of complex Actions, or of their natural Tendencys to Good or Evil : It only determines us to approve Benevolence, whenever it appears in any Action, and to hate the contrary. So our Sense of Beauty does not, without Reflection, Instruction, or Observation, give us Ideas of the regular Solids, Temples, Cirques, and Theatres ; but determines us to approve and delight in Uniformity amidst Variety, wherever we observe it.   Let us read the Preambles of any Laws we count unjust, or the Vindications of any disputed Practice by the Moralists, and we shall find no doubt, that Men are often mistaken in computing the Excess of the natural Good, or evil Consequences of certain Actions ; but the Ground on which any Action is approv'd, is still some Tendency to the greater natural Good of others, apprehended by those who approve it.

137   The same Reason may remove also the Objections against the Universality of this Sense, from some Storys of Travellers, concerning strange Crueltys practis'd toward the Aged, or Children, in certain Countrys.   If such Actions be done in sudden angry Passions, they only prove, that other Motives, or Springs of Action, may overpower Benevolence in its strongest Ties ; and if they really be universally allow'd, look'd upon as innocent, and vindicated ; it is certainly under some Appearance of Benevolence ; such as to secure them from Insults of Enemys, to avoid the Infirmitys of Age, which perhaps appear greater Evils than Death, or to free the vigorous and useful Citizens from the Charge of maintaining them, or the Troubles of Attendance upon them.   A love of Pleasure and Ease, may, in the immediate Agents, be stronger in some Instances, than Gratitude toward Parents, or natural Affection to Children. But that such Nations are continu'd, notwithstanding all the Toil in educating their Young, is still a sufficient Proof of natural Affection : For I fancy we are not to imagine any nice Laws in such places, compelling Parents to a proper Education of some certain number of their Offspring.   We know very well that an Appearance of publick Good, was the Ground of Laws, equally barbarous, enacted by LYCURGUS and SOLON, of killing the deform'd, or weak, to prevent a burdensome Croud of useless Citizens.

*   *   *   *   *   *   *

138   Men have Reason given them, to judge of the Tendencys of their Actions, that they may not stupidly follow the first Appearance of publick Good ; but it is still some Appearance of Good which they pursue.   And it is strange, that Reason is universally allow'd to Men, notwithstanding all the stupid, ridiculous Opinions receiv'd in many Places, and yet absurd Practices, founded upon those very Opinions, shall seem an Argument against any moral Sense ; altho the bad Conduct is not owing to any Irregularity in the moral Sense, but to a wrong Judgment or Opinion.   If putting the Aged to death, with all its Consequences, really tends to the publick Good, and to the lesser Misery of the Aged, it is no doubt justifiable ; nay, perhaps the Aged chuse it, in hopes of a future State.   If a deform'd, or weak Race, could never, by Ingenuity and Art, make themselves useful to Mankind, but should grow an absolutely unsupportable Burden, so as to involve a whole State in Misery, it is just to put them to death.   This all allow to be just, in the Case of an over-loaded Boat in a Storm.   And as for killing of their Children, when Parents are sufficiently stock'd, it is perhaps practis'd, and allow'd from Self-love ; but I can scarce think it passes for a good Action any where.   If Wood, or Stone, or Metal

be a DEITY, have Government, and Power, and have been
the Authors of Benefits to us; it is morally amiable to praise
and worship them.   Or if the true DEITY be pleas'd with
Worship before Statues, or any other Symbol of some more
immediate Presence, or Influence;   Image-Worship is virtuous.
If he delights in Sacrifices, Penances, Ceremonys, Cringings;
they are all laudable.   Our Sense of Virtue, generally leads us
exactly enough according to our Opinions; and therefore the
absurd Practices which prevail in the World, are much better
Arguments that Men have no Reason, than that they have no
moral Sense of Beauty in Actions.

139   IV. The next Ground of Diversity in Sentiments, is the
Diversity of Systems, to which Men, from foolish Opinions,
confine their Benevolence.   We insinuated above[1], that it is
regular and beautiful to have stronger Benevolence, toward
the morally good Parts of Mankind, who are useful to the
Whole, than toward the useless or pernicious.   Now if Men
receive a low, or base Opinion of any Body, or Sect of Men;
if they imagine them bent upon the Destruction of the more
valuable Parts, or but useless Burdens of the Earth; Benevolence itself will lead them to neglect the Interests of such, and
to suppress them.   This is the Reason, why, among Nations
who have high Notions of Virtue, every Action toward an
Enemy may pass for just; why ROMANS, and GREEKS, could
approve of making those they call'd Barbarians, Slaves.

A late ingenious Author[2] justly observes, 'That the various
Sects, Partys, Factions, Cabals of Mankind in larger Societys,
are all influenced by a publick Spirit: That some generous
Notions of publick Good, some strong friendly Dispositions,
raise them at first, and excite Men of the same Faction or
Cabal to the most disinterested mutual Succour and Aid:
That all the Contentions of the different Factions, and even
the fiercest Wars against each other, are influenc'd by a sociable

---

[1] See *Sect.* iii. *Art.* 10. *Par.* 1 (§ 123).
[2] Ld. Shaftesbury's Essay on Wit and Humour, *Part.* iii. *Sect.* ii.

publick Spirit in a limited System.' But certain it is, that Men are little oblig'd to those, who often artfully raise and foment this Party Spirit; or cantonize them into several Sects for the Defence of very trifling Causes.

*   *   *   *   *   *   *

140   Were we freely conversant with Robbers, who shew a moral Sense in the equal or proportionable Division of their Prey, and in Faith to each other, we should find they have their own sublime moral Ideas of their Party, as Generous, Courageous, Trusty, nay Honest too; and that those we call Honest and Industrious, are imagin'd by them to be Mean-spirited, Selfish, Churlish, or Luxurious; on whom that Wealth is ill bestow'd which therefore they would apply to better Uses, to maintain gallanter Men, who have a Right to a Living as well as their Neighbours, who are their profess'd Enemys. Nay, if we observe the Discourse of our profess'd Debauchees, our most dissolute Rakes, we shall find their Vices cloth'd, in their Imaginations, with some amiable Dress of Liberty, Generosity, just Resentment against the Contrivers of artful Rules to enslave Men, and rob them of their Pleasures.

141   Perhaps never any Men pursu'd Vice long with Peace of Mind, without some such deluding Imagination of moral Good[1], while they may be still inadvertent to the barbarous and inhuman Consequences of their Actions. The Idea of an ill-natur'd Villain, is too frightful ever to become familiar to any Mortal. Here we shall find, that the basest Actions are dress'd in some tolerable Mask. What others call Avarice, appears to the Agent a prudent Care of a Family, or Friends; Fraud, artful Conduct; Malice and Revenge, a just Sense of Honour and a Vindication of our Right in Possessions, of Fame; Fire and Sword, and Desolation among Enemys, a just thorow Defence of our Country; Persecution, a Zeal for the Truth, and for the eternal Happiness of Men, which Hereticks oppose. In all these Instances, Men generally

[1] See below, *Sect.* vi. *Art.* 2. *Par.* 2 (§ 161).

act from a Sense of Virtue upon false Opinions, and mistaken Benevolence; upon wrong or partial Views of publick Good, and the means to promote it; or upon very narrow Systems form'd by like foolish Opinions. It is not a Delight in the Misery of others, or Malice, which occasions the horrid Crimes which fill our Historys; but generally an injudicious unreasonable Enthusiasm for some kind of limited Virtue.

> Insani sapiens nomen ferat, æquus iniqui,
> Ultra, quam satis est, VIRTUTEM si petat ipsam[1].

142 V. The last Ground of Diversity which occurs, are the false Opinions of the Will or Laws of the DEITY. To obey these we are determin'd from Gratitude, and a Sense of Right imagin'd in the DEITY, to dispose at pleasure the Fortunes of his Creatures. This is so abundantly known to have produc'd Follys, Superstitions, Murders, Devastations of Kingdoms, from a Sense of Virtue and Duty, that it is needless to mention particular Instances. Only we may observe, 'That all those Follys, or Barbaritys, rather confirm than destroy the Opinion of a moral Sense;' since the DEITY is believ'd to have a Right to dispose of his Creatures; and Gratitude to him, if he be conceiv'd good, must move us to Obedience to his Will: if he be not conceiv'd good, Self-Love may overcome our moral Sense of the Action which we undertake to avoid his Fury.

As for the Vices which commonly proceed from Love of Pleasure, or any violent Passion, since generally the Agent is soon sensible of their Evil, and that sometimes amidst the heat of the Action, they only prove, 'That this moral Sense, and Benevolence, may be overcome by the more importunate Sollicitations of other Desires.'

143 VI. Before we leave this Subject, it is necessary to remove one of the strongest Objections against what has been said so often, *viz.* 'That this Sense is natural, and independent on Custom and Education.' The Objection is this, 'That

[1] Hor. *Ep.* 6. *Lib.* i. *v.* 15.

we shall find some Actions always attended with the strongest Abhorrence, even at first View, in some whole Nations, in which there appears nothing contrary to Benevolence; and that the same Actions shall in another Nation be counted innocent, or honourable. Thus Incest, among Christians, is abhorr'd at first appearance as much as Murder; even by those who do not know or reflect upon any necessary tendency of it to the detriment of Mankind. Now we generally allow, that what is from Nature in one Nation, would be so in all. This Abhorrence therefore cannot be from Nature, since in GREECE, the marrying half Sisters was counted honourable; and among the Persian MAGI, the marrying of Mothers. Say they then, may not all our Approbation or Dislike of Actions arise the same way from Custom and Education?'

The Answer to this may be easily found from what is already said. Had we no moral Sense natural to us, we should only look upon Incest as hurtful to our selves, and shun it, and never hate other incestuous Persons, more than we do a broken Merchant; so that still this Abhorrence supposes a Sense of moral Good. And further, it is true, that many who abhor Incest do not know, or reflect upon the natural tendency of some sorts of Incest to the publick Detriment; but wherever it is hated, it is apprehended as offensive to the DEITY, and that it exposes the Persons concern'd to his just Vengeance. Now it is universally acknowledg'd to be the grossest Ingratitude and Baseness, in any Creature, to counteract the Will of the DEITY, to whom it is under such Obligations. This then is plainly a moral evil Quality apprehended in Incest, and reducible to the general Foundation of Malice, or rather Want of Benevolence. Nay further, where this Opinion, 'that Incest is offensive to the DEITY,' prevails, Incest must have another direct Contrariety to Benevolence; since we must apprehend the Incestuous, as exposing an Associate, who should be dear to him by the Ties of Nature, to the lowest State of Misery and Baseness, Infamy and Punishment. But in those Countrys where no such Opinion prevails of the DEITY's abhorring or prohibiting Incest; if no obvious natural Evils attend it, it may be look'd upon as innocent. And further, as Men who have the Sense of Tasting, may, by Company and Education, have Prejudices against Meats they never tasted, as unsavoury; so may Men, who have a moral Sense, acquire an Opinion by implicit Faith, of the moral Evil of Actions, altho they do not themselves discern in them any tendency to natural Evil; imagining that others do: or, by Education, they may have some Ideas associated, which raise an abhorrence without Reason. But without a moral Sense, we could receive no Prejudice against Actions, under any other View than as naturally disadvantageous to our selves.

144   VII. The Universality of this moral Sense, and that it is antecedent to Instruction, may appear from observing the Sentiments of Children, upon hearing the Storys with which they are commonly entertain'd as soon as they understand Language. They always passionately interest themselves on that side where Kindness and Humanity are found; and détest the Cruel, the Covetous, the Selfish, or the Treacherous. How strongly do we see their passions of Joy, Sorrow, Love, and Indignation, mov'd by these moral Representations, even tho there has been no pains taken to give them Ideas of a DEITY, of Laws, of a future State, or of the more intricate Tendency of the universal Good to that of each Individual!

Sect. V.

A FURTHER CONFIRMATION THAT WE HAVE PRACTICAL DIS-
POSITIONS TO VIRTUE IMPLANTED IN OUR NATURE; WITH
A FURTHER EXPLICATION OF OUR INSTINCT TO BENEVOLENCE
IN ITS VARIOUS DEGREES; WITH THE ADDITIONAL MOTIVES
OF INTEREST, VIZ. HONOUR, SHAME AND PITY.

145   I. We have already endeavour'd to prove, 'That there is a universal Determination to Benevolence in Mankind, even toward the most distant parts of the Species:' But we are not

to imagine that this Benevolence is equal, or in the same
degree toward all.   There are some nearer and stronger
Degrees of Benevolence, when the Objects stand in some
nearer relations to our selves, which have obtain'd distinct
Names ; such as natural Affection, and Gratitude ; or when
Benevolence is increas'd by greater Love of Esteem.

One Species of natural Affection, *viz.* that in Parents towards
their Children, has been consider'd already [1]; we shall only
observe further, that there is the same kind of affection among
collateral Relations, tho in a weaker degree; which is universally
observable where no Opposition of Interest produces contrary
Actions, or counterballances the Power of this natural affection.

We may also observe, that as to the Affection of Parents, it
cannot be entirely founded on Merit or Acquaintance ; not only
because it is antecedent to all Acquaintance, which might
occasion the Love of Esteem ; but because it operates where
Acquaintance would produce Hatred, even toward Children
apprehended to be vitious. And this Affection is further
confirm'd to be from NATURE, because it is always observ'd
to descend, and not ascend from Children to Parents mutually.
NATURE, who seems sometimes frugal in her Operations, has
strongly determin'd Parents to the Care of their Children,
because they universally stand in absolute need of Support
from them ; but has left it to Reflection, and a Sense of
Gratitude, to produce Returns of Love in Children, toward
such tender kind Benefactors, who very seldom stand in such
absolute need of Support from their Posterity, as their Children
did from them. Now did Acquaintance, or Merit produce
natural Affection, we surely should find it strongest in Children,
on whom all the Obligations are laid by a thousand good
Offices ; which yet is quite contrary to Observation.   Nay, this
Principle seems not confin'd to Mankind, but extends to other
Animals, where yet we scarcely ever suppose any Ideas of

---

[1] See above, *Sect.* ii. *Art.* 9. *Par.* 2, 3 (§ 122).

Merit ; and is observ'd to continue in them no longer than the Necessitys of their Young require. Nor could it be of any service to the Young that it should, since when they are grown up, they can receive little Benefit from the Love of their Dams. But as it is otherwise with rational Agents, so their Affections are of longer continuance, even during their whole lives.

146 II. But nothing will give us a juster Idea of the wise Order in which human Nature is form'd for universal Love, and mutual good Offices, than considering that strong attraction of Benevolence, which we call Gratitude. Every one knows that Beneficence toward our selves makes a much deeper Impression upon us, and raises Gratitude, or a stronger Love toward the Benefactor, than equal Beneficence toward a third Person [1]. Now because of the vast Numbers of Mankind, their distant Habitations, and the Incapacity of any one to be remarkably useful to vast Multitudes ; that our Benevolence might not be quite distracted with a multiplicity of Objects, whose equal Virtues would equally recommend them to our regard ; or become useless, by being equally extended to Multitudes at vast distances, whose Interests we could not understand, nor be capable of promoting, having no Intercourse of Offices with them ; NATURE has more powerfully determin'd us to admire, and love the moral Qualitys of others which affect our selves, and has given us more powerful Impressions of Good-will toward those who are beneficent to our selves. This we call Gratitude. And thus a Foundation is laid for joyful Associations in all kinds of Business, and virtuous Friendships.

By this Constitution also the Benefactor is more encourag'd in his Beneficence, and better secur'd of an increase of Happiness by grateful Returns [2], than if his Virtue were only to be honour'd by the colder general Sentiments of Persons unconcern'd, who could not know his Necessitys, nor how to be profitable to him ; especially, when they would all be equally

---

[1] See above, *Sect.* ii. *Art.* 6. *Par.* 3 (§ 100).
[2] See above, *Sect.* iii. *Art.* 2. *Par.* 2 (§ 93).

determin'd to love innumerable Multitudes, whose equal Virtues would have the same Pretensions to their Love, were there not an increase of Love, according as the Object is more nearly attach'd to us, or our Friends, by good Offices which affect our selves, or them.

147   This universal Benevolence toward all Men, we may compare to that Principle of Gravitation, which perhaps extends to all Bodys in the Universe; but, like the Love of Benevolence, increases as the Distance is diminish'd, and is strongest when Bodys come to touch each other. Now this increase of Attraction upon nearer Approach, is as necessary to the Frame of the Universe, as that there should be any Attraction at all. For a general Attraction, equal in all Distances, would by the Contrariety of such multitudes of equal Forces, put an end to all Regularity of Motion, and perhaps stop it altogether.

This increase of Love toward the Benevolent, according to their nearer Approaches to our selves by their Benefits, is observable in the high degree of Love, which Heroes and Lawgivers universally obtain in their own Countrys, above what they find abroad, even among those who are not insensible of their Virtues; and in all the strong Ties of Friendship, Acquaintance, Neighbourhood, Partnership; which are exceedingly necessary to the Order and Happiness of human Society.

148   III. From considering that strong Determination in our Nature to Gratitude, and Love toward our Benefactors, which was already shewn to be disinterested[1]; we are easily led to consider another Determination of our Minds, equally natural with the former, which is to delight in the good Opinion and Love of others, even when we expect no other Advantage from them, except what flows from this Constitution, whereby HONOUR is made an immediate Good. This Desire of Honour I would call AMBITION, had not Custom join'd some evil Ideas to that Word, making it denote such a violent desire of Honour, and of Power also, as will make us stop at no base Means

---

[1] See above, *Sect.* ii. *Art.* 6 (§ 98–100).

to obtain them.   On the other hand, we are by NATURE subjected to a grievous Sensation of Misery, from the unfavourable Opinions of others concerning us, even when we dread no other Evil from them.   This we call SHAME; which in the same manner is constituted an immediate Evil, as we said Honour was an immediate Good.

Now were there no moral Sense, or had we no other Idea of Actions but as advantageous or hurtful, I see no reason why we should be delighted with Honour, or subjected to the uneasiness of Shame; or how it could ever happen, that a Man, who is secure from Punishment for any Action, should ever be uneasy at its being known to all the World.   The World may have the worse Opinion of him for it; but what subjects my Ease to the Opinion of the World?   Why, perhaps, we shall not be so much trusted henceforward in Business, and so suffer Loss.   If this be the only reason of Shame, and it has no immediate Evil, or Pain in it, distinct from Fear of Loss; then wherever we expose ourselves to Loss, we should be asham'd and endeavour to conceal the Action : and yet it is quite otherwise.

A Merchant, for instance, lest it should impair his Credit, conceals a Shipwrack, or a very bad Market, which he has sent his Goods to.   But is this the same with the Passion of SHAME?   Has he that Anguish, that Dejection of Mind, and Self-condemnation, which one shall have whose Treachery is detected?   Nay, how will Men sometimes glory in their Losses, when in a Cause imagin'd morally good, tho they really weaken their Credit in the Merchant's Sense; that is, the Opinion of their Wealth, or fitness for Business?   Was any Man ever asham'd of impoverishing himself to serve his Country, or his Friend?

149   IV. The Opinions of our Country are by some made the first Standard of Virtue.   They alledge, 'That by comparing Actions to them, we first distinguish between moral Good, and Evil : And then, say they, AMBITION, or the Love of HONOUR, is our chief Motive.'   But what is Honour?   It is not the being

universally known, no matter how. A covetous Man is not
honour'd by being universally known as covetous; nor a weak,
selfish, or luxurious Man, when he is known to be so: Much
less can a treacherous, cruel, or ungrateful Man, be said to be
honour'd for his being known as such. A Posture-master,
a Fire-eater, or Practiser of Leger-de-main, is not honour'd for
these publick Shews, unless we consider him as a Person
capable of giving the Pleasures of Admiration and Surprize to
Multitudes. Honour then is the Opinion of others concerning
our morally good Actions, or Abilitys presum'd to be apply'd
that way; for Abilitys constantly apply'd to other Purposes,
procure the greatest Infamy. Now, it is certain, that Ambition,
or Love of Honour is really selfish; but then this Determination to love Honour, presupposes a Sense of moral Virtue,
both in the Persons who confer the Honour, and in him
who pursues it.

And let it be observ'd, that if we knew an Agent had no
other Motive of Action than Ambition, we should apprehend
no Virtue even in his most useful Actions, since they flow'd
not from any Love to others, or Desire of their Happiness.
When Honour is thus constituted by NATURE pleasant to us,
it may be an additional Motive to Virtue, as we said above [1],
the Pleasure arising from Reflection on our Benevolence was:
but the Person whom we imagine perfectly virtuous, acts
immediately from the Love of others; however these refin'd
Interests may be joint Motives to him to set about such
a Course of Actions, or to cultivate every kind Inclination,
and to despise every contrary Interest, as giving a smaller
Happiness than Reflection on his own Virtue, and Consciousness of the Esteem of others.

Shame is in the same manner constituted an immediate
Evil, and influences us the same way to abstain from moral
Evil; not that any Action or Omission would appear virtuous,
where the sole Motive was Fear of Shame.

[1] See *Sect.* iii. *Art.* 15. *Par.* 2 (§ 131).

150 V. But to enquire further, how far the Opinions of our Company can raise a Sense of moral Good or Evil. If any Opinion be universal in any Country, Men of little Reflection will probably embrace it. If an Action be believ'd to be advantageous to the Agent, we may be led to believe so too, and then Self-Love may make us undertake it; or may, the same way, make us shun an Action reputed pernicious to the Agent. If an Action pass for advantageous to the Publick, we may believe so too; and what next? If we have no disinterested Benevolence, what shall move us to undertake it? 'Why, we love Honour; and to obtain this Pleasure, we will undertake the Action from Self-Interest.' Now, is Honour only the Opinion of our Country that an Action is advantageous to the Publick? No: we see no Honour paid to the useful Treachery of an Enemy whom we have brib'd to our Side, to casual undesign'd Services, or to the most useful Effects of Compulsion on Cowards; and yet we see Honour paid to unsuccessful Attempts to serve the Publick from sincere Love to it. Honour then presupposes a Sense of something amiable besides Advantage, *viz.* a Sense of Excellence in a publick Spirit; and therefore the first Sense of moral Good must be antecedent to Honour, for Honour is founded upon it. The Company we keep may lead us, without examining, to believe that certain Actions tend to the publick Good; but that our Company honours such Actions, and loves the Agent, must flow from a Sense of some Excellence in this Love of the Publick, and serving its Interests.

151 'We therefore, say they again, pretend to love the Publick, altho we only desire the Pleasure of Honour; and we will applaud all who seem to act in that manner, either that we may reap Advantage from their Actions, or that others may believe we really love the Publick.' But shall any Man ever really love the Publick, or study the Good of others in his heart, if Self-love be the only spring of his Actions? No: that is impossible. Or, shall we ever really love Men who appear to love the Publick, without a moral Sense? No : we could form no Idea of such a Temper ; and as for these Pretenders to publick Love, we should hate them as Hypocrites, and our Rivals in Fame. Now this is all which could be effected by the Opinions of our Country, even supposing they had a moral Sense, provided we had none our selves : They never could make us admire Virtue, or virtuous Characters in others; but could only give us Opinions of Advantage, or Disadvantage in Actions, according as they tended to procure us the Pleasures of Honour, or the Pain of Shame.

But if we suppose that Men have, by NATURE, a moral Sense of Goodness in Actions, and that they are capable of disinterested Love ; all is easy. The Opinions of our Company may make us rashly conclude, that certain Actions tend to the universal Detriment, and are morally Evil, when perhaps they are not so ; and then our Sense may determine us to have an Aversion to them, and their Authors ; or we may, the same way, be led into implicit Prejudices in favour of Actions as good ; and then our desire of Honour may co-operate with Benevolence, to move us to such Actions : but had we no Sense of moral Qualitys in Actions, nor any Conceptions of them, except as advantageous or hurtful, we never could have honour'd or lov'd Agents for publick Love, or had any regard to their Actions, further than they affected our selves in particular. We might have form'd the metaphysical Idea of publick Good, but we had never desir'd it, further than it tended to our own private Interest, without a Principle of Benevolence; nor admir'd and lov'd those who were studious of it, without a moral Sense. So far is Virtue from being (in the Language of a late [1] Author) the Offspring of Flattery, begot upon Pride ; that Pride, in the bad meaning of that Word, is the spurious Brood of Ignorance by our moral Sense, and Flattery only an Engine, which the Cunning may use to turn this moral Sense in others, to the Purposes of Self-love in the Flatterer.

[1] Author of the Fable of the Bees, *pag.* 37. *3rd Ed.*

152   VI. To explain what has been said of the Power of Honour. Suppose a STATE or PRINCE, observing the Money which is drawn out of England by Italian Musicians, should decree Honours, Statues, Titles, for great Musicians : This would certainly excite all who had hopes of Success, to the Study of Musick; and Men of a good Ear would approve of the good Performers as useful Subjects, as well as very entertaining. But would this give all Men a good Ear, or make them delight in Harmony?   Or could it ever make us really love a Musician, who study'd nothing but his own Gain, in the same manner we do a Patriot, or a generous Friend?   I doubt not.   And yet Friendship, without the Assistance of Statues, or Honours, can make Persons appear exceedingly amiable.

Let us take another Instance.   Suppose Statues, and triumphal Arches were decreed, as well as a large Sum of Money, to the Discoverer of the Longitude, or any other useful Invention in Mathematicks: This would raise a universal Desire of such Knowledge from Self-Love; but would Men therefore love a Mathematician as they do a virtuous Man? Would a Mathematician love every Person who had attain'd Perfection in that Knowledge, wherever he observ'd it, altho he knew that it was not accompany'd with any Love to Mankind, or Study of their Good, but with Ill-nature, Pride, Covetousness?   In short, let us honour other Qualitys by external Shew as much as we please, if we do not discern a benevolent Intention in the Application, or presume upon it; we may look upon these Qualitys as useful, enriching, or otherwise advantageous to any one who is possess'd of them ; but they shall never meet with those endearing Sentiments of Esteem and Love, which our Nature determines us to appropriate to Benevolence, or Virtue.

153   Love of Honour, and Aversion to Shame, may often move us to do Actions for which others profess to honour us, even tho we see no Good in them our selves : And Compliance with the Inclinations of others, as it evidences Humanity, may procure some Love to the Agent, from Spectators who see no moral Good in the Action it self.   But without some Sense of Good in the Actions, Men shall never be fond of such Actions in Solitude, nor ever love any one for Perfection in them, or for practising them in Solitude ; and much less shall they be dissatisfy'd with themselves when they act otherwise in Solitude. Now this is the case with us, as to Virtue ; and therefore we must have, by NATURE, a moral Sense of it antecedent to Honour.

This will shew us with what Judgment a late [1] Author compares the Original of our Ideas of Virtue, and Approbation of it, to the manner of regulating the Behaviour of aukard Children by Commendation.   It shall appear afterward [2], that our Approbation of some Gestures, and what we call Decency in Motion, depends upon some moral Ideas in People of advanc'd Years.   But before Children come to observe this Relation, it is only good Nature, an Inclination to please, and Love of Praise, which makes them endeavour to behave as they are desir'd; and not any Perception of Excellence in this Behaviour. Hence they are not sollicitous about Gestures when alone, unless with a View to please when they return to Company ; nor do they ever love or approve others for any Perfection of this kind, but rather envy or hate them ; till they either discern the Connexion between Gestures, and moral Qualitys ; or reflect on the good Nature, which is evidenc'd by such a Compliance with the desire of the Company.

154   VII. The considering Honour in the manner above explain'd, may shew us the reason, why Men are often asham'd for things which are not vitious, and honour'd for what is not virtuous. For, if any Action only appears vitious to any Persons or Company, altho it be not so, they will have a bad Idea of the Agent ; and then he may be asham'd, or suffer Uneasiness in being thought morally Evil.   The same way, those who look upon an Action as morally good, will honour the Agent, and he

---

[1] See the Fable of the Bees, *page* 38. *3rd Ed.*
[2] See *Sect*. vi. *Art*. 4 (§ 163).

may be pleas'd with the Honour, altho he does not himself perceive any moral Good in what has procur'd it.

Again, we shall be asham'd of every Evidence of moral Incapacity, or Want of Ability ; and with good ground, when this Want is occasion'd by our own Negligence. Nay further, if any Circumstance be look'd upon as indecent in any Country, offensive to others, or deform'd ; we shall, out of our Love to the good Opinions of others, be asham'd to be found in such Circumstances, even when we are sensible that this Indecency or Offence is not founded on Nature, but is merely the Effect of Custom. Thus being observ'd in those Functions of Nature which are counted indecent and offensive, will make us uneasy, altho we are sensible that they really do not argue any Vice or Weakness. But on the contrary, since moral Abilitys of any kind, upon the general Presumption of a good Application, procure the Esteem of others, we shall value our selves upon them, or grow proud of them, and be asham'd of any Discovery of our want of such Abilitys. This is the reason that Wealth and Power, the great Engines of Virtue, when presum'd to be intended for benevolent Purposes, either toward our Friends or our Country, procure Honour from others, and are apt to beget Pride in the Possessor ; which, as it is a general Passion which may be either good or evil, according as it is grounded, we may describe to be the Joy which arises from the real or imagin'd Possession of Honour, or Claim to it. The same are the Effects of Knowledge, Sagacity, Strength ; and hence it is that Men are apt to boast of them.

But whenever it appears that Men have only their private Advantage in view, in the application of these Abilitys, or natural Advantages, the Honour ceases, and we study to conceal them, or at least are not fond of displaying them ; and much more when there is any Suspicion of an ill-natur'd Application. Thus some Misers are asham'd of their Wealth, and study to conceal it ; as the malicious or selfish do their Power : Nay, this is very often done where there is no positive evil Intention; because the diminishing their Abilitys, increases the moral Good of any little kind Action, which they can find in their hearts to perform.

In short, we always see Actions which flow from publick Love, accompany'd with generous Boldness and Openness; and not only malicious, but even selfish ones, the matter of Shame and Confusion; and that Men study to conceal them. The Love of private Pleasure is the ordinary occasion of Vice; and when Men have got any lively Notions of Virtue, they generally begin to be asham'd of every thing which betrays Selfishness, even in Instances where it is innocent. We are apt to imagine, that others observing us in such Pursuits, form mean Opinions of us, as too much set on private Pleasure; and hence we shall find such Enjoyments, in most polite Nations, conceal'd from those who do not partake with us. Such are venereal Pleasures between Persons marry'd, and even eating and drinking alone, any nicer sorts of Meats or Drinks; whereas a hospitable Table is rather matter of boasting; and so are all other kind, generous Offices between marry'd Persons, where there is no Suspicion of Self-love in the Agent; but he is imagin'd as acting from Love to his Associate. This, I fancy, first introduc'd Ideas of Modesty in polite Nations, and Custom has strengthen'd them wonderfully; so that we are now asham'd of many things, upon some confus'd implicit Opinions of moral Evil, tho we know not upon what account.

Here too we may see the reason, why we are not asham'd of any of the Methods of Grandeur, or high-Living. There is such a Mixture of moral Ideas, of Benevolence, of Abilitys kindly employ'd; so many Dependants supported, so many Friends entertain'd, assisted, protected; such a Capacity imagin'd for great and amiable Actions, that we are never asham'd, but rather boast of such things: We never affect Obscurity or Concealment, but rather desire that our State and Magnificence should be known. Were it not for this Conjunction of moral Ideas, no Mortal could bear the Drudgery of

State, or abstain from laughing at those who did. Could any Man be pleas'd with a Company of Statues surrounding his Table, so artfully contriv'd as to consume his various Courses, and inspir'd by some Servant, like so many Puppets, to give the usual trifling Returns in praise of their Fare? Or with so many Machines to perform the Cringes and Whispers of a Levee?

The Shame we suffer from the Meanness of Dress, Table, Equipage, is entirely owing to the same reason. This Meanness is often imagin'd to argue Avarice, Meanness of Spirit, want of Capacity, or Conduct in Life, of Industry, or moral Abilitys of one kind or other. To confirm this, let us observe that Men will glory in the Meanness of their Fare, when it was occasion'd by a good Action. How many would be asham'd to be surpriz'd at a Dinner of cold Meat, who will boast of their having fed upon Dogs and Horses at the Siege of Derry? And they will all tell you that they were not, nor are asham'd of it.

This ordinary Connexion in our Imagination, between external Grandeur, Regularity in Dress, Equipage, Retinue, Badges of Honour, and some moral Abilitys greater than ordinary, is perhaps of more consequence in the World than some recluse Philosophers apprehend, who pique themselves upon despising these external Shews. This may possibly be a great, if not the only Cause of what some count miraculous, *viz.* That Civil Governors of no greater Capacity than their Neighbours, by some inexpressible Awe, and Authority, quell the Spirits of the Vulgar, and keep them in subjection by such small Guards, as might easily be conquer'd by those Associations which might be rais'd among the Disaffected, or Factious of any State; who are daring enough among their Equals, and shew a sufficient Contempt of Death for undertaking such an Enterprize.

155   Hence also we may discover the reason, why the gratifying our superior Senses of Beauty and Harmony, or the Enjoyment of the Pleasures of Knowledge, never occasions any Shame or Confusion, tho our Enjoyment were known to all the World.   The Objects which furnish this Pleasure, are of such a nature, as to afford the same Delights to multitudes; nor is there any thing in the Enjoyment of them by one, which excludes any Mortal from a like Enjoyment.   So that altho we pursue these Enjoyments from Self-love, yet, since our Enjoyment cannot be prejudicial to others, no Man is imagin'd any way inhumanly selfish, from the fullest Enjoyment of them which is possible.   The same Regularity or Harmony which delights me, may at the same time delight multitudes; the same Theorem shall be equally fruitful of Pleasure, when it has entertain'd thousands.   Men therefore are not asham'd of such Pursuits, since they never, of themselves, seduce us into any thing malicious, envious, or ill-natur'd; nor does any one apprehend another too selfish, from his pursuing Objects of unexhausted universal Pleasure.

This View of Honour and Shame may also let us see the reason, why most Men are uneasy at being prais'd, when they themselves are present.   Every one is delighted with the Esteem of others, and must enjoy great Pleasure when he hears himself commended; but we are unwilling others should observe our Enjoyment of this Pleasure, which is really selfish; or that they should imagine us fond of it, or influenc'd by hopes of it in our good Actions: and therefore we chuse Secrecy for the Enjoyment of it, as we do with respect to other Pleasures, in which others do not share with us.

156   VIII. Let us next consider another Determination of our Mind, which strongly proves Benevolence to be natural to us, and that is COMPASSION; by which we are dispos'd to study the Interest of others, without any Views of private Advantage. This needs little Illustration.   Every Mortal is made uneasy by any grievous Misery he sees another involv'd in, unless the Person be imagin'd evil, in a moral Sense: Nay, it is almost impossible for us to be unmov'd, even in that Case.   Advantage may make us do a cruel Action, or may overcome Pity; but it scarce ever extinguishes it.   A sudden Passion of Hatred

or Anger may represent a Person as absolutely evil, and so extinguish Pity; but when the Passion is over, it often returns. Another disinterested View may even in cold blood overcome Pity; such as Love to our Country, or Zeal for Religion. Persecution is generally occasion'd by Love of Virtue, and a Desire of the eternal Happiness of Mankind, altho our Folly makes us chuse absurd Means to promote it; and is often accompany'd with Pity enough to make the Persecutor uneasy, in what, for prepollent Reasons, he chuses; unless his Opinion leads him to look upon the Heretick as absolutely and entirely evil.

We may here observe how wonderfully the Constitution of human Nature is adapted to move Compassion. Our Misery or Distress immediately appears in our Countenance, if we do not study to prevent it, and propagates some Pain to all Spectators; who from Observation, universally understand the meaning of those dismal Airs. We mechanically send forth Shrieks and Groans upon any surprizing Apprehension of Evil; so that no regard to Decency can sometimes restrain them. This is the voice of NATURE, understood by all Nations, by which all who are present are rous'd to our Assistance, and sometimes our injurious Enemy is made to relent.

157 We observ'd above [1], that we are not immediately excited by Compassion to desire the Removal of our own Pain: we think it just to be so affected upon the Occasion, and dislike those who are not so. But we are excited directly to desire the Relief of the Miserable; without any imagination that this Relief is a private Good to our selves: And if we see this impossible, we may by Reflection discern it to be vain for us to indulge our Compassion any further; and then Self-love prompts us to retire from the Object which occasions our Pain, and to endeavour to divert our Thoughts. But where there is no such Reflection, People are hurry'd by a natural, kind Instinct, to see Objects of Compassion, and expose themselves

---

[1] See *Sect.* ii. *Art.* 8. *Par.* 2 (§ 104).

to this Pain when they can give no reason for it ; as in the Instance of publick Executions.

This same Principle leads men to Tragedys ; only we are to observe, that another strong reason of this, is the moral Beauty of the Characters and Actions which we love to behold. For I doubt, whether any Audience would be pleas'd to see fictitious Scenes of Misery, if they were kept strangers to the moral Qualitys of the Sufferers, or their Characters and Actions. As in such a case, there would be no Beauty to raise Desire of seeing such Representations, I fancy we would not expose our selves to Pain alone, from Misery which we knew to be fictitious.

It was the same Cause which crouded the Roman Theatres to see Gladiators. There the People had frequent Instances of great Courage, and Contempt of Death, two great moral Abilitys, if not Virtues. Hence CICERO looks upon them as great Instructions in Fortitude. The Antagonist Gladiator bore all the blame of the Cruelty committed, among People of little Reflection ; and the courageous and artful one, really obtain'd a Reputation of Virtue, and Favour among the Spectators, and was vindicated by the Necessity of Self-defence. In the mean time they were inadvertent to this, that their crouding to such Sights, and favouring the Persons who presented them with such Spectacles of Courage, and with Opportunitys of following their natural Instinct to Compassion, was the true occasion of all the real Distress, or Assaults which they were sorry for.

What Sentiments can we imagine a Candidate would have rais'd of himself, had he presented his Countrymen only with Scenes of Misery ; had he drain'd Hospitals and Infirmarys of all their pityable Inhabitants, or had he bound so many Slaves, and without any Resistance, butcher'd them with his own Hands? I should very much question the Success of his Election, (however Compassion might cause his Shews still to be frequented) if his Antagonist chose a Diversion apparently more virtuous, or with a Mixture of Scenes of Virtue.

How independent this Disposition to Compassion is on Custom, Education, or Instruction, will appear from the Prevalence of it in Women and Children, who are less influenc'd by these. That Children delight in some Actions which are cruel and tormenting to Animals which they have in their Power, flows not from Malice, or want of Compassion, but from their Ignorance of those signs of Pain which many Creatures make ; together with a Curiosity to see the various Contortions of their Bodys. For when they are more acquainted with these Creatures, or come by any means to know their Sufferings, their Compassion often becomes too strong for their Reason ; as it generally does in beholding Executions, where as soon as they observe the evidences of Distress, or Pain in the Malefactor, they are apt to condemn this necessary Method of Self-defence in the State.

Sect. VI.

CONCERNING THE IMPORTANCE OF THIS MORAL SENSE TO THE PRESENT HAPPINESS OF MANKIND, AND ITS INFLUENCE ON HUMAN AFFAIRS.

158 It may now probably appear, that notwithstanding the Corruption of Manners so justly complain'd of every where, this moral Sense has a greater Influence on Mankind than is generally imagin'd, altho it is often directed by very partial imperfect Views of publick Good, and often overcome by Self-love. But we shall offer some further Considerations, to prove, 'That it gives us more Pleasure and Pain than all our other Facultys.' And to prevent Repetitions, let us observe, 'That wherever any morally good Quality gives Pleasure from Reflection, or from Honour, the contrary evil one will give proportionable Pain, from Remorse and Shame.' Now we shall consider the moral Pleasures, not only separately, but as they are the most delightful Ingredient in the ordinary Pleasures of Life.

159 All Men seem persuaded of some Excellency in the Possession of good moral Qualitys, which is superior to all other

Enjoyments ; and on the contrary, look upon a State of moral
Evil, as worse and more wretched than any other whatsoever.
We must not form our Judgment in this matter from the
Actions of Men ; for however they may be influenc'd by moral
Sentiments, yet it is certain, that Self-interested Passions
frequently overcome them, and partial Views of the Tendency
of Actions, make us do what is really morally evil, appre-
hending it to be good. But let us examine the Sentiments
which Men universally form of the State of others, when they
are no way immediately concern'd ; for in these Sentiments
human Nature is calm and undisturb'd, and shews its true Face.

Now should we imagine a rational Creature in a sufficiently
happy State, tho his Mind was, without Interruption, wholly
occupy'd with pleasant Sensations of Smell, Taste, Touch, &c.
if at the same time all other Ideas were excluded ? Should we
not think the State low, mean and sordid, if there were no
Society, no Love or Friendship, no Good Offices ? What then
must that State be wherein there are no Pleasures but those of
the external Senses, with such long Intervals as human Nature
at present must have ? Do these short Fits of Pleasure make
the Luxurious happy ? How insipid and joyless are the Reflections on past Pleasure ? And how poor a Recompence is the
Return of the transient Sensation, for the nauseous Satietys,
and Languors in the Intervals ? This Frame of our Nature, so incapable of long Enjoyments of the external Senses, points out
to us, ' That there must be some other more durable Pleasure,
without such tedious Interruptions, and nauseous Reflections.'

Let us even join with the Pleasures of the external Senses,
the Perceptions of Beauty, Order, Harmony. These are no
doubt more noble Pleasures, and seem to inlarge the Mind ;
and yet how cold and joyless are they, if there be no moral
Pleasures of Friendship, Love and Beneficence ? Now if the
bare Absence of moral Good, makes, in our Judgment, the
State of a rational Agent contemptible ; the Presence of
contrary Dispositions is always imagin'd by us to sink him into

a degree of Misery, from which no other Pleasures can relieve him. Would we ever wish to be in the same Condition with a wrathful, malicious, revengeful, or envious Being, tho we were at the same time to enjoy all the Pleasures of the external and internal Senses? The internal Pleasures of Beauty and Harmony, contribute greatly indeed toward soothing the Mind into a forgetfulness of Wrath, Malice or Revenge; and they must do so, before we can have any tolerable Delight or Enjoyment: for while these Affections possess the Mind, there is nothing but Torment and Misery.

What Castle-builder, who forms to himself imaginary Scenes of Life, in which he thinks he should be happy, ever made acknowledg'd Treachery, Cruelty, or Ingratitude, the Steps by which he mounted to his wish'd for Elevation, or Parts of his Character, when he had attain'd it? We always conduct our selves in such Resveries, according to the Dictates of Honour, Faith, Generosity, Courage; and the lowest we can sink, is hoping we may be enrich'd by some innocent Accident.

> O si urnam Argenti FORS quà mihi monstret [1]!——

But Labour, Hunger, Thirst, Poverty, Pain, Danger, have nothing so detestable in them, that our Self-love cannot allow us to be often expos'd to them. On the contrary, the Virtues which these give us occasions of displaying, are so amiable and excellent, that scarce ever is any imaginary Hero in Romance, or Epic, brought to his highest Pitch of Happiness, without going thro them all. Where there is no Virtue, there is nothing worth Desire or Contemplation; the Romance, or Epos must end. Nay, the Difficulty[2], or natural Evil, does so much increase the Virtue of the good Action which it accompanys, that we cannot easily sustain these Works after the Distress is over; and if we continue the Work, it must be by presenting a new Scene of Benevolence in a prosperous Fortune. A Scene of external Prosperity or natural Good,

---

[1] Hor. *Lib.* 2. *Sat.* 6. *v.* 10.
[2] *Sect.* iii. *Art.* 11. *Axiom* 6 (§ 126).

without any thing moral or virtuous, cannot entertain a Person
of the dullest Imagination, had he ever so much interested
himself in the Fortunes of his Hero ; for where Virtue ceases,
there remains nothing worth wishing to our Favourite, or
which we can be delighted to view his Possession of, when we
are most studious of his Happiness.

160   Let us take a particular Instance, to try how much we prefer
the Possession of Virtue to all other Enjoyments, and how
we look upon Vice as worse than any other Misery. Who
could ever read the History of REGULUS, without concerning
himself in the Fortunes of that gallant Man, sorrowing at his
Sufferings, and wishing him a better Fate ? But how a better
Fate ? Should he have comply'd with the Terms of the CAR-
THAGINIANS, and preserv'd himself from the intended Tortures,
tho to the detriment of his Country ? Or should he have
violated his plighted Faith and Promise of returning ? Will any
Man say, that either of these is the better Fate he wishes his
Favourite ? Had he acted thus, that Virtue would have been
gone, which interests every one in his Fortunes.—' Let him
take his Fate like other common Mortals.'—What else do we
wish then, but that the CARTHAGINIANS had relented of their
Cruelty, or that PROVIDENCE, by some unexpected EVENT, had
rescued him out of their hands.

Now may not this teach us, that we are indeed determin'd
to judge Virtue with Peace and Safety, preferable to Virtue
with Distress ; but that at the same time we look upon the
State of the Virtuous, the Publick-spirited, even in the utmost
natural Distress, as preferable to all affluence of other Enjoyments ? For this is what we chuse to have our Favourite Hero
in, notwithstanding all its Pains and natural Evils. We should
never have imagin'd him happier, had he acted otherwise ; or
thought him in a more eligible State, with Liberty and Safety,
at the expence of his Virtue. We secretly judge the Purchase
too dear ; and therefore we never imagine he acted foolishly
in securing his Virtue, his Honour, at the expence of his Ease,

his Pleasure, his Life. Nor can we think these latter Enjoyments worth the keeping, when the former are entirely lost.

161 II. Let us in the same manner examine our Sentiments of the Happiness of others in common Life. WEALTH AND EXTERNAL PLEASURES bear no small bulk in our Imaginations; but does there not always accompany this Opinion of Happiness in Wealth, some suppos'd beneficent Intention of doing good Offices to Persons dear to us, at least to our Familys, or Kinsmen? And in our imagin'd Happiness from external Pleasure, are not some Ideas always included of some moral Enjoyments of Society, some Communication of Pleasure, something of Love, of Friendship, of Esteem, of Gratitude? Who ever pretended to a Taste of these Pleasures without Society? Or if any seem violent in pursuit of them, how base and contemptible do they appear to all Persons, even to those who could have no expectation of Advantage from their having a more generous Notion of Pleasure?

Now were there no moral Sense, no Happiness in Benevolence, and did we act from no other Principle than Self-love; sure there is no Pleasure of the external Senses, which we could not enjoy alone, with less trouble and expence than in Society. But a Mixture of the moral Pleasures is what gives the alluring Relish; 'tis some Appearance of Friendship, of Love, of communicating Pleasure to others, which preserves the Pleasures of the Luxurious from being nauseous and insipid. And this partial Imagination of some good moral Qualitys, some Benevolence, in Actions which have many cruel, inhuman, and destructive Consequences toward others, is what has kept Vice more in countenance than any other Consideration [1].

But to convince us further wherein the Happiness of Wealth, and external Pleasure lies; let us but suppose Malice, Wrath, Revenge; or only Solitude, Absence of Friendship, of Love, of Society, of Esteem, join'd with the Possession of them;

---

[1] See above, *Sect.* iv. *Art.* 4. *Par.* 4, 5 (§ 141).

and all the Happiness vanishes like a Dream.   And yet Love, Friendship, Society, Humanity, tho accompany'd with Poverty and Toil, nay even with smaller degrees of Pain, such as do not wholly occupy the Mind, are not only the Object of Love from others, but even of a sort of Emulation: which plainly shews, 'That Virtue is the chief Happiness in the Judgment of all Mankind.'

162   III. There is a further Consideration which must not be pass'd over, concerning the EXTERNAL BEAUTY of Persons, which all allow to have a great Power over human Minds.   Now it is some apprehended Morality, some natural or imagin'd Indication of concomitant Virtue, which gives it this powerful Charm above all other kinds of Beauty.   Let us consider the Characters of Beauty, which are commonly admir'd in Countenances, and we shall find them to be Sweetness, Mildness, Majesty, Dignity, Vivacity, Humility, Tenderness, Good-nature ; that is, that certain Airs, Proportions, je ne scai quoy's are natural Indications of such Virtues, or of Abilitys or Dispositions toward them.   As we observ'd above [1] of Misery, or Distress appearing in Countenances ; so it is certain, almost all habitual Dispositions of Mind, form the Countenance in such a manner, as to give some Indications of them to the Spectator.   Our violent Passions are obvious at first view in the Countenance ; so that sometimes no Art can conceal them : and smaller degrees of them give some less obvious Turns to the Face, which an accurate Eye will observe.   Now when the natural Air of a Face approaches to that which any Passion would form it unto, we make a conjecture from this concerning the leading Disposition of the Person's Mind.

As to those Fancys which prevail in certain Countrys toward large Lips, little Noses, narrow Eyes ; unless we knew from themselves under what Idea such Features are admir'd, whether as naturally beautiful in Form, or Proportion to the rest of the Face ; or as presum'd Indications of some moral

[1] See *Sect.* v. *Art.* 8. *Par.* 2 (§ 156).

Qualitys ; we may more probably conclude that it is the latter ; since this is so much the Ground of Approbation, or Aversion towards Faces among our selves. And as to those Features which we count naturally disagreeable as to Form, we know the Aversion on this account is so weak, that moral Qualitys shall procure a liking, even to the Face, in Persons who are sensible of the Irregularity, or want of that Regularity which is common in others. With us, certain Features are imagin'd to denote Dulness; as hollow Eyes, large Lips ; a Colour of Hair, Wantonness : and may we not conclude the like Association of Ideas, perhaps in both Cases without Foundation in Nature, to be the Ground of those Approbations which appear unaccountable to us ?

In the same manner, when there is nothing grosly disproportion'd in any Face, what is it we dispraise ? It is Pride, Haughtiness, Sourness, Ill-nature, Discontent, Folly, Levity, Wantonness ; which some Countenances discover in the manner above hinted at ? And these Airs, when brought by Custom upon the most regular Set of Features, have often made them very disagreeable ; as the contrary Airs have given the strongest Charms to Countenances, which were far from Perfection in external Beauty.

One cannot but observe the Judgment of HOMER, in his Character of HELEN. Had he ever so much rais'd our Idea of her external Beauty, it would have been ridiculous to have engag'd his Countrymen in a War for such a HELEN as VIRGIL has drawn her. He therefore still retains something amiable in a moral Sense, amidst all her Weakness, and often suggests to his Reader,

$$\text{—'Ελένης ὁρμήματά τε σοναχάς τε}[1],$$

as the Spring of his Countrymens Indignation and Revenge.

This Consideration may shew us one Reason, among many others, for Mens different Fancys, or Relishes of Beauty. The Mind of Man, however generally dispos'd to esteem Benevo-

[1] See Homer, *Iliad* 2. *v.* 356, 590.

lence and Virtue, yet by more particular Attention to some
kinds of it than others, may gain a stronger Admiration of
some moral Dispositions than others.   Military Men, may
admire Courage more than other Virtues ; Persons of smaller
Courage, may admire Sweetness of Temper ; Men of Thought
and Reflection, who have more extensive Views, will admire
the like Qualitys in others ; Men of keen Passions, expect
equal Returns of all the kind Affections, and are wonderfully
charm'd by Compliance : the Proud, may like those of higher
Spirit, as more suitable to their Dignity ; tho Pride, join'd
with Reflection and good Sense, will recommend to them
Humility in the Person belov'd.   Now as the various Tempers
of Men make various Tempers of others agreeable to them, so
they must differ in their Relishes of Beauty, according as it
denotes the several Qualitys most agreeable to themselves.

This may also shew us, how in virtuous Love there may be
the greatest Beauty, without the least Charm to engage a
Rival.   Love it self gives a Beauty to the Lover, in the Eyes
of the Person belov'd, which no other Mortal is much affected
with.   And this perhaps is the strongest Charm possible, and
that which will have the greatest Power, where there is not
some very great Counter-ballance from worldly Interest, Vice,
or gross Deformity.

163   IV. This same Consideration may be extended to the whole
Air and Motion of any Person.   Every thing we count agreeable, some way denotes Chearfulness, Ease, a Condescension
and Readiness to oblige, a Love of Company, with a Freedom
and Boldness which always accompanys an honest, undesigning
Heart.   On the contrary, what is shocking in Air, or Motion,
is Roughness, Ill-nature, a Disregard to others, or a foolish
Shame-facedness, which evidences a Person to be unexperienc'd
in Society, or Offices of Humanity.

With relation to these Airs, Motions, Gestures, we may
observe, that considering the different Ceremonys, and Modes
of shewing respect, which are practis'd in different Nations, we

may indeed probably conclude that there is no natural Connexion between any of these Gestures, or Motions, and the
Affections of Mind which they are by Custom made to express.
But when Custom has made any of them pass for Expressions
of such Affections, by a constant Association of Ideas, some
shall become agreeable and lovely, and others extremely offensive, altho they were both, in their own Nature, perfectly
indifferent.

164   V. Here we may remark the manner in which NATURE leads
Mankind to the Continuance of their Race, and by its
strongest Power engages them to what occasions the greatest
Toil and Anxiety of Life ; and yet supports them under it
with an inexpressible delight.   We might have been excited
to the Propagation of our Species, by such an uneasy Sensation
as would have effectually determin d us to it, without any great
prospect of Happiness ; as we see Hunger and Thirst determine us to preserve our Bodys, tho few look upon eating and
drinking as any considerable Happiness.   The Sexes might have
been engag'd to Concurrence, as we imagine the Brutes are,
by Desire only, or by a Love of sensual Pleasure.   But how
dull and insipid had Life been, were there no more in
MARRIAGE ? Who would have had Resolution enough to bear
all the Cares of a Family, and Education of Children ? Or who,
from the general Motive of Benevolence alone, would have
chosen to subject himself to natural Affection toward an Offspring, when he could so easily foresee what Troubles it might
occasion ?

This Inclination therefore of the Sexes, is founded on
something stronger, and more efficacious and joyful, than the
Sollicitations of Uneasiness, or the bare desire of sensible
Pleasure.   BEAUTY gives a favourable Presumption of good
moral Dispositions, and Acquaintance confirms this into a real
Love of Esteem, or begets it, where there is little Beauty.
This raises an expectation of the greatest moral Pleasures along
with the sensible, and a thousand tender Sentiments of

Humanity and Generosity ; and makes us impatient for a Society which we imagine big with unspeakable moral Pleasures : where nothing is indifferent, and every trifling Service, being an Evidence of this strong Love of Esteem, is mutually receiv'd with the Rapture and Gratitude of the greatest Benefit, and of the most substantial Obligation. And where Prudence and Good-nature influence both sides, this Society may answer all their Expectations.

165   Nay, let us examine those of looser Conduct with relation to the fair Sex, and we shall find, that Love of sensible Pleasure is not the chief Motive of Debauchery, or false Gallantry. Were it so, the meanest Prostitutes would please as much as any. But we know sufficiently, that Men are fond of Good-nature, Faith, Pleasantry of Temper, Wit, and many other moral Qualitys, even in a Mistress. And this may furnish us with a Reason for what appears pretty unaccountable, *viz.* ' That Chastity it self has a powerful Charm in the Eyes of the Dissolute, even when they are attempting to destroy it.'

This powerful Determination even to a limited Benevolence, and other moral Sentiments, is observ'd to give a strong biass to our Minds toward a universal Goodness, Tenderness, Humanity, Generosity, and Contempt of private Good in our whole Conduct ; besides the obvious Improvement it occasions in our external Deportment, and in our relish of Beauty, Order, and Harmony. As soon as a Heart, before hard and obdurate, is soften'd in this Flame, we shall observe, arising along with it, a Love of Poetry, Musick, the Beauty of Nature in rural Scenes, a Contempt of other selfish Pleasures of the external Senses, a neat Dress, a humane Deportment, a Delight in and Emulation of every thing which is gallant, generous and friendly.

In the same manner we are determin'd to common Friendships and Acquaintances, not by the sullen Apprehensions of our Necessitys, or Prospects of Interest ; but by an incredible variety of little agreeable, engaging Evidences of Love, Good-nature, and other morally amiable Qualitys in those we converse with. And among the rest, none of the least considerable is an Inclination to Chearfulness, a Delight to raise Mirth in others, which procures a secret Approbation and Gratitude toward the Person who puts us in such an agreeable, innocent, good-natur'd, and easy state of Mind, as we are conscious of while we enjoy pleasant Conversation, enliven'd by moderate Laughter.

Sect. VII.

A DEDUCTION OF SOME COMPLEX MORAL IDEAS, VIZ. OF OBLIGA-
TION, AND RIGHT, PERFECT, IMPERFECT, AND EXTERNAL,
ALIENABLE, AND UNALIENABLE, FROM THIS MORAL SENSE.

166 I. To conclude this Subject, we may, from what has been said, see the true Original of moral Ideas, *viz.* This moral Sense of Excellence in every Appearance, or Evidence of Benevolence. It remains to be explain'd, how we acquire more particular Ideas of Virtue and Vice, abstracting from any Law, Human, or Divine.

If any one ask, Can we have any Sense of OBLIGATION, abstracting from the Laws of a Superior? We must answer according to the various Senses of the word Obligation. If by Obligation we understand a Determination, without regard to our own Interest, to approve Actions, and to perform them; which Determination shall also make us displeas'd with our selves, and uneasy upon having acted contrary to it; in this meaning of the word Obligation, there is naturally an Obligation upon all Men to Benevolence; and they are still under its Influence, even when by false, or partial Opinions of the natural Tendency of their Actions, this moral Sense leads them to Evil; unless by long inveterate Habits it be exceedingly weaken'd. For it scarce seems possible wholly to extinguish it. Or, which is to the same purpose, this internal Sense, and Instinct toward Benevolence, will either influence our Actions, or else make us very uneasy and dissatisfy'd; and we shall be conscious that we are in a base unhappy State, even without considering any Law whatsoever, or any external Advantages lost, or Disadvantages impending from its Sanctions. And further, there are still such Indications given us of what is in the whole benevolent, and what not; as may probably discover to us the true Tendency of every Action, and let us see, some time or other, the evil Tendency of what upon a partial View appear'd benevolent : or if we have no Friends so faithful as to admonish us, the Persons injur'd will not fail to upbraid us. So that no Mortal can secure to himself a perpetual Serenity, Satisfaction, and Self-approbation, but by a serious Inquiry into the Tendency of his Actions, and a perpetual Study of universal Good, according to the justest Notions of it.

167   But if by Obligation, we understand a Motive from Self-interest, sufficient to determine all those who duly consider it, and pursue their own Advantage wisely, to a certain Course of Actions; we may have a Sense of such an Obligation, by reflecting on this Determination of our Nature to approve Virtue, to be pleas'd and happy when we reflect upon our having done virtuous Actions, and to be uneasy when we are conscious of having acted otherwise ; and also by considering how much superior we esteem the Happiness of Virtue to any other Enjoyment[1]. We may likewise have a Sense of this sort of Obligation, by considering those Reasons which prove a constant Course of benevolent and social Actions, to be the most probable means of promoting the natural Good of every Individual; as CUMBERLAND and PUFFENDORF have prov'd : And all this without Relation to a Law.

But further, if our moral Sense be suppos'd exceedingly weaken'd, and the selfish Passions grown strong, either thro some general Corruption of Nature, or inveterate Habits ; if our Understanding be weak, and we be often in danger of being hurry'd by our Passions into precipitate and rash Judgments, that malicious Actions shall promote our Advantage more than

[1] See above, *Sect.* vi. *Art.* 1, 2 (§ 158-161).

Beneficence; in such a Case, if it be inquir'd what is necessary to engage Men to beneficent Actions, or induce a steady Sense of an Obligation to act for the publick Good; then, no doubt, 'A Law with Sanctions, given by a superior Being, of sufficient Power to make us happy or miserable, must be necessary to counter-ballance those apparent Motives to Interest, to calm our Passions, and give room for the recovery of our moral Sense, or at least for a just View of our Interest.'

168 II. Now the principal Business of the moral Philosopher is to shew, from solid Reasons, 'That universal Benevolence tends to the Happiness of the Benevolent, either from the Pleasures of Reflection, Honour, natural Tendency to engage the good Offices of Men, upon whose Aid we must depend for our Happiness in this World; or from the Sanctions of divine Laws discover'd to us by the Constitution of the Universe;' that so no apparent Views of Interest may counteract this natural Inclination: but not to attempt proving, 'That Prospects of our own Advantage of any kind, can raise in us real Love to others.' Let the Obstacles from Self-love be only remov'd, and NATURE it self will incline us to Benevolence. Let the Misery of excessive Selfishness, and all its Passions, be but once explain'd, that so Self-love may cease to counteract our natural Propensity to Benevolence, and when this noble Disposition gets loose from these Bonds of Ignorance, and false Views of Interest, it shall be assisted even by Self-love, and grow strong enough to make a noble virtuous Character. Then he is to enquire, by Reflection upon human Affairs, what Course of Action does most effectually promote the universal Good, what universal Rules or Maxims are to be observ'd, and in what Circumstances the Reason of them alters, so as to admit Exceptions; that so our good Inclinations may be directed by Reason, and a just Knowledge of the Interests of Mankind. But Virtue it self, or good Dispositions of Mind, are not directly taught, or produc'd by Instruction; they must be originally implanted in our Nature, by its great AUTHOR;

and afterwards strengthen'd and confirm'd by our own Cultivation.

169   III. We are often told, 'That there is no need of supposing such a Sense of Morality given to Men, since Reflection, and Instruction would recommend the same Actions from Arguments of Self-Interest, and engage us, from the acknowledg'd Principle of Self-love, to the Practice of them, without this unintelligible Determination to Benevolence, or the occult Quality of a moral Sense.'

It is perhaps true, that Reflection and Reason might lead us to approve the same Actions as advantageous. But would not the same Reflection and Reason likewise, generally recommend the same Meats to us which our Taste represents as pleasant? And shall we thence conclude that we have no Sense of Tasting? Or that such a Sense is useless? No: The use is plain in both Cases. Notwithstanding the mighty Reason we boast of above other Animals, its Processes are too slow, too full of doubt and hesitation, to serve us in every Exigency, either for our own Preservation, without the external Senses, or to direct our Actions for the Good of the Whole, without this moral Sense. Nor could we be so strongly determin'd at all times to what is most conducive to either of these Ends, without these expeditious Monitors, and importunate Sollicitors; nor so nobly rewarded, when we act vigorously in pursuit of these Ends, by the calm dull Reflections of Self-Interest, as by those delightful Sensations.

170   This natural Determination to approve and admire, or hate and dislike Actions, is no doubt an occult Quality. But is it any way more mysterious that the Idea of an Action should raise Esteem, or Contempt, than that the motion, or tearing of Flesh should give Pleasure, or Pain; or the Act of Volition should move Flesh and Bones? In the latter Case, we have got the Brain, and elastic Fibres, and animal Spirits, and elastic Fluids, like the Indian's Elephant, and Tortoise, to bear the Burden of the Difficulty: but go one step further, and you find the whole as difficult as at first, and equally a Mystery with this Determination to love and approve, or hate and despise Actions and Agents, without any Views of Interest, as they appear benevolent, or the contrary.

171   When they offer it as a Presumption that there can be no such Sense, antecedent to all Prospect of Interest, 'That these Actions for the most part are really advantageous, one way or other, to the Actor, the Approver, or Mankind in general, by whose Happiness our own State may be some way made better;' may we not ask, supposing the DEITY intended to impress such a Sense of something amiable in Actions, (which is no impossible Supposition) what sort of Actions would a good GOD determine us to approve? Must we deny the possibility of such a Determination, if it did not lead us to admire Actions of no Advantage to Mankind, or to love Agents for their being eminent Triflers? If then the Actions which a wife and good GOD must determine us to approve, if he give us any such Sense at all, must be Actions useful to the Publick, this Advantage can never be a Reason against the Sense it self. After the same manner, we should deny all Revelation which taught us good Sense, Humanity, Justice, and a rational Worship, because Reason and Interest confirm and recommend such Principles, and Services; and should greedily embrace every Contradiction, Foppery, and Pageantry, as a truly divine Institution, without any thing humane, or useful to Mankind.

172   IV. The Writers upon opposite Schemes, who deduce all Ideas of Good and Evil from the private Advantage of the Actor, or from Relation to a Law and its Sanctions, either known from Reason, or Revelation, are perpetually recurring to this moral Sense which they deny; not only in calling the Laws of the DEITY just and good, and alledging Justice and Right in the DEITY to govern us; but by using a set of Words which import something different from what they will allow to be their only meaning. Obligation, with them, is only such a Constitution, either of Nature, or some governing Power, as

makes it advantageous for the Agent to act in a certain manner. Let this Definition be substituted, wherever we meet with the words, ought, should, must, in a moral Sense, and many of their Sentences would seem very strange; as that the DEITY must act rationally, must not, or ought not to punish the Innocent, must make the state of the Virtuous better than that of the Wicked, must observe Promises; substituting the Definition of the Words, must, ought, should, would make these Sentences either ridiculous, or very disputable.

173 V. But that our first Ideas of moral Good depend not on Laws, may plainly appear from our constant Inquirys into the Justice of Laws themselves; and that not only of human Laws, but of the divine. What else can be the meaning of that universal Opinion, 'That the Laws of GOD are just, and holy, and good?' Human Laws may be call'd good, because of their Conformity to the Divine. But to call the Laws of the supreme DEITY good, or holy, or just, if all Goodness, Holiness, and Justice be constituted by Laws, or the Will of a Superior any way reveal'd, must be an insignificant Tautology, amounting to no more than this, 'That GOD wills what he wills.'

It must then first be suppos'd, that there is something in Actions which is apprehended absolutely good; and this is Benevolence, or a Tendency to the publick natural Happiness of rational Agents; and that our moral Sense perceives this Excellence: and then we call the Laws of the DEITY good, when we imagine that they are contriv'd to promote the publick Good in the most effectual and impartial manner. And the DEITY is call'd good, in a moral Sense, when we apprehend that his whole Providence tends to the universal Happiness of his Creatures; whence we conclude his Benevolence, and Delight in their Happiness.

Some tell us, 'That the Goodness of the divine Laws, consists in their Conformity to some essential Rectitude of his Nature.' But they must excuse us from assenting to this, till they make us understand the meaning of this Metaphor, essential Rectitude, and till we discern whether any thing more is meant by it than a perfectly wise, uniform, impartial Benevolence.

174 Hence we may see the Difference between Constraint, and Obligation. There is indeed no difference between Constraint, and the second Sense of the word Obligation, *viz.* a Constitution which makes an Action eligible from Self-Interest, if we only mean external Interest, distinct from the delightful Consciousness which arises from the moral Sense. The Reader need scarcely be told, that by Constraint, we do not understand an external Force moving our Limbs without our Consent, for in that Case we are not Agents at all; but that Constraint which arises from the threatning and presenting some Evil, in order to make us act in a certain manner. And yet there seems a universally acknowledg'd Difference between even this sort of Constraint, and Obligation. We never say we are oblig'd to do an Action which we count base, but we may be constrain'd to it; we never say that the divine Laws, by their Sanctions, constrain us, but oblige us; nor do we call Obedience to the DEITY Constraint, unless by a Metaphor, tho many own they are influenc'd by fear of Punishments. And yet supposing an almighty evil Being should require, under grievous Penaltys, Treachery, Cruelty, Ingratitude, we would call this Constraint. The difference is plainly this. When any Sanctions co-operate with our moral Sense, in exciting us to Actions which we count morally good, we say we are oblig'd; but when Sanctions of Rewards or Punishments oppose our moral Sense, then we say we are brib'd or constrain'd. In the former Case we call the Lawgiver good, as designing the publick Happiness; in the latter we call him evil, or unjust, for the suppos'd contrary Intention. But were all our Ideas of moral Good or Evil, deriv'd solely from Opinions of private Advantage or Loss in Actions, I see no possible difference which could be made in the meaning of these words.

175 VI. From this Sense too we derive our Ideas of RIGHTS. Whenever it appears to us, that a Faculty of doing, demanding, or possessing any thing, universally allow'd in certain Circumstances, would in the whole tend to the general Good, we say that any Person in such Circumstances, has a Right to do, possess, or demand that Thing. And according as this Tendency to the publick Good is greater or less, the Right is greater or less.

The Rights call'd perfect, are of such necessity to the publick Good, that the universal Violation of them would make human Life intolerable; and it actually makes those miserable, whose Rights are thus violated. On the contrary, to fulfil these Rights in every Instance, tends to the publick Good, either directly, or by promoting the innocent Advantage of a Part. Hence it plainly follows, 'That to allow a violent Defence, or Prosecution of such Rights, before Civil Government be constituted, cannot in any particular Case be more detrimental to the Publick, than the Violation of them with Impunity.' And as to the general Consequences, the universal Use of Force in a State of Nature, in pursuance of perfect Rights, seems exceedingly advantageous to the Whole, by making every one dread any Attempts against the perfect Rights of others.

This is the moral Effect which attends proper Injury, or a Violation of the perfect Rights of others, *viz.* A Right to War, and all Violence which is necessary to oblige the Injurious to repair the Damage, and give Security against such Offences for the future. This is the sole Foundation of the Rights of punishing Criminals, and of violent Prosecutions of our Rights, in a State of Nature. And these Rights, belonging originally to the Persons injur'd, or their voluntary, or invited Assistants, according to the Judgment of indifferent Arbitrators, in a State of Nature, being by the Consent of the Persons injur'd, transferr'd to the Magistrate in a Civil State, are the true Foundation of his Right of Punishment.

Instances of perfect Rights are those to our Lives; to the Fruits of our Labours; to demand Performance of Contracts upon valuable Considerations, from Men capable of performing them; to direct our own Actions either for publick, or innocent private Good, before we have submitted them to the Direction of others in any measure; and many others of like nature.

176 Imperfect Rights are such as, when universally violated, would not necessarily make Men miserable. These Rights tend to the improvement and increase of positive Good in any Society, but are not absolutely necessary to prevent universal Misery. The Violation of them, only disappoints Men of the Happiness expected from the Humanity or Gratitude of others; but does not deprive Men of any Good which they had before. From this Description it appears, 'That a violent Prosecution of such Rights, would generally occasion greater Evil than the Violation of them.' Besides, the allowing of Force in such Cases, would deprive Men of the greatest Pleasure in Actions of Kindness, Humanity, Gratitude; which would cease to appear amiable, when Men could be constrain'd to perform them. Instances of imperfect Rights are those which the Poor have to the Charity of the Wealthy; which all Men have to Offices of no trouble or expence to the Performer; which Benefactors have to returns of Gratitude, and such like.

The Violation of imperfect Rights, only argues a Man to have such weak Benevolence, as not to study advancing the positive Good of others, when in the least opposite to his own: but the Violation of perfect Rights, argues the injurious Person to be positively evil or cruel; or at least so immoderately selfish, as to be indifferent about the positive Misery and Ruin of others, when he imagines he can find his Interest in it. In violating the former, we shew a weak Desire of publick Happiness, which every small view of private Interest over-ballances; but in violating the latter, we shew our selves so entirely negligent of the Misery of others, that Views of increasing our own Good, overcome all our Compassion toward their Sufferings. Now as the absence of Good, is more easily born than the presence of Misery; so our good Wishes toward the positive Good of others, are weaker than our Compassion toward their Misery. He then who violates imperfect Rights, shews that his Self-love overcomes only the Desire of positive Good to others; but he who violates perfect Rights, betrays such a selfish Desire of advancing his own positive Good, as overcomes all Compassion toward the Misery of others.

177   Beside these two sorts of Rights, there is a third call'd External; as when the doing, possessing, or demanding of any thing is really detrimental to the Publick in any particular Instance, as being contrary to the imperfect Right of another; but yet the universally denying Men this Faculty of doing, possessing, or demanding that Thing, or of using Force in pursuance of it, would do more mischief than all the Evils to be fear'd from the Use of this Faculty. And hence it appears, 'That there can be no Right to use Force in opposition even to external Rights, since it tends to the universal Good to allow Force in pursuance of them.'

CIVIL Societys substitute Actions in Law, instead of the Force allow'd in the State of Nature.

Instances of external Rights are these; that of a wealthy Miser to recal his Loan from the most industrious poor Tradesman at any time; that of demanding the Performance of a Covenant too burdensom on one side; the Right of a wealthy Heir to refuse Payment of any Debts which were contracted by him under Age, without Fraud in the Lender; the Right of taking advantage of a positive Law, contrary to what was Equity antecedent to that Law; as when a register'd Deed takes place of one not register'd, altho prior to it, and known to be so before the second Contract.

178   Now whereas no Action, Demand, or Possession, can at

once be either necessary to the publick Good, or conducive to it, and at the same time its contrary be either necessary or conducive to the same end; it follows, 'That there can be no Opposition of perfect Rights among themselves, of imperfect among themselves, or between perfect and imperfect Rights.' But it may often tend to the publick Good, to allow a Right of doing, possessing, or demanding, and of using Force in pursuance of it, while perhaps it would have been more humane and kind in any Person to have acted otherwise, and not have claim'd his Right. But yet a violent Opposition to these Rights, would have been vastly more pernicious than all the Inhumanity in the use of them. And therefore, tho external Rights cannot be opposite among themselves; yet they may be opposite to imperfect Rights; but imperfect Rights, tho violated, give no Right to Force. Hence it appears, 'That there can never be a Right to Force on both Sides, or a just War on both Sides at the same time.'

179 VII. There is another important Difference of Rights, according as they are Alienable, or Unalienable. To determine what Rights are alienable, and what not, we must take these two Marks:

1st. If the Alienation be within our natural Power, so that it be possible for us in Fact to transfer our Right; and if it be so, then,

2dly. It must appear, that to transfer such Rights may serve some valuable Purpose.

By the first Mark it appears, 'That the Right of private Judgment, or of our inward Sentiments, is unalienable;' since we cannot command ourselves to think what either we our selves, or any other Person pleases. So are also our internal Affections, which necessarily arise according to our Opinions of their Objects. By the second Mark it appears, 'That our Right of serving GOD, in the manner which we think acceptable, is not alienable;' because it can never serve any valuable purpose, to make Men worship him in a way which seems to them displeasing to him. The same way, a direct Right over our Lives or Limbs, is not alienable to any Person ; so that he might at Pleasure put us to death, or maim us. We have indeed a Right to hazard our Lives in any good Action which is of importance to the Publick ; and it may often serve a most valuable end, to subject the direction of such perilous Actions to the Prudence of others in pursuing a publick Good; as Soldiers do to their General, or to a Council of War : and so far this Right is alienable. These may serve as Instances to shew the Use of the two Marks of alienable Rights, which must both concur to make them so, and will explain the manner of applying them in other Cases.

180   VIII. That we may see the Foundation of some of the more important Rights of Mankind, let us observe, that probably nine Tenths, at least, of the things which are useful to Mankind, are owing to their Labour and Industry ; and consequently, when once Men become so numerous, that the natural Product of the Earth is not sufficient for their Support, or Ease, or innocent Pleasure ; a necessity arises, for the support of the increasing System, that such a Tenour of Conduct be observ'd, as shall most effectually promote Industry ; and that Men abstain from all Actions which would have the contrary effect. It is well known, that general Benevolence alone, is not a Motive strong enough to Industry, to bear Labour and Toil, and many other Difficultys which we are averse to from Self-love. For the strengthning therefore our Motives to Industry, we have the strongest Attractions of Blood, of Friendship, of Gratitude, and the additional Motives of Honour, and even of external Interest. Self-love is really as necessary to the Good of the Whole, as Benevolence ; as that Attraction which causes the Cohesion of the Parts, is as necessary to the regular State of the Whole, as Gravitation. Without these additional Motives, Self-love would generally oppose the Motions of Benevolence, and concur with Malice, or influence us to the same Actions which Malice would. 'That Tenour of Action then, which would take away the stronger Ties of Benevolence, or the additional Motives of Honour and Advantage, from our Minds, and so hinder us from pursuing industriously that Course which really increases the Good of the Whole, is evil; and we are oblig'd to shun it.'

First then, the depriving any Person of the Fruits of his own innocent Labour, takes away all Motives to Industry from Self-love, or the nearer Ties; and leaves us no other Motive than general Benevolence: nay, it exposes the Industrious as a constant Prey to the Slothful, and sets Self-love against Industry. This is the Ground of our Right of Dominion and Property in the Fruits of our Labours; without which Right, we could scarce hope for any Industry, or any thing beyond the Product of uncultivated Nature. Industry will be confin'd to our present Necessitys, and cease when they are provided for; at least it will only continue from the weak Motive of general Benevolence, if we are not allow'd to store up beyond present Necessity, and to dispose of what is above our Necessitys, either in Barter for other kinds of Necessarys, or for the Service of our Friends or Familys. And hence appears the Right which Men have to lay up for the future, the Goods which will not be spoil'd by it; of alienating them in Trade; of Donation to Friends, Children, Relations: otherwise we deprive Industry of all the Motives of Self-love, Friendship, Gratitude, and natural Affection. The same Foundation there is for the Right of Disposition by Testament. The Presumption of this Disposition, is the Ground of the Right of Succession to the Intestate.

The external Right of the Miser to his useless Hoards, is founded also on this, that allowing Persons by Violence, or without Consent of the Acquirer, to take the Use of his Acquisitions, would discourage Industry, and take away all the Pleasures of Generosity, Honour, Charity, which cease when Men can be forc'd to these Actions. Besides, there is no determining in many Cases, who is a Miser, and who is not.

Marriage must be so constituted as to ascertain the Offspring ; otherwise we take away from the Males one of the strongest Motives to publick Good, *viz.* natural Affection ; and discourage Industry, as has been shewn above.

The Labour of each Man cannot furnish him with all Necessarys, tho it may furnish him with a needless Plenty of one sort : Hence the Right of Commerce, and alienating our Goods ; and also the Rights from Contracts and Promises, either to the Goods acquir'd by others, or to their Labours.

The great Advantages which accrue to Mankind from unprejudic'd Arbitrators, impower'd to decide the Controversys which ordinarily arise, thro the partiality of Self-love, among Neighbours ; as also from prudent Directors, who should not only instruct the Multitude in the best Methods of promoting the publick Good, and of defending themselves against mutual or foreign Injurys ; but also be arm'd with Force sufficient to make their Decrees or Orders effectual at home, and the Society formidable abroad : these Advantages, I say, sufficiently shew the Right Men have to constitute Civil Government, and to subject their alienable Rights to the Disposal of their Governours, under such Limitations as their Prudence suggests. And as far as the People have subjected their Rights, so far their Governours have an external Right at least, to dispose of them, as their Prudence shall direct, for attaining the Ends of their Institution ; and no further.

181   IX. These Instances may shew how our moral Sense, by a little Reflection upon the tendencys of Actions, may adjust the Rights of Mankind.   Let us now apply the general Canon laid down above [1], for comparing the Degrees of Virtue and Vice in Actions, in a few Corollarys besides that one already deduc'd [2].

1. The Disappointment, in whole or in part, of any Attempt, Good or Evil, if it be occasion'd only by external Force, or

---

[1] See *Sect.* iii. *Art.* 11, 12. (§§ 126, 127).
[2] See *Sect.* iii. *Art.* 15. *Par.* 3. (§132).

any unforeseen Accident, does not vary the moral Good, or Evil; for as in good Attempts, the Moment of Good, or [M] is diminish'd, or vanishes in such a case, so does the Ability, or [A] likewise : The Quotient then may still be the same. This holds equally in evil Attempts. So that Actions are not to be judg'd good or evil by the Events, and further than they might have been foreseen by the Agent in evil Attempts; or were actually intended, if they were good, in good Actions; for then only they argue either Love or Hatred in the Agent.

2. Secular Rewards annex'd to Virtue, and actually influencing the Agent further than his Benevolence would, diminish the moral Good as far as they were necessary to move the Agent to the Action, or to make him do more Good than otherwise he would have done ; for by increasing the Interest, or [I] positive, to be subtracted, they diminish the Benevolence. But additional Interests which were not necessary to have mov'd the Agent, such as the Rewards of a good Being for Actions which he would have undertaken without a Reward, do not diminish the Virtue. In this however no Mortal is capable of judging another. Nor do the Prospects of grateful Returns for Benefits which we would have conferr'd gratuitously, diminish the Generosity. This Corollary may be apply'd to the Rewards of a future State, if any Person conceives them distinct from the Pleasures of Virtue itself : If they be not conceiv'd as something distinct from those Pleasures, then the very Desire of them is a strong Evidence of a virtuous Disposition.

3. External Advantage exciting us to Actions of evil Tendency to others, if without this Prospect of Advantage we would not have undertaken them, diminishes the Evil of the Action ; such as the Prospects of great Rewards, of avoiding Tortures, or even the uneasy Sollicitations of violent selfish Passions. This is commonly call'd the greatness of Temptation. The reason of this is the same with that in the former

Case, since $H = \dfrac{\mu - I}{A}$. We may here also remember again, that we are more uneasy upon the presence of Pain, than upon the absence of Good ; and hence Torture is a more extenuating Circumstance than Bribes, engaging us to Evil, because [I] is greater.

4. The surmounting the uneasy Sollicitations of the selfish Passions, increases the Virtue of a benevolent Action, and much more worldly Losses, Toil, &c. for now the Interest becomes negative ; the Subtraction of which increases the Quantity.

5. A malicious Action is made the more odious by all its foreseen Disadvantages to the Agent, for the same reason : particularly,

6. The Knowledge of a Law prohibiting an evil Action, increases the Evil by increasing the negative Interest to be subtracted ; for then the ill-natur'd Inclination must be so strong as to surmount all the Motives of Self-love, to avoid the Penaltys, and all the Motives of Gratitude toward the Law-giver. This is commonly call'd sinning against Conscience.

7. Offices of no Toil or Expence, have little Virtue generally, because the Ability is very great, and there is no contrary Interest surmounted.

8. But the refusing of them may be very vitious, as it argues an absence of good Affection, and often produces a great enough Moment of natural Evil. And,

9. In general, the fulfilling the perfect Rights of others has little Virtue in it ; for thereby no Moment of Good is produc'd more than there was before ; and the Interest engaging to the Action is very great, even the avoiding all the Evils of War in a State of Nature.

10. But the violating perfect, or even external Rights, is always exceedingly evil, either in the immediate, or more remote Consequences of the Action ; and the selfish Motives

surmounted by this vitious Inclination, are the same with those in the former Case.

11. The truest Matter of Praise are those Actions or Offices which others claim from us by an imperfect Right; and generally, the stronger their Right is, there is the less Virtue in fulfilling it, but the greater Vice in violating it.

LEMMA. The stronger Ties of Benevolence, in equal Abilitys, must produce a greater Moment of Good, in equally good Characters, than the weaker Ties. Thus, natural Affections, Gratitude, Friendship, have greater Effects than general Benevolence. Hence,

12. In equal Moments of Good produc'd by two Agents, when one acts from general Benevolence, and the other from a nearer Tie; there is greater Virtue in the Agent, who produces equal Good from the weaker Attachment, and less Virtue, where there is the stronger Attachment, which yet produces no more.

13. But the Omission of the good Offices of the stronger Ties, or Actions contrary to them, have greater Vice in them, than the like Omissions or Actions contrary to the weaker Ties; since our Selfishness or Malice must appear the greater, by the strength of the contrary Attachment which it surmounts. Thus, in co-operating with Gratitude, natural Affection, or Friendship, we evidence less Virtue in any given Moment of Good produc'd, than in equally important Actions of general Benevolence: But Ingratitude to a Benefactor, Negligence of the Interests of a Friend, or Relation; or Returns of evil Offices, are vastly more odious, than equal Negligence, or evil Offices toward Strangers.

14. When we cannot at once follow two different Inclinations of Benevolence, we are to prefer gratifying the stronger Inclination; according to the wise Order of NATURE, who has constituted these Attachments. Thus, we are rather to be Grateful than Liberal, rather serve a Friend, or Kinsman, than a Stranger of only equal Virtue, when we cannot do both.

15. Or more generally, since there can be no Right, Claim, or Obligation to Impossibilitys; when two Actions to be done by any Agent, would both tend to the good of Mankind, but they cannot be perform'd both at once; that which occasions most Good is to be done, if the Omission of the other occasions no prepollent Evil. If the omission of either, will occasion some new natural Evil, that is to be omitted, whose Omission will occasion the least Evil. Thus, if two Persons of unequal Dignity be in Danger, we are to relieve the more valuable, when we cannot relieve both. Ingratitude, as it evidences a worse Temper than neglect of Beneficence; so it raises worse Sentiments in the Benefactor, and greater Diffidence, and Suspicion of his Fellow-Creatures, than an Omission of an Act of Beneficence: we ought therefore to be Grateful, rather than Beneficent, when we cannot (in any particular Case) evidence both Dispositions. If omitting of one Action will occasion new positive Evil, or continuance in a State of Pain, whereas the Omission of another would only prevent some new positive Good; since a State of Pain is a greater Evil, than the absence of Good, we are to follow Compassion, rather than Kindness; and relieve the Distressed, rather than increase the Pleasures of the Easy; when we cannot do both at once, and other Circumstances of the Objects are equal. In such Cases, we should not suppose contrary Obligations, or Dutys; the more important Office is our present Duty, and the Omission of the less important inconsistent Office at present, is no moral Evil.

182   X. From Art. vii. it follows, 'That all human Power, or Authority, must consist in a Right transferr'd to any Person or Council, to dispose of the alienable Rights of others, and that consequently, there can be no Government so absolute, as to have even an external Right to do or command every thing.' For wherever any Invasion is made upon unalienable Rights, there must arise either a perfect, or external Right to Resistance. The only Restraints of a moral Kind upon Subjects

in such cases, are, when they foresee that, thro their want of
Force, they shall probably by Resistance occasion greater Evils
to the Publick, than those they attempt to remove; or when
they find that Governours, in the main very useful to the
Publick, have by some unadvised Passion, done an Injury too
small to overballance the Advantages of their Administration, or the Evils which Resistance would in all likelihood
occasion; especially when the Injury is of a private Nature,
and not likely to be made a Precedent to the ruin of others.
Unalienable Rights are essential Limitations in all Govern-
ments.

But by absolute Government, either in Prince, or Council,
or in both jointly, we understand a Right to dispose of the
natural Force, and Goods of a whole People, as far as they are
naturally alienable, according to the Prudence of the Prince,
Council, or of both jointly, for the publick Good of the State,
or whole People; without any Reservation as to the Quantity
of the Goods, manner of Levying, or the proportion of the
Labours of the Subject, which they shall demand. But in all
States this tacit Trust is presuppos'd, 'that the Power conferr'd
shall be employ'd according to the best Judgment of the
Rulers for the publick Good.' So that whenever the Governours openly profess a Design of destroying the State, or act in
such a manner as will necessarily do it; the essential Trust,
suppos'd in all conveyance of Civil Power, is violated, and the
Grant thereby made void.

A Prince, or Council, or both jointly, may be variously
Limited; either when the Consent of the one may be necessary
to the validity of the Acts of the other; or when, in the very
Constitution of this supreme Power, certain Affairs are expressly
exempted from the Jurisdiction of the Prince, or Council, or
both jointly : as when several independent States uniting, form
a general Council, from whose Cognizance they expressly
reserve certain Privileges, in the very Formation of this
Council; or when in the very Constitution of any State,

a certain Method of Election of the Person of the Prince, or of the Members of the supreme Council is determin'd, and the Intention of their Assembling declar'd.   In all such cases, it is not in the Power of such Prince, Council, or both jointly, to alter the very Form of Government, or to take away that Right which the People have to be govern'd in such a manner, by a Prince, or Council thus elected, without the universal Consent of the very People who have subjected themselves to this Form of Government.   So that there may be a very regular State, where there is no universal absolute Power, lodg'd either in one Person, or Council, or in any other Assembly beside that of the whole People associated into that State.   To say, that upon a Change attempted in the very Form of the Government, by the supreme Power, the People have no Remedy according to the Constitution itself, will not prove that the supreme Power has such a Right; unless we confound all Ideas of Right with those of external Force.   The only Remedy indeed in that Case, is an universal Insurrection against such perfidious Trustees.

Despotick Power, is that which Persons injur'd may acquire over those Criminals, whose Lives, consistently with the publick Safety, they may prolong, that by their Labours they may repair the Damages they have done; or over those who stand oblig'd to a greater Value, than all their Goods and Labours can possibly amount to.   This Power itself, is limited to the Goods and Labours only of the Criminals or Debtors; and includes no Right to Tortures, Prostitution, or any Rights of the Governed which are naturally Unalienable; or to any thing which is not of some Moment toward Repair of Damage, Payment of Debt, or Security against future Offences.   The Characteristick of despotick Power, is this, 'that it is solely intended for the good of the Governours, without any tacit Trust of consulting the good of the Governed.'   Despotick Government, in this Sense, is directly inconsistent with the Notion of Civil Government.

183   From the Idea of Right, as above explain'd, we must necessarily conclude, 'that there can be no Right, or Limitation of Right, inconsistent with, or opposite to the greatest publick Good.'   And therefore in Cases of extreme Necessity, when the State cannot otherwise be preserv'd from Ruin, it must certainly be Just and Good in limited Governours, or in any other Persons who can do it, to use the Force of the State for its own preservation, beyond the Limits fix'd by the Constitution, in some transitory Acts, which are not to be made Precedents.   And on the other hand, when an equal Necessity to avoid Ruin requires it, the Subjects may justly resume the Powers ordinarily lodg'd in their Governours, or may counteract them.   This Privilege of flagrant Necessity, we all allow in defence of the most perfect private Rights : And if publick Rights are of more extensive Importance, so are also publick Necessitys.   These Necessitys must be very grievous and flagrant, otherwise they can never over-ballance the Evils of violating a tolerable Constitution, by an arbitrary act of Power, on the one hand ; or by an Insurrection, or Civil War, on the other.   No Person, or State can be happy, where they do not think their important Rights are secur'd from the Cruelty, Avarice, Ambition, or Caprice of their Governours.   Nor can any Magistracy be safe, or effectual for the ends of its Institution, where there are frequent Terrors of Insurrections.   Whatever temporary Acts therefore may be allow'd in extraordinary Cases ; whatever may be lawful in the transitory Act of a bold Legislator, who without previous Consent should rescue a slavish Nation, and place their Affairs so in the Hands of a Person, or Council, elected, or limited by themselves, that they should soon have Confidence in their own Safety, and in the Wisdom of the Administration ; yet, as to the fixed State which should ordinarily obtain in all Communitys, since no Assumer of Government, can so demonstrate his superior Wisdom or Goodness to the satisfaction and security of the Governed,

as is necessary to their Happiness; this must follow, That except when Men, for their own Interest, or out of publick Love, have by Consent subjected their Actions, or their Goods within certain Limits to the Disposal of others; no Mortal can have a Right from his superior Wisdom, or Goodness, or any other Quality, to give Laws to others without their Consent, express or tacit; or to dispose of the Fruits of their Labours, or of any other Right whatsoever.' And therefore superior Wisdom, or Goodness, gives no Right to Men to govern others.

184   But then with relation to the DEITY, suppos'd omniscient and benevolent, and secure from Indigence, the ordinary Cause of Injurys toward others; it must be amiable in such a Being, to assume the Government of weak, inconstant Creatures, often misled by Selfishness; and to give them Laws. To these Laws every Mortal should submit from publick Love, as being contriv'd for the Good of the Whole, and for the greatest private Good consistent with it; and every one may be sure, that he shall be better directed how to attain these Ends by the Divine Laws, than by his own greatest Prudence and Circumspection. Hence we imagine, 'That a good and wise GOD must have a perfect Right to govern the Universe; and that all Mortals are oblig'd to universal Obedience.'

The Justice of the DEITY is only a Conception of his universal impartial Benevolence, as it shall influence him, if he gives any Laws, to attemper them to the universal Good, and inforce them with the most effectual Sanctions of Rewards and Punishments.

185   XI. Some imagine that the Property the Creator has in all his Works, must be the true Foundation of his Right to govern. Among Men indeed, we find it necessary for the publick Good, that none should arbitrarily dispose of the Goods acquir'd by the Labour of another, which we call his Property; and hence we imagine that Creation is the only

Foundation of GOD's Dominion. But if the Reason[1] of establishing the Rights of Property does not hold against a perfectly wise and benevolent Being, I see no Reason why Property should be necessary to his Dominion. Now the Reason does not hold: For an infinitely wise and good Being, could never employ his assumed Authority to counteract the universal Good. The tie of Gratitude is stronger indeed than bare Benevolence; and therefore supposing two equally wise and good Beings, the one our Creator, and the other not, we should think our selves more oblig'd to obey our Creator. But supposing our Creator malicious, and a good Being condescending to rescue us, or govern us better, with sufficient Power to accomplish his kind Intentions; his Right to govern would be perfectly good. But this is rather matter of curious Speculation than Use; since both Titles of Benevolence and Property concur in the one only true DEITY, as far as we can know, join'd with infinite Wisdom and Power.

186   XII. If it be here enquir'd 'Could not the DEITY have given us a different or contrary determination of Mind, *viz.* to approve Actions upon another Foundation than Benevolence?' It is certain, there is nothing in this surpassing the natural Power of the DEITY. But as in the first Treatise, we resolv'd the Constitution of our present Sense of Beauty into the divine Goodness, so with much more obvious Reason may we ascribe the present Constitution of our moral Sense to his Goodness. For if the DEITY be really benevolent, or delights in the Happiness of others, he could not rationally act otherwise, or give us a moral Sense upon another Foundation, without counteracting his own benevolent Intentions. For, even upon the Supposition of a contrary Sense, every rational Being must still have been sollicitous in some degree about his own external Happiness: Reflection on the Circumstances of Mankind in this World would have suggested, that

---

[1] See *Art.* 10. *Par.* 6. of this Section (§ 184).

universal Benevolence and a social Temper, or a certain
Course of external Actions, would most effectually promote
the external Good of every one, according to the Reasonings
of CUMBERLAND and PUFFENDORF ; while at the same time
this perverted Sense of Morality would have made us uneasy
in such a Course, and inclin'd us to the quite contrary,
viz. Barbarity, Cruelty, and Fraud ; and universal War, according to Mr. HOBBS, would really have been our natural State ;
so that in every Action we must have been distracted by two
contrary Principles, and perpetually miserable, and dissatisfy'd
when we follow'd the Directions of either.

187   XIII. It has often been taken for granted in these Papers,
'That the ˌDEITY is morally good ;' tho the Reasoning is not
at all built upon this Supposition. If we enquire into the
Reason of the great Agreement of Mankind in this Opinion,
we shall perhaps find no demonstrative Arguments *à priori*,
from the Idea of an Independent Being, to prove his Goodness.   But there is abundant Probability, deduc'd from the
whole Frame of Nature, which seems, as far as we know,
plainly contriv'd for the Good of the Whole ; and the casual
Evils seem the necessary Concomitants of some Mechanism
design'd for vastly prepollent Good.   Nay, this very moral
Sense, implanted in rational Agents, to delight in, and admire
whatever Actions flow from a Study of the Good of others,
is one of the strongest Evidences of Goodness in the AUTHOR
of Nature.

But these Reflections are no way so universal as the
Opinion, nor are they often inculcated by any one. What
then more probably leads Mankind into that Opinion, is
this.   The obvious Frame of the World gives us Ideas of
boundless Wisdom and Power in its AUTHOR.   Such a Being
we cannot conceive indigent, and must conclude happy, and
in the best State possible, since he can still gratify himself.
The best State of rational Agents, and their greatest and
most worthy Happiness, we are necessarily led to imagine

must consist in universal efficacious Benevolence : and hence we conclude the DEITY benevolent in the most universal impartial manner. Nor can we well imagine what else deserves the Name of Perfection but Benevolence, and those Capacitys or Abilitys which are necessary to make it effectual ; such as Wisdom, and Power : at least we can have no other valuable Conception of it.

BUTLER

SERMONS AND DISSERTATION
UPON VIRTUE

Sermons, first edition, 1726 : reprinted here from the second edition, 1729. (Preface dated Sept. 16, 1729.)

Dissertation upon Virtue appended to the ' Analogy,' first edition, 1736.

BUTLER

Sermons

—••—

PREFACE.

*   *   *   *   *   *   *

188 THERE are two ways in which the subject of morals may be treated. One begins from inquiring into the abstract relations of things: the other from a matter of fact, namely, what the particular nature of man is, its several parts, their economy or constitution; from whence it proceeds to determine what course of life it is, which is correspondent to this whole nature. In the former method the conclusion is expressed thus, that vice is contrary to the nature and reason of things: in the latter, that it is a violation or breaking in upon our own nature. Thus they both lead us to the same thing, our obligations to the practice of virtue; and thus they exceedingly strengthen and enforce each other. The first seems the most direct formal proof, and in some respects the least liable to cavil and dispute: the latter is in a peculiar manner adapted to satisfy a fair mind; and is more easily applicable to the several particular relations and circumstances in life.

189 The following Discourses proceed chiefly in this latter method. The three first wholly. They were intended to explain what is meant by the nature of man, when it is said

that virtue consists in following, and vice in deviating from it ;
and by explaining to shew that the assertion is true. That
the ancient moralists had some inward feeling or other, which
they chose to express in this manner, that man is born to
virtue, that it consists in following nature, and that vice is
more contrary to this nature than tortures or death, their works
in our hands are instances. Now a person' who found no
mystery in this way of speaking of the ancients ; who, without
being very explicit with himself, kept to his natural feeling,
went along with them, and found within himself a full conviction, that what they laid down was just and true ; such an
one would probably wonder to see a point, in which he never
perceived any difficulty, so laboured as this is, in the second
and third Sermons ; insomuch perhaps as to be at a loss for
the occasion, scope, and drift of them. But it need not be
thought strange that this manner of expression, though familiar
with them, and, if not usually carried so far, yet not uncommon
amongst ourselves, should want explaining ; since there are
several perceptions daily felt and spoken of, which yet it may
not be very easy at first view to explicate, to distinguish from
all others, and ascertain exactly what the idea or perception is.
The many treatises upon the passions are a proof of this ; since
so many would never have undertaken to unfold their several
complications, and trace and resolve them into their principles,
if they had thought, what they were endeavouring to shew was
obvious to every one, who felt and talked of those passions.
Thus, though there seems no ground to doubt, but that the
generality of mankind have the inward perception expressed so
commonly in that manner by the ancient moralists, more than
to doubt whether they have those passions ; yet it appeared of
use to unfold that inward conviction, and lay it open in a more
explicit manner, than I had seen done ; especially when there
were not wanting persons, who manifestly mistook the whole
thing, and so had great reason to express themselves dissatis-
fied with it. A late author of great and deserved reputation

says, that to place virtue in following nature, is at best a loose way of talk. And he has reason to say this, if what I think he intends to express, though with great decency, be true, that scarce any other sense can be put upon those words, but acting as any of the several parts, without distinction, of a man's nature happened most to incline him [1].

190   Whoever thinks it worth while to consider this matter thoroughly, should begin with stating to himself exactly the idea of a system, economy, or constitution of any particular nature, or particular any thing : and he will, I suppose, find, that it is an one or a whole, made up of several parts ; but yet, that the several parts even considered as a whole do not complete the idea, unless in the notion of a whole you include the relations and respects which those parts have to each other. Every work both of nature and of art is a system : and as every particular thing, both natural and artificial, is for some use or purpose out of and beyond itself, one may add, to what has been already brought into the idea of a system, its conduciveness to this one or more ends. Let us instance in a watch—Suppose the several parts of it taken to pieces, and placed apart from each other : let a man have ever so exact a notion of these several parts, unless he considers the respects and relations which they have to each other, he will not have any thing like the idea of a watch. Suppose these several parts brought together and anyhow united : neither will he yet, be the union ever so close, have an idea which will bear any resemblance to that of a watch. But let him view those several parts put together, or consider them as to be put together in the manner of a watch ; let him form a notion of the relations which those several parts have to each other—all conducive in their respective ways to this purpose, shewing the hour of the day ; and then he has the idea of a watch. Thus it is with regard to the inward frame of man. Appetites, passions, affections, and the principle of

[1] Rel. of Nature Delin., § 1. art. ix. pp. 22, 23, edit. 1725.

reflection, considered merely as the several parts of our inward nature, do not at all give us an idea of the system or constitution of this nature ; because the constitution is formed by somewhat not yet taken into consideration, namely, by the relations which these several parts have to each other ; the chief of which is the authority of reflection or conscience. It is from considering the relations which the several appetites and passions in the inward frame have to each other, and, above all, the supremacy of reflection or conscience, that we get the idea of the system or constitution of human nature. And from the idea itself it will as fully appear, that this our nature, i. e. constitution, is adapted to virtue, as from the idea of a watch it appears, that its nature, i. e. constitution or system, is adapted to measure time. What in fact or event commonly happens is nothing to this question. Every work of art is apt to be out of order : but this is so far from being according to its system, that let the disorder increase, and it will totally destroy it. This is merely by way of explanation, what an economy, system, or constitution is. And thus far the cases are perfectly parallel. If we go further, there is indeed a difference, nothing to the present purpose, but too important a one ever to be omitted. A machine is inanimate and passive : but we are agents. Our constitution is put in our own power. We are charged with it; and therefore are accountable for any disorder or violation of it.

191   Thus nothing can possibly be more contrary to nature than vice ; meaning by nature not only the *several parts* of our internal frame, but also the *constitution* of it. Poverty and disgrace, tortures and death, are not so contrary to it. Misery and injustice are indeed equally contrary to some different parts of our nature taken singly : but injustice is moreover contrary to the whole constitution of the nature.

If it be asked, whether this constitution be really what those philosophers meant, and whether they would have explained themselves in this manner ; the answer is the same, as if it should be asked, whether a person, who had often used the word *resentment,* and felt the thing, would have explained this passion exactly in the same manner, in which it is done in one of these Discourses.   As I have no doubt, but that this is a true account of that passion, which he referred to and intended to express by the word *resentment ;* so I have no doubt, but that this is the true account of the ground of that conviction which they referred to, when they said, vice was contrary to nature.   And though it should be thought that they meant no more than that vice was contrary to the higher and better part of our nature ; even this implies such a constitution as I have endeavoured to explain.   For the very terms, higher and better, imply a relation or respect of parts to each other ; and these relative parts, being in one and the same nature, form a constitution, and are the very idea of it.   They had a perception that injustice was contrary to their nature, and that pain was so also. They observed these two perceptions totally different, not in degree, but in kind : and the reflecting upon each of them, as they thus stood in their nature, wrought a full intuitive conviction, that more was due and of right belonged to one of these inward perceptions, than to the other ; that it demanded in all cases to govern such a creature as man.   So that, upon the whole, this is a fair and true account of what was the ground of their conviction ; of what they intended to refer to, when they said, virtue consisted in following nature : a manner of speaking not loose and undeterminate, but clear and distinct, strictly just and true.

192   Though I am persuaded the force of this conviction is felt by almost every one ; yet since, considered as an argument and put in words, it appears somewhat abstruse, and since the connexion of it is broken in the three first Sermons, it may not be amiss to give the reader the whole argument here in one view.

Mankind has various instincts and principles of action, as brute creatures have ; some leading most directly and immediately to the good of the community, and some most directly to private good.

Man has several which brutes have not ; particularly reflection or conscience, an approbation of some principles or actions, and disapprobation of others.

Brutes obey their instincts or principles of action, according to certain rules ; suppose the constitution of their body, and the objects around them.

The generality of mankind also obey their instincts and principles, all of them ; those propensions we call good, as well as the bad, according to the same rules ; namely, the constitution of their body, and the external circumstances which they are in.   [Therefore it is not a true representation of mankind to affirm, that they are wholly governed by self-love, the love of power and sensual appetites : since, as on the one hand they are often actuated by these, without any regard to right or wrong ; so on the other it is manifest fact, that the same persons, the generality, are frequently influenced by friendship, compassion, gratitude ; and even a general abhorrence of what is base, and liking of what is fair and just, takes its turn amongst the other motives of action.   This is the partial inadequate notion of human nature treated of in the first Discourse : and it is by this nature, if one may speak so, that the world is in fact influenced, and kept in that tolerable order, in which it is.]

193   Brutes in acting according to the rules before mentioned, their bodily constitution and circumstances, act suitably to their whole nature.   [It is however to be distinctly noted, that the reason why we affirm this is not merely that brutes in fact act so ; for this alone, however universal, does not at all determine, whether such course of action be correspondent to their whole nature : but the reason of the assertion is, that as in acting thus they plainly act conformably to somewhat in their nature, so, from all observations we are able to make upon them, there does not appear the least ground to imagine them to have any thing else in their nature, which requires a different rule or course of action.]

Mankind also in acting thus would act suitably to their

whole nature, if no more were to be said of man's nature than what has been now said ; if that, as it is a true, were also a complete, adequate account of our nature.

194　But that is not a complete account of man's nature. Somewhat further must be brought in to give us an adequate notion of it ; namely, that one of those principles of action, conscience or reflection, compared with the rest as they all stand together in the nature of man, plainly bears upon it marks of authority over all the rest, and claims the absolute direction of them all, to allow or forbid their gratification : a disapprobation of reflection being in itself a principle manifestly superior to a mere propension. And the conclusion is, that to allow no more to this superior principle or part of our nature, than to other parts ; to let it govern and guide only occasionally in common with the rest, as its turn happens to come, from the temper and circumstances one happens to be in ; this is not to act comformably to the constitution of man : neither can any human creature be said to act conformably to his constitution of nature, unless he allows to that superior principle the absolute authority which is due to it. And this conclusion is abundantly confirmed from hence, that one may determine what course of action the economy of man's nature requires, without so much as knowing in what degrees of *strength* the several principles prevail, or which of them have actually the greatest influence.

195　The practical reason of insisting so much upon this natural authority of the principle of reflection or conscience is, that it seems in great measure overlooked by many, who are by no means the worse sort of men. It is thought sufficient to abstain from gross wickedness, and to be humane and kind to such as happen to come in their way. Whereas in reality the very constitution of our nature requires, that we bring our whole conduct before this superior faculty ; wait its determination ; enforce upon ourselves its authority, and make it the business of our lives, as it is absolutely the whole business of a moral agent, to conform ourselves to it. This is the true meaning of that ancient precept, *Reverence thyself.*

The not taking into consideration this authority, which is implied in the idea of reflex approbation or disapprobation, seems a material deficiency or omission in lord Shaftesbury's Inquiry concerning Virtue. He has shewn beyond all contradiction, that virtue is naturally the interest or happiness, and vice the misery, of such a creature as man, placed in the circumstances which we are in this world. But suppose there are particular exceptions; a case which this author was unwilling to put, and yet surely it is to be put: or suppose a case which he has put and determined, that of a sceptic not convinced of this happy tendency of virtue, or being of a contrary opinion. His determination is, that it would be *without remedy*[1]. One may say more explicitly, that leaving out the authority of reflex approbation or disapprobation, such an one would be under an obligation to act viciously; since interest, one's own happiness, is a manifest obligation, and there is not supposed to be any other obligation in the case. 'But does it much mend the matter, to take in that natural authority of reflection? There indeed would be an obligation to virtue; but would not the obligation from supposed interest on the side of vice remain?' If it should, yet to be under two contrary obligations, i. e. under none at all, would not be exactly the same, as to be under a formal obligation to be vicious, or to be in circumstances in which the constitution of man's nature plainly required that vice should be preferred. But the obligation on the side of interest really does not remain. For the natural authority of the principle of reflection is an obligation the most near and intimate, the most certain and known: whereas the contrary obligation can at the utmost appear no more than probable; since no man can be *certain* in any circumstances that vice is his

[1] 'Inquiry,' B. i. part 3, § 3.

interest in the present world, much less can he be certain
against another : and thus the certain obligation would entirely
supersede and destroy the uncertain one ; which yet would
have been of real force without the former.

196   In truth, the taking in this consideration totally changes
the whole state of the case ; and shews, what this author
does not seem to have been aware of, that the greatest degree
of scepticism which he thought possible will still leave men
under the strictest moral obligations, whatever their opinion
be concerning the happiness of virtue. For that mankind
upon reflection felt an approbation of what was good, and
disapprobation of the contrary, he thought a plain matter
of fact, as it undoubtedly is, which none could deny, but
from mere affectation.   Take in then that authority and obligation, which is a constituent part of this reflex approbation,
and it will undeniably follow, though a man should doubt
of every thing else, yet, that he would still remain under
the nearest and most certain obligation to the practice of
virtue ; and obligation implied in the very idea of virtue,
in the very idea of reflex approbation.

And how little influence soever this obligation alone can
be expected to have in fact upon mankind, yet one may
appeal even to interest and self-love, and ask, since from
man's nature, condition, and the shortness of life, so little,
so very little indeed, can possibly in any case be gained
by vice ; whether it be so prodigious a thing to sacrifice
that little to the most intimate of all obligations ; and which
a man cannot transgress without being self-condemned, and,
unless he has corrupted his nature, without real self-dislike :
this question, I say, may be asked, even upon supposition
that the prospect of a future life were ever so uncertain.

The observation, that man is thus by his very nature
a law to himself, pursued to its just consequences, is of the
utmost importance ; because from it it will follow, that though
men should, through stupidity or speculative scepticism, be

ignorant of, or disbelieve, any authority in the universe to punish the violation of this law; yet, if there should be such authority, they would be as really liable to punishment, as though they had been beforehand convinced, that such punishment would follow. For in whatever sense we understand justice, even supposing, what I think would be very presumptuous to assert, that the end of divine punishment is no other than that of civil punishment, namely, to prevent future mischief; upon this bold supposition, ignorance or disbelief of the sanction would by no means exempt even from this justice: because it is not foreknowledge of the punishment which renders us obnoxious to it; but merely violating a known obligation.

197   And here it comes in one's way to take notice of a manifest error or mistake in the author now cited, unless perhaps he has incautiously expressed himself so as to be misunderstood; namely, that *it is malice only, and not goodness, which can make us afraid.* Whereas in reality, goodness is the natural and just object of the greatest fear to an ill man. Malice may be appeased or satiated; humour may change, but goodness is a fixed, steady, immovable principle of action. If either of the former holds the sword of justice, there is plainly ground for the greatest of crimes to hope for impunity: but if it be goodness, there can be no possible hope, whilst the reasons of things, or the ends of government, call for punishment. Thus every one sees how much greater chance of impunity an ill man has in a partial administration, than in a just and upright one. It is said, that *the interest or good of the whole must be the interest of the universal Being, and that he can have no other.* Be it so. This author has proved, that vice is naturally the misery of mankind in this world. Consequently it was for the good of the whole that it should be so. What shadow of reason then is there to assert, that this may not be the case hereafter? Danger of future punishment (and if there be danger, there

is ground of fear) no more supposes malice, than the present
feeling of punishment does.

198   The chief design of the eleventh Discourse is to state the
notion of self-love and disinterestedness, in order to shew that
benevolence is not more unfriendly to self-love, than any other
particular affection whatever.   There is a strange affectation in
many people of explaining away all particular affections, and
representing the whole of life as nothing but one continued
exercise of self-love.   Hence arises that surprising confusion
and perplexity in the Epicureans[1] of old, Hobbes, the author
of *Reflexions, Sentences, et Maximes Morales,* and this whole
set of writers; the confusion of calling actions interested which
are done in contradiction to the most manifest known interest,
merely for the gratification of a present passion.   Now all this
confusion might easily be avoided, by stating to ourselves
wherein the idea of self-love in general consists, as distinguished
from all particular movements towards particular external
objects; the appetites of sense, resentment, compassion,
curiosity, ambition, and the rest[2].   When this is done, if the
words *selfish* and *interested* cannot be parted with, but must be
applied to every thing; yet, to avoid such total confusion of
all language, let the distinction be made by epithets: and the
first may be called cool or settled selfishness, and the other
passionate or sensual selfishness.   But the most natural way of
speaking plainly is, to call the first only, self-love, and the
actions proceeding from it, interested: and to say of the latter,
that they are not love to ourselves, but movements towards

[1] One need only look into Torquatus's account of the Epicurean system,
in Cicero's first book *De Finibus,* to see in what a surprising manner this
was done by them.   Thus the desire of praise, and of being beloved, he
explains to be no other than desire of safety: regard to our country, even
in the most virtuous character, to be nothing but regard to ourselves.   The
author of *Reflexions, &c. Morales,* says, Curiosity proceeds from interest or
pride; which pride also would doubtless have been explained to be self-
love.   Page 85, ed. 1725.   As if there were no such passions in mankind as
desire of esteem, or of being beloved, or of knowledge.   Hobbes's account
of the affections of good-will and pity are instances of the same kind.

[2] Inf. §§ 228-9.

somewhat external : honour, power, the harm or good of
another : and that the pursuit of these external objects, so far
as it proceeds from these movements, (for it may proceed from
self-love ,) is no otherwise interested, than as every action of
every creature must, from the nature of the thing, be ; for no
one can act but from a desire, or choice, or preference of
his own.

199   Self-love and any particular passion may be joined together ;
and from this complication, it becomes impossible in numberless
instances to determine precisely, how far an action, perhaps
even of one's own, has for its principle general self-love, or
some particular passion.   But this need create no confusion in
the ideas themselves of self-love and particular passions.   We
distinctly discern what one is, and what the other are : though
we may be uncertain how far one or the other influences us.
And though, from this uncertainty, it cannot but be that there
will be different opinions concerning mankind, as more or less
governed by interest ; and some will ascribe actions to self-love,
which others will ascribe to particular passions : yet it is absurd
to say that mankind are wholly actuated by either ; since it is
manifest that both have their influence.   For as, on the one
hand, men form a general notion of interest, some placing it in
one thing, and some in another, and have a considerable regard
to it throughout the course of their life, which is owing to self-
love ; so, on the other hand, they are often set on work by the
particular passions themselves, and a considerable part of life
is spent in the actual gratification of them, i. e. is employed, not
by self-love, but by the passions.

Besides, the very idea of an interested pursuit necessarily
presupposes particular passions or appetites ; since the very
idea of interest or happiness consists in this, that an appetite
or affection enjoys its object.   It is not because we love
ourselves that we find delight in such and such objects, but
because we have particular affections towards them.   Take

[1] See the note, § 205, pp. 199-200.

away these affections, and you leave self-love absolutely nothing at all to employ itself about[1]; no end or object for it to pursue, excepting only that of avoiding pain. Indeed the Epicureans, who maintained that absence of pain was the highest happiness, might, consistently with themselves, deny all affection, and, if they had so pleased, every sensual appetite too; but the very idea of interest or happiness other than absence of pain implies particular appetites or passions; these being necessary to constitute that interest or happiness.

200   The observation, that benevolence is no more disinterested than any of the common particular passions[2], seems in itself worth being taken notice of; but is insisted upon to obviate that scorn, which one sees rising upon the faces of people who are said to know the world, when mention is made of a disinterested, generous, or public-spirited action. The truth of that observation might be made appear in a more formal manner of proof: for whoever will consider all the possible respects and relations which any particular affection can have to self-love and private interest, will, I think, see demonstrably, that benevolence is not in any respect more at variance with self-love, than any other particular affection whatever, but that it is in every respect, at least, as friendly to it.

If the observation be true, it follows, that self-love and benevolence, virtue and interest, are not to be opposed, but only to be distinguished from each other; in the same way as virtue and any other particular affection, love of arts, suppose, are to be distinguished. Every thing is what it is, and not another thing. The goodness or badness of actions does not arise from hence, that the epithet, interested or disinterested, may be applied to them, any more than that any other indifferent epithet, suppose inquisitive or jealous, may or may not be applied to them; not from their being attended with present or future pleasure or pain; but from their being what they are; namely, what becomes such creatures as we are,

---

[1] § 231.   [2] § 233, &c.

what the state of the case requires, or the contrary. Or in
other words, we may judge and determine, that an action is
morally good or evil, before we so much as consider, whether
it be interested or disinterested.   This consideration no more
comes in to determine whether an action be virtuous, than to
determine whether it be resentful.   Self-love in its due degree
is as just and morally good, as any affection whatever.   Benevolence towards particular persons may be to a degree of
weakness, and so be blamable : and disinterestedness is so far
from being in itself commendable, that the utmost possible
depravity which we can in imagination conceive, is that of disinterested cruelty.

201   Neither does there appear any reason to wish self-love were
weaker in the generality of the world than it is.   The influence
which it has seems plainly owing to its being constant and
habitual, which it cannot but be, and not to the degree
or strength of it.   Every caprice of the imagination, every
curiosity of the understanding, every affection of the heart,
is perpetually shewing its weakness, by prevailing over it.   Men
daily, hourly sacrifice the greatest known interest, to fancy,
inquisitiveness, love, or hatred, any vagrant inclination.   The
thing to be lamented is, not that men have so great regard to
their own good or interest in the present world, for they have
not enough[1]; but that they have so little to the good of others.
And this seems plainly owing to their being so much engaged
in the gratification of particular passions unfriendly to benevolence, and which happen to be most prevalent in them, much
more than to self-love.   As a proof of this may be observed,
that there is no character more void of friendship, gratitude,
natural affection, love to their country, common justice, or
more equally and uniformly hard-hearted, than the *abandoned*
in, what is called, the way of pleasure—hard-hearted and totally
without feeling in behalf of others ; except when they cannot
escape the sight of distress, and so are interrupted by it in

[1] § 22.

their pleasures. And yet it is ridiculous to call such an abandoned course of pleasure interested, when the person engaged in it knows beforehand, and goes on under the feeling and apprehension, that it will be as ruinous to himself, as to those who depend upon him.

Upon the whole, if the generality of mankind were to cultivate within themselves the principle of self-love; if they were to accustom themselves often to set down and consider, what was the greatest happiness they were capable of attaining for themselves in this life, and if self-love were so strong and prevalent, as that they would uniformly pursue this their supposed chief temporal good, without being diverted from it by any particular passion; it would manifestly prevent numberless follies and vices. This was in a great measure the Epicurean system of philosophy. It is indeed by no means the religious or even moral institution of life. Yet, with all the mistakes men would fall into about interest, it would be less mischievous than the extravagances of mere appetite, will, and pleasure : for certainly self-love, though confined to the interest of this life, is, of the two, a much better guide than passion [1], which has absolutely no bound or measure, but what is set to it by this self-love, or moral considerations.

202 From the distinction above made between self-love, and the several particular principles or affections in our nature, we may see how good ground there was for that assertion, maintained by the several ancient schools of philosophy against the Epicureans, namely, that virtue is to be pursued as an end, eligible in and for itself. For, if there be any principles or affections in the mind of man distinct from self-love, that the things those principles tend towards, or that the objects of those affections are, each of them, in themselves eligible, to be pursued upon its own account, and to be rested in as an end, is implied in the very idea of such principle or affection. They indeed asserted much higher things of virtue, and with

[1] § 217.

very good reason; but to say thus much of it, that it is to be pursued for itself, is to say no more of it, than may truly be said of the object of every natural affection whatever.

The question, which was a few years ago disputed in France, concerning *the love of God*, which was there called enthusiasm, as it will every where by the generality of the world; this question, I say, answers in religion to that old one in morals now mentioned. And both of them are, I think, fully determined by the same observation, namely, that the very nature of affection, the idea itself, necessarily implies resting in its object as an end.

     *   *   *   *   *   *

SERMON I.

UPON THE SOCIAL NATURE OF MAN.

For as we have many members in one body, and all members have not the same office: so we being many are one body in Christ, and every one members one of another.—ROM. xii. 4, 5.

     *   *   *   *   *   *

203 The relation which the several parts or members of the natural body have to each other and to the whole body, is here compared to the relation which each particular person in society has to other particular persons and to the whole society; and the latter is intended to be illustrated by the former. And if there be a likeness between these two relations, the consequence is obvious : that the latter shews us we were intended to do good to others, as the former shews us that the several members of the natural body were intended to be instruments of good to each other and to the whole body. But as there is scarce any ground for a comparison between society and the mere material body, this without the mind being a dead unactive thing; much less can the comparison be carried to any length. And since the apostle speaks of the several members as having distinct offices, which implies the mind; it cannot be thought an unallowable liberty; instead of the *body* and *its members*, to substitute the *whole nature of man,*

and *all the variety of internal principles which belong to it.*
And then the comparison will be between the nature of man
as respecting self, and tending to private good, his own preservation and happiness ; and the nature of man as having respect
to society, and tending to promote public good, the happiness
of that society. These ends do indeed perfectly coincide ;
and to aim at public and private good are so far from being
inconsistent, that they mutually promote each other : yet in
the following discourse they must be considered as entirely
distinct ; otherwise the nature of man as tending to one, or as
tending to the other cannot be compared. There can no comparison be made, without considering the things compared as
distinct and different.

From this review and comparison of the nature of man as
respecting self, and as respecting society, it will plainly appear,
that *there are as real and the same kind of indications in human
nature, that we were made for society and to do good to our
fellow-creatures ; as that we were intended to take care of our
own life and health and private good : and that the same objections lie against one of these assertions, as against the other.* For,

204   First, there is a natural principle of *benevolence* [1] in man ;

---

[1] Suppose a man of learning to be writing a grave book upon *human
nature*, and to shew in several parts of it that he had an insight into the
subject he was considering ; amongst other things, the following one would
require to be accounted for ; the appearance of benevolence or good-will
in men towards each other in the instances of natural relation, and in
others *. Cautious of being deceived with outward show, he retires within
himself to see exactly, what that is in the mind of man from whence this
appearance proceeds ; and, upon deep reflection, asserts the principle in
the mind to be only the love of power, and delight in the exercise of it.
Would not every body think here was a mistake of one word for another ?
that the philosopher was contemplating and accounting for some other
human actions, some other behaviour of man to man ? And could any one
be thoroughly satisfied, that what is commonly called benevolence or
good-will was really the affection meant, but only by being made to
understand that this learned person had a general hypothesis, to which the
appearance of good-will could no otherwise be reconciled ? That what
has this appearance is often nothing but ambition ; that delight in
superiority often (suppose always) mixes itself with benevolence, only
makes it more specious to call it ambition than hunger, of the two : but
* Hobbes of Human Nature, c. ix. § 7.

which is in some degree to *society*, what *self-love* is to the *individual*. And if there be in mankind any disposition to

in reality that passion does no more account for the whole appearances of good-will, than this appetite does. Is there not often the appearance of one man's wishing that good to another, which he knows himself unable to procure him; and rejoicing in it, though bestowed by a third person? And can love of power any way possibly come in to account for this desire or delight? Is there not often the appearance of men's distinguishing between two or more persons, preferring one before another, to do good to, in cases where love of power cannot in the least account for the distinction and preference? For this principle can no otherwise distinguish between objects, than as it is a greater instance and exertion of power to do good to one rather than to another. Again, suppose good-will in the mind of man to be nothing but delight in the exercise of power: men might indeed be restrained by distant and accidental consideration; but these restraints being removed, they would have a disposition to, and delight in mischief as an exercise and proof of power: and this disposition and delight would arise from, or be the same principle in the mind, as a disposition to, and delight in charity. Thus cruelty, as distinct from envy and resentment, would be exactly the same in the mind of man as good-will: that one tends to the happiness, the other to the misery of our fellow-creatures, is, it seems, merely an accidental circumstance, which the mind has not the least regard to. These are the absurdities which even men of capacity run into, when they have occasion to belie their nature, and will perversely disclaim that image of God which was originally stamped upon it, the traces of which, however faint, are plainly discernible upon the mind of man.

If any person can in earnest doubt, whether there be such a thing as good-will in one man towards another; (for the question is not concerning either the degree or extensiveness of it, but concerning the affection itself:) let it be observed, that *whether man be thus, or otherwise constituted, what is the inward frame in this particular,* is a mere question of fact or natural history, not proveable immediately by reason. It is therefore to be judged of and determined in the same way other facts or matters of natural history are : by appealing to the external senses, or inward perceptions, respectively, as the matter under consideration is cognizable by one or the other : by arguing from acknowledged facts and actions; for a great number of actions in the same kind, in different circumstances, and respecting different objects, will prove, to a certainty, what principles they do not, and, to the greatest probability, what principles they do proceed from : and lastly, by the testimony of mankind. Now that there is some degree of benevolence amongst men, may be as strongly and plainly proved in all these ways, as it could possibly be proved, supposing there was this affection in our nature. And should any one think fit to assert, that resentment in the mind of man was absolutely nothing but reasonable concern for our own safety, the falsity of this, and what is the real nature of that passion, could be shewn in no other ways than those in which it may be shewn, that there is such a thing in *some degree* as *real* good-will, in man towards man. It is sufficient that the seeds of it be implanted in our nature by God. There is, it is owned, much left for us to do upon our own heart

friendship; if there be any such thing as compassion, for compassion is momentary love; if there be any such thing as the
paternal or filial affections ; if there be any affection in human
nature, the object and end of which is the good of another,
this is itself benevolence or the love of another.   Be it ever so
short, be it in ever so low a degree, or ever so unhappily confined ; it proves the assertion, and points out what we were
designed for, as really as though it were in a higher degree and
more extensive.   I must, however, remind you that though
benevolence and self-love are different ; though the former tends
most directly to public good, and the latter to private : yet they
are so perfectly coincident that the greatest satisfactions to
ourselves depend upon our having benevolence in a due degree ;
and that self-love is one chief security of our right behaviour
towards society.   It may be added, that their mutual coinciding, so that we can scarce promote one without the other, is
equally a proof that we were made for both.

205   Secondly, This will further appear, from observing that the
several passions and *affections*, which are distinct [1] both from

and temper; to cultivate, to improve, to call it forth, to exercise it in
a steady, uniform manner.   This is our work : this is virtue and religion.
    [1] Every body makes a distinction between self-love, and the several par-
ticular passions, appetites, and affections ; and yet they are often confounded
again.   That they are totally different, will be seen by any one who will
distinguish between the passions and appetites *themselves*, and *endeavouring*
after the means of their gratification.   Consider the appetite of hunger,
and the desire of esteem : these being the occasion both of pleasure and
pain, the coolest *self-love*, as well as the appetites and passions themselves,
may put us upon making use of the *proper methods of obtaining* that
pleasure, and avoiding that pain ; but the *feelings themselves*, the pain
of hunger and shame, and the delight from esteem, are no more self-love
than they are any thing in the world.   Though a man hated himself, he
would as much feel the pain of hunger as he would that of the gout :
and it is plainly supposable there may be creatures with self-love in
them to the highest degree, who may be quite insensible and indifferent
(as men in some cases are) to the contempt and esteem of those, upon
whom their happiness does not in some further respects depend.   And
as self-love and the several particular passions and appetites are in themselves totally different ; so, that some actions proceed from one, and
some from the other, will be manifest to any who will observe the two
following very supposable cases.   One man rushes upon certain ruin for
the gratification of a present desire : nobody will call the principle of this

benevolence and self-love, do in general contribute and lead us
to *public* good as really as to *private*. It might be thought too
minute and particular, and would carry us too great a length,
to distinguish between and compare together the several
passions or appetites distinct from benevolence, whose primary
use and intention is the security and good of society; and
the passions distinct from self-love, whose primary intention
and design is the security and good of the individual [1]. It is
enough to the present argument, that desire of esteem from
others, contempt and esteem of them, love of society as distinct
from affection to the good of it, indignation against successful
vice, that these are public affections or passions; have an
immediate respect to others, naturally lead us to regulate our
behaviour in such a manner as will be of service to our fellow-
creatures. If any or all of these may be considered likewise
as private affections, as tending to private good; this does not
hinder them from being public affections too, or destroy the
good influence of them upon society, and their tendency to
public good. It may be added, that as persons without any
conviction from reason of the desirableness of life, would yet of

action self-love. Suppose another man to go through some laborious
work upon promise of a great reward, without any distinct knowledge what
the reward will be : this course of action cannot be ascribed to any
particular passion. The former of these actions is plainly to be imputed to
some particular passion or affection, the latter as plainly to the general
affection or principle of self-love. That there are some particular pursuits
or actions concerning which we cannot determine how far they are owing
to one, and how far to the other, proceeds from this, that the two principles
are frequently mixed together, and run up into each other. This distinction
is further explained in the eleventh sermon.

[1] If any desire to see this distinction and comparison made in a particular
instance, the appetite and passion now mentioned may serve for one.
Hunger is to be considered as a private appetite; because the end for
which it was given us is the preservation of the individual. Desire of
esteem is a public passion; because the end for which it was given us
is to regulate our behaviour towards society. The respect which this has
to private good is as remote as the respect that has to public good: and
the appetite is no more self-love, than the passion is benevolence. The
object and end of the former is merely food; the object and end of the
latter is merely esteem: but the latter can no more be gratified, without
contributing to the good of society; than the former can be gratified,
without contributing to the preservation of the individual.

course preserve it merely from the appetite of hunger ; so by acting merely from regard (suppose) to reputation, without any consideration of the good of others, men often contribute to public good.　In both these instances they are plainly instruments in the hands of another, in the hands of Providence, to carry on ends, the preservation of the individual and good of society, which they themselves have not in their view or intention.　The sum is, men have various appetites, passions, and particular affections, quite distinct both from self-love and from benevolence : all of these have a tendency to promote both public and private good, and may be considered as respecting others and ourselves equally and in common : but some of them seem most immediately to respect others, or tend to public good ; others of them most immediately to respect self, or tend to private good : as the former are not benevolence, so the latter are not self-love : neither sort are instances of our love either to ourselves or others ; but only instances of our Maker's care and love both of the individual and the species, and proofs that he intended we should be instruments of good to each other, as well as that we should be so to ourselves.

206　　Thirdly, There is a principle of reflection in men, by which they distinguish between, approve and disapprove their own actions.　We are plainly constituted such sort of creatures as to reflect upon our own nature.　The mind can take a view of what passes within itself, its propensions, aversions, passions, affections, as respecting such objects, and in such degrees ; and of the several actions consequent thereupon.　In this survey it approves of one, disapproves of another, and towards a third is affected in neither of these ways, but is quite indifferent. This principle in man, by which he approves or disapproves his heart, temper, and actions, is conscience ; for this is the strict sense of the word, though sometimes it is used so as to take in more.　And that this faculty tends to restrain men from doing mischief to each other, and leads them to do good, is too manifest to need being insisted upon.　Thus a parent

has the affection of love to his children : this leads him to take
care of, to educate, to make due provision for them ; the
natural affection leads to this : but the reflection that it is his
proper business, what belongs to him, that it is right and commendable so to do ; this added to the affection becomes a
much more settled principle, and carries him on through more
labour and difficulties for the sake of his children, than he
would undergo from that affection alone, if he thought it, and
the course of action it led to, either indifferent or criminal.
This indeed is impossible, to do that which is good and not to
approve of it ; for which reason they are frequently not considered as distinct, though they really are : for men often
approve of the actions of others, which they will not imitate,
and likewise do that which they approve not. It cannot possibly be denied, that there is this principle of reflection or
conscience in human nature. Suppose a man to relieve an
innocent person in great distress ; suppose the same man
afterwards, in the fury of anger, to do the greatest mischief to
a person who had given no just cause of offence ; to aggravate
the injury, add the circumstances of former friendship, and obligation from the injured person ; let the man who is supposed to
have done these two different actions, coolly reflect upon them
afterwards, without regard to their consequences to himself :
to assert that any common man would be affected in the same
way towards these different actions, that he would make no
distinction between them, but approve or disapprove them
equally, is too glaring a falsity to need being confuted. There
is therefore this principle of reflection or conscience in mankind. It is needless to compare the respect it has to private
good, with the respect it has to public ; since it plainly tends
as much to the latter as to the former, and is commonly thought
to tend chiefly to the latter. This faculty is now mentioned
merely as another part in the inward frame of man, pointing
out to us in some degree what we are intended for, and as
what will naturally and of course have some influence. The

particular place assigned to it by nature, what authority it has, and how great influence it ought to have, shall be hereafter considered.

207   From this comparison of benevolence and self-love, of our public and private affections, of the courses of life they lead to, and of the principle of reflection or conscience as respecting each of them, it is as manifest, that *we were made for society, and to promote the happiness of it; as that we were intended to take care of our own life, and health, and private good.*

And from this whole review must be given a different draught of human nature from what we are often presented with.   Mankind are by nature so closely united, there is such a correspondence between the inward sensations of one man and those of another, that disgrace is as much avoided as bodily pain, and to be the object of esteem and love as much desired as any external goods: and in many particular cases persons are carried on to do good to others, as the end their affection tends to and rests in; and manifest that they find real satisfaction and enjoyment in this course of behaviour. There is such a natural principle of attraction in man towards man, that having trod the same tract of land, having breathed in the same climate, barely having been born in the same artificial district or division, becomes the occasion of contracting acquaintances and familiarities many years after : for any thing may serve the purpose.   Thus relations merely nominal are sought and invented, not by governors, but by the lowest of the people; which are found sufficient to hold mankind together in little fraternities and copartnerships : weak ties indeed, and what may afford fund enough for ridicule, if they are absurdly considered as the real principles of that union : but they are in truth merely the occasions, as any thing may be of any thing, upon which our nature carries us on according to its own previous bent and bias; which occasions therefore would be nothing at all, were there not this prior disposition and bias of nature.   Men are so much one body, that in a peculiar manner they feel for each other, shame, sudden danger, resentment, honour, prosperity, distress ; one or another, or all of these, from the social nature in general, from benevolence, upon the occasion of natural relation, acquaintance, protection, dependence ; each of these being distinct cements of society.   And therefore to have no restraint from, no regard to others in our behaviour, is the speculative absurdity of considering ourselves as single and independent, as having nothing in our nature which has respect to our fellow-creatures, reduced to action and practice.   And this is the same absurdity, as to suppose a hand, or any part to have no natural respect to any other, or to the whole body.

208   But allowing all this, it may be asked, ' Has not man dispositions and principles within, which lead him to do evil to others, as well as to do good ? Whence come the many miseries else, which men are the authors and instruments of to each other ? ' These questions, so far as they relate to the foregoing discourse, may be answered by asking, Has not man also dispositions and principles within, which lead him to do evil to himself, as well as good ? Whence come the many miseries else, sickness, pain, and death, which men are instruments and authors of to themselves ?

It may be thought more easy to answer one of these questions than the other, but the answer to both is really the same ; that mankind have ungoverned passions which they will gratify at any rate, as well to the injury of others, as in contradiction to known private interest : but that as there is no such thing as self-hatred, so neither is there any such thing as ill-will in one man towards another, emulation and resentment being away ; whereas there is plainly benevolence or good-will : there is no such thing as love of injustice, oppression, treachery, ingratitude ; but only eager desires after such and such external goods ; which, according to a very ancient observation, the most abandoned would choose to obtain by innocent means, if they were as easy, and as effectual to their end: that even emulation and resentment, by any one who will consider what these passions really are in nature [1], will be found nothing to the purpose of this objection: and that the principles and passions in the mind of man, which are distinct both from self-love and benevolence, primarily and most directly lead to right behaviour with regard to others as well as himself, and only secondarily and accidentally to what is evil. Thus, though men, to avoid the shame of one villany, are sometimes guilty of a greater, yet it is easy to see, that the original tendency of shame is to prevent the doing of shameful actions; and its leading men to conceal such actions when done, is only in consequence of their being done; i. e. of the passion's not having answered its first end.

209 If it be said, that there are persons in the world, who are in great measure without the natural affections towards their fellow-creatures: there are likewise instances of persons without the common natural affections to themselves: but the nature of man is not to be judged of by either of these, but by what appears in the common world, in the bulk of mankind.

I am afraid it would be thought very strange, if to confirm the truth of this account of human nature, and make out the justness of the foregoing comparison, it should be added, that, from what appears, men in fact as much and as often contradict that *part* of their nature which respects *self*, and which leads them to their *own private* good and happiness;

---

[1] Emulation is merely the desire and hope of equality with, or superiority over others, with whom we compare ourselves. There does not appear to be any *other grief* in the natural passion, but only *that want* which is implied in desire. However this may be so strong as to be the occasion of great *grief*. To desire the attainment of this equality or superiority by the *particular means* of others, being brought down to our own level, or below it, is, I think, the distinct notion of envy. From whence it is easy to see, that the real end, which the natural passion emulation, and which the unlawful one envy aims at, is exactly the same; namely, that equality or superiority: and consequently, that to do mischief is not the end of envy, but merely the means it makes use of to attain its end. As to resentment, see the eighth sermon.

as they contradict that *part* of it which respects *society*, and tends to *public* good : that there are as few persons, who attain the greatest satisfaction and enjoyment which they might attain in the present world ; as who do the greatest good to others which they might do ; nay, that there are as few who can be said really and in earnest to aim at one, as at the other.   Take a survey of mankind : the world in general, the good and bad, almost without exception, equally are agreed, that were religion out of the case, the happiness of the present life would consist in a manner wholly in riches, honours, sensual gratifications ; insomuch that one scarce hears a reflection made upon prudence, life, conduct, but upon this supposition.   Yet on the contrary, that persons in the greatest affluence of fortune are no happier than such as have only a competency ; that the cares and disappointments of ambition for the most part far exceed the satisfactions of it ; as also the miserable intervals of intemperance and excess, and the many untimely deaths occasioned by a dissolute course of life : these things are all seen, acknowledged, by every one acknowledged ; but are thought no objections against, though they expressly contradict, this universal principle, that the happiness of the present life consists in one or other of them   Whence is all this absurdity and contradiction?   Is not the middle way obvious?   Can any thing be more manifest, than that the happiness of life consists in these possessed and enjoyed only to a certain degree ; that to pursue them beyond this degree, is always attended with more inconvenience than advantage to a man's self, and often with extreme misery and unhappiness.   Whence then, I say, is all this absurdity and contradiction?   It is really the result of consideration in mankind, how they may become most easy to themselves, most free from care, and enjoy the chief happiness attainable in this world?   Or is it not manifestly owing either to this, that they have not cool and reasonable concern enough for themselves to consider wherein their chief happiness in the present life consists; or else, if they do consider it, that they will not act conformably to what is the result of that consideration: i. e. reasonable concern for themselves, or cool self-love is prevailed over by passion and appetite. So that from what appears, there is no ground to assert that those principles in the nature of man, which most directly lead to promote the good of our fellow-creatures, are more generally or in a greater degree violated, than those, which most directly lead us to promote our own private good and happiness.

210   The sum of the whole is plainly this. The nature of man considered in his single capacity, and with respect only to the present world, is adapted and leads him to attain the greatest happiness he can for himself in the present world. The nature of man considered in his public or social capacity leads him to a right behaviour in society, to that course of life which we call virtue. Men follow or obey their nature in both these capacities and respects to a certain degree, but not entirely : their actions do not come up to the whole of what their nature leads them to in either of these capacities or respects: and they often violate their nature in both, i. e. as they neglect the duties they owe to their fellow-creatures, to which their nature leads them; and are injurious, to which their nature is abhorrent; so there is a manifest negligence in men of their real happiness or interest in the present world, when that interest is inconsistent with a present gratification; for the sake of which they negligently, nay, even knowingly, are the authors and instruments of their own misery and ruin. Thus they are as often unjust to themselves as to others, and for the most part are equally so to both by the same actions.

SERMON II, III,

UPON THE NATURAL SUPREMACY OF CONSCIENCE.

For when the Gentiles, which have not the law, do by nature the things contained in the law, these, having not the law, are a law unto themselves.—Rom. ii. 14.

211 As speculative truth admits of different kinds of proof, so likewise moral obligations may be shewn by different methods. If the real nature of any creature leads him and is adapted to such and such purposes only, or more than to any other ; this is a reason to believe the author of that nature intended it for those purposes. Thus there is no doubt the eye was intended for us to see with. And the more complex any constitution is, and the greater variety of parts there are which thus tend to some one end, the stronger is the proof that such end was designed. However, when the inward frame of man is considered as any guide in morals, the utmost caution must be used that none make peculiarities in their own temper, or any thing which is the effect of particular customs, though observable in several, the standard of what is common to the species ; and above all, that the highest principle be not forgot or excluded, that to which belongs the adjustment and correction of all other inward movements and affections : which principle will of course have some influence, but which being in nature supreme, as shall now be shewn, ought to preside over and govern all the rest. The difficulty of rightly observing the two former cautions ; the appearance there is of some small diversity amongst mankind with respect to this faculty, with respect to their natural sense of moral good and evil ; and the attention necessary to survey with any exactness what passes within, have occasioned that it is not so much agreed what is the standard of the internal nature of man, as of his external form. Neither is this last exactly settled. Yet we understand one another when we speak of the shape of a human body : so likewise we do when we speak of the heart

and inward principles, how far soever the standard is from
212 being exact or precisely fixed. There is therefore ground for
an attempt of shewing men to themselves, of shewing them
what course of life and behaviour their real nature points out
and would lead them to. Now obligations of virtue shewn,
and motives to the practice of it enforced, from a review of
the nature of man, are to be considered as an appeal to
each particular person's heart and natural conscience: as the
external senses are appealed to for the proof of things cognizable by them. Since then our inward feelings, and the perceptions we receive from our external senses, are equally real;
to argue from the former to life and conduct is as little
liable to exception, as to argue from the latter to absolute
speculative truth. A man can as little doubt whether his eyes
were given him to see with, as he can doubt of the truth of the
science of *optics*, deduced from ocular experiments. And
allowing the inward feeling, shame; a man can as little doubt
whether it was given him to prevent his doing shameful actions,
as he can doubt whether his eyes were given him to guide his
steps. And as to these inward feelings themselves; that
they are real, that man has in his nature passions and
affections, can no more be questioned, than that he has
external senses. Neither can the former be wholly mistaken;
though to a certain degree liable to greater mistakes than the
latter.

213   There can be no doubt but that several propensions or
instincts, several principles in the heart of man, carry him to
society, and to contribute to the happiness of it, in a sense
and a manner in which no inward principle leads him to evil.
These principles, propensions, or instincts which lead him to
do good, are approved of by a certain faculty within, quite
distinct from these propensions themselves. All this hath
been fully made out in the foregoing discourse.

But it may be said, 'What is all this, though true, to the
purpose of virtue and religion? these require, not only that we

do good to others when we are led this way, by benevolence or reflection, happening to be stronger than other principles, passions, or appetites; but likewise that the *whole* character be formed upon thought and reflection; that *every* action be directed by some determinate rule, some other rule than the strength and prevalency of any principle or passion. What sign is there in our nature (for the inquiry is only about what is to be collected from thence) that this was intended by its Author? Or how does so various and fickle a temper as that of man appear adapted thereto? It may indeed be absurd and unnatural for men to act without any reflection; nay, without regard to that particular kind of reflection which you call conscience; because this does belong to our nature. For as there never was a man but who approved one place, prospect, building, before another: so it does not appear that there ever was a man who would not have approved an action of humanity rather than of cruelty; interest and passion being quite out of the case. But interest and passion do come in, and are often too strong for and prevail over reflection and conscience. Now as brutes have various instincts, by which they are carried on to the end the Author of their nature intended them for: is not man in the same condition; with this difference only, that to his instincts (i. e. appetites and passions) is added the principle of reflection or conscience? And as brutes act agreeably to their nature, in following that principle or particular instinct which for the present is strongest in them : does not man likewise act agreeably to his nature, or obey the law of his creation, by following that principle, be it passion or conscience, which for the present happens to be strongest in him? Thus different men are by their particular nature hurried on to pursue honour or riches or pleasure : there are also persons whose temper leads them in an un- common degree to kindness, compassion, doing good to their fellow-creatures : as there are others who are given to suspend their judgment, to weigh and consider things, and to act upon

thought and reflection. Let every one then quietly follow
his nature; as passion, reflection, appetite, the several parts
of it, happen to be strongest: but let not the man of virtue
take upon him to blame the ambitious, the covetous, the
dissolute; since these equally with him obey and follow
their nature. Thus, as in some cases we follow our nature
in doing the works *contained in the law,* so in other cases
we follow nature in doing contrary.'

214 Now all this licentious talk entirely goes upon a supposition, that men follow their nature in the same sense, in
violating the known rules of justice and honesty for the
sake of a present gratification, as they do in following those
rules when they have no temptation to the contrary. And
if this were true, that could not be so which St. Paul asserts,
that men are *by nature a law to themselves.* If by following
nature were meant only acting as we please, it would indeed
be ridiculous to speak of nature as any guide in morals:
nay the very mention of deviating from nature would be
absurd; and the mention of following it, when spoken by
way of distinction, would absolutely have no meaning. For
did ever any one act otherwise than as he pleased? And
yet the ancients speak of deviating from nature as vice; and
of following nature so much as a distinction, that according
to them the perfection of virtue consists therein. So that
language itself should teach people another sense to the words
following nature, than barely acting as we please. Let it
however be observed, that though the words *human nature*
are to be explained, yet the real question of this discourse
is not concerning the meaning of words, any other than
as the explanation of them may be needful to make out and
explain the assertion, that *every man is naturally a law to
himself,* that *every one may find within himself the rule of
right, and obligations to follow it.* This St. Paul affirms in the
words of the text, and this the foregoing objection really
denies by seeming to allow it. And the objection will be

fully answered, and the text before us explained, by observing that *nature* is considered in different views, and the word used in different senses; and by shewing in what view it is considered, and in what sense the word is used, when intended to express and signify that which is the guide of life, that by which men are a law to themselves. I say, the explanation of the term will be sufficient, because from thence it will appear, that in some senses of the word *nature* cannot be, but that in another sense it manifestly is, a law to us.

215   I. By nature is often meant no more than some principle in man, without regard either to the kind or degree of it. Thus the passion of anger, and the affection of parents to their children, would be called equally *natural*. And as the same person hath often contrary principles, which at the same time draw contrary ways, he may by the same action both follow and contradict his nature in this sense of the word; he may follow one passion and contradict another.

II. *Nature* is frequently spoken of as consisting in those passions which are strongest, and most influence the actions; which being vicious ones, mankind is in this sense naturally vicious, or vicious by nature. Thus St. Paul says of the Gentiles, *who were dead in trespasses and sins, and walked according to the spirit of disobedience, that they were by nature the children of wrath*[1]. They could be no otherwise *children of wrath* by nature, than they were vicious by nature.

Here then are two different senses of the word *nature*, in neither of which men can at all be said to be a law to themselves. They are mentioned only to be excluded; to prevent their being confounded, as the latter is in the objection, with another sense of it, which is now to be inquired after and explained.

216   III. The apostle asserts, that the Gentiles *do by NATURE the things contained in the law*. Nature is indeed here put by way of distinction from revelation, but yet it is not a mere

[1] Ephes. ii. 3.

negative. He intends to express more than that by which they *did not*, that by which they *did* the works of the law; namely, by *nature*. It is plain the meaning of the word is not the same in this passage as in the former, where it is spoken of as evil; for in this latter it is spoken of as good; as that by which they acted, or might have acted virtuously. What that is in man by which he is *naturally a law to himself*, is explained in the following words: *Which shew the work of the law written in their hearts, their consciences also bearing witness, and their thoughts the mean while accusing or else excusing one another.* If there be a distinction to be made between the *works written in their hearts*, and the *witness of conscience*; by the former must be meant the natural disposition to kindness and compassion, to do what is of good report, to which this apostle often refers: that part of the nature of man, treated of in the foregoing discourse, which with very little reflection and of course leads him to society, and by means of which he naturally acts a just and good part in it, unless other passions or interest lead him astray. Yet since other passions, and regards to private interest, which lead us (though indirectly, yet they lead us) astray, are themselves in a degree equally natural, and often most prevalent; and since we have no method of seeing the particular degrees in which one or the other is placed in us by nature; it is plain the former, considered merely as natural, good and right as they are, can no more be a law to us than the latter. But there is a superior principle of reflection or conscience in every man, which distinguishes between the internal principles of his heart, as well as his external actions: which passes judgment upon himself and them; pronounces determinately some actions to be in themselves just, right, good; others to be in themselves evil, wrong, unjust: which, without being consulted, without being advised with, magisterially exerts itself, and approves or condemns him the doer of them accordingly: and which, if not forcibly stopped, naturally and always of course goes on to anticipate a higher and more effectual sentence, which shall hereafter second and affirm its own. But this part of the office of conscience is beyond my present design explicitly to consider. It is by this faculty, natural to man, that he is a moral agent, that he is a law to himself: but this faculty, I say, not to be considered merely as a principle in his heart, which is to have some influence as well as others; but considered as a faculty in kind and in nature supreme over all others, and which bears its own authority of being so.

217   This *prerogative*, this *natural supremacy*, of the faculty which surveys, approves or disapproves the several affections of our mind and actions of our lives, being that by which men *are a law to themselves*, their conformity or disobedience to which law of our nature renders their actions, in the highest and most proper sense, natural or unnatural; it is fit it be further explained to you: and I hope it will be so, if you will attend to the following reflections.

Man may act according to that principle or inclination which for the present happens to be strongest, and yet act in a way disproportionate to, and violate his real proper nature. Suppose a brute creature by any bait to be allured into a snare, by which he is destroyed. He plainly followed the bent of his nature, leading him to gratify his appetite: there is an entire correspondence between his whole nature and such an action: such action therefore is natural. But suppose a man, foreseeing the same danger of certain ruin, should rush into it for the sake of a present gratification; he in this instance would follow his strongest desire, as did the brute creature: but there would be as manifest a disproportion, between the nature of a man and such an action, as between the meanest work of art and the skill of the greatest master in that art: which disproportion arises, not from considering the action singly in *itself*, or in its *consequences*; but from *comparison* of it with the nature of the agent. And since such an action is utterly disproportionate to the nature of man, it is in the strictest and most proper sense unnatural; this word expressing that disproportion. Therefore instead of the words *disproportionate to his nature*, the word *unnatural* may now be put; this being more familiar to us : but let it be observed, that it stands for the same thing precisely.

Now what is it which renders such a rash action unnatural? Is it that he went against the principle of reasonable and cool self-love, considered *merely* as a part of his nature? No : for if he had acted the contrary way, he would equally have gone against a principle, or part of his nature, namely, passion or appetite. But to deny a present appetite, from foresight that the gratification of it would end in immediate ruin or extreme misery, is by no means an unnatural action : whereas to contradict or go against cool self-love for the sake of such gratification, is so in the instance before us. Such an action then being unnatural; and its being so not arising from a man's going against a principle or desire barely, nor in going against that principle or desire which happens for the present to be strongest; it necessarily follows, that there must be some other difference or distinction to be made between these two principles, passion and cool self-love, than what I have yet taken notice of. And this difference, not being a difference in strength or degree, I call a difference in *nature* and in *kind*. And since, in the instance still before us, if passion prevails over self-love, the consequent action is unnatural; but if self-love prevails over passion, the action is natural : it is manifest that self-love is in human nature a superior principle to passion. This may be contradicted without violating that nature; but the former cannot. So that, if we will act conformably to the economy of man's nature, reasonable self-love must govern. Thus, without particular consideration of conscience, we may have a clear

conception of the *superior nature* of one inward principle
to another ; and see that there really is this natural superiority,
quite distinct from degrees of strength and prevalency.

218   Let us now take a view of the nature of man, as consisting partly of various appetites, passions, affections, and partly
of the principle of reflection or conscience; leaving quite out
all consideration of the different degrees of strength, in which
either of them prevail, and it will further appear that there
is this natural superiority of one inward principle to another,
and that it is even part of the idea of reflection or conscience.

Passion or appetite implies a direct simple tendency towards
such and such objects, without distinction of the means by
which they are to be obtained.   Consequently it will often
happen there will be a desire of particular objects, in cases
where they cannot be obtained without manifest injury to
others.   Reflection or conscience comes in, and disapproves
the pursuit of them in these circumstances; but the desire
remains.   Which is to be obeyed, appetite or reflection?
Cannot this question be answered, from the economy and
constitution of human nature merely, without saying which
is strongest?   Or need this at all come into consideration?
Would not the question be *intelligibly* and fully answered
by saying, that the principle of reflection or conscience being
compared with the various appetites, passions, and affections
in men, the former is manifestly superior and chief, without
regard to strength?   And how often soever the latter happens
to prevail, it is mere *usurpation* : the former remains in nature
and in kind its superior; and every instance of such prevalence of the latter is an instance of breaking in upon and
violation of the constitution of man.

219   All this is no more than the distinction, which every body
is acquainted with, between *mere power* and *authority* : only
instead of being intended to express the difference between
what is possible, and what is lawful in civil government ; here
it has been shewn applicable to the several principles in the

mind of man. Thus that principle, by which we survey, and either approve or disapprove our own heart, temper, and actions, is not only to be considered as what is in its turn to have some influence ; which may be said of every passion, of the lowest appetites ; but likewise as being superior ; as from its very nature manifestly claiming superiority over all others : insomuch that you cannot form a notion of this faculty, conscience, without taking in judgment, direction, superintendency. This is a constituent part of the idea, that is, of the faculty itself : and, to preside and govern, from the very economy and constitution of man, belongs to it. Had it strength, as it had right ; had it power, as it had manifest authority, it would absolutely govern the world.

This gives us a further view of the nature of man ; shews us what course of life we were made for : not only that our real nature leads us to be influenced in some degree by reflection and conscience ; but likewise in what degree we are to be influenced by it, if we will fall in with, and act agreeably to the constitution of our nature : that this faculty was placed within to be our proper governor ; to direct and regulate all under principles, passions, and motives of action. This is its right and office : thus sacred is its authority. And how often soever men violate and rebelliously refuse to submit to it, for supposed interest which they cannot otherwise obtain, or for the sake of passion which they cannot otherwise gratify ; this makes no alteration as to the *natural right* and *office* of conscience.

220 Let us now turn this whole matter another way, and suppose there was no such thing at all as this natural supremacy of conscience ; that there was no distinction to be made between one inward principle and another, but only that of strength ; and see what would be the consequence.

Consider then what is the latitude and compass of the actions of man with regard to himself, his fellow-creatures, and the Supreme Being ? What are their bounds, besides that of our natural power ? With respect to the two first, they are plainly no other than these : no man seeks misery as such for himself; and no one unprovoked does mischief to another for its own sake.   For in every degree within these bounds, mankind knowingly from passion or wantonness bring ruin and misery upon themselves and others.   And impiety and profaneness, I mean, what every one would call so who believes the being of God, have absolutely no bounds at all. Men blaspheme the Author of nature, formally and in words renounce their allegiance to their Creator.   Put an instance then with respect to any one of these three.   Though we should suppose profane swearing, and in general that kind of impiety now mentioned, to mean nothing, yet it implies wanton disregard and irreverence towards an infinite Being, our Creator ; and is this as suitable to the nature of man, as reverence and dutiful submission of heart towards that Almighty Being?   Or suppose a man guilty of parricide, with all the circumstances of cruelty which such an action can admit of.   This action is done in consequence of its principle being for the present strongest ; and if there be no difference between inward principles, but only that of strength ; the strength being given, you have the whole nature of the man given, so far as it relates to this matter.   The action plainly corresponds to the principle, the principle being in that degree of strength it was ; it therefore corresponds to the whole nature of the man.   Upon comparing the action and the whole nature, there arises no disproportion, there appears no unsuitableness between them.   Thus the *murder of a father* and the *nature of man* correspond to each other, as the same nature and an act of filial duty.   If there be no difference between inward principles, but only that of strength ; we can make no distinction between these two actions considered as the actions of such a creature ; but in our coolest hours must approve or disapprove them equally : than which nothing can be reduced to a greater absurdity.

SERMON III.

221 THE natural supremacy of reflection or conscience being thus established; we may from it form a distinct notion of what is meant by *human nature*, when virtue is said to consist in following it, and vice in deviating from it.

As the idea of a civil constitution implies in it united strength, various subordinations, under one direction, that of the supreme authority; the different strength of each particular member of the society not coming into the idea; whereas, if you leave out the subordination, the union, and the one direction, you destroy and lose it: so reason, several appetites, passions, and affections, prevailing in different degrees of strength, is not *that* idea or notion of *human nature*; but *that nature* consists in these several principles considered as having a natural respect to each other, in the several passions being naturally subordinate to the one superior principle of reflection or conscience. Every bias, instinct, propension within, is a natural part of our nature, but not the whole: add to these the superior faculty, whose office it is to adjust, manage, and preside over them, and take in this its natural superiority, and you complete the idea of human nature. And as in civil government the constitution is broken in upon, and violated by power and strength prevailing over authority; so the constitution of man is broken in upon and violated by the lower faculties or principles within prevailing over that which is in its nature supreme over them all. Thus, when it is said by ancient writers, that tortures and death are not so contrary to human nature as injustice; by this to be sure is not meant, that the aversion to the former in mankind is less strong and prevalent than their aversion to the latter: but that the former is only contrary to our nature considered in a partial view, and which takes in only the lowest part of it, that which we have in common with the brutes; whereas the latter is contrary to our nature, considered in a higher sense, as a system and constitution contrary to the whole economy of man [1].

222   And from all these things put together, nothing can be more evident, than that, exclusive of revelation, man cannot be considered as a creature left by his Maker to act at random, and live at large up to the extent of his natural power, as passion, humour, wilfulness, happen to carry him ; which is the condition brute creatures are in : but that *from his make, constitution, or nature, he is in the strictest and most proper sense a law to himself.* He hath the rule of right within : what is wanting is only that he honestly attends to it.

[1] Every man in his physical nature is one individual single agent. He has likewise properties and principles, each of which may be considered separately, and without regard to the respects which they have to each other. Neither of these are the nature we are taking a view of. But it is the inward frame of man considered as a *system* or *constitution* : whose several parts are united, not by a physical principle of individuation, but by the respects they have to each other ; the chief of which is the subjection which the appetites, passions, and particular affections have to the one supreme principle of reflection or conscience. The system or constitution is formed by and consists in these respects and this subjection. Thus the body is a *system* or *constitution*: so is a tree: so is every machine. Consider all the several parts of a tree without the natural respects they have to each other, and you have not at all the idea of a tree; but add these respects, and this gives you the idea The body may be impaired by sickness, a tree may decay, a machine be out of order, and yet the system and constitution of them not totally dissolved. There is plainly somewhat which answers to all this in the moral constitution of man. Whoever will consider his own nature, will see that the several appetites, passions, and particular affections, have different respects among themselves. They are restraints upon, and are in a proportion to each other. This proportion is just and perfect, when all those under principles are perfectly coincident with conscience, so far as their nature permits, and in all cases under its absolute and entire direction. The least excess or defect, the least alteration of the due proportions amongst themselves, or of their coincidence with conscience, though not proceeding into action, is some degree of disorder in the moral constitution. But perfection, though plainly intelligible and unsupposable, was never attained by any man. If the higher principle of reflection maintains its place, and as much as it can corrects that disorder, and hinders it from breaking out into action, this is all that can be expected in such a creature as man. And though the appetites and passions have not their exact due proportion to each other; though they often strive for mastery with judgment or reflection : yet, since the superiority of this principle to all others is the chief respect which forms the constitution, so far as this superiority is maintained, the character, the man, is good, worthy, virtuous.

The inquiries which have been made by men of leisure after some general rule, the conformity to, or disagreement from which, should denominate our actions good or evil, are in many respects of great service. Yet let any plain honest man, before he engages in any course of action, ask himself, Is this I am going about right, or is it wrong? Is it good, or is it evil? I do not in the least doubt, but that this question would be answered agreeably to truth and virtue, by almost any fair man in almost any circumstance. Neither do there appear any cases which look like exceptions to this; but those of superstition, and of partiality to ourselves. Superstition may perhaps be somewhat of an exception: but partiality to ourselves is not; this being itself dishonesty. For a man to judge that to be the equitable, the moderate, the right part for him to act, which he would see to be hard, unjust, oppressive in another; this is plain vice, and can proceed only from great unfairness of mind.

223 But allowing that mankind hath the rule of right within himself, yet it may be asked, 'What obligations are we under to attend to and follow it?' I answer: it has been proved that man by his nature is a law to himself, without the particular distinct consideration of the positive sanctions of that law; the rewards and punishments which we feel, and those which from the light of reason we have ground to believe, are annexed to it. The question then carries its own answer along with it. Your obligation to obey this law, is its being the law of your nature. That your conscience approves of and attests to such a course of action, is itself alone an obligation. Conscience does not only offer itself to shew us the way we should walk in, but it likewise carries its own authority with it, that it is our natural guide; the guide assigned us by the Author of our nature: it therefore belongs to our condition of being, it is our duty to walk in that path, and follow this guide, without looking about to see whether we may not possibly forsake them with impunity.

224   However, let us hear what is to be said against obeying this law of our nature.   And the sum is no more than this : ' Why should we be concerned about any thing out of and beyond ourselves ?   If we do find within ourselves regards to others, and restraints of we know not how many different kinds ; yet these being embarrassments, and hindering us from going the nearest way to our own good, why should we not endeavour to suppress and get over them ? '

Thus people go on with words, which, when applied to human nature, and the condition in which it is placed in this world, have really no meaning.   For does not all this kind of talk go upon supposition, that our happiness in this world consists in somewhat quite distinct from regard to others ; and that it is the privilege of vice to be without restraint or confinement?   Whereas, on the contrary, the enjoyments, in a manner all the common enjoyments of life, even the pleasures of vice, depend upon these regards of one kind or another to our fellow-creatures.   Throw off all regards to others, and we should be quite indifferent to infamy and to honour; there could be no such thing at all as ambition; and scarce any such thing as covetousness ; for we should likewise be equally indifferent to the disgrace of poverty, the several neglects and kinds of contempt which accompany this state ; and to the reputation of riches, the regard and respect they usually procure.   Neither is restraint by any means peculiar to one course of life ; but our very nature, exclusive of conscience and our condition, lays us under an absolute necessity of it. We cannot gain any end whatever without being confined to the proper means, which is often the most painful and uneasy confinement.   And in numberless instances a present appetite cannot be gratified without such apparent and immediate ruin and misery, that the most dissolute man in the world chooses to forego the pleasure, rather than endure the pain.

225   Is the meaning then, to indulge those regards to our fellow-creatures, and submit to those restraints, which upon the whole are attended with more satisfaction than uneasiness, and get over only those which bring more uneasiness and inconvenience than satisfaction? 'Doubtless this was our meaning.' You have changed sides then. Keep to this; be consistent with yourselves; and you and the men of virtue are *in general* perfectly agreed. But let us take care and avoid mistakes. Let it not be taken for granted that the temper of envy, rage, resentment, yields greater delight than meekness, forgiveness, compassion, and good-will; especially when it is acknowledged that rage, envy, resentment, are in themselves mere misery; and the satisfaction arising from the indulgence of them is little more than relief from that misery; whereas the temper of compassion and benevolence is itself delightful; and the indulgence of it, by doing good, affords new positive delight and enjoyment. Let it not be taken for granted, that the satisfaction arising from the reputation of riches and power, however obtained, and from the respect paid to them, is greater than the satisfaction arising from the reputation of justice, honesty, charity, and the esteem which is universally acknowledged to be their due. And if it be doubtful which of these satisfactions is the greatest, as there are persons who think neither of them very considerable, yet there can be no doubt concerning ambition and covetousness, virtue and a good mind, considered in themselves, and as leading to different courses of life; there can, I say, be no doubt, which temper and which course is attended with most peace and tranquillity of mind, which with most perplexity, vexation, and inconvenience. And both the virtues and vices which have been now mentioned, do in a manner equally imply in them regards of one kind or another to our fellow-creatures. And with respect to restraint and confinement: whoever will consider the restraints from fear and shame, the dissimulation, mean arts of concealment, servile compliances, one or other of which belong to almost every course of vice, will soon be convinced that the man of virtue is by no means upon a disadvantage in this respect. How many instances are there in which men feel and own and cry aloud under the chains of vice with which they are enthralled, and which yet they will not shake off! How many instances, in which persons manifestly go through more pains and self-denial to gratify a vicious passion, than would have been necessary to the conquest of it! To this is to be added, that when virtue is become habitual, when the temper of it is acquired, what was before confinement ceases to be so, by becoming choice and delight. Whatever restraint and guard upon ourselves may be needful to unlearn any unnatural distortion or odd gesture; yet, in all propriety of speech, natural behaviour must be the most easy and unrestrained. It is manifest that, in the common course of life, there is seldom any inconsistency between our duty and what is *called* interest: it is much seldomer that there is an inconsistency between duty and what is really our present interest; meaning by interest, happiness and satisfaction. Self-love then, though confined to the interest of the present world, does in general perfectly coincide with virtue; and leads us to one and the same course of life. But, whatever exceptions there are to this, which are much fewer than they are commonly thought, all shall be set right at the final distribution of things. It is a manifest absurdity to suppose evil prevailing finally over good, under the conduct and administration of a perfect mind.

226 The whole argument, which I have been now insisting upon, may be thus summed up, and given you in one view. The nature of man is adapted to some course of action or other. Upon comparing some actions with this nature, they appear suitable and correspondent to it: from comparison of other actions with the same nature, there arises to our view some unsuitableness or disproportion. The correspondence of actions to the nature of the agent renders them natural: their disproportion to it, unnatural. That an action is correspondent to the nature of the agent, does not arise

from its being agreeable to the principle which happens to be the strongest: for it may be so, and yet be quite disproportionate to the nature of the agent. The correspondence therefore, or disproportion, arises from somewhat else. This can be nothing but a difference in nature and kind, altogether distinct from strength, between the inward principles. Some then are in nature and kind superior to others. And the correspondence arises from the action being conformable to the higher principle; and the unsuitableness from its being contrary to it. Reasonable self-love and conscience are the chief or superior principles in the nature of man : because an action may be suitable to this nature, though all other principles be violated; but becomes unsuitable, if either of those are. Conscience and self-love, if we understand our true happiness, always lead us the same way. Duty and interest are perfectly coincident; for the most part in this world, but entirely and in every instance if we take in the future, and the whole; this being implied in the notion of a good and perfect administration of things. Thus they who have been so wise in their generation as to regard only their own supposed interest, at the expense and to the injury of others, shall at last find, that he who has given up all the advantages of the present world, rather than violate his conscience and the relations of life, has infinitely better provided for himself, and secured his own interest and happiness.

SERMONS XI, XII.

UPON THE LOVE OF OUR NEIGHBOUR.

And if there be any other commandment, it is briefly comprehended in this saying, namely, Thou shalt love thy neighbour as thyself.—ROM. xiii. 9.

227 IT is commonly observed, that there is a disposition in men to complain of the viciousness and corruption of the age in which they live, as greater than that of former ones; which

is usually followed with this further observation, that mankind
has been in that respect much the same in all times. Now, not
to determine whether this last be not contradicted by the
accounts of history; thus much can scarce be doubted, that
vice and folly takes different turns, and some particular kinds
of it are more open and avowed in some ages than in others;
and, I suppose, it may be spoken of as very much the distinction of the present to profess a contracted spirit, and greater
regards to self-interest, than appears to have been done formerly. Upon this account it seems worth while to inquire,
whether private interest is likely to be promoted in proportion to the degree in which self-love engrosses us, and prevails over all other principles; *or whether the contracted affection
may not possibly be so prevalent as to disappoint itself, and even
contradict its own end, private good.*

And since, further, there is generally thought to be some
peculiar kind of contrariety between self-love and the love of
our neighbour, between the pursuit of public and of private
good; insomuch that when you are recommending one of these,
you are supposed to be speaking against the other; and from
hence arises a secret prejudice against, and frequently open
scorn of all talk of public spirit, and real good-will to our
fellow-creatures; it will be necessary to *inquire what respect
benevolence hath to self-love, and the pursuit of private interest
to the pursuit of public*: or whether there be any thing of that
peculiar inconsistence and contrariety between them, over and
above what there is between self-love and other passions and
particular affections, and their respective pursuits.

These inquiries, it is hoped, may be favourably attended
to: for there shall be all possible concessions made to the
favourite passion, which hath so much allowed to it, and whose
cause is so universally pleaded: it shall be treated with the
utmost tenderness and concern for its interests.

228   In order to this, as well as to determine the forementioned
questions, it will be necessary to *consider the nature, the object,*

and end of that self-love, as distinguished from other principles
or affections in the mind, and their respective objects.

Every man hath a general desire of his own happiness; and
likewise a variety of particular affections, passions, and appetites to particular external objects. The former proceeds
from, or is self-love; and seems inseparable from all sensible
creatures, who can reflect upon themselves and their own
interest or happiness, so as to have that interest an object to
their minds: what is to be said of the latter is, that they
proceed from, or together make up that particular nature,
according to which man is made. The object the former
pursues it somewhat internal, our own happiness, enjoyment,
satisfaction; whether we have, or have not, a distinct particular
perception what it is, or wherein it consists: the objects of the
latter are this or that particular external thing, which the affections tend towards, and of which it hath always a particular
idea or perception. The principle we call self-love never seeks
any thing external for the sake of the thing, but only as a means
of happiness or good: particular affections rest in the external
things themselves. One belongs to man as a reasonable
creature reflecting upon his own interest or happiness. The
other, though quite distinct from reason, are as much a part of
human nature.

229   That all particular appetites and passions are towards *external*
things themselves, distinct from the *pleasure arising from them*,
is manifested from hence; that there could not be this pleasure, were it not for that prior suitableness between the object
and the passion: there could be no enjoyment or delight from
one thing more than another, from eating food more than from
swallowing a stone, if there were not an affection or appetite to
one thing more than another.

Every particular affection, even the love of our neighbour, is
as really our own affection, as self-love; and the pleasure
arising from its gratification is as much my own pleasure, as
the pleasure self-love would have, from knowing I myself

should be happy some time hence, would be my own pleasure. And if, because every particular affection is a man's own, and the pleasure arising from its gratification his own pleasure, or pleasure to himself, such particular affection must be called self-love; according to this way of speaking, no creature whatever can possibly act but merely from self-love; and every action and every affection whatever is to be resolved up into this one principle. But then this is not the language of mankind: or if it were, we should want words to express the difference, between the principle of an action, proceeding from cool consideration that it will be to my own advantage; and an action, suppose of revenge, or of friendship, by which a man runs upon certain ruin, to do evil or good to another. It is manifest the principles of these actions are totally different, and so want different words to be distinguished by: all that they agree in is, that they both proceed from, and are done to gratify an inclination in a man's self. But the principle or inclination in one case is self-love; in the other, hatred or love of another. There is then a distinction between the cool principle of self-love, or general desire of our own happiness, as one part of our nature, and one principle of action; and the particular affections towards particular external objects, as another part of our nature, and another•principle of action. How much soever therefore is to be allowed to self-love, yet it cannot be allowed to be the whole of our inward constitution; because, you see, there are other parts or principles which come into it.

230   Further, private happiness or good is all which self-love can make us desire, or be concerned about: in having this consists its gratification: it is an affection to ourselves; a regard to our own interest, happiness, and private good: and in the proportion a man hath this, he is interested, or a lover of himself. Let this be kept in mind; because there is commonly, as I shall presently have occasion to observe, another sense put upon these words. On the other hand, particular affections

tend towards particular external things : these are their objects : having these is their end : in this consists their gratification : no matter whether it be, or be not, upon the whole, our interest or happiness. An action done from the former of these principles is called an interested action. An action proceeding from any of the latter has its denomination of passionate, ambitious, friendly, revengeful, or any other, from the particular appetite or affection from which it proceeds. Thus self-love as one part of human nature, and the several particular principles as the other part, are, themselves, their objects and ends, stated and shewn.

231 From hence it will be easy to see, how far, and in what ways, each of these can contribute and be subservient to the private good of the individual. Happiness does not consist in self-love. The desire of happiness is no more the thing itself, than the desire of riches is the possession or enjoyment of them. People may love themselves with the most entire and unbounded affection, and yet be extremely miserable. Neither can self-love any way help them out, but by setting them on work to get rid of the causes of their misery, to gain or make use of those objects.which are by nature adapted to afford satisfaction. Happiness or satisfaction consists only in the enjoyment of those objects, which are by nature suited to our several particular appetites, passions, and affections. So that if self-love wholly engrosses us, and leaves no room for any other principle, there can be absolutely no such thing at all as happiness, or enjoyment of any kind whatever ; since happiness consists in the gratification of particular passions, which supposes the having of them. Self-love then does not constitute *this* or *that* to be our interest or good ; but, our interest or good being constituted by nature and supposed, self-love only puts us upon obtaining and securing it. Therefore, if it be possible, that self-love may prevail and exert itself in a degree or manner which is not subservient to this end ; then it will not follow, that our interest will be promoted in proportion to the degree in which that principle engrosses us, and prevails over others. Nay further, the private and contracted affection, when it is not subservient to this end, private good, may, for any thing that appears, have a direct contrary tendency and effect. And if we will consider the matter, we shall see that it often really has. *Disengagement* is absolutely necessary to enjoyment: and a person may have so steady and fixed an eye upon his own interest, whatever he places it in, as may hinder him from *attending* to many gratifications within his reach, which others have their minds *free* and *open* to. Over-fondness for a child is not generally thought to be for its advantage : and, if there be any guess to be made from appearances, surely that character we call selfish is not the most promising for happiness. Such a temper may plainly be, and exert itself in a degree and manner which may give unnecessary and useless solicitude and anxiety, in a degree and manner which may prevent obtaining the means and materials of enjoyment, as well as the making use of them. Immoderate self-love does very ill consult its own interest: and, how much soever a paradox it may appear, it is certainly true, that even from self-love we should endeavour to get over all inordinate regard to, and consideration of ourselves. Every one of our passions and affections hath its natural stint and bound, which may easily be exceeded ; whereas our enjoyments can possibly be but in a determinate measure and degree. Therefore such excess of the affection, since it cannot procure any enjoyment, must in all cases be useless ; but is generally attended with inconveniences, and often is downright pain and misery. This holds as much with regard to self-love as to all other affections. The natural degree of it, so far as it sets us on work to gain and make use of the materials of satisfaction, may be to our real advantage ; but beyond or besides this, it is in several respects an inconvenience and disadvantage. Thus it appears, that private interest is so far from being likely to be promoted in proportion to the degree in which self-love engrosses us, and prevails over all other principles ; that *the contracted affection may be so prevalent as to disappoint itself, and even contradict its own end, private good.*

232 'But who, except the most sordidly covetous, ever thought there was any rivalship between the love of greatness, honour, power, or between sensual appetites, and self-love ? No, there is a perfect harmony between them. It is by means of these particular appetites and affections that self-love is gratified in enjoyment, happiness, and satisfaction. The competition and rivalship is between self-love and the love of our neighbour : that affection which leads us out of ourselves, makes us regardless of our own interest, and substitute that of another in its stead.' Whether then there be any peculiar competition and contrariety in this case, shall now be considered.

Self-love and interestedness was stated to consist in or be an affection to ourselves, a regard to our own private good : it is therefore distinct from benevolence, which is an affection to the good of our fellow-creatures. But that benevolence is distinct from, that is, not the same thing with self-love, is no reason for its being looked upon with any peculiar suspicion ; because every principle whatever, by means of which self-love is gratified, is distinct from it : and all things which are distinct from each other are equally so. A man has an affection or aversion to another : that one of these tends to, and is gratified by doing good, that the other tends to, and is gratified by doing harm, does not in the least alter the respect which either one or the other of these inward feelings has to self-love. We use the word *property* so as to exclude any other persons having an interest in that of which we say a particular man has the property. And we often use the word *selfish* so as to exclude in the same manner all regards to the good of others. But the cases are not parallel : for though that exclusion is really part of the idea of property; yet such positive exclusion, or bringing this peculiar disregard to the good of others into the idea of self-love, is in reality adding to the idea, or changing

it from what it was before stated to consist in, namely, in an
233 affection to ourselves [1].   This being the whole idea of self-love,
it can no otherwise exclude good-will or love of others, than
merely by not including it, no otherwise, than it excludes love
of arts or reputation, or of any thing else.   Neither on the
other hand does benevolence, any more than love of arts or of
reputation, exclude self-love.   Love of our neighbour then has
just the same respect to, is no more distant from, self-love,
than hatred of our neighbour, or than love or hatred of any
thing else.   Thus the principles, from which men rush upon
certain ruin for the destruction of an enemy, and for the
preservation of a friend, have the same respect to the private
affection, and are equally interested, or equally disinterested :
and it is of no avail, whether they are said to be one or the
other.   Therefore to those who are shocked to hear virtue
spoken of as disinterested, it may be allowed that it is indeed
absurd to speak thus of it; unless hatred, several particular
instances of vice, and all the common affections and aversions
in mankind, are acknowledged to be disinterested too.   Is
there any less inconsistence, between the love of inanimate
things, or of creatures merely sensitive, and self-love; than
between self-love and the love of our neighbour?   Is desire of
and delight in the happiness of another any more a diminution
of self-love, than desire of and delight in the esteem of another?
They are both equally desire of and delight in somewhat
external to ourselves : either both or neither are so.   The
object of self-love is expressed in the term self : and every
appetite of sense, and every particular affection of the heart,
are equally interested or disinterested, because the objects
of them all are equally self or somewhat else.   Whatever
ridicule therefore the mention of a disinterested principle or
action may be supposed to lie open to, must, upon the matter
being thus stated, relate to ambition, and every appetite and
particular affection, as much as to benevolence.   And indeed

[1] P. 228.

all the ridicule, and all the grave perplexity, of which this subject hath had its full share, is merely from words. The most intelligible way of speaking of it seems to be this : that self-love and the actions done in consequence of it (for these will presently appear to be the same as to this question) are interested ; that particular affections towards external objects, and the actions done in consequence of those affections, are not so. But every one is at liberty to use words as he pleases. All that is here insisted upon is, that ambition, revenge, benevolence, all particular passions whatever, and the actions they produce, are equally interested or disinterested.

234   Thus it appears that there is no peculiar contrariety between self-love and benevolence ; no greater competition between these, than between any other particular affections and self-love. This relates to the affections themselves. Let us now see whether there be any peculiar contrariety between the respective courses of life which these affections lead to ; whether there be any greater competition between the pursuit of private and of public good, than between any other particular pursuits and that of private good.

There seems no other reason to suspect that there is any such peculiar contrariety, but only that the course of action which benevolence leads to, has a more direct tendency to promote the good of others, than that course of action which love of reputation, suppose, or any other particular affection leads to. But that any affection tends to the happiness of another, does not hinder its tending to one's own happiness too. That others enjoy the benefit of the air and the light of the sun, does not hinder but that these are as much one's own private advantage now, as they would be if we had the property of them exclusive of all others. So a pursuit which tends to promote the good of another, yet may have as great tendency to promote private interest, as a pursuit which does not tend to the good of another at all, or which is mischievous to him. All particular affections whatever, resentment,

benevolence, love of arts, equally lead to a course of action for
their own gratification, i. e. the gratification of ourselves ; and
the gratification of each gives delight : so far then it is manifest
they have all the same respect to private interest.   Now take
into consideration further, concerning these three pursuits,
that the end of the first is the harm, of the second, the good
of another, of the last, somewhat indifferent ; and is there any
necessity, that these additional considerations should alter the
respect, which we before saw these three pursuits had to private
interest ; or render any one of them less conducive to it, than
any other?   Thus one man's affection is to honour as his end ;
in order to obtain which he thinks no pains too great.   Suppose
another, with such a singularity of mind, as to have the same
affection to public good as his end, which he endeavours with
the same labour to obtain.   In case of success, surely the man
of benevolence hath as great enjoyment as the man of
ambition ; they both equally having the end their affections, in
the same degree, tended to : but in case of disappointment,
the benevolent man has clearly the advantage ; since endeavouring to do good considered as a virtuous pursuit, is gratified
by its own consciousness, i. e. is in a degree its own reward.

235   And as to these two, or benevolence and any other particular
passions whatever, considered in a further view, as forming
a general temper, which more or less disposes us for enjoyment
of all the common blessings of life, distinct from their own
gratification : is benevolence less the temper of tranquillity and
freedom than ambition or covetousness?   Does the benevolent man appear less easy with himself, from his love to his
neighbour?   Does he less relish his being?   Is there any
peculiar gloom seated on his face?   Is his mind less open
to entertainment, to any particular gratification ?   Nothing is
more manifest, than that being in good humour, which is
benevolence whilst it lasts, is itself the temper of satisfaction
and enjoyment.

Suppose then a man sitting down to consider how he might

become most easy to himself, and attain the greatest pleasure
he could ; all that which is his real natural happiness. This
can only consist in the enjoyment of those objects, which are
by nature adapted to our several faculties. These particular
enjoyments make up the sum total of our happiness : and they
are supposed to arise from riches, honours, and the gratification of sensual appetites : be it so : yet none profess themselves so completely happy in these enjoyments, but that there
is room left in the mind for others, if they were presented to
them : nay, these, as much as they engage us, are not thought
so high, but that human nature is capable even of greater.
Now there have been persons in all ages, who have professed
that they found satisfaction in the exercise of charity, in the
love of their neighbour, in endeavouring to promote the happiness of all they had to do with, and in the pursuit of what is
just and right and good, as the general bent of their mind, and
end of their life ; and that doing an action of baseness or
cruelty, would be as great violence to *their* self, as much
breaking in upon their nature, as any external force. Persons
of this character would add, if they might be heard, that they
consider themselves as acting in the view of an infinite Being,
who is in a much higher sense the object of reverence and of
love, than all the world besides ; and therefore they could
have no more enjoyment from a wicked action done under his
eye, than the persons to whom they are making their apology
could, if all mankind were the spectators of it ; and that the
satisfaction of approving themselves to his unerring judgment,
to whom they thus refer all their actions, is a more continued
settled satisfaction than any this world can afford ; as also that
they have, no less than others, a mind free and open to all the
common innocent gratifications of it, such as they are. And
if we go no further, does there appear any absurdity in this ?
Will any one take upon him to say, that a man cannot find his
account in this general course of life, as much as in the most
unbounded ambition, and the excesses of pleasure ? Or that

such a person has not consulted so well for himself, for the satisfaction and peace of his own mind, as the ambitious or dissolute man ?　And though the consideration, that God himself will in the end justify their taste, and support their cause, is not formally to be insisted upon here ; yet thus much comes in, that all enjoyments whatever are much more clear and unmixed from the assurance that they will end well.　Is it certain then that there is nothing in these pretensions to happiness ? especially when there are not wanting persons, who have supported themselves with satisfactions of this kind in sickness, poverty, disgrace, and in the very pangs of death ; whereas it is manifest all other enjoyments fail in these circumstances.　This surely looks suspicious of having somewhat in it.　Self-love methinks should be alarmed.　May she not possibly pass over greater pleasures, than those she is so wholly taken up with ?

236　The short of the matter is no more than this.　Happiness consists in the gratification of certain affections, appetites, passions, with objects which are by nature adapted to them. Self-love may indeed set us on work to gratify these : but happiness or enjoyment has no immediate connection with self-love, but arises from such gratification alone.　Love of our neighbour is one of those affections.　This, considered as a *virtuous principle*, is gratified by a consciousness of *endeavouring* to promote the good of others ; but considered as a natural affection, its gratification consists in the actual accomplishment of this endeavour.　Now indulgence or gratification of this affection, whether in that consciousness or this accomplishment, has the same respect to interest, as indulgence of any other affection ; they equally proceed from or do not proceed from self-love, they equally include or equally exclude this principle.　Thus it appears, that *benevolence and the pursuit of public good hath at least as great respect to self-love and the pursuit of private good, as any other particular passions, and their respective pursuits.*

237　　Neither is covetousness, whether as a temper or pursuit, any exception to this. For if by covetousness is meant the desire and pursuit of riches for their owń sake, without any regard to, or consideration of, the uses of them ; this hath as little to do with self-love, as benevolence hath. But by this word is usually meant, not such madness and total distraction of mind, but immoderate affection to and pursuit of riches as possessions in order to some further end ; namely, satisfaction, interest, or good. This therefore is not a particular affection, or particular pursuit, but it is the general principle of self-love, and the general pursuit of our own interest ; for which reason, the word *selfish* is by every one appropriated to this temper and pursuit. Now as it is ridiculous to assert, that self-love and the love of our neighbour are the same ; so neither is it asserted, that following these different affections hath the same tendency and respect to our own interest. The comparison is not beween self-love and the love of our neighbour ; between pursuit of our own interest, and the interest of others ; but between the several particular affections in human nature towards external objects, as one part of the comparison ; and the one particular affection to the good of our neighbour, as the other part of it : and it has been shewn, that all these have the same respect to self-love and private interest.

238　　There is indeed frequently an inconsistence or interfering between self-love or private interest, and the several particular appetites, passions, affections, or the pursuits they lead to. But this competition or interfering is merely accidental ; and happens much oftener between pride, revenge, sensual gratifications, and private interest, than between private interest and benevolence. For nothing is more common, than to see men give themselves up to a passion or an affection to their known prejudice and ruin, and in direct contradiction to manifest and real interest, and the loudest calls of self-love : whereas the seeming competitions and interfering, between benevolence and private interest, relate much more to the materials or means of enjoyment, than to enjoyment itself. There is often an interfering in the former, when there is none in the latter. Thus as to riches : so much money as a man gives away, so much less will remain in his possession. Here is a real inter- fering. But though a man cannot possibly give without lessening his fortune, yet there are multitudes might give without lessening their own enjoyment; because they may have more than they can turn to any real use or advantage to themselves. Thus, the more thought and time any one employs about the interests and good of others, he must necessarily have less to attend his own; but he may have so ready and large a supply of his own wants, that such thought might be really useless to himself, though of great service and assistance to others.

The general mistake, that there is some greater inconsistence between endeavouring to promote the good of another and self-interest, than between self-interest and pursuing any thing else, seems, as hath already been hinted, to arise from our notions of property; and to be carried on by this property's being supposed to be itself our happiness or good. People are so very much taken up with this one subject, that they seem from it to have formed a general way of thinking, which they apply to other things that they have nothing to do with. Hence, in a confused and slight way, it might well be taken for granted, that another's having no interest in an affection (i. e. his good not being the object of it), renders, as one may speak, the proprietor's interest in it greater; and that if another had an interest in it, this would render his less, or occasion that such affection could not be so friendly to self-love, or conducive to private good, as an affection or pursuit which has not a regard to the good of another. This, I say, might be taken for granted, whilst it was not attended to, that the object of every particular affection is equally somewhat external to ourselves; and whether it be the good of another person, or whether it be any other external thing, makes no alteration

with regard to its being one's own affection, and the gratification of it one's own private enjoyment. And so far as it is
taken for granted, that barely having the means and materials
of enjoyment is what constitutes interest and happiness ; that
our interest or good consists in possessions themselves, in
having the property of riches, houses, lands, gardens, not
in the enjoyment of them ; so far it will even more strongly
be taken for granted, in the way already explained, that an
affection's conducing to the good of another, must even
necessarily occasion it to conduce less to private good, if not
to be positively detrimental to it. For, if property and happiness are one and the same thing, as by increasing the property
of another you lessen your own property, so by promoting the
happiness of another you must lessen your own happiness.
But whatever occasioned the mistake, I hope it has been fully
proved to be one ; as it has been proved, that there is no
peculiar rivalship or competition between self-love and benevolence : that as there may be a competition between these
two, so there may also between any particular affection whatever and self-love ; that every particular affection, benevolence
among the rest, is subservient to self-love by being the instrument of private enjoyment ; and that in one respect benevolence
contributes more to private interest, i. e. enjoyment or satisfaction, than any other of the particular common affections, as
it is in a degree its own gratification.

239 And to all these things may be added, that religion, from
whence arises our strongest obligation to benevolence, is so
far from disowning the principle of self-love, that it often
addresses itself to that very principle, and always to the mind
in that state when reason presides ; and there can no access
be had to the understanding, but by convincing men, that the
course of life we would persuade them to is not contrary
to their interest. It may be allowed, without any prejudice to
the cause of virtue and religion, that our ideas of happiness
and misery are of all our ideas the nearest and most important

to us; that they will, nay, if you please, that they ought to prevail over those of order, and beauty, and harmony, and proportion, if there should ever be, as it is impossible there ever should be, any inconsistence between them : though these last too, as expressing the fitness of actions, are real as truth itself. Let it be allowed, though virtue or moral rectitude does indeed consist in affection to and pursuit of what is right and good, as such ; yet, that when we sit down in a cool hour, we can neither justify to ourselves this or any other pursuit, till we are convinced that it will be for our happiness, or at least not contrary to it.

Common reason and humanity will have some influence upon mankind, whatever becomes of speculations ; but, so far as the interests of virtue depend upon the theory of it being secured from open scorn, so far its very being in the world depends upon its appearing to have no contrariety to private interest and self-love. The foregoing observations, therefore, it is hoped, may have gained a little ground in favour of the precept before us ; the particular explanation of which shall be the subject of the next discourse.

*   *   *   *   *   *   *

SERMON XII.

*   *   *   *   *   *   *

240   I PROCEED to consider, lastly, what is affirmed of the precept now explained, that it comprehends in it all others; i. e. that to love our neighbour as ourselves includes in it all virtues.

Now the way in which every maxim of conduct, or general speculative assertion, when it is to be explained at large, should be treated, is, to shew what are the particular truths which were designed to be comprehended under such a general observation, how far it is strictly true ; and then the limitations, restrictions, and exceptions, if there be exceptions, with which it is to be understood. But it is only the former of these ;

namely, how far the assertion in the text holds, and the ground of the pre-eminence assigned to the precept of it, which in strictness comes into our present consideration.

However, in almost every thing that is said, there is somewhat to be understood beyond what is explicitly laid down, and which we of course supply ; somewhat, I mean, which would not be commonly called a restriction, or limitation. Thus, when benevolence is said to be the sum of virtue, it is not spoken of as a blind propension, but as a principle in reasonable creatures, and so to be directed by their reason : for reason and reflection comes into our notion of a moral agent. And that will lead us to consider distant consequences, as well as the immediate tendency of an action : it will teach us, that the care of some persons, suppose children and families, is particularly committed to our charge by Nature and Providence ; as also that there are other circumstances, suppose friendship or former obligations, which require that we do good to some, preferably to others. Reason, considered merely as subservient to benevolence, as assisting to produce the greatest good, will teach us to have particular regard to these relations and circumstances ; because it is plainly for the good of the world that they should be regarded. And as there are numberless cases, in which, notwithstanding appearances, we are not competent judges, whether a particular action will upon the whole do good or harm ; reason in the same way will teach us to be cautious how we act in these cases of uncertainty. It will suggest to our consideration, which is the safer side ; how liable we are to be led wrong by passion and private interest ; and what regard is due to laws, and the judgment of mankind. All these things must come into consideration, were it only in order to determine which way of acting is likely to produce the greatest good. Thus, upon supposition that it were in the strictest sense true, without limitation, that benevolence includes in it all virtues ; yet reason must come in as its guide and director, in order to attain its own end, the end of benevolence, the greatest public good. Reason then being thus included, let us now consider the truth of the assertion itself.

241 First, It is manifest that nothing can be of consequence to mankind or any creature, but happiness. This then is all which any person can, in strictness of speaking, be said to have a right to. We can therefore *owe no man any thing*, but only to further and promote his happiness, according to our abilities. And therefore a disposition and endeavour to do good to all with whom we have to do, in the degree and manner which the different relations we stand in to them require, is a discharge of all the obligations we are under to them.

As human nature is not one simple uniform thing, but a composition of various parts, body, spirit, appetites, particular passions, and affections ; for each of which reasonable self-love would lead men to have due regard, and make suitable provision : so society consists of various parts, to which we stand in different respects and relations ; and just benevolence would as surely lead us to have due regard to each of these, and behave as the respective relations require. Reasonable good-will, and right behaviour towards our fellow-creatures, are in a manner the same : only that the former expresseth the principle as it is in the mind ; the latter, the principle as it were become external, i. e. exerted in actions.

And so far as temperance, sobriety, and moderation in sensual pleasures, and the contrary vices, have any respect to our fellow-creatures, any influence upon their quiet, welfare, and happiness ; as they always have a real, and often a near influence upon it ; so far it is manifest those virtues may be produced by the love of our neighbour, and that the contrary vices would be prevented by it. Indeed if men's regard to themselves will not restrain them from excess ; it may be thought little probable, that their love to others will be sufficient : but the reason is, that their love to others is not, any more than their regard to themselves, just, and in its due degree. There are however manifest instances of persons kept sober and temperate from regard to their affairs, and the welfare of those who depend upon them.   And it is obvious to every one, that habitual excess, a dissolute course of life, implies a general neglect of the duties we owe towards our friends, our families, and our country.

242   From hence it is manifest that the common virtues, and the common vices of mankind, may be traced up to benevolence, or the want of it.   And this entitles the precept, *Thou shalt love thy neighbour as thyself*, to the preeminence given to it ; and is a justification of the apostle's assertion, that all other commandments are comprehended in it ; whatever cautions and restrictions[1] there are, which might require to be considered, if we were to state particularly and at length, what is virtue and right behaviour in mankind.   But,

[1] For instance: as we are not competent judges, what is upon the whole for the good of the world, there may be other immediate ends appointed us to pursue, besides that one of doing good, or producing happiness. Though the good of the creation be the only end of the Author of it, yet he may have laid us under particular obligations, which we may discern and feel ourselves under, quite distinct from a perception, that the observance or violation of them is for the happiness or misery of our fellow-creatures.   And this is in fact the case.   For there are certain dispositions of mind, and certain actions, which are in themselves approved or disapproved by mankind, abstracted from the consideration of their tendency to the happiness or misery of the world; approved or disapproved by reflection, by that principle within, which is the guide of life, the judge of right and wrong.   Numberless instances of this kind might be mentioned. There are pieces of treachery, which in themselves appear base and detestable to every one.   There are actions, which perhaps can scarce have any other general name given them than indecencies, which yet are odious and shocking to human nature.   There is such a thing as meanness, a little mind ; which, as it is quite distinct from incapacity, so it raises a dislike and disapprobation quite different from that contempt, which men are too apt to have, of mere folly.   On the other hand ; what we call greatness of mind is the object of another sort of approbation, than superior understanding.   Fidelity, honour, strict justice, are themselves approved in the highest degree, abstracted from the consideration of their tendency.   Now, whether it be thought that each of these are connected with benevolence in our nature, and so may be considered as the same thing with it ; or whether some of them be thought an inferior kind of virtues and vices, somewhat like natural beauties and deformities ; or lastly, plain exceptions to the general rule : thus much however is certain, that the things now instanced in, and numberless others, are approved or disapproved by mankind in general, in quite another view than as conducive to the happiness or misery of the world.

243 Secondly, It might be added, that in a higher and more general way of consideration, leaving out the particular nature of creatures, and the particular circumstances in which they are placed, benevolence seems in the strictest sense to include in it all that is good and worthy; all that is good, which we have any distinct particular notion of. We have no clear conception of any positive moral attribute in the supreme Being, but what may be resolved up into goodness. And, if we consider a reasonable creature or moral agent, without regard to the particular relations and circumstances in which he is placed; we cannot conceive any thing else to come in towards determining whether he is to be ranked in an higher or lower class of virtuous beings, but the higher or lower degree in which that principle, and what is manifestly connected with it, prevail in him.

That which we more strictly call piety, or the love of God, and which is an essential part of a right temper, some may perhaps imagine no way connected with benevolence: yet surely they must be connected, if there be indeed in being an object infinitely good. Human nature is so constituted, that every good affection implies the love of itself; i. e. becomes the object of a new affection in the same person. Thus, to be righteous, implies in it the love of righteousness; to be benevolent, the love of benevolence; to be good, the love of goodness; whether this righteousness, benevolence, or goodness, be viewed as in our own mind, or in another's: and the love of God as a being perfectly good, is the love of perfect goodness contemplated in a being or person. Thus morality and religion, virtue and piety, will at last necessarily coincide, run up into one and the same point, and *love* will be in all senses *the end of the commandment.*

DISSERTATION II.

OF THE NATURE OF VIRTUE.

244　　That which renders beings capable of moral government, is their having a moral nature, and moral faculties of perception and of action.　Brute creatures are impressed and actuated by various instincts and propensions : so also are we.　But additional to this, we have a capacity of reflecting upon actions and characters, and making them an object to our thought ; and on doing this, we naturally and unavoidably approve some actions, under the peculiar view of their being virtuous and of good desert ; and disapprove others, as vicious and of ill desert.　That we have this moral approving and disapproving [1] faculty, is certain from our experiencing it in ourselves, and recognising it in each other.　It appears from our exercising it unavoidably, in the approbation and disapprobation even of feigned characters : from the words, right and wrong, odious and amiable, base and worthy, with many others of like signification in all languages, applied to actions and characters : from the many written systems of morals which suppose it ; since it cannot be imagined, that all these authors, throughout all these treatises, had absolutely no meaning at all to their words, or a meaning merely chimerical : from our natural sense of gratitude, which implies a distinction between merely being the instrument of good, and intending it :

[1] This way of speaking is taken from Epictetus,* and is made use of as seeming the most full, and least liable to cavil.　And the moral faculty may be understood to have these two epithets, δοκιμαστικὴ and ἀποδοκιμαστικὴ, upon a double account ; because, upon a survey of actions, whether before or after they are done, it determines them to be good or evil ; and also because it determines itself to be the guide of action and of life, in contradistinction from all other faculties, or natural principles of action : in the very same manner as speculative reason *directly* and naturally judges of speculative truth and falsehood ; and at the same time is attended with a consciousness upon *reflection*, that the natural right to judge of them belongs to it.

* Arr. Epict. lib. i. cap. i.

from the like distinction, every one makes, between injury and mere harm, which Hobbes says, is peculiar to mankind ; and between injury and just punishment, a distinction plainly natural, prior to the consideration of human laws.   It is manifest great part of common language, and of common behaviour over the world, is formed upon supposition of such a moral faculty ; whether called conscience, moral reason, moral sense, or divine reason ; whether considered as a sentiment of the understanding, or as a perception of the heart ; or, which seems the truth, as including both.   Nor is it at all doubtful, in the general, what course of action this faculty, or practical discerning power within us, approves, and what it disapproves.   For as much as it has been disputed wherein virtue consists, or whatever ground for doubt there may be about particulars ; yet, in general, there is in reality an universally acknowledged standard of it.   It is that which all ages and all countries have made profession of in public ; it is that which every man you meet puts on the show of ; it is that which the primary and fundamental laws of all civil constitutions over the face of the earth make it their business and endeavour to enforce the practice of upon mankind ; namely, justice, veracity, and regard to common good.   It being manifest then, in general, that we have such a faculty or discernment as this, it may be of use to remark some things more distinctly concerning it.

245   First, It ought to be observed, that the object of this faculty is actions[1], comprehending under that name active or practical principles ; those principles from which men would act, if occasions and circumstances gave them power ; and which, when fixed and habitual in any person, we call his character. It does not appear that brutes have the least reflex sense of actions, as distinguished from events ; or that will and design, which constitute the very nature of actions as such, are at all

---

[1] Οὐδὲ ἡ ἀρετὴ καὶ κακία—ἐν πείσει, ἀλλὰ ἐνεργείᾳ. M. Anton. lib. ix. 16. Virtutis laus omnis in actione consistit.   Cic. Off. lib. i. cap. 6.

an object to their perception.   But to ours they are ; and they are the object, and the only one, of the approving and disapproving faculty.   Acting, conduct, behaviour, abstracted from all regard to what is, in fact and event, the consequence of it, is itself the natural object of the moral discernment, as speculative truth and falsehood is of speculative reason. Intention of such and such consequences, indeed, is always included ; for it is part of the action itself : but though the intended good or bad consequences do not follow, we have exactly the same sense of the action as if they did.   In like manner, we think well or ill of characters, abstracted from all consideration of the good or the evil, which persons of such characters have it actually in their power to do.   We never, in the moral way, applaud or blame either ourselves or others, for what we enjoy or what we suffer, or for having impressions made upon us which we consider as altogether out of our power ;   but only for what we do, or would have done, had it been in our power ;   or for what we leave undone, which we might have done, or would have left undone, though we could have done it.

246   Secondly :   Our sense or discernment of actions as morally good or evil, implies in it a sense or discernment of them as of good or ill desert.   It may be difficult to explain this perception, so as to answer all the questions which may be asked concerning it ;   but every one speaks of such and such actions as deserving punishment ;   and it is not, I suppose, pretended, that they have absolutely no meaning at all to the expression. Now the meaning plainly is not, that we conceive it for the good of society, that the doer of such actions should be made to suffer.   For if unhappily it were resolved, that a man who, by some innocent action, was infected with the plague, should be left to perish, lest, by other people's coming near him, the infection should spread ;   no one would say he deserved this treatment.   Innocence and ill desert are inconsistent ideas. Ill desert always supposes guilt ; and if one be no part of the other, yet they are evidently and naturally connected in our mind. The sight of a man in misery raises our compassion towards him ; and, if this misery be inflicted on him by another, our indignation against the author of it. But when we are informed that the sufferer is a villain, and is punished only for his treachery or cruelty, our compassion exceedingly lessens, and in many instances our indignation wholly subsides. Now what produces this effect is the conception of that in the sufferer, which we call ill desert. Upon considering then, or viewing together, our notion of vice and that of misery, there results a third, that of ill desert. And thus there is in human creatures an association of the two ideas, natural and moral evil, wickedness and punishment. If this association were merely artificial or accidental, it were nothing ; but being most unquestionably natural, it greatly concerns us to attend to it, instead of endeavouring to explain it away.

It may be observed further, concerning our perception of good and of ill desert, that the former is very weak with respect to common instances of virtue. One reason of which may be, that it does not appear to a spectator, how far such instances of virtue proceed from a virtuous principle, or in what degree this principle is prevalent : since a very weak regard to virtue may be sufficient to make men act well in many common instances. And on the other hand, our perception of ill desert in vicious actions lessens in proportion to the temptations men are thought to have had to such vices. For vice in human creatures consisting chiefly in the absence or want of the virtuous principle ; though a man be overcome, suppose, by tortures, it does not from thence appear to what degree the virtuous principle was wanting. All that appears is, that he had it not in such a degree as to prevail over the temptation ; but possibly he had it in a degree which would have rendered him proof against common temptations.

247   Thirdly : Our perception of vice and ill desert arises from, and is the result of, a comparison of actions with the nature and

capacities of the agent.　For the mere neglect of doing what
we ought to do would, in many cases, be determined by all men
to be in the highest degree vicious.　And this determination
must arise from such comparison, and be the result of it ;
because such neglect would not be vicious in creatures of other
natures and capacities, as brutes.　And it is the same also with
respect to positive vices, or such as consist in doing what we
ought not.　For every one has a different sense of harm done
by an idiot, madman, or child, and by one of mature and
common understanding ; though the action of both, including
the intention, which is part of the action, be the same ; as it
may be, since idiots and madmen, as well as children, are
capable not only of doing mischief, but also of intending it.
Now this difference must arise from somewhat discerned in
the nature or capacities of one, which renders the action
vicious ; and the want of which, in the other, renders the same
action innocent or less vicious : and this plainly supposes
a comparison, whether reflected upon or not, between the
action and capacities of the agent, previous to our determining
an action to be vicious.　And hence arises a proper application
of the epithets, incongruous, unsuitable, disproportionate,
unfit, to actions which our moral faculty determines to be
vicious.

248　Fourthly : It deserves to be considered, whether men are
more at liberty, in point of morals, to make themselves
miserable without reason, than to make other people so ; or
dissolutely to neglect their own greater good, for the sake
of a present lesser gratification, than they are to neglect the
good of others, whom nature has committed to their care.
It should seem, that a due concern about our own interest
or happiness, and a reasonable endeavour to secure and
promote it, which is, I think, very much the meaning of
the word prudence in our language; it should seem that
this is virtue, and the contrary behaviour faulty and blameable ; since, in the calmest way of reflection, we approve

of the first, and condemn the other conduct, both in ourselves and others. This approbation and disapprobation are altogether different from mere desire of our own, or of their happiness, and from sorrow upon missing it. For the object or occasion of this last kind of perception is satisfaction or uneasiness; whereas the object of the first is active behaviour. In one case, what our thoughts fix upon is our condition; in the other, our conduct. It is true, indeed, that nature has not given us so sensible a disapprobation of imprudence and folly, either in *ourselves* or *others*, as of falsehood, injustice, and cruelty; I suppose, because that constant habitual sense of private interest and good, which we always carry about with us, renders such sensible disapprobation less necessary, less wanting, to keep us from imprudently neglecting our own happiness, and foolishly injuring ourselves, than it is necessary and wanting to keep us from injuring others, to whose good we cannot have so strong and constant a regard; and also, because imprudence and folly, appearing to bring its own punishment more immediately and constantly than injurious behaviour, it less needs the additional punishment, which would be inflicted upon it by others, had they the same sensible indignation against it, as against injustice, and fraud, and cruelty. Besides, unhappiness being in itself the natural object of compassion, the unhappiness which people bring upon themselves, though it be wilfully, excites in us some pity for them; and this, of course, lessens our displeasure against them. But still it is matter of experience, that we are formed so as to reflect very severely upon the greater instances of imprudent neglects and foolish rashness, both in ourselves and others. In instances of this kind, men often say of themselves with remorse, and of others with some indignation, that they deserved to suffer such calamities, because they brought them upon themselves, and would not take warning. Particularly when persons come to poverty and distress by a long course of extravagance, and after frequent admonitions, though without falsehood or injustice; we plainly do not regard such people as alike objects of compassion with those who are brought into the same condition by unavoidable accidents. From these things it appears, that prudence is a species of virtue, and folly of vice: meaning by *folly*, somewhat quite different from mere incapacity; a thoughtless want of that regard and attention to our own happiness, which we had capacity for. And this the word properly includes; and, as it seems, in its usual acceptation; for we scarcely apply it to brute creatures.

However, if any person be disposed to dispute the matter, I shall very willingly give him up the words virtue and vice, as not applicable to prudence and folly; but must beg leave to insist, that the faculty within us, which is the judge of actions, approves of prudent actions, and disapproves imprudent ones; I say prudent and imprudent *actions* as such, and considered distinctly from the happiness or misery which they occasion. And by the way, this observation may help to determine what justness there is in that objection against religion, that it teaches us to be interested and selfish.

249 Fifthly: Without inquiring how far, and in what sense, virtue is resolvable into benevolence, and vice into the want of it; it may be proper to observe, that benevolence, and the want of it, singly considered, are in no sort the whole of virtue and vice. For if this were the case, in the review of one's own character, or that of others, our moral understanding and moral sense would be indifferent to every thing, but the degrees in which benevolence prevailed, and the degrees in which it was wanting. That is, we should neither approve of benevolence to some persons rather than to others, nor disapprove injustice and falsehood upon any other account, than merely as an overbalance of happiness was foreseen likely to be produced by the first, and of misery by the second. But now, on the contrary, suppose two men com-

petitors for any thing whatever, which would be of equal
advantage to each of them; though nothing, indeed, would
be more impertinent, than for a stranger to busy himself to
get one of them preferred to the other; yet such endeavour
would be virtue, in behalf of a friend or benefactor, abstracted from all consideration of distant consequences : as
that examples of gratitude, and the cultivation of friendship,
would be of general good to the world.   Again, suppose
one man should, by fraud or violence, take from another
the fruit of his labour, with intent to give it to a third,
who he thought would have as much pleasure from it as
would balance the pleasure which the first possessor would
have had in the enjoyment, and his vexation in the loss of
it ; suppose, also, that no bad consequences would follow ;
yet such an action would surely be vicious.   Nay, further,
were treachery, violence, and injustice, no otherwise vicious,
than as foreseen likely to produce an overbalance of misery
to society ; then, if in any case a man could procure to
himself as great advantage by an act of injustice, as the
whole foreseen inconvenience, likely to be brought upon
others by it, would amount to, such a piece of injustice
would not be faulty or vicious at all ; because it would be
no more than, in any other case, for a man to prefer his
own satisfaction to another's in equal degrees.   The fact
then appears to be, that we are constituted so as to condemn
falsehood, unprovoked violence, injustice, and to approve of
benevolence to some preferably to others, abstracted from all
consideration, which conduct is likeliest to produce an overbalance of happiness or misery.   And therefore, were the
Author of nature to propose nothing to himself as an end
but the production of happiness, were his moral character
merely that of benevolence ; yet ours is not so.   Upon that
supposition, indeed, the only reason of his giving us the
above-mentioned approbation of benevolence to some persons
rather than others, and disapprobation of falsehood, unpro-

voked violence, and injustice, must be, that he foresaw this constitution of our nature would produce more happiness, than forming us with a temper of mere general benevolence. But still, since this is our constitution, falsehood, violence, injustice, must be vice in us, and benevolence to some, preferably to others, virtue ; abstracted from all consideration of the overbalance of evil or good, which they may appear likely to produce.

Now if human creatures are endued with such a moral nature as we have been explaining, or with a moral faculty, the natural object of which is actions ; moral government must consist in rendering them happy and unhappy, in rewarding and punishing them, as they follow, neglect, or depart from, the moral rule of action interwoven in their nature, or suggested and enforced by this moral faculty ; in rewarding and punishing them upon account of their so doing.

250 I am not sensible that I have, in this fifth observation, contradicted what any author designed to assert. But some of great and distinguished merit have, I think, expressed themselves in a manner, which may occasion some danger, to careless readers, of imagining the whole of virtue to consist in singly aiming, according to the best of their judgment, at promoting the happiness of mankind in the present state ; and the whole of vice, in doing what they foresee, or might foresee, is likely to produce an overbalance of unhappiness in it ; than which mistakes none can be conceived more terrible. For it is certain, that some of the most shocking instances of injustice, adultery, murder, perjury, and even of persecution, may, in many supposable cases, not have the appearance of being likely to produce an overbalance of misery in the present state ; perhaps sometimes may have the contrary appearance. For this reflection might easily be carried on, but I forbear——The happiness of the world is the concern of him who is the lord and the proprietor of it ; nor do we know what we are about, when we endeavour to

promote the good of mankind in any ways but those which
he has directed; that is, indeed, in all ways not contrary to
veracity and justice. I speak thus upon supposition of persons
really endeavouring, in some sort, to do good without regard
to these. But the truth seems to be, that such supposed
endeavours proceed, almost always, from ambition, the spirit
of party, or some indirect principle, concealed perhaps in
great measure from persons themselves. And though it is
our business and our duty to endeavour, within the bounds
of veracity and justice, to contribute to the ease, convenience,
and even cheerfulness and diversion of our fellow creatures;
yet from our short views, it is greatly uncertain, whether this
endeavour will, in particular instances, produce an overbalance
of happiness upon the whole; since so many and distant things
must come into the account. And that which makes it our
duty is, that there is some appearance that it will, and no
positive appearance sufficient to balance this, on the contrary
side; and also, that such benevolent endeavour is a cultivation
of that most excellent of all virtuous principles, the active
principle of benevolence.

However, though veracity, as well as justice, is to be our rule
of life, it must be added, otherwise a snare will be laid in the way
of some plain men, that the use of common forms of speech,
generally understood, cannot be falsehood; and, in general,
that there can be no designed falsehood without designing
to deceive. It must likewise be observed, that in numberless
cases, a man may be under the strictest obligations to what he
foresees will deceive, without his intending it. For it is
impossible not to foresee, that the words and actions of men,
in different ranks and employments, and of different educa-
tions, will perpetually be mistaken by each other; and it
cannot but be so, whilst they will judge with the utmost careless-
ness, as they daily do, of what they are not, perhaps, enough
informed to be competent judges of, even though they considered it with great attention.

ADAM SMITH

THE
THEORY OF MORAL SENTIMENTS

[First published, 1759.   Reprinted here from the 6th edition, 1790.]

SMITH

The Theory of Moral Sentiments

——◆◆——

PART I.

OF THE PROPRIETY OF ACTION.

——◆◆——

SECTION I.—OF THE SENSE OF PROPRIETY.

CHAPTER I.—OF SYMPATHY.

251 How selfish soever man may be supposed, there are
evidently some principles in his nature, which interest him
in the fortune of others, and render their happiness necessary
to him, though he derives nothing from it except the pleasure
of seeing it. Of this kind is pity or compassion, the emotion
which we feel for the misery of others, when we either see it,
or are made to conceive it in a very lively manner. That we
often derive sorrow from the sorrow of others, is a matter of
fact too obvious to require any instances to prove it; for this
sentiment, like all the other original passions of human
nature, is by no means confined to the virtuous and humane,
though they perhaps may feel it with the most exquisite
sensibility. The greatest ruffian, the most hardened violator
of the laws of society, is not altogether without it.

252 As we have no immediate experience of what other men feel,
we can form no idea of the manner in which they are

affected, but by conceiving what we ourselves should feel in the like situation. Though our brother is upon the rack, as long as we ourselves are at our ease, our senses will never inform us of what he suffers. They never did, and never can, carry us beyond our own person, and it is by the imagination only that we can form any conception of what are his sensations. Neither can that faculty help us to this any other way, than by representing to us what would be our own, if we were in his case. It is the impressions of our own senses only, not those of his, which our imaginations copy. By the imagination we place ourselves in his situation, we conceive ourselves enduring all the same torments, we enter as it were into his body, and become in some measure the same person with him, and thence form some idea of his sensations, and even feel something which, though weaker in degree, is not altogether unlike them. His agonies, when they are thus brought home to ourselves, when we have thus adopted and made them our own, begin at last to affect us, and we then tremble and shudder at the thought of what he feels. For as to be in pain or distress of any kind excites the most excessive sorrow, so to conceive or to imagine that we are in it, excites some degree of the same emotion, in proportion to the vivacity or dulness of the conception.

253　　That this is the source of our fellow-feeling for the misery of others, that it is by changing places in fancy with the sufferer, that we come either to conceive or to be affected by what he feels, may be demonstrated by many obvious observations, if it should not be thought sufficiently evident of itself. When we see a stroke aimed and just ready to fall upon the leg or arm of another person, we naturally shrink and draw back our own leg or our own arm ; and when it does fall, we feel it in some measure, and are hurt by it as well as the sufferer. The mob, when they are gazing at a dancer on the slack rope, naturally writhe and twist and balance their own bodies, as they see him do, and as they feel that they themselves must do it in his situation. Persons of delicate fibres, and a weak constitution of body, complain, that in looking on the sores and ulcers which are exposed by beggars in the streets, they are apt to feel an itching or uneasy sensation in the correspondent part of their own bodies. The horror which they conceive at the misery of those wretches affects that particular part in themselves more than any other; because that horror arises from conceiving what they themselves would suffer, if they really were the wretches whom they are looking upon, and if that particular part in themselves was actually affected in the same miserable manner. The very force of this conception is sufficient, in their feeble frames, to produce that itching or uneasy sensation complained of. Men of the most robust make observe, that in looking upon sore eyes they often feel a very sensible soreness in their own, which proceeds from the same reason ; that organ being in the strongest man more delicate than any other part of the body is in the weakest.

Neither is it those circumstances only, which create pain or sorrow, that call forth our fellow-feeling. Whatever is the passion which arises from any object in the person principally concerned, an analogous emotion springs up, at the thought of his situation, in the breast of every attentive spectator. Our joy for the deliverance of those heroes of tragedy or romance who interest us, is as sincere as our grief for their distress, and our fellow-feeling with their misery is not more real than that with their happiness. We enter into their gratitude towards those faithful friends who did not desert them in their difficulties ; and we heartily go along with their resentment against those perfidious traitors who injured, abandoned, or deceived them. In every passion of which the mind of man is susceptible, the emotions of the by-stander always correspond to what, by bringing the case home to himself, he imagines should be the sentiments of the sufferer.

Pity and compassion are words appropriated to signify our

fellow-feeling with the sorrow of others. Sympathy, though its meaning was, perhaps, originally the same, may now, however, with much impropriety, be made use of to denote our fellow-feeling with any passion whatever.

254 Upon some occasions sympathy may seem to arise merely from the view of a certain emotion in another person. The passions, upon some occasions, may seem to be transfused from one man to another, instantaneously, and antecedent to any knowledge of what excited them in the person principally concerned. Grief and joy, for example, strongly expressed in the look and gestures of any one, at once affect the spectator with some degree of a like painful or agreeable emotion. A smiling face is, to every body that sees it, a cheerful object; as a sorrowful countenance, on the other hand, is a melancholy one.

This, however, does not hold universally, or with regard to every passion. There are some passions of which the expressions excite no sort of sympathy, but before we are acquainted with what gave occasion to them, serve rather to disgust and provoke us against them. The furious behaviour of an angry man is more likely to exasperate us against himself than against his enemies. As we are unacquainted with his provocation, we cannot bring his case home to ourselves, nor conceive any thing like the passions which it excites. But we plainly see what is the situation of those with whom he is angry, and to what violence they may be exposed from so enraged an adversary. We readily, therefore, sympathize with their fear or resentment, and are immediately disposed to take part against the man from whom they appear to be in so much danger.

255 If the very appearances of grief and joy inspire us with some degree of the like emotions, it is because they suggest to us the general idea of some good or bad fortune that has befallen the person in whom we observe them: and in these passions this is sufficient to have some little influence upon us. The effects of grief and joy terminate in the person who feels those emotions, of which the expressions do not, like those of resentment, suggest to us the idea of any other person for whom we are concerned, and whose interests are opposite to his. The general idea of good or bad fortune, therefore, creates some concern for the person who has met with it, but the general idea of provocation excites no sympathy with the anger of the man who has received it. Nature, it seems, teaches us to be more averse to enter into this passion, and, till informed of its cause, to be disposed rather to take part against it.

Even our sympathy with the grief or joy of another, before we are informed of the cause of either, is always extremely imperfect. General lamentations, which express nothing but the anguish of the sufferer, create rather a curiosity to inquire into his situation, along with some disposition to sympathize with him, than any actual sympathy that is very sensible. The first question which we ask is, What has befallen you ? Till this be answered, though we are uneasy both from the vague idea of his misfortune, and still more from torturing ourselves with conjectures about what it may be, yet our fellow-feeling is not very considerable.

256 Sympathy, therefore, does not arise so much from the view of the passion, as from that of the situation which excites it. We sometimes feel for another, a passion of which he himself seems to be altogether incapable ; because, when we put ourselves in his case, that passion arises in our breast from the imagination, though it does not in his from the reality. We blush for the impudence and rudeness of another, though he himself appears to have no sense of the impropriety of his own behaviour ; because we cannot help feeling with what confusion we ourselves should be covered had we behaved in so absurd a manner.

Of all the calamities to which the condition of morality exposes mankind, the loss of reason appears, to those who have the least spark of humanity, by far the most dreadful; and they behold that last stage of human wretchedness with deeper commiseration than any other. But the poor wretch, who is in it, laughs and sings perhaps, and is altogether insensible of his own misery. The anguish which humanity feels, therefore, at the sight of such an object, cannot be the reflection of any sentiment of the sufferer.' The compassion of the spectator must arise altogether from the consideration of what he himself would feel if he was reduced to the same unhappy situation, and, what perhaps is impossible, was at the same time able to regard it with his present reason and judgment.

What are the pangs of a mother when she hears the moanings of her infant that during the agony of disease cannot express what it feels? In her idea of what it suffers, she joins, to its real helplessness, her own consciousness of that helplessness, and her own terrors for the unknown consequences of its disorder; and, out of all these, forms, for her own sorrow, the most complete image of misery and distress. The infant, however, feels only the uneasiness of the present instant, which can never be great. With regard to the future, it is perfectly secure, and in its thoughtlessness and want of foresight, possesses an antidote against fear and anxiety, the great tormentors of the human breast, from which reason and philosophy will, in vain, attempt to defend it, when it grows up to a man.

257 We sympathize even with the dead, and overlooking what is of real importance in their situation, that awful futurity which awaits them, we are chiefly affected by those circumstances which strike our senses, but can have no influence upon their happiness. It is miserable, we think, to be deprived of the light of the sun; to be shut out from life and conversation; to be laid in the cold grave, a prey to corruption and the reptiles of the earth; to be no more thought of in this world, but to be obliterated, in a little time, from the affections, and almost from the memory, of their dearest friends and relations. Surely, we imagine, we can never feel too much for those who have suffered so dreadful a calamity.   The tribute of our fellow feeling seems doubly due to them now, when they are in danger of being forgot by every body; and, by the vain honours which we pay to their memory, we endeavour, for our own misery, artificially to keep alive our melancholy remembrance of their misfortune.   That our sympathy can afford them no consolation seems to be an addition to their calamity; and to think that all we can do is unavailing, and that, what alleviates all other distress, the regret, the love, and the lamentations of their friends, can yield no comfort to them, serves only to exasperate our sense of their misery.   The happiness of the dead, however, most assuredly, is affected by none of these circumstances; nor is it the thought of these things which can ever disturb the profound security of their repose.   The idea of that dreary and endless melancholy which the fancy naturally ascribes to their condition, arises altogether from our joining to the change which has been produced upon them, our own consciousnes of that change, from our putting ourselves in their situation, and from our lodging, if I may be allowed to say so, our own living souls in their inanimated bodies, and thence conceiving what would be our emotions in this case.   It is from this very illusion of the imagination, that the foresight of our own dissolution is so terrible to us, and that the idea of those circumstances, which undoubtedly can give us no pain when we are dead, makes us miserable while we are alive.   And from thence arises one of the most important principles in human nature, the dread of death, the great poison to the happiness, but the great restraint upon the injustice of mankind, which, while it afflicts and mortifies the individual, guards and protects the society.

Chapter II.—Of the Pleasure of Mutual Sympathy.

258   But whatever may be the cause of sympathy, or however it may be excited, nothing pleases us more than to observe in other men a fellow-feeling with all the emotions of our own breast; nor are we ever so much shocked as by the appearance of the contrary. Those who are fond of deducing all our sentiments from certain refinements of self-love, think themselves at no loss to account, according to their own principles, both for this pleasure and this pain. Man, say they, conscious of his own weakness, and of the need which he has for the assistance of others, rejoices whenever he observes that they adopt his own passions, because he is then assured of that assistance; and grieves whenever he observes the contrary, because he is then assured of their opposition. But both the pleasure and the pain are always felt so instantaneously, and often upon such frivolous occasions, that it seems evident that neither of them can be derived from any such self-interested consideration. A man is mortified when, after having endeavoured to divert the company, he looks round and sees that nobody laughs at his jests but himself. On the contrary, the mirth of the company is highly agreeable to him, and he regards this correspondence of their sentiments with his own as the greatest applause.

259   Neither does his pleasure seem to arise altogether from the additional vivacity which his mirth may receive from sympathy with theirs, nor his pain from the disappointment he meets with when he misses this pleasure; though both the one and the other, no doubt, do in some measure. When we have read a book or poem so often that we can no longer find any amusement in reading it by ourselves, we can still take pleasure in reading it to a companion. To him it has all the graces of novelty; we enter into the surprise and

admiration which it naturally excites in him, but which it is
no longer capable of exciting in us; we consider all the ideas
which it presents, rather in the light in which they appear
to him, than in that in which they appear to ourselves, and
we are amused by sympathy with his amusement, which thus
enlivens our own. On the contrary, we should be vexed if
he did not seem to be entertained with it, and we could no
longer take any pleasure in reading it to him. It is the same
case here. The mirth of the company, no doubt, enlivens
our own mirth; and their silence, no doubt, disappoints us.
But though this may contribute both to the pleasure which
we derive from the one, and to the pain which we feel from
the other, it is by no means the sole cause of either; and this
correspondence of the sentiments of others with our own
appears to be a cause of pleasure, and the want of it a cause
of pain, which cannot be accounted for in this manner.
The sympathy, which my friends express with my joy, might
indeed give me pleasure by enlivening that joy: but that
which they express with my grief could give me none, if it
served only to enliven that grief. Sympathy, however,
enlivens joy and alleviates grief. It enlivens joy by presenting
another source of satisfaction; and it alleviates grief by
insinuating into the heart almost the only agreeable sensation
which it is at that time capable of receiving.

260 It is to be observed, accordingly, that we are still more
anxious to communicate to our friends our disagreeable, than
our agreeable passions, that we derive still more satisfaction
from their sympathy with the former than from that with
the latter, and that we are still more shocked by the want
of it.

How are the unfortunate relieved when they have found
out a person to whom they can communicate the cause of
their sorrow? Upon his sympathy they seem to disburthen
themselves of a part of their distress: he is not improperly
said to share it with them. He not only feels a sorrow of

the same kind with that which they feel, but as if he had derived a part of it to himself, what he feels seems to alleviate the weight of what they feel. Yet by relating their misfortunes they in some measure renew their grief. They awaken in their memory the remembrance of those circumstances which occasion their affliction. Their tears accordingly flow faster than before, and they are apt to abandon themselves to all the weakness of sorrow. They take pleasure, however, in all this, and, it is evident, are sensibly relieved by it ; because the sweetness of his sympathy more than compensates the bitterness of that sorrow, which, in order to excite this sympathy, they had thus enlivened and renewed. The cruelest insult, on the contrary, which can be offered to the unfortunate, is to appear to make light of their calamities. To seem not to be affected with the joy of our companions, is but want of politeness ; but not to wear a serious countenance when they tell us their afflictions, is real and gross inhumanity.

Love is an agreeable ; resentment, a disagreeable passion ; and accordingly we are not half so anxious that our friends should adopt our friendships, as that they should enter into our resentments. We can forgive them though they seem to be little affected with the favours which we may have received, but lose all patience if they seem indifferent about the injuries which may have been done to us : nor are we half so angry with them for not entering into our gratitude, as for not sympathizing with our resentment. They can easily avoid being friends to our friends, but can hardly avoid being enemies to those with whom we are at variance. We seldom resent their being at enmity with the first, though upon that account we may sometimes affect to make an awkward quarrel with them ; but we quarrel with them in good earnest if they live in friendship with the last. The agreeable passions of love and joy can satisfy and support the heart without any auxiliary pleasure. The bitter and painful emotions of grief and resentment more strongly require the healing consolation of sympathy.

261   As the person who is principally interested in any event is pleased with our sympathy, and hurt by the want of it, so we, too, seem to be pleased when we are able to sympathize with him, and to be hurt when we are unable to do so.   We run not only to congratulate the successful, but to condole with the afflicted; and the pleasure which we find in the conversation of one whom in all the passions of his heart we can entirely sympathize with, seems to do more than compensate the painfulness of that sorrow with which the view of his situation affects us.   On the contrary, it is always disagreeable to feel that we cannot sympathize with him, and instead of being pleased with this exemption from sympathetic pain, it hurts us to find that we cannot share his uneasiness.   If we hear a person loudly lamenting his misfortunes, which however, upon bringing the case home to ourselves, we feel, can produce no such violent effect upon us, we are shocked at his grief; and, because we cannot enter into it, call it pusillanimity and weakness.   It gives us the spleen, on the other hand, to see another too happy, or too much elevated, as we call it, with any little piece of good fortune.   We are disobliged even with his joy; and, because we cannot go along with it, call it levity and folly.   We are even put out of humour if our companion laughs louder or longer at a joke than we think it deserves; that is, than we feel that we ourselves could laugh at it.

CHAPTER III.—OF THE MANNER IN WHICH WE JUDGE OF THE PROPRIETY OR IMPROPRIETY OF THE AFFECTIONS OF OTHER MEN BY THEIR CONCORD OR DISSONANCE WITH OUR OWN.

262   WHEN the original passions of the person principally concerned are in perfect concord with the sympathetic emotions of the spectator, they necessarily appear to this last just and

proper, and suitable to their objects ; and, on the contrary, when, upon bringing the case home to himself, he finds that they do not coincide with what he feels, they necessarily appear to him unjust and improper, and unsuitable to the causes which excite them.   To approve of the passions of another, therefore, as suitable to their objects, is the same thing as to observe that we entirely sympathize with them ; and not to approve of them as such, is the same thing as to observe that we do not entirely sympathize with them.   The man who resents the injuries that have been done to me, and observes that I resent them precisely as he does, necessarily approves of my resentment.   The man whose sympathy keeps time to my grief, cannot but admit the reasonableness of my sorrow.   He who admires the same poem, or the same picture, and admires them exactly as I do, must surely allow the justness of my admiration. He who laughs at the same joke, and laughs along with me, cannot well deny the propriety of my laughter.   On the contrary, the person who, upon these different occasions, either feels no such emotion as that which I feel, or feels none that bears any proportion to mine, cannot avoid disapproving my sentiments on account of their dissonance with his own.   If my animosity goes beyond what the indignation of my friend can correspond to ; if my grief exceeds what his most tender compassion can go along with ; if my admiration is either too high or too low to tally with his own ; if I laugh loud and heartily when he only smiles, or, on the contrary, only smile when he laughs loud and heartily ; in all these cases, as soon as he comes from considering the object, to observe how I am affected by it, according as there is more or less disproportion between his sentiments and mine, I must incur a greater or less degree of his disapprobation : and upon all occasions his own sentiments are the standards and measures by which he judges of mine.

263   To approve of another man's opinions is to adopt those opinions, and to adopt them is to approve of them.   If the same arguments which convince you, convince me likewise, I necessarily approve of your conviction ; and if they do not, I necessarily disapprove of it : neither can I possibly conceive that I should do the one without the other. To approve or disapprove, therefore, of the opinions of others is acknowledged, by every body, to mean no more than to observe their agreement or disagreement with our own. But this is equally the case with regard to our approbation or disapprobation of the sentiments, or passions of others.

264   There are, indeed, some cases in which we seem to approve without any sympathy or correspondence of sentiments, and in which, consequently, the sentiment of approbation would seem to be different from the perception of this coincidence. A little attention, however, will convince us that even in these cases our approbation is ultimately founded upon a sympathy or correspondence of this kind. I shall give an instance in things of a very frivolous nature, because in them the judgments of mankind are less apt to be perverted by wrong systems. We may often approve of a jest, and think the laughter of the company quite just and proper, though we ourselves do not laugh, because, perhaps, we are in a grave humour, or happen to have our attention engaged with other objects. We have learned, however, from experience, what sort of pleasantry is upon most occasions capable of making us laugh, and we observe that this is one of that kind. We approve, therefore, of the laughter of the company, and feel that it is natural and suitable to its object ; because, though in our present mood we cannot easily enter into it, we are sensible that upon most occasions we should very heartily join in it.

The same thing often happens with regard to all the other passions. A stranger passes by us in the street with all the marks of the deepest affliction ; and we are immediately told that he has just received the news of the death of his father. It is impossible that, in this case, we should not approve of his grief. Yet it may often happen, without any defect of humanity on our part, that, so far from entering into the violence of his sorrow, we should scarce conceive the first movements of concern upon his account. Both he and his father, perhaps, are entirely unknown to us, or we happen to be employed about other things, and do not take time to picture out in our imagination the different circumstances of distress which must occur to him. We have learned, however, from experience, that such a misfortune naturally excites such a degree of sorrow, and we know that if we took time to consider his situation fully and in all its parts, we should without doubt most sincerely sympathize with him. It is upon the consciousness of this conditional sympathy, that our approbation of his sorrow is founded, even in those cases in which that sympathy does not actually take place ; and the general rules derived from our preceding experience of what our sentiments would commonly correspond with, correct upon this, as upon many other occasions, the impropriety of our present emotions.

265   The sentiment or affection of the heart from which any action proceeds, and upon which its whole virtue or vice must ultimately depend, may be considered under two different aspects, or in two different relations ; first, in relation to the cause which excites it, or the motive which gives occasion to it ; and secondly, in relation to the end which it proposes, or the effect which it tends to produce.

In the suitableness or unsuitableness, in the proportion or disproportion which the affection seems to bear to the cause or object which excites it, consists the propriety or impropriety, the decency or ungracefulness of the consequent action.

In the beneficial or hurtful nature of the effects which the affection aims at, or tends to produce, consists the merit or demerit of the action, the qualities by which it is entitled to reward, or is deserving of punishment.

266   Philosophers have, of late years, considered chiefly the tendency of affections, and have given little attention to the relation which they stand in to the cause which excites them.

In common life, however, when we judge of any person's conduct, and of the sentiments which directed it, we constantly consider them under both these aspects. When we blame in another man the excesses of love, of grief, of resentment, we not only consider the ruinous effects which they tend to produce, but the little occasion which was given for them. The merit of his favourite, we say, is not so great, his misfortune is not so dreadful, his provocation is not so extraordinary as to justify so violent a passion. We should have indulged, we say; perhaps, have approved of the violence of his emotion, had the cause been in any respect proportioned to it.

267   When we judge in this manner of any affection as proportioned or disproportioned to the cause which excites it, it is scarce possible that we should make use of any other rule or canon but the correspondent affection in ourselves. If upon bringing the case home to our own breast, we find that the sentiments which it gives occasion to, coincide and tally with our own, we necessarily approve of them, as proportioned and suitable to their objects; if otherwise, we necessarily disapprove of them, as extravagant and out of proportion.

Every faculty in one man is the measure by which he judges of the like faculty in another. I judge of your sight by my sight, of your ear by my ear, of your reason by my reason, of your resentment by my resentment, of your love by my love. I neither have, nor can have, any other way of judging about them.

CHAPTER IV.—THE SAME SUBJECT CONTINUED.

268   WE may judge of the propriety or impropriety of the sentiments of another person by their correspondence or disagreement with our own, upon two different occasions; either, first, when the objects which excite them are considered without any particular relation either to ourselves or to the

person whose sentiments we judge of; or, secondly, when they are considered as peculiarly affecting one or other of us.

1. With regard to those objects which are considered without any peculiar relation either to ourselves or to the person whose sentiments we judge of; wherever his sentiments entirely correspond with our own, we ascribe to him the qualities of taste and good judgment. The beauty of a plain, the greatness of a mountain, the ornaments of a building, the expression of a picture, the composition of a discourse, the conduct of a third person, the proportions of different quantities and numbers, the various appearances which the great machine of the universe is perpetually exhibiting, with the secret wheels and springs which produce them; all the general subjects of science and taste, are what we and our companions regard as having no peculiar relation to either of us. We both look at them from the same point of view, and we have no occasion for sympathy, or for that imaginary change of situations from which it arises, in order to produce, with regard to these, the most perfect harmony of sentiments and affections. If, notwithstanding, we are often differently affected, it arises either from the different degrees of attention which our different habits of life allow us to give easily to the several parts of those complex objects, or from the different degrees of natural acuteness in the faculty of the mind to which they are addressed.

269   When the sentiments of our companion coincide with our own in things of this kind, which are obvious and easy, and in which, perhaps, we never found a single person who differed from us, though we, no doubt, must approve of them, yet he seems to deserve no praise or admiration on account of them. But when they not only coincide with our own, but lead and direct our own; when in forming them he appears to have attended to many things which we had overlooked, and to have adjusted them to all the various circumstances of their objects; we not only approve of them, but wonder and are surprised at their uncommon and unexpected acuteness and comprehensiveness, and he appears to deserve a very high degree of admiration and applause. For approbation, heightened by wonder and surprise, constitutes the sentiment which is properly called admiration, and of which applause is the natural expression. The decision of the man who judges that exquisite beauty is preferable to the grossest deformity, or that twice two are equal to four, must certainly be approved of by all the world, but will not, surely, be much admired. It is the acute and delicate discernment of the man of taste, who distinguishes the minute, and scarce perceptible differences of beauty and deformity; it is the comprehensive accuracy of the experienced mathematician, who unravels with ease the most intricate and perplexed proportions; it is the great leader in science and taste, the man who directs and conducts our own sentiments, the extent and superior justness of whose talents astonish us with wonder and surprise, who excites our admiration, and seems to deserve our applause; and upon this foundation is grounded the greater part of the praise which is bestowed upon what are called the intellectual virtues.

270　　The utility of those qualities, it may be thought, is what first recommends them to us; and, no doubt, the consideration of this, when we come to attend to it, gives them a new value. Originally, however, we approve of another man's judgment, not as something useful, but as right, as accurate, as agreeable to truth and reality : and it is evident we attribute those qualities to it for no other reason but because we find that it agrees with our own. Taste, in the same manner, is originally approved of, not as useful, but as just, as delicate, and as precisely suited to its object. The idea of the utility of all qualities of this kind, is plainly an after-thought, and not what first recommends them to our approbation.

271　　2. With regard to those objects, which affect in a particular manner either ourselves or the person whose sentiments we judge of, it is at once more difficult to preserve this harmony and correspondence, and, at the same time, vastly more important. My companion does not naturally look upon the misfortune that has befallen me, or the injury that has been done me, from the same point of view in which I consider them. They affect me much more nearly. We do not view them from the same station, as we do a picture, or a poem, or a system of philosophy, and are, therefore, apt to be very differently affected by them. But I can much more easily overlook the want of this correspondence of sentiments with regard to such indifferent objects as concern neither me nor my companion, than with regard to what interests me so much as the misfortune that has befallen me, or the injury that has been done me. Though you despise that picture, or that poem, or even that system of philosophy, which I admire, there is little danger of our quarrelling upon that account. Neither of us can reasonably be much interested about them. They ought all of them to be matters of great indifference to us both; so that, though our opinions may be opposite, our affections may still be very nearly the same. But it is quite otherwise with regard to those objects by which either you or I are particularly affected. Though your judgments in matters of speculation, though your sentiments in matters of taste, are quite opposite to mine, I can easily overlook this opposition; and if I have any degree of temper, I may still find some entertainment in your conversation, even upon those very subjects. But if you have either no fellow-feeling for the misfortunes I have met with, or none that bears any proportion to the grief which distracts me; or if you have either no indignation at the injuries I have suffered, or none that bears any proportion to the resentment which transports me, we can no longer converse upon these subjects. We become intolerable to one another. I can neither support your company, nor you mine. You are confounded at my violence and passion, and I am enraged at your cold insensibility and want of feeling.

272   In all such cases, that there may be some correspondence of

sentiments between the spectator and the person principally
concerned, the spectator must, first of all, endeavour, as much as
he can, to put himself in the situation of the other, and to bring
home to himself every little circumstance of distress which can
possibly occur to the sufferer.   He must adopt the whole case
of his companion with all its minutest incidents ; and strive to
render as perfect as possible that imaginary change of situation
upon which his sympathy is founded.

273   After all this, however, the emotions of the spectator will
still be very apt to fall short of the violence of what is felt
by the sufferer.   Mankind, though naturally sympathetic,
never conceive, for what has befallen another, that degree
of passion which naturally animates the person principally
concerned.   That imaginary change of situation, upon which
their sympathy is founded, is but momentary.   The thought of
their own safety, the thought that they themselves are not
really the sufferers, continually intrudes itself upon them ;
and though it does not hinder them from conceiving
a passion somewhat analogous to what is felt by the
sufferer, hinders them from conceiving any thing that
approaches to the same degree of violence.   The person
principally concerned is sensible of this, and at the same
time passionately desires a more complete sympathy.   He
longs for that relief which nothing can afford him but the
entire concord of the affections of the spectators with his
own.   To see the emotions of their hearts, in every respect,
beat time to his own, in the violent and disagreeable passions,
constitutes his sole consolation.   But he can only hope to
obtain this by lowering his passion to that pitch in which the
spectators are capable of going along with him.   He must
flatten, if I may be allowed to say so, the sharpness of its
natural tone, in order to reduce it to harmony and concord
with the emotions of those who are about him.   What they
feel, will indeed always be, in some respects, different from
what he feels, and compassion can never be exactly the

same with original sorrow; because the secret consciousness
that the change of situations, from which the sympathetic
sentiment arises, is but imaginary, not only lowers it in degree,
but, in some measure, varies it in kind, and gives it a quite
different modification.   These two sentiments, however, may,
it is evident, have such a correspondence with one another,
as is sufficient for the harmony of society.   Though they will
never be unisons, they may be concords, and this is all that
is wanted or required.

274   In order to produce this concord, as nature teaches the
spectators to assume the circumstances of the person principally
concerned, so she teaches this last in some measure to assume
those of the spectators.   As they are continually placing themselves in his situation, and thence conceiving emotions similar
to what he feels; so he is as constantly placing himself in
theirs, and thence conceiving some degree of that coolness
about his own fortune, with which he is sensible that they will
view it.   As they are constantly considering what they themselves would feel, if they actually were the sufferers, so he is as
constantly led to imagine in what manner he would be affected
if he was only one of the spectators of his own situation.   As
their sympathy makes them look at it, in some measure, with
his eyes, so his sympathy makes him look at it, in some
measure, with theirs, especially when in their presence and
acting under their observation : and as the reflected passion,
which he thus conceives, is much weaker than the original one,
it necessarily abates the violence of what he felt before he
came into their presence, before he began to recollect in what
manner they would be affected by it, and to view his situation
in this candid and impartial light.

275   The mind, therefore, is rarely so disturbed but that the
company of a friend will restore it to some degree of tranquillity
and sedateness.   The breast is, in some measure, calmed and
composed the moment we come into his presence.   We are
immediately put in mind of the light in which he will view

our situation, and we begin to view it ourselves in the same light; for the effect of sympathy is instantaneous. We expect less sympathy from a common acquaintance than from a friend : we cannot open to the former all those little circumstances which we can unfold to the latter : we assume, therefore, more tranquillity before him, and endeavour to fix our thoughts upon those general outlines of our situation which he is willing to consider. We expect still less sympathy from an assembly of strangers, and we assume, therefore, still more tranquillity before them, and always endeavour to bring down our passion to that pitch, which the particular company we are in may be expected to go along with. Nor is this only an assumed appearance : for if we are at all masters of ourselves, the presence of a mere acquaintance will really compose us still more than that of a friend ; and that of an assembly of strangers, still more than that of an acquaintance.

Society and conversation, therefore, are the most powerful remedies for restoring the mind to its tranquillity, if, at any time, it has unfortunately lost it ; as well as the best preservatives of that equal and happy temper, which is so necessary to self-satisfaction and enjoyment. Men of retirement and speculation, who are apt to sit brooding at home over either grief or resentment, though they may often have more humanity, more generosity, and a nicer sense of honour, yet seldom possess that equality of temper which is so common among men of the world.

CHAPTER V.—OF THE AMIABLE AND RESPECTABLE VIRTUES.

276   UPON these two different efforts, upon that of the spectator to enter into the sentiments of the person principally concerned, and upon that of the person principally concerned, to bring down his emotions to what the spectator can go along with, are founded two different sets of virtues. The soft, the gentle, the amiable virtues, the virtues of candid condescension and

indulgent humanity, are founded upon the one : the great, the awful and respectable, the virtues of self-denial, of self-government, of that command of the passions which subjects all the movements of our nature to what our own dignity and honour, and the propriety of our own conduct require, take their origin from the other.

How amiable does he appear to be, whose sympathetic heart seems to re-echo all the sentiments of those with whom he converses, who grieves for their calamities, who resents their injuries, and who rejoices at their good fortune ! When we bring home to ourselves the situation of his companions, we enter into their gratitude, and feel what consolation they must derive from the tender sympathy of so affectionate a friend. And for a contrary reason, how disagreeable does he appear to be, whose hard and obdurate heart feels for himself only, but is altogether insensible to the happiness or misery of others ! We enter, in this case too, into the pain which his presence must give to every mortal with whom he converses, to those especially with whom we are most apt to sympathize, the unfortunate and the injured.

277   On the other hand, what noble propriety and grace do we feel in the conduct of those who, in their own case, exert that recollection and self-command which constitute the dignity of every passion, and which bring it down to what others can enter into ? We are disgusted with that clamorous grief which, without any delicacy, calls upon our compassion with sighs and tears and importunate lamentations. But we reverence that reserved, that silent and majestic sorrow, which discovers itself only in the swelling of the eyes, in the quivering of the lips and cheeks, and in the distant, but affecting coldness of the whole behaviour. It imposes the like silence upon us. We regard it with respectful attention, and watch with anxious concern over our whole behaviour, lest by any impropriety we should disturb that concerted tranquillity, which it requires so great an effort to support.

The insolence and brutality of anger, in the same manner when we indulge its fury without check or restraint, is, of all objects, the most detestable. But we admire that noble and generous resentment which governs its pursuit of the greatest injuries, not by the rage which they are apt to excite in the breast of the sufferer, but by the indignation which they naturally call forth in that of the impartial spectator ; which allows no word, no gesture, to escape it beyond what this more equitable sentiment would dictate ; which never, even in thought, attempts any greater vengeance, nor desires to inflict any greater punishment, than what every indifferent person would rejoice to see executed.

278   And hence it is, that to feel much for others and little for ourselves, that to restrain our selfish, and to indulge our benevolent affections, constitutes the perfection of human nature ; and can alone produce among mankind that harmony of sentiments and passions in which consists their whole grace and propriety. As to love our neighbour as we love ourselves is the great law of Christianity, so it is the great precept of nature to love ourselves only as we love our neighbour, or what comes to the same thing, as our neighbour is capable of loving us.

As taste and good judgment, when they are considered as qualities which deserve praise and admiration, are supposed to imply a delicacy of sentiment and an acuteness of understanding not commonly to be met with ; so the virtues of sensibility and self-command are not apprehended to consist in the ordinary, but in the uncommon degrees of those qualities. The amiable virtue of humanity requires, surely, a sensibility much beyond what is possessed by the rude vulgar of mankind. The great and exalted virtue of magnanimity undoubtedly demands much more than that degree of self-command, which the weakest of mortals is capable of exerting. As in the common degree of the intellectual qualities, there are no abilities ; so in the common degree of the moral, there is no virtue. Virtue is excellence, something uncommonly great and beautiful, which rises far above what is vulgar and ordinary. The amiable virtues consist in that degree of sensibility which surprises by its exquisite and unexpected delicacy and tenderness : the awful and respectable, in that degree of self-command which astonishes by its amazing superiority over the most ungovernable passions of human nature.

279   There is, in this respect, a considerable difference between virtue and mere propriety; between those qualities and actions which deserve to be admired and celebrated, and those which simply deserve to be approved of. Upon many occasions, to act with the most perfect propriety, requires no more than that common and ordinary degree of sensibility or self-command which the most worthless of mankind are possest of, and sometimes even that degree is not necessary. Thus, to give a very low instance, to eat when we are hungry, is certainly, upon ordinary occasions, perfectly right and proper, and cannot miss being approved of as such by every body. Nothing, however, could be more absurd than to say it was virtuous.

On the contrary, there may frequently be a considerable degree of virtue in those actions which fall short of the most perfect propriety; because they may still approach nearer to perfection than could well be expected upon occasions on which it was so extremely difficult to attain it : and this is very often the case upon these occasions which require the greatest exertions of self-command. There are some situations which bear so hard upon human nature, that the greatest degree of self-government, which can belong to so imperfect a creature as man, is not able to stifle, altogether, the voice of human weakness, or reduce the violence of the passions to that pitch of moderation, in which the impartial spectator can entirely enter into them. Though in those cases, therefore, the behaviour of the sufferer fall short of the most perfect propriety, it may still deserve some applause, and, even, in a certain sense, may be denominated virtuous. It may still manifest an effort of generosity and magnanimity of which the greater part of men are incapable ; and though it fails of absolute perfection, it may be a much nearer approximation towards perfection, than what, upon such trying occasions, is commonly either to be found or to be expected.

280   In cases of this kind, when we are determining the degree of blame or applause which seems due to any action, we very frequently make use of two different standards. The first is the idea of complete propriety and perfection, which, in those difficult situations, no human conduct ever did, or ever can come up to ; and in comparison with which the actions of all men must for ever appear blameable and imperfect. The second is the idea of that degree of proximity or distance from this complete perfection, which the actions of the greater part of men commonly arrive at. Whatever goes beyond this degree, how far soever it may be removed from absolute perfection, seems to deserve applause ; and whatever falls short of it, to deserve blame.

281   It is in the same manner that we judge of the productions of all the arts which address themselves to the imagination. When a critic examines the work of any of the great masters in poetry or painting, he may sometimes examine it by an idea of perfection, in his own mind, which neither that nor any other human work will ever come up to ; and as long as he compares it with this standard, he can see nothing in it but faults and imperfections. But when he comes to consider the rank which it ought to hold among other works of the same kind, he necessarily compares it with a very different standard, the common degree of excellence which is usually attained in this particular art ; and when he judges of it by this new measure, it may often appear to deserve the highest applause, upon account of its approaching much nearer to perfection than the greater part of those works which can be brought into competition with it.

SECTION II.—Of the Degrees of the different
Passions which are consistent with
Propriety.

INTRODUCTION.

282   THE propriety of every passion excited by objects peculiarly
related to ourselves, the pitch which the spectator can go along
with, must lie, it is evident, in a certain mediocrity. If the
passion is too high, or if it is too low, he cannot enter into it.
Grief and resentment for private misfortunes and injuries may
easily, for example, be too high, and in the greater part of
mankind, they are so. They may likewise, though this more
rarely happens, be too low. We denominate the excess,
weakness and fury : and we call the defect, stupidity, insensibility, and want of spirit. We can enter into neither of
them, but are astonished and confounded to see them.

   This mediocrity, however, in which the point of propriety
consists, is different in different passions. It is high in some,
and low in others. There are some passions which it is indecent to express very strongly, even upon those occasions, in
which it is acknowledged that we cannot avoid feeling them
in the highest degree. And there are others of which the
strongest expressions are upon many occasions extremely
graceful, even though the passions themselves do not, perhaps,
arise so necessarily. The first are those passions with which,
for certain reasons, there is little or no sympathy : the second
are those with which, for other reasons, there is the greatest.
And if we consider all the different passions of human nature,
we shall find that they are regarded as decent or indecent, just
in proportion as mankind are more or less disposed to
sympathize with them.

                *   *   *   *   *   *   *

CHAPTER IV.—OF THE SOCIAL PASSIONS.

283 As it is a divided sympathy which renders the whole set of passions just now mentioned, upon most occasions, so ungraceful and disagreeable ; so there is another set opposite to these, which a redoubled sympathy renders almost always peculiarly agreeable and becoming. Generosity, humanity, kindness, compassion, mutual friendship, and esteem, all the social and benevolent affections, when expressed in the countenance or behaviour, even towards those who are not peculiarly connected with ourselves, please the indifferent spectator upon almost every occasion. His sympathy with the person who feels those passions exactly coincides with his concern for the person who is the object of them. The interest, which, as a man, he is obliged to take in the happiness of this last, enlivens his fellow-feeling with the sentiments of the other, whose emotions are employed about the same object. We have always, therefore, the strongest disposition to sympathize with the benevolent affections. They appear in every respect agreeable to us. We enter into the satisfaction both of the person who feels them, and of the person who is the object of them. For as to be the object of hatred and indignation gives more pain than all the evil which a brave man can fear from his enemies ; so there is a satisfaction in the consciousness of being beloved, which, to a person of delicacy and sensibility, is of more importance to happiness than all the advantage which he can expect to derive from it. What character is so detestable as that of one who takes pleasure to sow dissension among friends, and to turn their most tender love into mortal hatred ? Yet wherein does the atrocity of this so much abhorred injury consist ? Is it in depriving them of the frivolous good offices, which, had their friendship continued, they might have expected from one another ? It is in depriving them of that friendship itself, in robbing them of each other's affections, from which both derived so much satisfaction ; it is

in disturbing the harmony of their hearts, and putting an end
to that happy commerce which had before subsisted between
them. These affections, that harmony, this commerce, are felt,
not only by the tender and the delicate, but by the rudest vulgar
of mankind, to be of more importance to happiness than all
the little services which could be expected to flow from them.

284   The sentiment of love is, in itself, agreeable to the person
who feels it. It soothes and composes the breast, seems to
favour the vital motions, and to promote the healthful state
of the human constitution; and it is rendered still more
delightful by the consciousness of the gratitude and satisfaction
which it must excite in him who is the object of it. Their
mutual regard renders them happy in one another, and sympathy, with this mutual regard, makes them agreeable to every
other person.

PART II.

OF MERIT AND DEMERIT; OR, OF THE OBJECTS
OF REWARD AND PUNISHMENT.

SECTION I.—OF THE SENSE OF MERIT AND DEMERIT.

CHAPTER I.—THAT WHATEVER APPEARS TO BE THE PROPER
OBJECT OF GRATITUDE, APPEARS TO DESERVE REWARD;
AND THAT, IN THE SAME MANNER, WHATEVER APPEARS
TO BE THE PROPER OBJECT OF RESENTMENT, APPEARS TO
DESERVE PUNISHMENT.

285   To us, therefore, that action must appear to deserve reward,
which appears to be the proper and approved object of that
sentiment, which most immediately and directly prompts us to
reward, or to do good to another. And in the same manner,
that action must appear to deserve punishment, which appears
to be the proper and approved object of that sentiment which

most immediately and directly prompts us to punish, or to inflict evil upon another.

The sentiment which most immediately and directly prompts us to reward, is gratitude; that which most immediately and directly prompts us to punish, is resentment.

To us, therefore, that action must appear to deserve reward, which appears to be the proper and approved object of gratitude; as, on the other hand, that action must appear to deserve punishment, which appears to be the proper and approved object of resentment.

To reward is to recompense, to remunerate, to return good for good received. To punish, too, is to recompense, to remunerate, though in a different manner; it is to return evil for evil that has been done.

286 There are some other passions, besides gratitude and resentment, which interest us in the happiness or misery of others; but there are none which so directly excite us to be the instruments of either. The love and esteem which grow upon acquaintance and habitual approbation, necessarily lead us to be pleased with the good fortune of the man who is the object of such agreeable emotions, and consequently, to be willing to lend a hand to promote it. Our love, however, is fully satisfied, though his good fortune should be brought about without our assistance. All that this passion desires is to see him happy, without regarding who was the author of his prosperity. But gratitude is not to be satisfied in this manner. If the person to whom we owe many obligations is made happy without our assistance, though it pleases our love, it does not content our gratitude. Till we have recompensed him, till we ourselves have been instrumental in promoting his happiness, we feel ourselves still loaded with that debt which his past services have laid upon us.

287 The hatred and dislike, in the same manner, which grow upon habitual disapprobation, would often lead us to take a malicious pleasure in the misfortune of the man whose

conduct and character excite so painful a passion. But
though dislike and hatred harden us against all sympathy,
and sometimes dispose us even to rejoice at the distress
of another, yet, if there is no resentment in the case, if neither
we nor our friends have received any great personal provocation, these passions would not naturally lead us to wish to be
instrumental in bringing it about.

*   *   *   *   *   *   *

288   But it is quite otherwise with resentment: if the person
who has done us some great injury, who had murdered our
father or our brother, for example, should soon afterwards
die of a fever, or even be brought to the scaffold upon
account of some other crime, though it might sooth our
hatred, it would not fully gratify our resentment. Resentment
would prompt us to desire, not only that he should be punished, but that he should be punished by our means, and
upon account of that particular injury which he had done
to us.   Resentment cannot be fully gratified unless the
offender is not only made to grieve in his turn, but to grieve
for that particular wrong which we have suffered from him.
He must be made to repent and be sorry for this very action,
that others, through fear of the like punishment, may be
terrified from being guilty of the like offence.   The natural
gratification of this passion tends, of its own accord, to produce
all the political ends of punishment; the correction of the
criminal, and the example to the public.

289   Gratitude and resentment, therefore, are the sentiments
which most immediately and directly prompt to reward and
to punish.   To us, therefore, he must appear to deserve
reward, who appears to be the proper and approved object
of gratitude; and he to deserve punishment, who appears
to be that of resentment.

CHAPTER II.—OF THE PROPER OBJECTS OF GRATITUDE AND RESENTMENT.

290   To be the proper and approved object either of gratitude or resentment, can mean nothing but to be the object of that gratitude, and of that resentment which naturally seems proper, and is approved of.

But these, as well as all the other passions of human nature, seem proper and are approved of, when the heart of every impartial spectator entirely sympathizes with them, when every indifferent by-stander entirely enters into, and goes along with them.

291   He, therefore, appears to deserve reward, who, to some person or persons, is the natural object of a gratitude which every human heart is disposed to beat time to, and thereby applaud : and he, on the other hand, appears to deserve punishment, who in the same manner is to some person or persons the natural object of a resentment which the breast of every reasonable man is ready to adopt and sympathize with.   To us, surely, that action must appear to deserve reward which every body who knows of it would wish to reward, and therefore delights to see rewarded : and that action must as surely appear to deserve punishment which every body who hears of it is angry with, and upon that account rejoices to see punished.

292   1. As we sympathize with the joy of our companions when in prosperity, so we join with them in the complacency and satisfaction with which they naturally regard whatever is the cause of their good fortune.   We enter into the love and affection which they conceive for it, and begin to love it too. We should be sorry for their sakes if it was destroyed, or even if it was placed at too great a distance from them, and out of the reach of their care and protection, though they should lose nothing by its absence except the pleasure of seeing it.

If it is man who has thus been the fortunate instrument of the happiness of his brethren, this is still more peculiarly the case. When we see one man assisted, protected, relieved by another, our sympathy with the joy of the person who receives the benefit serves only to animate our fellow-feeling with his gratitude towards him who bestows it. When we look upon the person who is the cause of his pleasure with the eyes with which we imagine he must look upon him, his benefactor seems to stand before us in the most engaging and amiable light. We readily therefore sympathize with the grateful affection which he conceives for a person to whom he has been so much obliged; and consequently applaud the returns which he is disposed to make for the good offices conferred upon him. As we entirely enter into the affection from which these returns proceed, they necessarily seem every way proper and suitable to their object.

293   2. In the same manner, as we sympathize with the sorrow of our fellow-creature whenever we see his distress, so we likewise enter into his abhorrence and aversion for whatever has given occasion to it. Our heart, as it adopts and beats time to his grief, so it is likewise animated with that spirit by which he endeavours to drive away or destroy the cause of it. The indolent and passive fellow-feeling by which we accompany him in his sufferings, readily gives way to that more vigorous and active sentiment by which we go along with him in the effort he makes, either to repel them, or to gratify his aversion to what has given occasion to them. This is still more peculiarly the case, when it is man who has caused them. When we see one man oppressed or injured by another, the sympathy which we feel with the distress of the sufferer seems to serve only to animate our fellow-feeling with his resentment against the offender. We are rejoiced to see him attack his adversary in his turn, and are eager and ready to assist him whenever he exerts bimself for defence, or even for vengeance within a certain degree. If the injured should perish in the quarrel, we not only sympathize with the real resentment of his friends and relations, but with the imaginary resentment which in fancy we lend to the dead, who is no longer capable of feeling or any other human sentiment.

* * * * * * *

The horrors which are supposed to haunt the bed of the murderer, the ghosts which superstition imagines rise from their graves to demand vengeance upon those who brought them to an untimely end, all take their origin from this natural sympathy with the imaginary resentment of the slain. And with regard, at least, to this most dreadful of crimes, Nature, antecedent to all reflections upon the utility of punishment, has in this manner stamped upon the human heart, in the strongest and most indelible characters, an immediate and instinctive approbation of the sacred and necessary law of retaliation.

CHAPTER III.—THAT WHERE THERE IS NO APPROBATION OF THE CONDUCT OF THE PERSON WHO CONFERS THE BENEFIT, THERE IS LITTLE SYMPATHY WITH THE GRATITUDE OF HIM WHO RECEIVES IT: AND THAT, ON THE CONTRARY, WHERE THERE IS NO DISAPPROBATION OF THE MOTIVES OF THE PERSON WHO DOES THE MISCHIEF, THERE IS NO SORT OF SYMPATHY WITH THE RESENTMENT OF HIM WHO SUFFERS IT.

294 IT is to be observed, however, that, how beneficial soever on the one hand, or how hurtful soever on the other, the actions or intentions of the person who acts may have been to the person who is, if I may say so, acted upon, yet if in the one case there appears to have been no propriety in the motives of the agent, if we cannot enter into the affections which influenced his conduct, we have little sympathy with the gratitude of the person who receives the benefit: or if, in the other case, there appears to have been no impropriety in the motives of the agent, if, on the contrary, the affections which influenced his conduct are such as we must necessarily enter into, we can have no sort of sympathy with the resentment of the person who suffers. Little gratitude seems due in the one case, and all sort of resentment seems unjust in the other. The one action seems to merit little reward, the other to deserve no punishment.

295 1. First, I say, That wherever we cannot sympathize with the affections of the agent, wherever there seems to be no propriety in the motives which influenced his conduct, we are less disposed to enter into the gratitude of the person who received the benefit of his actions. A very small return seems due to that foolish and profuse generosity which confers the greatest benefits from the most trivial motives, and gives an estate to a man merely because his name and sirname happen to be the same with those of the giver. Such services do not seem to demand any proportionable recompense. Our contempt for the folly of the agent hinders us from thoroughly entering into the gratitude of the person to whom the good office has been done. His benefactor seems unworthy of it. As when we place ourselves in the situation of the person obliged, we feel that we could conceive no great reverence for such a benefactor, we easily absolve him from a great deal of that submissive veneration and esteem which we should think due to a more respectable character ; and provided he always treats his weak friend with kindness and humanity, we are willing to excuse him from many attentions and regards which we should demand to a worthier patron. Those Princes, who have heaped, with the greatest profusion, wealth, power, and honours, upon their favourites, have seldom excited that degree of attachment to their persons which has often been experienced by those who were more frugal of their favours. The well-natured, but injudicious prodigality of James the First of Great Britain seems to have attached nobody to his person ; and that Prince, notwithstanding his social and harmless disposition, appears to have lived and died without a friend. The whole gentry and nobility of

England exposed their lives and fortunes in the cause of his more frugal and distinguishing son, notwithstanding the coldness and distant severity of his ordinary deportment.

296   2. Secondly, I say, That wherever the conduct of the agent appears to have been entirely directed by motives and affections which we thoroughly enter into and approve of, we can have no sort of sympathy with the resentment of the sufferer, how great soever the mischief which may have been done to him. When two people quarrel, if we take part with, and entirely adopt the resentment of one of them, it is impossible that we should enter into that of the other. Our sympathy with the person whose motives we go along with, and whom therefore we look upon as in the right, cannot but harden us against all fellow-feeling with the other, whom we necessarily regard as in the wrong. Whatever this last, therefore, may have suffered, while it is no more than what we ourselves should have wished him to suffer, while it is no more than what our own sympathetic indignation would have prompted us to inflict upon him, it cannot either displease or provoke us. When an inhuman murderer is brought to the scaffold, though we have some compassion for his misery, we can have no sort of fellow-feeling with his resentment, if he should be so absurd as to express any against either his prosecutor or his judge. The natural tendency of their just indignation against so vile a criminal is indeed the most fatal and ruinous to him. But it is impossible that we should be displeased with the tendency of a sentiment, which, when we bring the case home to ourselves, we feel that we cannot avoid adopting.

CHAPTER IV.—RECAPITULATION OF THE FOREGOING CHAPTERS.

297   1. WE do not, therefore, thoroughly and heartily sympathize with the gratitude of one man towards another, merely because this other has been the cause of his good fortune, unless he has been the cause of it from motives which we entirely go along with. Our heart must adopt the principles of the agent, and go along with all the affections which influenced his conduct, before it can entirely sympathize with, and beat time to, the gratitude of the person who has been benefited by his actions. If in the conduct of the benefactor there appears to have been no propriety, how beneficial soever its effects, it does not seem to demand, or necessarily to require, any proportionable recompense.

298   But when to the beneficent tendency of the action is joined the propriety of the affection from which it proceeds, when we entirely sympathize and go along with the motives of the agent, the love which we conceive for him upon his own account, enhances and enlivens our fellow-feeling with the gratitude of those who owe their prosperity to his good conduct. His actions seem then to demand, and, if I may say so, to call aloud for a proportionable recompense. We then entirely enter into that gratitude which prompts to bestow it. The benefactor seems then to be the proper object of reward, when we thus entirely sympathize with, and approve of, that sentiment which prompts to reward him. When we approve of, and go along with, the affection from which the action proceeds, we must necessarily approve of the action, and regard the person towards whom it is directed as its proper and suitable object.

*   *   *   *   *   *   *

CHAPTER V.—THE ANALYSIS OF THE SENSE OF MERIT AND DEMERIT.

299   1. As our sense, therefore, of the propriety of conduct arises from what I shall call a direct sympathy with the affections and motives of the person who acts, so our sense of its merits arises from what I shall call an indirect sympathy with the gratitude of the person who is, if I may say so, acted upon.

As we cannot indeed enter thoroughly into the gratitude of the person who receives the benefit, unless we beforehand approve of the motives of the benefactor, so, upon this account, the sense of merit seems to be a compounded sentiment, and to be made up of two distinct emotions; a direct sympathy with the sentiments of the agent, and an indirect sympathy with the gratitude of those who receive the benefit of his actions.

300   We may, upon many different occasions, plainly distinguish those two different emotions combining and uniting together in our sense of the good desert of a particular character or action.   When we read in history concerning actions of proper and beneficent greatness of mind, how eagerly do we enter into such designs?   How much are we animated by that high-spirited generosity which directs them?   How keen are we for their success?   How grieved at their disappointment?   In imagination we become the very person whose actions are represented to us : we transport ourselves in fancy to the scenes of those distant and forgotten adventures, and imagine ourselves acting the part of a Scipio or a Camillus, a Timeleon or an Aristides.   So far our sentiments are founded upon the direct sympathy with the person who acts.   Nor is the indirect sympathy with those who receive the benefit of such actions less sensibly felt.   Whenever we place ourselves in the situation of these last, with what warm and affectionate fellow-feeling do we enter into their gratitude towards those who served them so essentially ?   We embrace, as it were, their benefactor along with them.   Our heart readily sympathizes with the highest transports of their graceful affection.   No honours, no rewards, we think, can be too great for them to bestow upon him. When they make this proper return for his services, we heartily applaud and go along with them ; but are shocked beyond all measure, if by their conduct they appear to have little sense of the obligations conferred upon them.   Our whole sense, in short, of the merit and good desert of such actions, of the

propriety and fitness of recompensing them, and making the person who performed them rejoice in his turn, arises from the sympathetic emotions of gratitude and love, with which, when we bring home to our own breast the situation of those principally concerned, we feel ourselves naturally transported towards the man who could act with such proper and noble beneficence.

301 2. In the same manner, as our sense of the impropriety of conduct arises from a want of sympathy, or from a direct antipathy to the affections and motives of the agent, so our sense of its demerit arises from what I shall here too call an indirect sympathy with the resentment of the sufferer.

As we cannot indeed enter into the resentment of the sufferer, unless our heart beforehand disapproves the motives of the agent, and renounces all fellow-feeling with them; so upon this account the sense of demerit, as well as that of merit, seems to be a compounded sentiment, and to be made up of two distinct emotions; a direct antipathy to the sentiments of the agent, and an indirect sympathy with the resentment of the sufferer.

302 *Note.* To ascribe in this manner our natural sense of the ill desert of human actions to a sympathy with the resentment of the sufferer, may seem, to the greater part of people, to be a degradation of that sentiment. Resentment is commonly regarded as so odious a passion, that they will be apt to think it impossible that so laudable a principle, as the sense of the ill desert of vice, should in any respects be founded upon it. They will be more willing, perhaps, to admit that our sense of the merit of good actions is founded upon a sympathy with the gratitude of the persons who receive the benefit of them; because gratitude, as well as all the other benevolent passions, is regarded as an amiable principle, which can take nothing from the worth of whatever is founded upon it. Gratitude and resentment, however, are, in every respect, it is evident, counterparts to one another; and if our sense of merit arises from a sympathy with the one, our sense of demerit can scarce miss to proceed from a fellow-feeling with the other.

303 Let it be considered too that resentment, though, in the degrees in which we too often see it, the most odious, perhaps, of all the passions, is not disapproved of when properly humbled and entirely brought down to the level of the sympathetic indignation of the spectator. When we, who are the by-standers, feel that our own animosity entirely corresponds with that of the sufferer, when the resentment of this last does not in any respect go beyond our own, when no word, no gesture escapes him that denotes an emotion more violent than what we can keep time to, and when he never aims at inflicting any punishment beyond what we should rejoice to see inflicted, or what we ourselves would upon this account even desire to be the instruments of inflicting, it is impossible that we should not entirely approve of his sentiments. Our own emotion in this case must, in our eyes, undoubtedly justify his. And as experience teaches us how much the greater part of mankind are incapable of this moderation, and how great an effort must be made in order to bring down the rude and undisciplined impulse of resentment to this suitable temper, we cannot avoid conceiving a considerable degree of esteem and admiration for one who appears capable of exerting so much self-command over one of the most ungovernable passions of his nature. When indeed the animosity of the sufferer exceeds, as it almost always does, what we can go along with, as we cannot enter into it, we necessarily disapprove of it.   We even disapprove of it more than we should of an equal excess of almost any other passion derived from the imagination.   And this too violent resentment, instead of carrying us along with it, becomes itself the object of our resentment and indignation.   We enter into the opposite resentment of the person who is the object of this unjust emotion, and who is in danger of suffering from it.   Revenge, therefore, the excess of resentment, appears to be the most detestable of all the passions, and is the object of the horror and indignation of every body.   And as in the way in which this passion commonly discovers itself among mankind, it is excessive a hundred times for once that it is moderate, we are very apt to consider it as altogether odious and detestable, because in its most ordinary appearance it is so.   Nature, however, even in the present depraved state of mankind, does not seem to have dealt so unkindly with us, as to have endowed us with any principle which is wholly and in every respect evil, or which, in no degree and in no direction, can be the proper object of praise and approbation.   Upon some occasions we are sensible that this passion, which is generally too strong, may likewise be too weak. We sometimes complain that a particular person shows too little spirit, and has too little sense of the injuries that have been done to him ; and we are as ready to despise him for the defect, as to hate him for the excess of this passion.

The inspired writers would not surely have talked so frequently or so strongly of the wrath and anger of God, if they had regarded every degree of those passions as vicious and evil, even in so weak and imperfect a creature as man.

304   Let it be considered too, that the present inquiry is not concerning a matter of right, if I may say so, but concerning a matter of fact.   We are not at present examining upon what principles a perfect being would approve of the punishment of bad actions ; but upon what principles so weak and imperfect a creature as man actually and in fact approves of it. The principles which I have just now mentioned, it is evident, have a very great effect upon his sentiments ; and it seems wisely ordered that it should be so.   The very existence of society requires that unmerited and unprovoked malice should be restrained by proper punishments ; and consequently, that to inflict those punishments should be regarded as a proper and laudable action.   Though man, therefore, be naturally endowed with a desire of the welfare and preservation of society, yet the Author of Nature has not entrusted it to his reason to find out that a certain application of punishments is the proper means of attaining this end ; but has endowed him with an immediate and instinctive approbation of that very application which is most proper to attain it. The œconomy of Nature is in this respect exactly of a piece with what it is upon many other occasions. With regard to all those ends which, upon account of their peculiar importance, may be regarded, if such an expression is allowable, as the favourite ends of Nature, she has constantly in this manner not only endowed mankind with an appetite for the end which she proposes, but likewise with an appetite for the means by which alone this end can be brought about, for their own sakes, and independent of their tendency to produce it. Thus self-preservation, and the propagation of the species, and the great ends which Nature seems to have proposed in the formation of all animals. Mankind are endowed with a desire of those ends, and an aversion to the contrary ; with a love of life, and a dread of dissolution ; with a desire of the continuance and perpetuity of the species, and with an aversion to the thoughts of its entire extinction. But though we are in this manner endowed with a very strong desire of those ends, it has not been intrusted to the slow and uncertain determinations of our reason, to find out the proper means of bringing them about. Nature has directed us to the greater part of these by original and immediate instincts. Hunger, thirst, the passion which unites the two sexes, the love of pleasure and the dread of pain, prompt us to apply those means for their own sakes, and without any consideration of their tendency to those beneficent ends which the great Director of nature intended to produce by them.

305 Before I conclude this note, I must take notice of a difference between the approbation of propriety and that of merit or beneficence. Before we approve of the sentiments of any person as proper and suitable to their objects, we must not only be affected in the same manner as he is, but we must perceive this harmony and correspondence of sentiments between him and ourselves. Thus, though upon hearing of a misfortune that had befallen my friend, I should conceive precisely that degree of concern which he gives way to ; yet till I am informed of the manner in which he behaves, till I perceive the harmony between his emotions and mine, I cannot be said to approve of the sentiments which influence his behaviour. The approbation of propriety therefore requires, not only that we should entirely sympathize with the person who acts, but that we should perceive this present concord between his sentiments and our own. On the contrary, when I hear of a benefit that has been bestowed upon another person, let him who has received it be affected in what manner he pleases, if, by bringing his case home to myself, I feel gratitude arise in my own breast, I necessarily approve of the conduct of his benefactor, and regard it as meritorious, and the proper object of reward. Whether the person who has received the benefit conceives gratitude or not, cannot, it is evident, in any degree alter our sentiments with regard to the merit of him who has bestowed it. No actual correspondence of sentiments, therefore, is here required. It is sufficient that if he was grateful, they would correspond ; and our sense of merit is often founded upon one of those illusive sympathies, by which, when we bring home to ourselves the case of another, we are often affected in a manner in which the person principally concerned is incapable of being affected. There is a similar difference between our disapprobation of demerit, and that of impropriety.

* * * * * * *

PART III.

OF THE FOUNDATION OF OUR JUDGMENTS CONCERNING OUR OWN SENTIMENTS AND CONDUCT, AND OF THE SENSE OF DUTY.

—————•—————

CHAPTER I.—OF THE PRINCIPLE OF SELF-APPROBATION AND OF SELF-DISAPPROBATION.

306 IN the two foregoing parts of this discourse, I have chiefly considered the origin and foundation of our judgments concerning the sentiments and conduct of others. I come now to consider more particularly the origin of those concerning our own.

The principle by which we naturally either approve or disapprove of our own conduct seems to be altogether the same with that by which we exercise the like judgments concerning the conduct of other people. We either approve or disapprove of the conduct of another man according as we feel that, when we bring his case home to ourselves, we either can or cannot entirely sympathize with the sentiments and motives which directed it. And, in the same manner, we either approve or disapprove of our own conduct, according as we feel that, when we place ourselves in the situation of another man, and view it, as it were, with his eyes, and from his station, we either can or cannot entirely enter into and sympathize with the sentiments and motives which influenced it. We can never survey our own sentiments and motives, we can never form any judgment concerning them; unless we remove ourselves, as it were, from our own natural station, and endeavour to view them as at a certain distance from us. But we can do this in no other way than by endeavouring to view them with the eyes of other people, or as other people are likely to view them. Whatever judgment we can form concerning them, accordingly, must always bear some secret reference, either to what are, or to what, upon a certain condition, would be, or to what, we imagine, ought to be the judgment of others. We endeavour to examine our own conduct as we imagine any other fair and impartial spectator would examine it. If, upon placing ourselves in his situation, we thoroughly enter into all the passions and motives which influenced it, we approve of it, by sympathy with the approbation of this supposed equitable judge. If otherwise, we enter into his disapprobation, and condemn it.

307   Were it possible that a human creature could grow up to manhood in some solitary place, without any communication with his own species, he could no more think of his own character, of the propriety or demerit of his own sentiments and conduct, of the beauty or deformity of his own mind, than of the beauty or deformity of his own face. All these are objects which he cannot easily see, which naturally he does not look at, and with regard to which he is provided with no mirror which can present them to his view. Bring him into society, and he is immediately provided with the mirror which he wanted before. It is placed in the countenance and behaviour of those he lives with, which always mark when they enter into, and when they disapprove of his sentiments; and it is here that he first views the propriety and impropriety of his own passions, the beauty and deformity of his own mind. To a man who from his birth was a stranger to society, the objects of his passions, the external bodies which either pleased or hurt him, would occupy his whole attention. The passions themselves, the desires or aversions, the joys or sorrows, which those objects excited, though of all things the most immediately present to him, could scarce ever be the objects of his thoughts. The idea of them could never interest him so much as to call upon his attentive consideration. The consideration of his joy could in him excite no new joy, nor that of his sorrow any new sorrow, though the consideration of the

causes of those passions might often excite both.   Bring
him into society, and all his own passions will immediately
become the causes of new passions.   He will observe that
mankind approve of some of them, and are disgusted by
others.   He will be elevated in the one case, and cast down
in the other; his desires and aversions, his joys and sorrows,
will now often become the causes of new desires and new
aversions, new joys and new sorrows : they will now, therefore, interest him deeply, and often call upon his most attentive consideration.

308   Our first ideas of personal beauty and deformity are drawn
from the shape and appearance of others, not from our own.
We soon become sensible, however, that others exercise the
same criticism upon us.   We are pleased when they approve of
our figure, and are disobliged when they seem to be disgusted.
We become anxious to know how far our appearance deserves
either their blame or approbation.   We examine our persons
limb by limb, and by placing ourselves before a looking-glass,
or by some such expedient, endeavour, as much as possible,
to view ourselves at the distance and with the eyes of other
people.   If, after this examination, we are satisfied with our
own appearance, we can more easily support the most disadvantageous judgments of others.   If, on the contrary, we
are sensible that we are the natural objects of distaste, every
appearance of their disapprobation mortifies us beyond all
measure.   A man who is tolerably handsome, will allow you to
laugh at any little irregularity in his person ; but all such jokes
are commonly unsupportable to one who is really deformed.
It is evident, however, that we are anxious about our own
beauty and deformity, only upon account of its effect upon
others.   If we had no connexion with society, we should be
altogether indifferent about either.

309   In the same manner our first moral criticisms are exercised
upon the characters and conduct of other people ; and we are
all very forward to observe how each of these affects us.   But

we soon learn, that other people are equally frank with regard
to our own. We become anxious to know how far we deserve
their censure or applause, and whether to them we must
necessarily appear those agreeable or disagreeable creatures
which they represent us. We begin, upon this account, to
examine our own passions and conduct, and to consider how
these must appear to them, by considering how they would
appear to us if in their situation. We suppose ourselves the
spectators of our own behaviour, and endeavour to imagine
what effect it would, in this light, produce upon us. This is
the only looking-glass by which we can, in some measure, with
the eyes of other people, scrutinize the propriety of our own
conduct. If in this view it pleases us, we are tolerably
satisfied. We can be more indifferent about the applause,
and, in some measure, despise the censure of the world ;
secure that, however misunderstood or misrepresented, we are
the natural and proper objects of approbation. On the contrary, if we are doubtful about it, we are often upon that very
account, more anxious to gain their approbation, and provided
we have not already, as they say, shaken hands with infamy,
we are altogether distracted at the thoughts of their censure,
which then strikes us with double severity.

310   When I endeavour to examine my own conduct, when
I endeavour to pass sentence upon it, and either to approve or
condemn it, it is evident that, in all such cases, I divide myself,
as it were, into two persons ; and that I, the examiner and
judge, represent a different character from that other I, the
person whose conduct is examined into, and judged of. The
first is the spectator, whose sentiments with regard to my own
conduct I endeavour to enter into, by placing myself in his
situation, and by considering how it would appear to me,
when seen from that particular point of view. The second
is the agent, the person whom I properly call myself, and of
whose conduct, under the character of a spectator, I was
endeavouring to form some opinion. The first is the judge ;

the second the person judged of. But that the judge should, in every respect, be the same with the person judged of, is as impossible, as that the cause should, in every respect, be the same with the effect.

To be amiable and to be meritorious ; that is, to deserve love and to deserve reward, are the great characters of virtue ; and to be odious and punishable, of vice. But all these characters have an immediate reference to the sentiments of others. Virtue is not said to be amiable, or to be meritorious, because it is the object of its own love, or of its own gratitude ; but because it excites those sentiments in other men. The consciousness that it is the object of such favourable regards, is the source of that inward tranquillity and self-satisfaction with which it is naturally attended, as the suspicion of the contrary, gives occasion to the torments of vice. What so great happiness as to be beloved, and to know that we deserve to be beloved ? What so great misery as to be hated, and to know that we deserve to be hated ?

*　　*　　*　　*　　*　　*　　*

CHAPTER IV.—OF THE NATURE OF SELF-DECEIT, AND OF THE ORIGIN AND USE OF GENERAL RULES.

*　　*　　*　　*　　*　　*　　*

311　THERE are two different occasions upon which we examine our own conduct, and endeavour to view it in the light in which the impartial spectator would view it : first, when we are about to act ; and secondly, after we have acted. Our views are apt to be very partial in both cases ; but they are apt to be most partial when it is of most importance that they should be otherwise.

When we are about to act, the eagerness of passion will seldom allow us to consider what we are doing, with the candour of an indifferent person. The violent emotions which at that time agitate us, discolour our views of things, even when we are endeavouring to place ourselves in the situation of another, and to regard the objects that interest us in the light in which they will naturally appear to him. The fury of our own passions constantly calls us back to our own place, where every thing appears magnified and misrepresented by self-love. Of the manner in which those objects would appear to another, of the view which he would take of them, we can obtain, if I may say so, but instantaneous glimpses, which vanish in a moment, and which, even while they last, are not altogether just. We cannot even for that moment divest ourselves entirely of the heat and keenness with which our peculiar situation inspires us, nor consider what we are about to do with the complete impartiality of an equitable judge. The passions, upon this account, as father Malebranche says, all justify themselves, and seem reasonable and proportioned to their objects, as long as we continue to feel them.

312   When the action is over, indeed, and the passions which prompted it have subsided, we can enter more coolly into the sentiments of the indifferent spectator. What before interested us is now become almost as indifferent to us as it always was to him, and we can now examine our own conduct with his candour and impartiality. The man of to-day is no longer agitated by the same passions which distracted the man of yesterday: and when the paroxysm of emotion, in the same manner as when the paroxysm of distress, is fairly over, we can identify ourselves, as it were, with the ideal man within the breast, and, in our own character, view, as in the one case, our own situation, so in the other, our own conduct, with the severe eyes of the most impartial spectator. But our judgments now are often of little importance in comparison of what they were before; and can frequently produce nothing but vain regret and unavailing repentance; without always securing us from the like errors in time to come.

*   *   *   *   *   *   *

313   So partial are the views of mankind with regard to the

propriety of their own conduct, both at the time of action and after it ; and so difficult is it for them to view it in the light in which any indifferent spectator would consider it. But if it was by a peculiar faculty, such as the moral sense is supposed to be, that they judged of their own conduct, if they were endued with a particular power of perception, which distinguished the beauty or deformity of passions and affections ; as their own passions would be more immediately exposed to the view of this faculty, it would judge with more accuracy concerning them, than concerning those of other men, of which it had only a more distant prospect.

314   This self-deceit, this fatal weakness of mankind, is the source of half the disorders of human life.   If we saw ourselves in the light in which others see us, or in which they would see us if they knew all, a reformation would generally be unavoidable.   We could not otherwise endure the fight.

Nature, however, has not left this weakness, which is of so much importance, altogether without a remedy ; nor has she abandoned us entirely to the delusions of self-love.   Our continual observations upon the conduct of others, insensibly lead us to form to ourselves certain general rules concerning what is fit and proper either to be done or to be avoided. Some of their actions shock all our natural sentiments.   We hear every body about us express the like detestation against them.   This still further confirms, and even exasperates our natural sense of their deformity.   It satisfies us that we view them in the proper light, when we see other people view them in the same light.   We resolve never to be guilty of the like, nor ever, upon any account, to render ourselves in this manner the objects of universal disapprobation.   We thus naturally lay down to ourselves a general rule, that all such actions are to be avoided, as tending to render us odious, contemptible, or punishable, the objects of all those sentiments for which we have the greatest dread and aversion.   Other actions, on the contrary, call forth our approbation, and we hear every body around us express the same favourable opinion concerning them. Every body is eager to honour and reward them. They excite all those sentiments for which we have by nature the strongest desire ; the love, the gratitude, the admiration of mankind. We become ambitious of performing the like ; and thus naturally lay down to ourselves a rule of another kind, that every opportunity of acting in this manner is carefully to be sought after.

315 It is thus that the general rules of morality are formed. They are ultimately founded upon experience of what, in particular instances, our moral faculties, our natural sense of merit and propriety, approve, or disapprove of. We do not originally approve or condemn particular actions ; because, upon examination, they appear to be agreeable or inconsistent with a certain general rule. The general rule, on the contrary, is formed, by finding from experience, that all actions of a certain kind, or circumstanced in a certain manner, are approved or disapproved of. To the man who first saw an inhuman murder, committed from avarice, envy, or unjust resentment, and upon one too that loved and trusted the murderer, who beheld the last agonies of the dying person, who heard him, with his expiring breath, complain more of the perfidy and ingratitude of his false friend, than of the violence which had been done to him, there could be no occasion, in order to conceive how horrible such an action was, that he should reflect, that one of the most sacred rules of conduct was what prohibited the taking away the life of an innocent person, that this was a plain violation of that rule, and consequently a very blameable action. His detestation of this crime, it is evident, would arise instantaneously and antecedent to his having formed to himself any such general rule. The general rule, on the contrary, which he might afterwards form, would be founded upon the detestation which he felt necessarily arise in his own breast, at the thought of this, and every other particular action of the same kind.

    *   *   *   *   *   *   *

316 When these general rules, indeed, have been formed, when they are universally acknowledged and established, by the concurring sentiments of mankind, we frequently appeal to them as to the standards of judgment, in debating concerning the degree of praise or blame that is due to certain actions of a complicated and dubious nature. They are upon these occasions commonly cited as the ultimate foundations of what is just and unjust in human conduct; and this circumstance seems to have misled several very eminent authors, to draw up their systems in such a manner, as if they had supposed that the original judgments of mankind with regard to right and wrong, were formed like the decisions of a court of judicatory, by considering first the general rule, and then, secondly, whether the particular action under consideration fell properly within its comprehension.

317 Those general rules of conduct, when they have been fixed in our mind by habitual reflection, are of great use in correcting the misrepresentations of self-love concerning what is fit and proper to be done in our particular situation. The man of furious resentment, if he was to listen to the dictates of that passion, would perhaps regard the death of his enemy, as but a small compensation for the wrong, he imagines, he has received; which, however, may be no more than a very slight provocation. But his observations upon the conduct of others, have taught him how horrible all such sanguinary revenges appear. Unless his education has been very singular, he has laid it down to himself as an inviolable rule, to abstain from them upon all occasions. This rule preserves its authority with him, and renders him incapable of being guilty of such a violence. Yet the fury of his own temper may be such, that had this been the first time in which he considered such an action, he would undoubtedly have determined it to be quite just and proper, and what every impartial spectator would approve of. But that reverence for the rule which past experience has impressed upon him, checks the impetuosity of his

passion, and helps him to correct the too partial views which
self-love might otherwise suggest, of what was proper to be done
in his situation.

*   *   *   *   *   *   *

PART IV.

OF THE EFFECT OF UTILITY UPON THE
SENTIMENT OF APPROBATION.

CHAPTER I.—OF THE BEAUTY WHICH THE APPEARANCE OF
UTILITY BESTOWS UPON ALL THE PRODUCTIONS OF ART,
AND OF THE EXTENSIVE INFLUENCE OF THIS SPECIES OF
BEAUTY.

318   THAT utility is one of the principal sources of beauty has
been observed by every body, who has considered with any
attention what constitutes the nature of beauty. The conveniency of a house gives pleasure to the spectator as well
as its regularity, and he is as much hurt when he observes
the contrary defect, as when he sees the correspondent windows
of different forms, or the door not placed exactly in the middle
of the building. That the fitness of any system or machine
to produce the end for which it was intended, bestows a certain
propriety and beauty upon the whole, and renders the very
thought and contemplation of it agreeable, is so very obvious·
that nobody has overlooked it.

319   The cause too, why utility pleases, has of late been assigned
by an ingenious and agreeable philosopher, who joins the
greatest depth of thought to the greatest elegance of expression, and possesses the singular and happy talent of treating
the abstrusest subjects not only with the most perfect per-
spicuity, but with the most lively eloquence. The utility of
any object, according to him, pleases the master by perpetually
suggesting to him the pleasure or conveniency which it is fitted

to promote. Every time he looks at it, he is put in mind of this pleasure ; and the object in this manner becomes a source of perpetual satisfaction and enjoyment. The spectator enters by sympathy into the sentiments of the master, and necessarily views the object under the same agreeable aspect. When we visit the palaces of the great, we cannot help conceiving the satisfaction we should enjoy if we ourselves were the masters, and were possessed of so much artful and ingeniously contrived accommodation. A similar account is given why the appearance of inconveniency should render any object disagreeable both to the owner and to the spectator.

320 But that this fitness, this happy contrivance of any production of art, should often be more valued, than the very end for which it was intended ; and that the exact adjustment of the means for obtaining any conveniency or pleasure, should frequently be more regarded, than that very conveniency or pleasure, in the attainment of which their whole merit would seem to consist, has not, so far as I know, been yet taken notice of by any body. That this however is very frequently the case, may be observed in a thousand instances, both in the most frivolous and in the most important concerns of human life.

When a person comes into his chamber, and finds the chairs all standing in the middle of the room, he is angry with his servant, and rather than see them continue in that disorder, perhaps takes the trouble himself to set them all in their places with their backs to the wall. The whole propriety of this new situation arises from its superior conveniency in leaving the floor free and disengaged. To attain this conveniency he voluntarily puts himself to more trouble than all he could have suffered from the want of it ; since nothing was more easy, than to have set himself down upon one of them, which is probably what he does when his labour is over. What he wanted therefore, it seems, was not so much this conveniency, as that arrangement of things which promotes it. Yet it is

this conveniency which ultimately recommends that arrangement, and bestows upon it the whole of its propriety and beauty.

*　　*　　*　　*　　*　　*　　*

321　Nor is it only with regard to such frivolous objects that our
conduct is influenced by this principle ; it is often the secret
motive of the most serious and important pursuits of both
private and public life.

The poor man's son, whom heaven in its anger has visited
with ambition, when he begins to look around him, admires
the condition of the rich.

*　　*　　*　　*　　*　　*　　*

It appears in his fancy like the life of some superior rank of
beings, and, in order to arrive at it, he devotes himself for ever
to the pursuit of wealth and greatness.　To obtain the con-
veniencies which these afford, he submits in the first year, nay
in the first month of his application, to more fatigue of body
and more uneasiness of mind than he could have suffered
through the whole of his life from the want of them.　He
studies to distinguish himself in some laborious profession.
With the most unrelenting industry he labours night and day
to acquire talents superior to all his competitors.　He endeavours next to bring those talents into public view, and with
equal assiduity solicits every opportunity of employment.　For
this purpose he makes his court to all mankind ; he serves
those whom he hates, and is obsequious to those whom he
despises.　Through the whole of his life he pursues the idea
of a certain artificial and elegant repose which he may never
arrive at, for which he sacrifices a real tranquillity that is at
all times in his power, and which, if in the extremity of old age
he should at last attain to it, he will find to be in no respect
preferable to that humble security and contentment which he
had abandoned for it.　It is then, in the last dregs of life, his
body wasted with toil and diseases, his mind galled and ruffled
by the memory of a thousand injuries and disappointments
which he imagines he has met with from the injustice of his

enemies, or from the perfidy and ingratitude of his friends, that he begins at last to find that wealth and greatness are mere trinkets of frivolous utility, no more adapted for procuring ease of body or tranquillity of mind than the tweezer-cases of the lover of toys; and like them too, more troublesome to the person who carries them about with him than all the advantages they can afford him are commodious.

*   *   *   *   *   *   *

322   If we examine, however, why the spectator distinguishes with such admiration the condition of the rich and the great, we shall find that it is not so much upon account of the superior ease or pleasure which they are supposed to enjoy, as of the numberless artificial and elegant contrivances for promoting this ease or pleasure.   He does not even imagine that they are really happier than other people : but he imagines that they possess more means of happiness.   And it is the ingenious and artful adjustment of those means to the end for which they were intended, that is the principal source of his admiration.   But in the languor of disease and the weariness of old age, the pleasures of the vain and empty distinctions of greatness disappear.   To one, in this situation, they are no longer capable of recommending those toilsome pursuits in which they had formerly engaged him.   In his heart he curses ambition, and vainly regrets the ease and the indolence of youth, pleasures which are fled for ever, and which he has foolishly sacrificed for what, when he has got it, can afford him no real satisfaction.   In this miserable aspect does greatness appear to every man when reduced either by spleen or disease to observe with attention his own situation, and to consider what it is that is really wanting to his happiness. Power and riches appear then to be, what they are, enormous and operose machines contrived to produce a few trifling con-veniencies to the body, consisting of springs the most nice and delicate, which must be kept in order with the most anxious attention, and which in spite of all our care are ready every moment to burst into pieces, and to crush in their ruins their unfortunate possessor. They are immense fabrics, which it requires the labour of a life to raise, which threaten every moment to overwhelm the person that dwells in them, and which while they stand, though they may save him from some smaller inconveniencies, can protect him from none of the severer inclemencies of the season. They keep off the summer shower, not the winter storms, but leave him always as much, and sometimes more exposed than before, to anxiety, to fear, and to sorrow ; to diseases, to danger, and to death.

323   But though this splenetic philosophy, which in time of sickness or low spirits is familiar to every man, thus entirely depreciates those great objects of human desire, when in better health and in better humour, we never fail to regard them under a more agreeable aspect. Our imagination, which in pain and sorrow seems to be confined and cooped up within our own persons, in times of ease and prosperity expands itself to every thing around us. We are then charmed with the beauty of that accommodation which reigns in the palaces and œconomy of the great ; and admire how every thing is adapted to promote their ease, to prevent their wants, to gratify their wishes, and to amuse and entertain their most frivolous desires. If we consider the real satisfaction which all these things are capable of affording, by itself and separated from the beauty of that arrangement which is fitted to promote it, it will always appear in the highest degree contemptible and trifling. But we rarely view it in this abstract and philosophical light. We naturally confound it in our imagination with the order, the regular and harmonious movement of the system, the machine or œconomy by means of which it is produced. The pleasures of wealth and greatness, when considered in this complex view, strike the imagination as something grand and beautiful and noble, of which the attainment is well worth all the toil and anxiety which we are so apt to bestow upon it.

*   *   *   *   *   *   *

CHAPTER II.—OF THE BEAUTY WHICH THE APPEARANCE OF UTILITY BESTOWS UPON THE CHARACTERS AND ACTIONS OF MEN ; AND HOW FAR THE PERCEPTION OF THIS BEAUTY MAY BE REGARDED AS ONE OF THE ORIGINAL PRINCIPLES OF APPROBATION.

324 THE characters of men, as well as the contrivances of art, or the institutions of civil government, may be fitted either to promote or to disturb the happiness both of the individual and of the society. The prudent, the equitable, the active, resolute, and sober character promises prosperity and satisfaction, both to the person himself and to every one connected with him. The rash, the insolent, the slothful, effeminate, and voluptuous, on the contrary, forebodes ruin to the individual, and misfortune to all who have any thing to do with him. The first turn of mind has at least all the beauty which can belong to the most perfect machine that was ever invented for promoting the most agreeable purpose : and the second, all the deformity of the most awkward and clumsy contrivance. What institution of government could tend so much to promote the happiness of mankind as the general prevalence of wisdom and virtue ? All government is but an imperfect remedy for the deficiency of these. Whatever beauty, therefore, can belong to civil government upon account of its utility, must in a far superior degree belong to these. On the contrary, what civil policy can be so ruinous and destructive as the vices of men ? The fatal effects of bad government arise from nothing, but that it does not sufficiently guard against the mischiefs which human wickedness gives occasion to.

325 This beauty and deformity which characters appear to derive from their usefulness or inconveniency, are apt to strike, in a peculiar manner, those who consider, in an abstract and philosophical light, the actions and conduct of mankind. When a philosopher goes to examine why humanity is approved

of or cruelty condemned, he does not always form to himself, in a very clear and distinct manner, the conception of any one particular action either of cruelty or of humanity, but is commonly contented with the vague and indeterminate idea which the general names of those qualities suggest to him. But it is in particular instances only that the propriety or impropriety, the merit or demerit of actions is very obvious and discernible. It is only when particular examples are given that we perceive distinctly either the concord or disagreement between our own affections and those of the agent, or feel a social gratitude arise towards him in the one case, or a sympathetic resentment in the other. When we consider virtue and vice in an abstract and general manner, the qualities by which they excite these several sentiments seem in a great measure to disappear, and the sentiments themselves become less obvious and discernible. On the contrary, the happy effects of the one and the fatal consequences of the other seem then to rise up to the view, and as it were to stand out and distinguish themselves from all the other qualities of either.

326 The same ingenious and agreeable author who first explained why utility pleases, has been so struck with this view of things, as to resolve our whole approbation of virtue into a perception of this species of beauty which results from the appearance of utility. No qualities of the mind, he observes, are approved of as virtuous, but such as are useful or agreeable either to the person himself or to others ; and no qualities are disapproved of as vicious, but such as have a contrary tendency. And Nature, indeed, seems to have so happily adjusted our senti-ments of approbation and disapprobation, to the conveniency both of the individual and of the society, that after the strictest examination it will be found, I believe, that this is universally the case. But still I affirm, that it is not the view of this utility or hurtfulness which is either the first or principal source of our approbation and disapprobation. These sentiments are no doubt enhanced and enlivened by the perception of the beauty or deformity which results from this utility or hurtful-ness. But still, I say, they are originally and essentially different from this perception.

327   For first of all, it seems impossible that the approbation of virtue should be a sentiment of the same kind with that by which we approve of a convenient and well-contrived building ; or that we should have no other reason for praising a man than that for which we commend a chest of drawers.

328   And secondly, it will be found, upon examination, that the usefulness of any disposition of mind is seldom the first ground of our approbation ; and that the sentiment of approbation always involves in it a sense of propriety quite distinct from the perception of utility. We may observe this with regard to all the qualities which are approved of as virtuous, both those which, according to this system, are originally valued as useful to ourselves, as well as those which are esteemed on account of their usefulness to others.

329   The qualities most useful to ourselves are, first of all, superior reason and understanding, by which we are capable of discerning the remote consequences of all our actions, and of foreseeing the advantage or detriment which is likely to result from them : and secondly, self-command, by which we are enabled to abstain from present pleasure or to endure present pain, in order to obtain a greater pleasure or to avoid a greater pain in some future time. In the union of those two qualities consists the virtue of prudence, of all the virtues that which is most useful to the individual.

With regard to the first of those qualities, it has been observed on a former occasion, that superior reason and understanding are originally approved of as just and right and accurate, and not merely as useful or advantageous. It is in the abstruser sciences, particularly in the higher parts of mathematics, that the greatest and most admired exertions of human reason have been displayed. But the utility of those sciences, either to the individual or to the public, is not very obvious, and to prove it, requires a discussion which is not always very easily comprehended. It was not, therefore, their utility which first recommended them to the public admiration. This quality was but little insisted upon, till it became necessary to make some reply to the reproaches of those, who, having themselves no taste for such sublime discoveries, endeavoured to depreciate them as useless.

330 That self-command, in the same manner, by which we restrain our present appetites, in order to gratify them more fully upon another occasion, is approved of, as much under the aspect of propriety, as under that of utility. When we act in this manner, the sentiments which influence our conduct seem exactly to coincide with those of the spectator. The spectator does not feel the solicitations of our present appetites. To him the pleasure which we are to enjoy a week hence, or a year hence, is just as interesting as that which we are to enjoy this moment. When for the sake of the present, therefore, we sacrifice the future, our conduct appears to him absurd and extravagant in the highest degree, and he cannot enter into the principles which influence it. On the contrary, when we abstain from present pleasure, in order to secure greater pleasure to come, when we act as if the remote object interested us as much as that which immediately presses upon the senses, as our affections exactly correspond with his own, he cannot fail to approve of our behaviour: and as he knows from experience, how few are capable of this self-command, he looks upon our conduct with a considerable degree of wonder and admiration. Hence arises that eminent esteem with which all men naturally regard a steady perseverance in the practice of frugality, industry, and application, though directed to no other purpose than the acquisition of fortune. The resolute firmness of the person who acts in this manner, and, in order to obtain a great though remote advantage, not only gives up all present pleasures, but endures the greatest labour both of mind and body, necessarily commands our approbation. That view of his interest and happiness which appears to regulate his conduct, exactly tallies with the idea which we naturally form of it. There is the most perfect correspondence between his sentiments and our own, and at the same time, from our experience of the common weakness of human nature, it is a correspondence which we could not reasonably have expected. We not only approve, therefore, but in some measure admire his conduct, and think it worthy of a considerable degree of applause. It is the consciousness of this merited approbation and esteem which is alone capable of supporting the agent in this tenour of conduct. The pleasure which we are to enjoy ten years hence interests us so little in comparison with that which we may enjoy to-day, the passion which the first excites, is naturally so weak in comparison with that violent emotion which the second is apt to give occasion to, that the one could never be any balance to the other, unless it was supported by the sense of propriety, by the consciousness that we merited the esteem and approbation of every body, by acting in the one way, and that we became the proper objects of their contempt and derision by behaving in the other.

331 Humanity, justice, generosity, and public spirit, are the qualities most useful to others. Wherein consists the propriety of humanity and justice has been explained upon a former occasion, where it was shewn how much our esteem and approbation of those qualities depended upon the concord between the affections of the agent and those of the spectators.

The propriety of generosity and public spirit is founded upon the same principle with that of justice. Generosity is different from humanity. Those two qualities, which at first sight seem so nearly allied, do not always belong to the same person. Humanity is the virtue of a woman, generosity of a man. The fair-sex, who have commonly much more tenderness than ours, have seldom so much generosity. That women rarely make considerable donations, is an observation of the civil law¹.   Humanity consists merely in the exquisite fellow-feeling which the spectator entertains with the sentiments of the persons principally concerned, so as to grieve for their sufferings, to resent their injuries, and to rejoice at their good fortune.   The most humane actions require no self-denial, no self-command, no great exertion of the sense of propriety. They consist only in doing what this exquisite sympathy would of its own accord prompt us to do.   But it is otherwise with generosity.   We never are generous except when in some respect we prefer some other person to ourselves, and sacrifice some great and important interest of our own to an equal interest of a friend or of a superior.   The man who gives up his pretensions to an office that was the great object of his ambition, because he imagines that the services of another are better entitled to it; the man who exposes his life to defend that of his friend, which he judges to be of more importance, neither of them act from humanity, or because they feel more exquisitely what concerns that other person than what concerns themselves.   They both consider those opposite interests, not in the light in which they naturally appear to themselves, but in that in which they appear to others.   To every by-stander, the success or preservation of this other person may justly be more interesting than their own; but it cannot be so to themselves.   When to the interest of this other person, therefore, they sacrifice their own, they accommodate themselves to the sentiments of the spectator, and by an effort of magnanimity act according to those views of things which they feel, must naturally occur to any third person.   The soldier who throws away his life in order to defend that of his officer, would perhaps be but little affected by the death of that officer, if it should happen without any fault of his own; and a very small disaster which had befallen himself might excite a much more lively sorrow.   But when he endeavours to act so as to deserve applause, and to make

¹ Raro mulieres donare solent.

the impartial spectator enter into the principles of his conduct, he feels, that to every body but himself, his own life is a trifle compared with that of his officer, and that when he sacrifices the one to the other, he acts quite properly and agreeably to what would be the natural apprehensions of every impartial bystander.

332   It is the same case with the greater exertions of public spirit. When a young officer exposes his life to acquire some inconsiderable addition to the dominions of his sovereign, it is not because the acquisition of the new territory is, to himself, an object more desirable than the preservation of his own life. To him his own life is of infinitely more value than the conquest of a whole kingdom for the state which he serves. But when he compares those two objects with one another, he does not view them in the light in which they naturally appear to himself, but in that in which they appear to the nation he fights for. To them the success of the war is of the highest importance; the life of a private person of scarce any consequence. When he puts himself in their situation, he immediately feels that he cannot be too prodigal of his blood, if, by shedding it, he can promote so valuable a purpose. In thus thwarting, from a sense of duty and propriety, the strongest of all natural propensities, consists the heroism of his conduct. There is many an honest Englishman, who, in his private station, would be more seriously disturbed by the loss of a guinea, than by the loss of Minorca, who yet, had it been in his power to defend that fortress, would have sacrificed his life a thousand times rather than, through his fault, have let it fall into the hands of the enemy. When the first Brutus led forth his own sons to a capital punishment, because they had conspired against the rising liberty of Rome, he sacrificed what, if he had consulted his own breast only, would appear to be the stronger to the weaker affection. Brutus ought naturally to have felt much more for the death of his own sons, than for all that probably

Rome could have suffered from the want of so great an example. But he viewed them, not with the eyes of a father, but with those of a Roman citizen. He entered so thoroughly into the sentiments of this last character, that he paid no regard to that tie, by which he himself was connected with them ; and to a Roman citizen, the sons even of Brutus seemed contemptible, when put into the balance with the smallest interest of Rome. In these and in all other cases of this kind, our admiration is not so much founded upon the utility, as upon the unexpected, and on that account the great, the noble, and exalted propriety of such actions. This utility, when we come to view it, bestows upon them, undoubtedly, a new beauty, and upon that account still further recommends them to our approbation. This beauty, however, is chiefly perceived by men of reflection and speculation, and is by no means the quality which first recommends such actions to the natural sentiments of the bulk of mankind.

333   It is to be observed, that so far as the sentiment of approbation arises from the perception of this beauty of utility, it has no reference of any kind to the sentiments of others. If it was possible, therefore, that a person should grow up to manhood without any communication with society, his own actions might, notwithstanding, be agreeable or disagreeable to him on account of their tendency to his happiness or disadvantage. He might perceive a beauty of this kind in prudence, temperance, and good conduct, and a deformity in the opposite behaviour ; he might view his own temper and character with that sort of satisfaction with which we consider a well contrived machine, in the one case ; or with that sort of distaste and dissatisfaction with which we regard a very aukward and clumsy contrivance, in the other. As these perceptions, however, are merely a matter of taste, and have all the feebleness and delicacy of that species of perceptions, upon the justness of which what is properly called taste is founded, they probably would not be much attended to by one in his solitary and miserable condition. Even though they should occur to him, they would by no means have the same effect upon him, antecedent to his connexion with society, which they would have in consequence of that connexion. He would not be cast down with inward shame at the thought of this deformity; nor would he be elevated with secret triumph of mind from the consciousness of the contrary beauty. He would not exult from the notion of deserving reward in the one case, nor tremble from the suspicion of meriting punishment in the other. All such sentiments suppose the idea of some other being, who is the natural judge of the person that feels them; and it is only by sympathy with the decisions of this arbiter of his conduct, that he can conceive, either the triumph of self-applause, or the shame of self-condemnation.

* * * * * * *

PART VII.

OF SYSTEMS OF MORAL PHILOSOPHY.

SECTION III.—OF THE DIFFERENT SYSTEMS WHICH HAVE BEEN FORMED CONCERNING THE PRINCIPLE OF APPROBATION.

INTRODUCTION.

334 AFTER the inquiry concerning the nature of virtue, the next question of importance in Moral Philosophy is concerning the principle of approbation, concerning the power or faculty of the mind which renders certain characters agreeable or disagreeable to us, makes us prefer one tenour of conduct to another, denominate the one right and the other wrong, and consider the one as the object of approbation, honour, and reward; the other as that of blame, censure and punishment.

Three different accounts have been given of this principle of approbation. According to some, we approve and disapprove both of our own actions and of those of others, from self-love only, or from some view of their tendency to our own happiness or disadvantage : according to others, reason, the same faculty by which we distinguish between truth and falsehood, enables us to distinguish between what is fit and unfit both in actions and affections : according to others this distinction is altogether the effect of immediate sentiment and feeling, and arises from the satisfaction or disgust with which the view of certain actions or affections inspires us. Self-love, reason, and sentiment, therefore, are the three different sources which have been assigned for the principle of approbation.

335 Before I proceed to give an account of those different systems, I must observe, that the determination of this second question, though of the greatest importance in speculation, is of none in practice. The question concerning the nature of virtue necessarily has some influence upon our notions of right and wrong in many particular cases. That concerning the principle of approbation can possibly have no such effect. To examine from what contrivance or mechanism within, those different notions or sentiments arise, is a mere matter of philosophical curiosity.

CHAPTER I.—OF THOSE SYSTEMS WHICH DEDUCE THE PRINCIPLE OF APPROBATION FROM SELF-LOVE.

336 THOSE who account for the principle of approbation from self-love, do not all account for it in the same manner, and there is a good deal of confusion and inaccuracy in all their different systems. According to Mr. Hobbes, and many of his followers[1], man is driven to take refuge in society, not by any natural love which he bears to his own kind, but

---

[1] Puffendorff, Mandeville.

because without the assistance of others he is incapable of
subsisting with ease or safety.   Society, upon this account,
becomes necessary to him, and whatever tends to its support
and welfare, he considers as having a remote tendency to his
own interest; and, on the contrary, whatever is likely to disturb
or destroy it, he regards as in some measure hurtful or pernicious to himself.   Virtue is the great support and vice the
great disturber of human society.   The former, therefore, is
agreeable and the latter offensive to every man ; as from the
one he foresees the prosperity, and from the other the ruin and
disorder of what is so necessary for the comfort and security
of his existence.

337   That the tendency of virtue to promote, and of vice to
disturb the order of society, when we consider it coolly and
philosophically, reflects a very great beauty upon the one,
and a very great deformity upon the other, cannot, as I have
observed upon a former occasion, be called in question.
Human society, when we contemplate it in a certain abstract
and philosophical light, appears like a great, an immense
machine, whose regular and harmonious movements produce
a thousand agreeable effects.   As in any other beautiful and
noble machine that was the production of human art, whatever tended to render its movements more smooth and easy,
would derive a beauty from this effect, and, on the contrary,
whatever tended to obstruct them would displease upon that
account : so virtue, which is, as it were, the fine polish to the
wheels of society, necessarily pleases ; while vice, like the vile
rust, which makes them jar and grate upon one another, is as
necessarily offensive.   This account, therefore, of the origin of
approbation and disapprobation, so far as it derives them from
a regard to the order of society, runs into that principle which
gives beauty to utility, and which I have explained upon
a former occasion ; and it is from thence that this system
derives all that appearance of probability which it possesses.
When those authors describe the innumerable advantages of

a cultivated and social, above a savage and solitary life; when they expatiate upon the necessity of virtue and good order for the maintenance of the one, and demonstrate how infallibly the prevalence of vice and disobedience to the laws tend to bring back the other, the reader is charmed with the novelty and grandeur of those views which they open to him : he sees plainly a new beauty in virtue, and a new deformity in vice, which he had never taken notice of before, and is commonly so delighted with the discovery, that he seldom takes time to reflect, that this political view having never occurred to him in his life before, cannot possibly be the ground of that approbation and disapprobation with which he has always been accustomed to consider those different qualities.

338   When those authors, on the other hand, deduce from self-love the interest which we take in the welfare of society, and the esteem which upon that account we bestow upon virtue, they do not mean, that when we in this age applaud the virtue of Cato, and detest the villany of Catiline, our sentiments are influenced by the notion of any benefit we receive from the one, or of any detriment we suffer from the other. It was not because the prosperity or subversion of society, in those remote ages and nations, was apprehended to have any influence upon our happiness or misery in the present times; that according to those philosophers, we esteemed the virtuous, and blamed the disorderly character. They never imagined that our sentiments were influenced by any benefit or damage which we supposed actually to redound to us, from either; but by that which might have redounded to us, had we lived in those distant ages and countries; or by that which might still redound to us, if in our own times we should meet with characters of the same kind. The idea, in short, which those authors were groping about, but which they were never able to unfold distinctly, was that indirect sympathy which we feel with the gratitude or resentment of those who received the benefit or suffered the damage resulting from such opposite characters: and it was this which they were indistinctly pointing at, when they said, that it was not the thought of what we had gained or suffered which prompted our applause or indignation, but the conception or imagination of what we might gain or suffer if we were to act in society with such associates.

339 Sympathy, however, cannot, in any sense, be regarded as a selfish principle. When I sympathize with your sorrow or your indignation, it may be pretended, indeed, that my emotion is founded in self-love, because it arises from bringing your case home to myself, from putting myself in your situation, and thence conceiving what I should feel in the like circumstances. But though sympathy is very properly said to arise from an imaginary change of situations with the person principally concerned, yet this imaginary change is not supposed to happen to me in my own person and character, but in that of the person with whom I sympathize. When I condole with you for the loss of your only son, in order to enter into your grief I do not consider what I, a person of such a character and profession, should suffer, if I had a son, and if that son was unfortunately to die: but I consider what I should suffer if I was really you, and I not only change circumstances with you, but I change persons and characters. My grief, therefore, is entirely upon your account, and not in the least upon my own. It is not, therefore, in the least selfish. How can that be regarded as a selfish passion, which does not arise even from the imagination of any thing that has befallen, or that relates to myself, in my own proper person and character, but which is entirely occupied about what relates to you? A man may sympathize with a woman in child-bed; though it is impossible that he should conceive himself as suffering her pains in his own proper person and character. That whole account of human nature, however, which deduces all sentiments and affections from self-love, which has made so much noise in the world,

but which, so far as I know, has never yet been fully and
distinctly explained, seems to me to have arisen from some
confused misapprehension of the system of sympathy.

CHAPTER II.—OF THOSE SYSTEMS WHICH MAKE REASON
THE PRINCIPLE OF APPROBATION.

340   IT is well known to have been the doctrine of Mr. Hobbes,
that a state of nature is a state of war; and that antecedent
to the institution of civil government, there could be no
safe or peaceable society among men.   To preserve society,
therefore, according to him, was to support civil government,
and to destroy civil government was the same thing as to put
an end to society.   But the existence of civil government
depends upon the obedience that is paid to the supreme
magistrate.   The moment he loses his authority, all government is at an end.   As self-preservation, therefore, teaches
men to applaud whatever tends to promote the welfare of
society, and to blame whatever is likely to hurt it; so the
same principle, if they would think and speak consistently,
ought to teach them to applaud upon all occasions obedience
to the civil magistrate, and to blame all disobedience and
rebellion.   The very ideas of laudable and blameable, ought
to be the same with those of obedience and disobedience.
The laws of the civil magistrate, therefore, ought to be
regarded as the sole ultimate standards of what was just and
unjust, of what was right and wrong.

341   It was the avowed intention of Mr. Hobbes, by propagating
these notions, to subject the consciences of men immediately
to the civil, and not to the ecclesiastical powers, whose
turbulence and ambition, he had been taught, by the example
of his own times, to regard as the principal source of the
disorders of society.   His doctrine, upon this account, was
peculiarly offensive to theologians, who accordingly did not
fail to vent their indignation against him with great asperity

and bitterness. It was likewise offensive to all sound moralists, as it supposed that there was no natural distinction between right and wrong, that these were mutable and changeable, and depended upon the mere arbitrary will of the civil magistrate. This account of things, therefore, was attacked from all quarters and by all sorts of weapons, by sober reason as well as by furious declamation.

342   In order to confute so odious a doctrine, it was necessary to prove, that antecedent to all law or positive institution, the mind was naturally endowed with a faculty, by which it distinguished in certain actions and affections, the qualities of right, laudable, and virtuous, and in others those of wrong, blameable, and vicious.

Law, it was justly observed by Dr. Cudworth[1], could not be the original source of those distinctions; since, upon the supposition of such a law, it must either be right to obey it, and wrong to disobey it, or indifferent whether we obeyed it, or disobeyed it. That law which it was indifferent whether we obeyed or disobeyed, could not, it was evident, be the source of those distinctions; neither could that which it was right to obey and wrong to disobey, since even this still supposed the antecedent notions or ideas of right and wrong, and that obedience to the law was conformable to the idea of right, and disobedience to that of wrong.

343   Since the mind, therefore, had a notion of those distinctions, antecedent to all law, it seemed necessarily to follow, that it derived this notion from reason, which pointed out the difference between right and wrong, in the same manner in which it did that between truth and falsehood: and this conclusion, which, though true in some respects, is rather hasty in others, was more easily received at a time when the abstract science of human nature was but in its infancy, and before the distinct offices and powers of the different faculties of the human mind had been carefully examined

---

[1] Immutable Morality, l. i.

and distinguished from one another. When this controversy
with Mr. Hobbes was carried on with the greatest warmth
and keenness, no other faculty had been thought of from
which any such ideas could possibly be supposed to arise.
It became at this time, therefore, the popular doctrine, that
the essence of virtue and vice did not consist in the conformity
or disagreement of human actions with the·law of a superior,
but in their conformity or disagreement with reason, which
was thus considered as the original source and principle of
approbation and disapprobation.

344   That virtue consists in conformity to reason, is true in some
respects, and this faculty may very justly be considered as,
in some sense, the source and principle of approbation and
disapprobation, and of all solid judgments concerning right
and wrong. It is by reason that we discover those general
rules of justice by which we ought to regulate our actions :
and it is by the same faculty that we form those more vague
and indeterminate ideas of what is prudent, of what is decent,
of what is generous or noble, which we carry constantly about
with us, and according to which we endeavour, as well as we
can, to model the tenour of our conduct. The general maxims
of morality are formed, like all other general maxims, from
experience and induction. We observe in a great variety
of particular cases what pleases or displeases our moral
faculties, what these approve or disapprove of, and, by
induction from this experience, we establish those general
rules. But induction is always regarded as one of the
operations of reason. From reason, therefore, we are very
properly said to derive all those general maxims and ideas.
It is by these, however, that we regulate the greater part of
our moral judgments, which would be extremely uncertain
and precarious if they depended altogether upon what is
liable to so many variations as immediate sentiment and
feeling, which the different states of health and humour are
capable of altering so essentially. As our most solid judg-

ments, therefore, with regard to right and wrong, are regulated by maxims and ideas derived from an induction of reason, virtue may very properly be said to consist in a conformity to reason, and so far this faculty may be considered as the source and principle of approbation and disapprobation.

345   But though reason is undoubtedly the source of the general rules of morality, and of all the moral judgments which we form by means of them ; it is altogether absurd and unintelligible to suppose that the first perceptions of right and wrong can be derived from reason, even in those particular cases upon the experience of which the general rules are formed. These first perceptions, as well as all other experiments upon which any general rules are founded, cannot be the object of reason but of immediate sense and feeling.   It is by finding in a vast variety of instances that one tenour of conduct constantly pleases in a certain manner, and that another as constantly displeases the mind, that we form the general rules of morality.   But reason cannot render any particular object either agreeable or disagreeable to the mind for its own sake.   Reason may show that this object is the means of obtaining some other which is naturally either pleasing or displeasing, and in this manner may render it either agreeable or disagreeable for the sake of something else.   But nothing can be agreeable or disagreeable for its own sake, which is not rendered such by immediate sense and feeling.   If virtue, therefore, in every particular instance, necessarily pleases for its own sake, and if vice as certainly displeases the mind, it cannot be reason, but immediate sense and feeling, which, in this manner, reconciles us to the one, and alienates us from the other.

Pleasure and pain are the great objects of desire and aversion : but these are distinguished not by reason, but by immediate sense and feeling.   If virtue, therefore, be desirable for its own sake, and if vice be, in the same manner, the object of aversion, it cannot be reason which originally distinguishes those different qualities, but immediate sense and feeling.

346   As reason, however, in a certain sense, may justly be considered as the principle of approbation and disapprobation, these sentiments were, through inattention, long regarded as originally flowing from the operations of this faculty. Dr. Hutcheson had the merit of being the first who distinguished with any degree of precision in what respect all moral distinctions may be said to arise from reason, and in what respect they are founded upon immediate sense and feeling. In his illustrations upon the moral sense he has explained this so fully, and, in my opinion, so unanswerably, that, if any controversy is still kept up about this subject, I can impute it to nothing, but either to inattention to what that gentleman has written, or to a superstitious attachment to certain forms of expression, a weakness not very uncommon among the learned, especially in subjects so deeply interesting as the present, in which a man of virtue is often loath to abandon, even the propriety of a single phrase which he has been accustomed to.

CHAPTER III.—OF THOSE SYSTEMS WHICH MAKE SENTIMENT THE PRINCIPLE OF APPROBATION.

347   THOSE systems which make sentiment the principle of approbation may be divided into two different classes.

I. According to some, the principle of approbation is founded upon a sentiment of a peculiar nature, upon a particular power of perception exerted by the mind at the view of certain actions or affections ; some of which affecting this faculty in an agreeable and others in a disagreeable manner, the former are stamped with the characters of right, laudable, and virtuous ; the latter with those of wrong, blameable, and vicious. This sentiment being of a peculiar nature distinct from every other, and the effect of a particular power of perception, they give it a particular name, and call it a moral sense.

II. According to others, in order to account for the principle of approbation, there is no occasion for supposing any new power of perception which had never been heard of before : Nature, they imagine, acts here, as in all other cases, with the strictest œconomy, and produces a multitude of effects from one and the same cause ; and sympathy, a power which has always been taken notice of, and with which the mind is manifestly endowed, is, they think, sufficient to account for all the effects ascribed to this peculiar faculty.

348   I. Dr. Hutcheson [1] had been at great pains to prove that the principle of approbation was not founded on self-love. He had demonstrated too that it could not arise from any operation of reason.   Nothing remained, he thought, but to suppose it a faculty of a peculiar kind, with which Nature had endowed the human mind, in order to produce this one particular and important effect.   When self-love and reason were both excluded, it did not occur to him that there was any other known faculty of the mind which could in any respect answer this purpose.

*   *   *   *   *   *   *

349   But notwithstanding all the pains which this ingenious philosopher has taken to prove that the principle of approbation is founded in a peculiar power of perception, somewhat analogous to the external senses, there are some consequences which he acknowledges to follow from this doctrine, that will, perhaps, be regarded by many as a sufficient confutation of it.   The qualities, he allows [2], which belong to the objects of any sense, cannot, without the greatest absurdity, be ascribed to the sense itself.   Who ever thought of calling the sense of seeing black or white, the sense of hearing loud or low, or the sense of tasting sweet or bitter?   And,

[1] Inquiry concerning Virtue.
[2] Illustrations upon the Moral Sense, sect. i.

according to him, it is equally absurd to call our moral faculties virtuous or vicious, morally good or evil. These qualities belong to the objects of those faculties, not to the faculties themselves. If any man, therefore, was so absurdly constituted as to approve of cruelty and injustice as the highest virtues, and to disapprove of equity and humanity as the most pitiful vices, such a constitution of mind might indeed be regarded as inconvenient both to the individual and to the society, and likewise as strange, surprising, and unnatural in itself; but it could not, without the greatest absurdity, be denominated vicious or morally evil.

350 Yet surely if we saw any man shouting with admiration and applause at a barbarous and unmerited execution, which some insolent tyrant had ordered, we should not think we were guilty of any great absurdity in denominating this behaviour vicious and morally evil in the highest degree, though it expressed nothing but depraved moral faculties, or an absurd approbation of this horrid action, as of what was noble, magnanimous, and great. Our heart, I imagine, at the sight of such a spectator, would forget for a while its sympathy with the sufferer, and feel nothing but horror and detestation, at the thought of so execrable a wretch. We should abominate him even more than the tyrant who might be goaded on by the strong passions of jealousy, fear, and resentment, and upon that account be more excusable. But the sentiments of the spectator would appear altogether without cause or motive, and therefore most perfectly and completely detestable. There is no perversion of sentiment or affection which our heart would be more averse to enter into, or which it would reject with greater hatred and indignation than one of this kind; and so far from regarding such a constitution of mind as being merely something strange or inconvenient, and not in any respect vicious or morally evil, we should rather consider it as the very last and most dreadful stage of moral depravity.

351 Correct moral sentiments, on the contrary, naturally appear in some degree laudable and morally good. The man, whose censure and applause are upon all occasions suited with the greatest accuracy to the value or unworthiness of the object, seems to deserve a degree even of moral approbation. We admire the delicate precision of his moral sentiments : they lead our own judgments, and, upon account of their uncommon and surprising justness, they even excite our wonder and applause. We cannot indeed be always sure that the conduct of such a person would be in any respect correspondent to the precision and accuracy of his judgments concerning the conduct of others. Virtue requires habit and resolution of mind, as well as delicacy of sentiment ; and unfortunately the former qualities are sometimes wanting, where the latter is in the greatest perfection. This disposition of mind, however, though it may sometimes be attended with imperfections, is incompatible with any thing that is grossly criminal, and is the happiest foundation upon which the superstructure of perfect virtue can be built. There are many men who mean very well, and seriously purpose to do what they think their duty, who notwithstanding are disagreeable on account of the coarseness of their moral sentiments.

352 It may be said, perhaps, that though the principle of approbation is not founded upon any power of perception that is in any respect analogous to the external senses, it may still be founded upon a peculiar sentiment which answers this one particular purpose and no other. Approbation and disapprobation, it may be pretended, are certain feelings or emotions which arise in the mind upon the view of different characters and actions ; and as resentment might be called a sense of injuries, or gratitude a sense of benefits, so these may very properly receive the name of a sense of right and wrong, or of a moral sense.

But this account of things, though it may not be liable to

the same objections with the foregoing, is exposed to others
which are equally unanswerable.

353   First of all, whatever variations any particular emotion may
undergo, it still preserves the general features which distinguish
it to be an emotion of such a kind, and these general features
are always more striking and remarkable than any variation
which it may undergo in particular cases. Thus anger is an
emotion of a particular kind: and accordingly its general features
are always more distinguishable than all the variations it undergoes in particular cases. Anger against a man is, no doubt,
somewhat different from anger against a woman, and that again
from anger against a child. In each of those three cases, the
general passion of anger receives a different modification from
the particular character of its object, as may easily be observed
by the attentive. But still the general features of the
passion predominate in all these cases. To distinguish these,
requires no nice observation : a very delicate attention, on
the contrary, is necessary to discover their variations, every
body takes notice of the former; scarce any body observes
the latter. If approbation and disapprobation, therefore,
were, like gratitude and resentment, emotions of a particular
kind, distinct from every other, we should expect that
in all the variations which either of them might undergo, it
would still retain the general features which mark it to be an
emotion of such a particular kind, clear, plain, and easily
distinguishable. But in fact it happens quite otherwise. If
we attend to what we really feel when upon different occasions
we either approve or disapprove, we shall find that our emotion
in one case is often totally different from that in another,
and that no common features can possibly be discovered
between them. Thus the approbation with which we view
a tender, delicate, and humane sentiment, is quite different
from that with which we are struck by one that appears great,
daring, and magnanimous. Our approbation of both may,
upon different occasions, be perfect and entire ; but we are

softened by the one, and we are elevated by the other, and there is no sort of resemblance between the emotions which they excite in us. But, according to that system which I have been endeavouring to establish, this must necessarily be the case. As the emotions of the person whom we approve of, are, in those two cases, quite opposite to one another, and as our approbation arises from sympathy with those opposite emotions, what we feel upon the one occasion, can have no sort of resemblance to what we feel upon the other. But this could not happen if approbation consisted in a peculiar emotion which had nothing in common with the sentiments we approved of, but which arose at the view of those sentiments, like any other passion at the view of its proper object. The same thing holds true with regard to disapprobation. Our horror for cruelty has no sort of resemblance to our contempt for mean-spiritedness. It is quite a different species of discord which we feel at the view of those two different vices, between our own minds and those of the person whose sentiments and behaviour we consider.

354   Secondly, I have already observed, that not only the different passions or affections of the human mind which are approved or disapproved of, appear morally good or evil, but that proper and improper approbation appear to our natural sentiments, to be stamped with the same characters. I would ask, therefore, how it is, that, according to this system, we approve or disapprove of proper or improper approbation? To this question there is, I imagine, but one reasonable answer, which can possibly be given. It must be said, that when the approbation with which our neighbour regards the conduct of a third person coincides with our own, we approve of his approbation, and consider it as, in some measure, morally good ; and that on the contrary, when it does not coincide with our own sentiments, we disapprove of it, and consider it as, in some measure, morally evil. It must be allowed, therefore, that, at least in this one case, the

coincidence or opposition of sentiments, between the observer and the person observed, constitutes moral approbation or disapprobation. And if it does so in this one case, I would ask, why not in every other? to what purpose imagine a new power of perception in order to account for those sentiments?

355 Against every account of the principle of approbation, which makes it depend upon a peculiar sentiment, distinct from every other, I would object; that it is strange that this sentiment, which Providence undoubtedly intended to be the governing principle of human nature, should hitherto have been so little taken notice of, as not to have got a name in any language. The word moral sense is of very late formation, and cannot yet be considered as making part of the English tongue. The word approbation has but within these few years been appropriated to denote peculiarly any thing of this kind. In propriety of language we approve of whatever is entirely to our satisfaction, of the form of a building, of the contrivance of a machine, of the flavour of a dish of meat. The word conscience does not immediately denote any moral faculty by which we approve or disapprove. Conscience supposes, indeed, the existence of some such faculty, and properly signifies our consciousness of having acted agreeably or contrary to its directions. When love, hatred, joy, sorrow, gratitude, resentment, with so many other passions which are all supposed to be the subjects of this principle, have made themselves considerable enough to get titles to know them by, is it not surprising that the sovereign of them all should hitherto have been so little heeded, that, a few philosophers excepted, nobody has yet thought it worth while to bestow a name upon it.

356 When we approve of any character or action, the sentiments which we feel are, according to the foregoing system, derived from four sources, which are in some respects different from one another. First, we sympathize with the motives of the agent ; secondly, we enter into the gratitude of those who receive the benefit of his actions ; thirdly, we observe that his conduct has been agreeable to the general rules by which those two sympathies generally act ; and, last of all, when we consider such actions as making a part of a system of behaviour which tends to promote the happiness either of the individual or of the society, they appear to derive a beauty from this utility, not unlike that which we ascribe to any well-contrived machine. After deducting, in any one particular case, all that must be acknowledged to proceed from some one or other of these four principles, I should be glad to know what remains, and I shall freely allow this overplus to be ascribed to a moral sense, or to any other peculiar faculty, provided any body will ascertain precisely what this overplus is. It might be expected, perhaps, that if there was any such peculiar principle, such as this moral sense is supposed to be, we should feel it, in some particular cases, separated and detached from every other, as we often feel joy, sorrow, hope, and fear, pure and unmixed with any other emotion. This however, I imagine, cannot even be pretended. I have never heard any instance alleged in which this principle could be said to exert itself alone and unmixed with sympathy or antipathy, with gratitude or resentment, with the perception of the agreement or disagreement of any action to an established rule, or last of all with that general taste for beauty and order which is excited by inanimated as well as by animated objects.

357 II. There is another system which attempts to account for the origin of our moral sentiments from sympathy, distinct from that which I have been endeavouring to establish. It is that which places virtue in utility, and accounts for the pleasure with which the spectator surveys the utility of any quality from sympathy with the happiness of those who are affected by it. This sympathy is different both from that by which we enter into the motives of the agent, and from that by which we go along with the gratitude of the persons who are benefited by his actions. It is the same principle with that by which we approve of a well-contrived machine. But no machine can be the object of either of those two last-mentioned sympathies. I have already, in the fourth part of this discourse, given some account of this system.

BENTHAM

AN INTRODUCTION TO THE PRINCIPLES OF MORALS AND LEGISLATION

[First printed, 1780; first published, 1789.
Reprinted here from the corrected edition, London, 1823.]

BENTHAM

An Introduction to the Principles of Morals and Legislation

———◆———

Chapter I.—Of the Principle of Utility.

358 I. Nature has placed mankind under the governance of two sovereign masters, *pain* and *pleasure*. It is for them alone to point out what we ought to do, as well as to determine what we shall do. On the one hand the standard of right and wrong, on the other the chain of causes and effects, are fastened to their throne. They govern us in all we do, in all we say, in all we think : every effort we can make to throw off our subjection, will serve but to demonstrate and confirm it. In words a man may pretend to abjure their empire : but in reality he will remain subject to it all the while. The *principle of utility*[1] recognises the subjection, and assumes

---

[1] Note by the Author, July 1812.

To this denomination has of late been added, or substituted, the *greatest happiness* or *greatest felicity* principle : this for shortness, instead of saying at length *that principle* which states the greatest happiness of all those whose interest is in question, as being the right and proper, and only right and proper and universally desirable, end of human action : of human action in every situation, and in particular in that of a functionary or set of functionaries exercising the powers of government. The word *utility* does not so clearly point to the ideas of *pleasure* and *pain* as the words *happiness* and *felicity* do : nor does it lead us to the consideration of the *number*, of

it for the foundation of that system, the object of which is to rear the fabric of felicity by the hands of reason and of law. Systems which attempt to question it, deal in sounds instead of sense, in caprice instead of reason, in darkness instead of light.

But enough of metaphor and declamation: it is not by such means that moral science is to be improved.

359   II. The principle of utility is the foundation of the present work: it will be proper therefore at the outset to give an explicit and determinate account of what is meant by it. By the principle [1] of utility is meant that principle which approves or disapproves of every action whatsoever, according to the tendency which it appears to have to augment or diminish the happiness of the party whose interest is in question: or, what is the same thing in other words, to promote or to oppose that happiness. I say of every action whatsoever; and therefore not only of every action of a private individual, but of every measure of government.

360   III. By utility is meant that property in any object, whereby it tends to produce benefit, advantage, pleasure, good, or happiness, (all this in the present case comes to the same thing) or (what comes again to the same thing) to prevent the happening of mischief, pain, evil, or unhappiness to the party whose interest is considered: if that party be the community in general, then the happiness of the community: if a particular individual, then the happiness of that individual.

the interests affected; to the *number*, as being the circumstance, which contributes, in the largest proportion. to the formation of the standard here in question; the *standard of right and wrong*, by which alone the propriety of human conduct, in every situation, can with propriety be tried. This want of a sufficiently manifest connexion between the ideas of *happiness* and *pleasure* on the one hand, and the idea of *utility* on the other, I have every now and then found operating, and with but too much efficiency, as a bar to the acceptance, that might otherwise have been given, to this principle.

[1] * * * The principle here in question may be taken for an act of the mind; a sentiment; a sentiment of approbation; a sentiment which, when applied to an action, approves of its utility, as that quality of it by which the measures of approbation or disapprobation bestowed upon it ought to be governed.

361   IV. The interest of the community is one of the most general expressions that can occur in the phraseology of morals : no wonder that the meaning of it is often lost. When it has a meaning, it is this. The community is a fictitious *body*, composed of the individual persons who are considered as constituting as it were its *members*. The interest of the community then is, what?—the sum of the interests of the several members who compose it.

V. It is in vain to talk of the interest of the community, without understanding what is the interest of the individual[1]. A thing is said to promote the interest, or to be *for* the interest, of an individual, when it tends to add to the sum total of his pleasures : or, what comes to the same thing, to diminish the sum total of his pains.

362   VI. An action then may be said to be conformable to the principle of utility, or, for shortness sake, to utility, (meaning with respect to the community at large) when the tendency it has to augment the happiness of the community is greater than any it has to diminish it.

VII. A measure of government (which is but a particular kind of action, performed by a particular person or persons) may be said to be conformable to or dictated by the principle of utility, when in like manner the tendency which it has to augment the happiness of the community is greater than any which it has to diminish it.

VIII. When an action, or in particular a measure of government, is supposed by a man to be conformable to the principle of utility, it may be convenient, for the purposes of discourse, to imagine a kind of law or dictate, called a law or dictate of utility : and to speak of the action in question, as being conformable to such law or dictate.

IX. A man may be said to be a partizan of the principle of utility, when the approbation or disapprobation he annexes

---

[1] Interest is one of those words, which not having any superior *genus*, cannot in the ordinary way be defined.

to any action, or to any measure, is determined by and
proportioned to the tendency which he conceives it to have
to augment or to diminish the happiness of the community :
or in other words, to its conformity or unconformity to the
laws or dictates of utility.

363   x. Of an action that is conformable to the principle of utility,
one may always say either that it is one that ought to be done,
or at least that it is not one that ought not to be done.   One
may say also, that it is right it should be done ; at least that
it is not wrong it should be done : that it is a right action ;
at least that it is not a wrong action.   When thus interpreted,
the words *ought*, and *right* and *wrong*, and others of that
stamp, have a meaning : when otherwise, they have none.

364   xi. Has the rectitude of this principle been ever formally
contested?   It should seem that it had, by those who have
not known what they have been meaning.   Is it susceptible
of any direct proof?   It should seem not : for that which is
used to prove every thing else, cannot itself be proved :
a chain of proofs must have their commencement somewhere.
To give such proof is as impossible as it is needless.

    xii. Not that there is or ever has been that human creature
breathing, however stupid or perverse, who has not on many,
perhaps on most occasions of his life, deferred to it.   By the
natural constitution of the human frame, on most occasions
of their lives men in general embrace this principle, without
thinking of it : if not for the ordering of their own actions,
yet for the trying of their own actions, as well as of those
of other men.   There have been, at the same time, not many,
perhaps, even of the most intelligent, who have been disposed
to embrace it purely and without reserve.   There are even
few who have not taken some occasion or other to quarrel
with it, either on account of their not understanding always
how to apply it, or on account of some prejudice or other
which they were afraid to examine into, or could not bear
to part with.   For such is the stuff that man is made of :

in principle and in practice, in a right track and in a wrong one, the rarest of all human qualities is consistency.

365 XIII. When a man attempts to combat the principle of utility, it is with reasons drawn, without his being aware of it, from that very principle itself[1]. His arguments, if they prove any thing, prove not that the principle is *wrong*, but that, according to the applications he supposes to be made of it, it is *misapplied*. Is it possible for a man to move the earth? Yes; but he must first find out another earth to stand upon.

366 To disprove the propriety of it by arguments is impossible; but, from the causes that have been mentioned, or from some confused or partial view of it, a man may happen to be disposed not to relish it. Where this is the case, if he thinks the settling of his opinions on such a subject worth the trouble, let him take the following steps, and at length, perhaps, he may come to reconcile himself to it.

1. Let him settle with himself, whether he would wish to discard this principle altogether; if so, let him consider what it is that all his reasonings (in matters of politics especially) can amount to?

2. If he would, let him settle with himself, whether he would judge and act without any principle, or whether there is any other he would judge and act by?

3. If there be, let him examine and satisfy himself whether the principle he thinks he has found is really any separate intelligible principle; or whether it be not a mere principle in words, a kind of phrase, which at bottom expresses neither more nor less than the mere averment of his own unfounded sentiments; that is, what in another person he might be apt to call caprice?

4. If he is inclined to think that his own approbation or

---

[1] 'The principle of utility, (I have heard it said) is a dangerous principle: it is dangerous on certain occasions to consult it.' This is as much as to say, what? that it is not consonant to utility, to consult utility: in short, that it is *not* consulting it, to consult it.

disapprobation, annexed to the idea of an act, without any regard to its consequences, is a sufficient foundation for him to judge and act upon, let him ask himself whether his sentiment is to be a standard of right and wrong, with respect to every other man, or whether every man's sentiment has the same privilege of being a standard to itself?

5. In the first case, let him ask himself whether his principle is not despotical, and hostile to all the rest of human race?

6. In the second case, whether it is not anarchial, and whether at this rate there are not as many different standards of right and wrong as there are men? and whether even to the same man, the same thing, which is right to-day, may not (without the least change in its nature) be wrong to-morrow? and whether the same thing is not right and wrong in the same place at the same time? and in either case, whether all argument is not at an end? and whether, when two men have said, 'I like this,' and 'I don't like it,' they can (upon such a principle) have any thing more to say?

7. If he should have said to himself, No: for that the sentiment which he proposes as a standard must be grounded on reflection, let him say on what particulars the reflection is to turn? if on particulars having relation to the utility of the act, then let him say whether this is not deserting his own principle, and borrowing assistance from that very one in opposition to which he sets it up: or if not on those particulars, on what other particulars?

8. If he should be for compounding the matter, and adopting his own principle in part, and the principle of utility in part, let him say how far he will adopt it?

9. When he has settled with himself where he will stop, then let him ask himself how he justifies to himself the adopting it so far? and why he will not adopt it any arther?

10. Admitting any other principle than the principle of

utility to be a right principle, a principle that it is right for a man to pursue; admitting (what is not true) that the word *right* can have a meaning without reference to utility, let him say whether there is any such thing as a *motive* that a man can have to pursue the dictates of it: if there is, let him say what that motive is, and how it is to be distinguished from those which enforce the dictates of utility : if not, then lastly let him say what it is this other principle can be good for?

CHAPTER II.—OF PRINCIPLES ADVERSE TO THAT OF UTILITY.

367   I. IF the principle of utility be a right principle to be governed by, and that in all cases, it follows from what has been just observed, that whatever principle differs from it in any case must necessarily be a wrong one.   To prove any other principle, therefore, to be a wrong one, there needs no more than just to show it to be what it is, a principle of which the dictates are in some point or other different from those of the principle of utility : to state it is to confute it.

II. A principle may be different from that of utility in two ways: 1. By being constantly opposed to it : this is the case with a principle which may be termed the principle of *asceticism*. 2. By being sometimes opposed to it, and sometimes not, as it may happen : this is the case with another, which may be termed the principle of *sympathy* and *antipathy*.

368   III. By the principle of asceticism I mean that principle, which, like the principle of utility, approves or disapproves of any action, according to the tendency which it appears to have to augment or diminish the happiness of the party whose interest is in question; but in an inverse manner : approving of actions in as far as they tend to diminish his happiness; disapproving of them in as far as they tend to augment it.

*   *   *   *   *   *   *

IX. The principle of asceticism seems originally to have been the reverie of certain hasty speculators, who having perceived, or fancied, that certain pleasures, when reaped in certain circumstances, have, at the long run, been attended with pains more than equivalent to them, took occasion to quarrel with every thing that offered itself under the name of pleasure. Having then got thus far, and having forgot the point which they set out from, they pushed on, and went so much further as to think it meritorious to fall in love with pain. Even this we see, is at bottom but the principle of utility misapplied.

x. The principle of utility is capable of being consistently pursued; and it is but tautology to say, that the more consistently it is pursued, the better it must ever be for humankind. The principle of asceticism never was, nor ever can be, consistently pursued by any living creature. Let but one tenth part of the inhabitants of this earth pursue it consistently, and in a day's time they will have turned it into a hell.

369   xi. Among principles adverse to that of utility, that which at this day seems to have most influence in matters of government, is what may be called the principle of sympathy and antipathy. By the principle of sympathy and antipathy, I mean that principle which approves or disapproves of certain actions, not on account of their tending to augment the happiness, nor yet on account of their tending to diminish the happiness of the party whose interest is in question, but merely because a man finds himself disposed to approve or disapprove of them : holding up that approbation or disapprobation as a sufficient reason for itself, and disclaiming the necessity of looking out for any extrinsic ground. Thus far in the general department of morals : and in the particular department of politics, measuring out the quantum (as well as determining the ground) of punishment, by the degree of the disapprobation.

370   xii. It is manifest, that this is rather a principle in name than in reality : it is not a positive principle of itself, so much as a term employed to signify the negation of all principle. What one expects to find in a principle is something that

points out some external consideration, as a means of warranting and guiding the internal sentiments of approbation and disapprobation: this expectation is but ill fulfilled by a proposition, which does neither more nor less than hold up each of those sentiments as a ground and standard for itself.

xiii. In looking over the catalogue of human actions (says a partizan of this principle) in order to determine which of them are to be marked with the seal of disapprobation, you need but to take counsel of your own feelings: whatever you find in yourself a propensity to condemn, is wrong for that very reason. For the same reason it is also meet for punishment : in what proportion it is adverse to utility, or whether it be adverse to utility at all, is a matter that makes no difference. In that same *proportion* also is it meet for punishment : if you hate much, punish much : if you hate little, punish little : punish as you hate. If you hate not at all, punish not at all : the fine feelings of the soul are not to be overborne and tyrannized by the harsh and rugged dictates of political utility.

371 xiv. The various systems that have been formed concerning the standard of right and wrong, may all be reduced to the principle of sympathy and antipathy. One account may serve for all of them. They consist all of them in so many contrivances for avoiding the obligation of appealing to any external standard, and for prevailing upon the reader to accept of the author's sentiment or opinion as a reason for itself. The phrases different, but the principle the same [1].

372 [1] It is curious enough to observe the variety of inventions men have hit upon, and the variety of phrases they have brought forward, in order to conceal from the world, and, if possible, from themselves, this very general and therefore very pardonable self-sufficiency.

1. One man says, he has a thing made on purpose to tell him what is right and what is wrong; and that it is called a *moral sense*: and then he goes to work at his ease, and says, such a thing is right, and such a thing is wrong—why ? ' because my moral sense tells me it is.'

2. Another man comes and alters the phrase : leaving out *moral*, and putting in *common*, in the room of it. He then tells you, that his common sense teaches him what is right and wrong, as surely as the other's moral sense did : meaning by common sense, a sense of some kind or other,

which, he says, is possessed by all mankind : the senso of those, whose sense is not the same as the author's, being struck out of the account as not worth taking. This contrivance does better than the other; for a moral sense, being a new thing, a man may feel about him a good while without being able to find it out : but common sense is as old as the creation ; and there is no man but would be ashamed to be thought not to have as much of it as his neighbours. It has another great advantage : by appearing to share power, it lessens envy : for when a man gets up upon this ground, in order to anathematize those who differ from him, it is not by a *sic volo sic jubeo*, but by a *velitis jubeatis*.

3. Another man comes, and says, that as to a moral sense indeed, he cannot find that he has any such thing : that however he has an *understanding*, which will do quite as well. This understanding, he says, is the standard of right and wrong : it tells him so and so. All good and wise men understand as he does : if other men's understandings differ in any point from his, so much the worse for them : it is a sure sign they are either defective or corrupt.

4. Another man says, that there is an eternal and immutable Rule of Right : that that rule of right dictates so and so : and then he begins giving you his sentiments upon any thing that comes uppermost : and these sentiments (you are to take for granted) are so many branches of the eternal rule of right.

5. Another man, or perhaps the same man (it's no matter) says, that there are certain practices conformable, and others repugnant, to the Fitness of Things ; and then he tells you, at his leisure, what practices are conformable and what repugnant : just as he happens to like a practice or dislike it.

6. A great multitude of people are continually talking of the Law of Nature ; and then they go on giving you their sentiments about what is right and what is wrong : and these sentiments, you are to understand, are so many chapters and sections of the Law of Nature.

7. Instead of the phrase, Law of Nature, you have sometimes, Law of Reason, Right Reason, Natural Justice, Natural Equity, Good Order. Any of them will do equally well. This latter is most used in politics. The last three are much more tolerable than the others, because they do not very explicitly claim to be any thing more than phrases ; they insist but feebly upon the being looked upon as so many positive standards of themselves, and seem content to be taken, upon occasion, for phrases expressive of the conformity of the thing in question to the proper standard, whatever that may be. On most occasions, however, it will be better to say *utility* : *utility* is clearer, as referring more explicitly to pain and pleasure.

8. We have one philosopher, who says, there is no harm in any thing in the world but in telling a lie : and that if, for example, you were to murder your own father, this would only be a particular way of saying, he was not your father. Of course, when this philosopher sees any thing that he does not like, he says, it is a particular way of telling a lie. It is saying, that the act ought to be done, or may be done, when, *in truth*, it ought not to be done.

9. The fairest and openest of them all is that sort of man who speaks out, and says, I am of the number of the Elect : now God himself takes care to inform the Elect what is right : and that with so good effect, that let them strive ever so, they cannot help not only knowing it but practising

it. If therefore a man wants to know what is right and what is wrong, he has nothing to do but to come to me.

373   It is upon the principle of antipathy that such and such acts are often reprobated on the score of their being *unnatural*: the practice of exposing children, established among the Greeks and Romans, was an unnatural practice. Unnatural, when it means any thing, means unfrequent: and there it means something; although nothing to the present purpose. But here it means no such thing: for the frequency of such acts is perhaps the great complaint. It therefore means nothing; nothing, I mean, which there is in the act itself. All it can serve to express is, the disposition of the person who is talking of it: the disposition he is in to be angry at the thoughts of it. Does it merit his anger? Very likely it may: but whether it does or no is a question, which, to be answered rightly, can only be answered upon the principle of utility.

Unnatural, is as good a word as moral sense, or common sense; and would be as good a foundation for a system. Such an act is unnatural; that is, repugnant to nature: for I do not like to practise it; and, consequently, do not practise it. It is therefore repugnant to what ought to be the nature of every body else.

*   *   *   *   *   *   *   *

374   'But is it never, then, from any other considerations than those of utility, that we derive our notions of right and wrong?' I do not know: I do not care. Whether a moral sentiment can be originally conceived from any other source than a view of utility, is one question: whether upon examination and reflection it can, in point of fact, be actually persisted in and justified on any other ground, by a person reflecting within himself, is another: whether in point of right it can possibly be justified on any other ground, by a person addressing himself to the community, is a third. The two first are questions of speculation: it matters not, comparatively speaking, how they are decided. The last is a question of practice: the decision of it is of as much importance as that of any can be.

'I feel in myself,' (say you) 'a disposition to approve of such or such an action in a moral view: but this is not owing to any notions I have of its being a useful one to the community. I do not pretend to know whether it be an useful one or not: it may be, for aught I know, a mischievous one.' 'But is it then,' (say I) 'a mischievous one? examine; and if you can make yourself sensible that it is so, then, if duty means any thing, that is, moral duty, it is your *duty* at least to abstain from it: and more than that, if it is what lies in your power, and can be done without too great a sacrifice, to endeavour to prevent it. It is not your cherishing the notion of it in your bosom, and giving it the name of virtue, that will excuse you.'

'I feel in myself,' (say you again) 'a disposition to detest such or such an action in a moral view; but this is not owing to any notions I have of its being a mischievous one to the community. I do not pretend to know whether it be a mischievous one or not: it may be not a mischievous one: it may be, for aught I know, an useful one?'—'May it indeed,' (say I) 'an useful one? but let me tell you then, that unless duty, and right and wrong, be just what you please to make them, if it really be not a mischievous one, and any body has a mind to do it, it is no duty of your's, but, on the contrary, it would be very wrong in you, to take upon you to prevent him: detest it within yourself as much as you please; that may be a very good reason (unless it be also a useful one) for your not doing it yourself: but if you go about, by word or deed, to do any thing to hinder him, or make him suffer for it, it is you, and not he, that have done wrong: it is not your setting yourself to blame his conduct, or branding it with the name of vice, that will make him culpable, or you blameless. Therefore, if you can make yourself content that he shall be of one mind, and you of another, about that matter, and so continue, it is well : but if nothing will serve you, but that you and he must needs be of the same mind, I'll tell you what you have to do: it is for you to get the better of your antipathy, not for him to truckle to it.'

375   xv. It is manifest, that the dictates of this principle will frequently coincide with those of utility, though perhaps without intending any such thing.   Probably more frequently than not : and hence it is that the business of penal justice is carried on upon that tolerable sort of footing upon which we see it carried on in common at this day.   For what more natural or more general ground of hatred to a practice can there be, than the mischievousness of such practice ?   What all men are exposed to suffer by, all men will be disposed to hate.   It is far yet, however, from being a constant ground : for when a man suffers, it is not always that he knows what it is he suffers by. A man may suffer grievously, for instance, by a new tax, without being able to trace up the cause of his sufferings to the injustice of some neighbour, who has eluded the payment of an old one.

　　　*　　*　　*　　*　　*　　*　　*

376   xviii. It may be wondered, perhaps, that in all this while no mention has been made of the *theological* principle ; meaning that principle which professes to recur for the standard of right and wrong to the will of God.   But the case is, this is not in fact a distinct principle.   It is never anything more or less than one or other of the three before-mentioned principles presenting itself under another shape.   The *will* of God here meant cannot be his revealed will, as contained in the sacred writings : for that is a system which nobody ever thinks of recurring to at this time of day, for the details of political administration : and even before it can be applied to the details of private conduct, it is universally allowed, by the most eminent divines of all persuasions, to stand in need of pretty ample interpretations; else to what use are the works of those divines? And for the guidance of these interpretations, it is also allowed, that some other standard must be assumed. The will then which is meant on this occasion, is that which may be called the *presumptive* will: that is to say, that which is presumed to be his will on account of the conformity of its dictates to those of some other principle. What then may be this other principle? it must be one or other of the three mentioned above: for there cannot, as we have seen, be any more. It is plain, therefore, that, setting revelation out of the question, no light can ever be thrown upon the standard of right and wrong, by any thing that can be said upon the question, what is God's will. We may be perfectly sure, indeed, that whatever is right is conformable to the will of God: but so far is that from answering the purpose of showing us what is right, that it is necessary to know first whether a thing is right, in order to know from thence whether it be conformable to the will of God [1].

377   XIX. There are two things which are very apt to be confounded, but which it imports us carefully to distinguish :—the motive or cause, which, by operating on the mind of an individual, is productive of any act : and the ground or reason which

---

[1] The principle of theology refers every thing to God's pleasure. But what is God's pleasure? God does not, he confessedly does not now, either speak or write to us. How then are we to know what is his pleasure? By observing what is our own pleasure, and pronouncing it to be his. Accordingly, what is called the pleasure of God is and must necessarily be (revelation apart) neither more nor less than the good pleasure of the person, whoever he be, who is pronouncing what he believes, or pretends, to be God's pleasure. How know you it to be God's pleasure that such or such an act should be abstained from? whence come you even to suppose as much? 'Because the engaging in it would, I imagine, be prejudicial upon the whole to the happiness of mankind;' says the partizan of the principle of utility: 'Because the commission of it is attended with a gross and sensual, or at least with a trifling and transient satisfaction;' says the partizan of the principle of asceticism : 'Because I detest the thoughts of it; and I cannot, neither ought I to be called upon to tell why;' says he who proceeds upon the principle of antipathy. In the words of one or other of these must that person necessarily answer (revelation apart) who professes to take for his standard the will of God.

warrants a legislator, or other by-stander, in regarding that act with an eye of approbation. When the act happens, in the particular instance in question, to be productive of effects which we approve of, much more if we happen to observe that the same motive may frequently be productive, in other instances, of the like effects, we are apt to transfer our approbation to the motive itself, and to assume, as the just ground for the approbation we bestow on the act, the circumstance of its originating from that motive. It is in this way that the sentiment of antipathy has often been considered as a just ground of action. Antipathy, for instance, in such or such a case, is the cause of an action which is attended with good effects: but this does not make it a right ground of action in that case, any more than in any other. Still farther. Not only the effects are good, but the agent sees beforehand that they will be so. This may make the action indeed a perfectly right action: but it does not make antipathy a right ground for action. For the same sentiment of antipathy, if implicitly deferred to, may be, and very frequently is, productive of the very worst effects. Antipathy, therefore, can never be a right ground of action. No more, therefore, can resentment, which, as will be seen more particularly hereafter, is but a modification of antipathy. The only right ground of action, that can possibly subsist, is, after all, the consideration of utility, which, if it is a right principle of action, and of approbation, in any one case, is so in every other. Other principles in abundance, that is, other motives, may be the reasons why such and such an act *has* been done: that is, the reasons or causes of its being done: but it is this alone that can be the reason why it might or ought to have been done. Antipathy or resentment requires always to be regulated, to prevent its doing mischief: to be regulated by what? always by the principle of utility. The principle of utility neither requires nor admits of any other regulator than itself.

CHAPTER III.—OF THE FOUR SANCTIONS OR SOURCES OF
PAIN AND PLEASURE.

378 I. IT has been shown that the happiness of the individuals, of
whom a community is composed, that is their pleasures and
their security, is the end and the sole end which the legislator
ought to have in view: the sole standard, in conformity to
which each individual ought, as far as depends upon the legislator, to be *made* to fashion his behaviour. But whether it be
this or any thing else that is to be *done*, there is nothing by
which a man can ultimately be *made* to do it, but either pain
or pleasure. Having taken a general view of these two grand
objects (*viz.* pleasure, and what comes to the same thing,
immunity from pain) in the character of *final* causes ; it will
be necessary to take a view of pleasure and pain itself, in the
character of *efficient* causes or means.

379 II. There are four distinguishable sources from which pleasure
and pain are in use to flow : considered separately, they may
be termed the *physical*, the *political*, the *moral*, and the
religious : and inasmuch as the pleasures and pains belonging
to each of them are capable of giving a binding force to any
law or rule of conduct, they may all of them be termed
sanctions [1].

III. If it be in the present life, and from the ordinary course
of nature, not purposely modified by the interposition of the
will of any human being, nor by any extraordinary interposition
of any superior invisible being, that the pleasure or the pain
takes place or is expected, it may be said to issue from or to
belong to the *physical sanction*.

[1] Sanctio, in Latin, was used to signify the *act of binding*, and, by
a common grammatical transition, *any thing which serves to bind a man* :
to wit, to the observance of such or such a mode of conduct.

*   *   *   *   *   *   *   *

A Sanction then is a source of obligatory powers or *motives* : that is, of
pains and *pleasures* ; which, according as they are connected with such or
such modes of conduct, operate, and are indeed the only things which can
operate, as *motives*. See Chap. x. [Motives].

IV. If at the hands of a *particular* person or set of persons in the community, who under names correspondent to that of *judge*, are chosen for the particular purpose of dispensing it, according to the will of the sovereign or supreme ruling power in the state, it may be said to issue from the *political sanction*.

V. If at the hands of such *chance* persons in the community, as the party in question may happen in the course of his life to have concerns with, according to each man's spontaneous disposition, and not according to any settled or concerted rule, it may be said to issue from the *moral* or *popular sanction* [1].

VI. If from the immediate hand of a superior invisible being, either in the present life, or in a futute, it may be said to issue from the *religious sanction*.

380   VII. Pleasures or pains which may be expected to issue from the *physical*, *political*, or *moral* sanctions, must all of them be expected to be experienced, if ever, in the *present* life : those which may be expected to issue from the *religious* sanction, may be expected to be experienced either in the *present* life or in a *future*.

VIII. Those which can be experienced in the present life, can of course be no others than such as human nature in the course of the present life is susceptible of : and from each of these sources may flow all the pleasures or pains of which, in the course of the present life, human nature is susceptible. With regard to these then (with which alone we have in this place any concern) those of them which belong to any one of those sanctions, differ not ultimately in kind from those which belong to any one of the other three : the only difference there is among them lies in the circumstances that accompany their production.

    *   *   *   *   *   *   *

[1] Better termed *popular*, as more directly indicative of its constituent cause ; as likewise of its relation to the more common phrase *public opinion*, in French *opinion publique*, the name there given to that tutelary power, of which of late so much is said, and by which so much is done. The latter appellation is however unhappy and inexpressive ; since if *opinion* is material, it is only in virtue of the influence it exercises over action, through the medium of the affections and the will.

381   IX. A man's goods, or his person, are consumed by fire.   If this happened to him by what is called an accident, it was a calamity : if by reason of his own imprudence (for instance, from his neglecting to put his candle out) it may be styled a punishment of the physical sanction : if it happened to him by the sentence of the political magistrate, a punishment belonging to the political sanction ; that is, what is commonly called a punishment : if for want of any assistance which his *neighbour* withheld from him out of some dislike to his *moral* character, a punishment of the *moral* sanction : if by an immediate act of *God's* displeasure, manifested on account of some *sin* committed by him, or through any distraction of mind, occasioned by the dread of such displeasure, a punishment of the *religious* sanction [1].

382   X. As to such of the pleasures and pains belonging to the religious sanction, as regard a future life, of what kind these may be we cannot know.   These lie not open to our observation.   During the present life they are matter only of expectation : and, whether that expectation be derived from natural or revealed religion, the particular kind of pleasure or pain, if it be different from all those which lie open to our observation, is what we can have no idea of.   The best ideas we can obtain of such pains and pleasures are altogether unliquidated in point of quality.   In what other respects our ideas of them *may* be liquidated will be considered in another place [2].

383   XI. Of these four sanctions the physical is altogether, we may observe, the ground-work of the political and the moral : so is it also of the religious, in as far as the latter bears relation to the present life.   It is included in each of those other three.   This may operate in any case, (that is, any of the pains or pleasures

---

[1] A suffering conceived to befal a man by the immediate act of God, as above, is often, for shortness sake, called a *judgment* : instead of saying, a suffering inflicted on him in consequence of a special judgment formed, and resolution thereupon taken, by the Deity.

[2] See ch. xiii. [Cases unmeet] par. 2. Note.

belonging to it may operate) independently of *them* : none of *them* can operate but by means of this. In a word, the powers of nature may operate of themselves ; but neither the magistrate, nor men at large, *can* operate, nor is God in the case in question *supposed* to operate, but through the powers of nature.

* * * * * * *

Chapter IV.—Value of a lot of Pleasure or Pain, how to be measured.

384 I. Pleasures then, and the avoidance of pains, are the *ends* which the legislator has in view : it behoves him therefore to understand their *value*. Pleasures and pains are the *instruments* he has to work with : it behoves him therefore to understand their force, which is again, in other words, their value.

385 II. To a person considered *by himself*, the value of a pleasure or pain considered *by itself*, will be greater or less, according to the four following circumstances [1] :

1. Its *intensity*.   3. Its *certainty* or *uncertainty*.
2. Its *duration*.   4. Its *propinquity* or *remoteness*.

386 III. These are the circumstances which are to be considered in estimating a pleasure or a pain considered each of them by itself. But when the value of any pleasure or pain is con-

---

[1] These circumstances have since been denominated *elements* or *dimensions* of *value* in a pleasure or a pain.

Not long after the publication of the first edition, the following memoriter verses were framed, in the view of lodging more effectually, in the memory, these points, on which the whole fabric of morals and legislation may be seen to rest.

> *Intense, long, certain, speedy, fruitful, pure—*
> Such marks in *pleasures* and in *pains* endure.
> Such pleasures seek, if *private* be thy end :
> If it be *public*, wide let them *extend*.
> Such *pains* avoid, whichever be thy view :
> If pains *must* come, let them *extend* to few.

sidered for the purpose of estimating the tendency of any *act* by which it is produced, there are two other circumstances to be taken into the account; these are,

5. Its *fecundity*, or the chance it has of being followed by sensations of the *same* kind : that is, pleasures, if it be a pleasure : pains, if it be a pain.

6. Its *purity*, or the chance it has of *not* being followed by sensations of the *opposite* kind : that is, pains, if it be a pleasure : pleasures, if it be a pain.

These two last, however, are in strictness scarcely to be deemed properties of the pleasures or the pain itself; they are not, therefore, in strictness to be taken into the account of the value of that pleasure or that pain. They are in strictness to be deemed properties only of the act, or other event, by which such pleasure or pain has been produced; and accordingly are only to be taken into the account of the tendency of such act or such event.

387   IV. To a *number* of persons, with reference to each of whom the value of a pleasure or a pain is considered, it will be greater or less, according to seven circumstances : to wit, the six preceding ones ; *viz.*

1. Its *intensity*.	4. Its *propinquity* or *remoteness*.
2. Its *duration*.	5. Its *fecundity*.
3. Its *certainty* or *uncertainty*.	6. Its *purity*.

And one other ; to wit :

7. Its *extent*; that is, the number of persons to whom it *extends*; or (in other words) who are affected by it.

388   V. To take an exact account then of the general tendency of any act, by which the interests of a community are affected, proceed as follows. Begin with any one person of those whose interests seem most immediately to be affected by it : and take an account,

1. Of the value of each distinguishable *pleasure* which appears to be produced by it in the *first* instance.

2. Of the value of each *pain* which appears to be produced by it in the *first* instance.

3. Of the value of each pleasure which appears to be produced by it *after* the first.   This constitutes the *fecundity* of the first *pleasure* and the *impurity* of the first *pain*.

4. Of the value of each *pain* which appears to be produced by it after the first.   This constitutes the *fecundity* of the first *pain*, and the *impurity* of the first pleasure.

5. Sum up all the values of all the *pleasures* on the one side, and those of all the pains on the other.   The balance, if it be on the side of pleasure, will give the *good* tendency of the act upon the whole, with respect to the interests of that *individual* person; if on the side of pain, the *bad* tendency of it upon the whole.

6. Take an account of the *number* of persons whose interests appear to be concerned; and repeat the above process with respect to each.   *Sum up* the numbers expressive of the degrees of *good* tendency, which the act has, with respect to each individual, in regard to whom the tendency of it is *good* upon the whole: do this again with respect to each individual, in regard to whom the tendency of it is *bad* upon the whole. Take the *balance*; which, if on the side of *pleasure*, will give the general *good tendency* of the act, with respect to the total number or community of individuals concerned; if on the side of pain, the general *evil tendency*, with respect to the same community.

389   VI. It is not to be expected that this process should be strictly pursued previously to every moral judgment, or to every legislative or judicial operation.   It may, however, be always kept in view: and as near as the process actually pursued on these occasions approaches to it, so near will such process approach to the character of an exact one.

VII. The same process is alike applicable to pleasure and plain in whatever shape they appear: and by whatever denomination they are distinguished: to pleasure, whether it be called *good* (which is properly the cause or instrument of pleasure) or *profit* (which is distant pleasure, or the cause or instrument of distant pleasure,) or *convenience*, or *advantage, benefit, emolument, happiness*, and so forth : to pain, whether it be called *evil*, (which corresponds to *good*) or *mischief*, or *inconvenience*, or *disadvantage*, or *loss*, or *unhappiness*, and so forth.

390   VIII. Nor is this a novel and unwarranted, any more than it is a useless theory. In all this there is nothing but what the practice of mankind, wheresoever they have a clear view of their own interest, is perfectly conformable to. An article of property, an estate in land, for instance, is valuable, on what account? On account of the pleasures of all kinds which it enables a man to produce, and what comes to the same thing the pains of all kinds which it enables him to avert. But the value of such an article of property is universally understood to rise or fall according to the length or shortness of the time which a man has in it : the certainty or uncertainty of its coming into possession : and the nearness or remoteness of the time at which, if at all, it is to come into possession. As to the *intensity* of the pleasures which a man may derive from it, this is never thought of, because it depends upon the use which each particular person may come to make of it; which cannot be estimated till the particular pleasures he may come to derive from it, or the particular pains he may come to exclude by means of it, are brought to view. For the same reason, neither does he think of the *fecundity* or *purity* of those pleasures.

*   *   *   *   *   *   *

CHAPTER VIII.—OF INTENTIONALITY.

391   I. So much with regard to the two first of the articles upon which the evil tendency of an action may depend : *viz.* the act itself, and the general assemblage of the circumstances with which it may have been accompanied. We come now to consider the ways in which the particular circumstances of *intention* may be concerned in it.

II. First, then, the intention or will may regard either of two objects: 1. The act itself: or, 2. Its consequences. Of these objects, that which the intention regards may be styled *intentional*. If it regards the act, then the act may be said to be intentional [1]: if the consequences, so also then may the consequences. If it regards both the act and consequences, the whole *action* may be said to be intentional. Whichever of those articles is not the object of the intention, may of course be said to be *unintentional*.

392 III. The act may very easily be intentional without the consequences; and often is so. Thus, you may intend to touch a man, without intending to hurt him: and yet, as the consequences turn out, you may chance to hurt him.

IV. The consequences of an act may also be intentional, without the act's being intentional throughout; that is, without its being intentional in every stage of it: but this is not so frequent a case as the former. You intend to hurt a man, suppose, by running against him, and pushing him down: and you run towards him accordingly: but a second man coming in on a sudden between you and the first man, before you can stop yourself, you run against the second man, and by him push down the first.

[1] On this occasion the words *voluntary* and *involuntary* are commonly employed. These, however, I purposely abstain from, on account of the extreme ambiguity of their signification. By a voluntary act is meant sometimes, any act, in the performance of which the will has had any concern at all; in this sense it is synonymous to *intentional*: sometimes such acts only, in the production of which the will has been determined by motives not of a painful nature; in this sense it is synonymous to unconstrained, or *uncoerced*: sometimes such acts only, in the production of which the will has been determined by motives, which, whether of the pleasurable or painful kind, occurred to a man himself, without being suggested by any body else; in this sense it is synonymous to *spontaneous*. The sense of the word involuntary does not correspond completely to that of the word voluntary. Involuntary is used in opposition to intentional; and to unconstrained: but not to spontaneous. It might be of use to confine the signification of the words voluntary and involuntary to one single and very narrow case, which will be mentioned in the next note.

393   V. But the consequences of an act cannot be intentional, without the act's being itself intentional in at least the first stage. If the act be not intentional in the first stage, it is no act of your's : there is accordingly no intention on your part to produce the consequences : that is to say, the individual consequences. All there can have been on your part is a distant intention to produce other consequences, of the same nature, by some act of your's, at a future time : or else, without any intention, a bare *wish* to see such event take place. The second man, suppose, runs of his own accord against the first, and pushes him down. You had intentions of doing a thing of the same nature : *viz.* To run against him, and push him down yourself ; but you had done nothing in pursuance of those intentions : the individual consequences therefore of the act, which the second man performed in pushing down the first, cannot be said to have been on your part intentional [1].

*   *   *   *   *   *   *

[1] To render the analysis here given of the possible states of the mind in point of intentionality absolutely complete, it must be pushed to such a farther degree of minuteness, as to some eyes will be apt to appear trifling. On this account it seemed advisable to discard what follows, from the text to a place where any one who thinks proper may pass by it. An act of the body, when of the positive kind, is a motion : now in motion there are always three articles to be considered : 1. The quantity of matter that moves : 2. The direction in which it moves : and, 3. The velocity with which it moves. Correspondent to these three articles, are so many modes of intentionality, with regard to an act, considered as being only in its first stage. To be completely unintentional, it must be unintentional with respect to every one of these three particulars. This is the case with those acts which alone are properly termed *involuntary* : acts, in the performance of which the will has no sort of share : such as the contraction of the heart and arteries.

Upon this principle, acts that are unintentional in their first stage, may be distinguished into such as are completely unintentional, and such as are incompletely unintentional : and these again may be unintentional, either in point of quantity of matter alone, in point of direction alone, in point of velocity alone, or in any two of these points together.

The example given further on may easily be extended to this part of the analysis, by any one who thinks it worth the while.

There seem to be occasions in which even these disquisitions, minute as they may appear, may not be without their use in practice. In the case of

394   XII. It is to be observed, that an act may be unintentional in any stage or stages of it, though intentional in the preceding : and, on the other hand, it may be intentional in any stage or stages of it, and yet unintentional in the succeeding[1]. But whether it be intentional or no in any preceding stage, is immaterial, with respect to the consequences, so it be unintentional in the last. The only point, with respect to which it is material, is the proof. The more stages the act is unintentional in, the more apparent it will commonly be, that it was unintentional with respect to the last. If a man, intending to strike you on the cheek, strikes you in the eye, and puts it out, it will probably be difficult for him to prove that it was not his intention to strike you in the eye. It will probably be easier, if his intention was really not to strike you, or even not to strike at all.

395   XIII. It is frequent to hear men speak of a good intention, of a bad intention ; of the goodness and badness of a man's intention : a circumstance on which great stress is generally laid. It is indeed of no small importance, when properly understood : but the import of it is to the last degree ambiguous and obscure. Strictly speaking, nothing can be said to be good or bad, but either in itself ; which is the case only with pain or pleasure : or on account of its effects ; which is the case only with things that are the causes or preventives of pain and pleasure. But in a figurative and less proper way of speech, a thing may also be styled good or bad, in consideration of its cause. Now the effects of an

---

homicide, for example, and other corporal injuries, all the distinctions here specified may occur, and in the course of trial may, for some purpose or other, require to be brought to mind, and made the subject of discourse. What may contribute to render the mention of them pardonable, is the use that might possibly be made of them in natural philosophy. In the hands of an expect metaphysician, these, together with the foregoing chapter on human actions, and the section on facts in general, in title Evidence of the Book of Procedure, might, perhaps, be made to contribute something towards an exhaustive analysis of the possible varieties of mechanical inventions.

[1] See ch. vii. [Actions] par. 14.

intention to do such or such an act, are the same objects which we have been speaking of under the appellation of its *consequences* : and the causes of intention are called *motives.* A man's intention then on any occasion may be styled good or bad, with reference either to the consequences of the act, or with reference to his motives. If it be deemed good or bad in any sense, it must be either because it is deemed to be productive of good or of bad consequences, or because it is deemed to originate from a good or from a bad motive. But the goodness or badness of the consequences depend upon the circumstances. Now the circumstances are no objects of the intention. A man intends the act : and by his intention produces the act : but as to the circumstances, he does not intend *them* : he does not, inasmuch as they are circumstances of it, produce them. If by accident there be a few which he has been instrumental in producing, it has been by former intentions, directed to former acts, productive of those circumstances as the consequences : at the time in question he takes them as he finds them. Acts, with their consequences, are objects of the will as well as of the understanding : circumstances, as such, are objects of the understanding only. All he can do with these, as such, is to know or not to know them : in other words, to be conscious of them, or not conscious. To the title of Consciousness belongs what is to be said of the goodness or badness of a man's intention, as resulting from the consequences of the act : and to the head of Motives, what is to be said of his intention, as resulting from the motive.

CHAPTER IX.—OF CONSCIOUSNESS.

*   *   *   *   *   *   *

396   XIII. In ordinary discourse, when a man does an act of which the consequences prove mischievous, it is a common thing to speak of him as having acted with a good intention or with a bad intention, of his intention's being a good one or a bad one. The epithets good and bad are all this while applied, we see, to the intention : but the application of them is most commonly governed by a supposition formed with regard to the nature of the motive. The act, though eventually it prove mischievous, is said to be done with a good intention, when it is supposed to issue from a motive which is looked upon as a good motive : with a bad intention, when it is supposed to be the result of a motive which is looked upon as a bad motive. But the nature of the consequences intended, and the nature of the motive which gave birth to the intention, are objects which, though intimately connected, are perfectly distinguishable. The intention might therefore with perfect propriety be styled a good one, whatever were the motive. It might be styled a good one, when not only the consequences of the act *prove* mischievous, but the motive which gave birth to it *was* what is called a bad one. To warrant the speaking of the intention as being a good one, it is sufficient if the consequences of the act, had they proved what to the agent they seemed likely to be, *would* have been of a beneficial nature. And in the same manner the intention may be bad, when not only the consequences of the act prove beneficial, but the motive which gave birth to it was a good one.

397 XIV. Now, when a man has a mind to speak of your *intention* as being good or bad, with reference to the consequences, if he speaks of it at all he must use the word intention, for there is no other. But if a man means to speak of the *motive* from which your intention originated, as being a good or a bad one, he is certainly not obliged to use the word intention : it is at least as well to use the word motive. By the supposition he means the motive ; and very likely he may *not* mean the intention. For what is true of the one is very often not true of the other. The motive may be good when the intention is bad : the intention may be good when the motive is bad : whether they are both good or both bad, or the one good and the other bad, makes, as we shall see hereafter, a very essential difference with regard to the consequences [1]. It is therefore much better, when motive is meant, never to say intention.

xv. An example will make this clear. Out of malice a man prosecutes you for a crime of which he believes you to be guilty, but of which in fact you are not guilty. Here the *consequences* of his conduct are mischievous : for they are mischievous to you at any rate, in virtue of the shame and anxiety which you are made to suffer while the prosecution is depending : to which is to be added, in case of your being convicted, the evil of the punishment. To you therefore they are mischievous ; nor is there any one to whom they are beneficial. The man's *motive* was also what is called a bad one : for malice will be allowed by every body to be a bad motive. However, the *consequences* of his conduct, had they proved such as he believed them likely to be, would have been good : for in them would have been included the punishment of a criminal, which is a benefit to all who are exposed to suffer by a crime of the like nature. The *intention* therefore, in this case, though not in a common way of speaking the motive, might be styled a *good* one. But of motives more particularly in the next chapter.

*   *   *   *   *   *   *

CHAPTER X.—MOTIVES.

§ I. *Different Senses of the word Motive* [2].

*   *   *   *   *   *   *

398   III. The motives with which alone we have any concern, are such as are of a nature to act upon the will. By a motive then, in this sense of the word, is to be understood any thing whatsoever, which, by influencing the will of a sensitive being, is supposed to serve as a means of determining him

[1] See ch. xii. [Consequences].
[2] Note by the author, July 1822.
The word *inducement* has of late presented itself, as being in its signification more comprehensive than the word *motive*, and on some occasions more apposite.

to act, or voluntarily to forbear to act[1], upon any occasion. Motives of this sort, in contradistinction to the former, may be styled *practical* motives, or motives applying to practice.

399   IV. Owing to the poverty and unsettled state of language, the word *motive* is employed indiscriminately to denote two kinds of objects, which, for the better understanding of the subject, it is necessary should be distinguished.   On some occasions it is employed to denote any of those really existing incidents from whence the act in question is supposed to take its rise. The sense it bears on these occasions may be styled its literal or *unfigurative* sense.   On other occasions it is employed to denote a certain fictitious entity, a passion, an affection of the mind, an ideal being which upon the happening of any such incident is considered as operating upon the mind, and prompting it to take that course, towards which it is impelled by the influence of such incident.   Motives of this class are Avarice, Indolence, Benevolence, and so forth ; as we shall see more particularly farther on.   This latter may be styled the *figurative* sense of the term *motive*.

400   V. As to the real incidents to which the name of the motive is also given, these too are of two very different kinds.   They may be either, 1. The *internal* perception of any individual lot of pleasure or pain, the expectation of which is looked upon as calculated to determine you to act in such or such a manner ; as the pleasure of acquiring such a sum of money, the pain of exerting yourself on such an occasion, and so forth : Or, 2. Any *external* event, the happening whereof is regarded as having a tendency to bring about the perception of such pleasure or

---

[1] When the effect or tendency of a motive is to determine a man to forbear to act, it may seem improper to make use of the term *motive* : since motive, properly speaking, means that which disposes an object to *move*. We must however use that improper term, or a term which. though proper enough, is scarce in use, the word *determinative*.   By way of justification, or at least apology, for the popular usage in this behalf, it may be observed, that even forbearance to act; or the negation of motion (that is, of bodily motion) supposes an act done, when such forbearance is voluntary. It supposes, to wit, an act of the will, which is as much a positive act, as much a motion, as any other act of the thinking substance.

such pain : for instance, the coming up of a lottery ticket, by which the possession of the money devolves to you ; or the breaking out of a fire in the house you are in, which makes it necessary for you to quit it.   The former kind of motives may be termed interior, or internal : the latter exterior, or external.

401   VI. Two other senses of the term *motive* need also to be distinguished.   Motive refers necessarily to action.   It is a pleasure, pain, or other event, that prompts to action.   Motive then, in one sense of the word, must be previous to such event.   But, for a man to be governed by any motive, he must in every case look beyond that event which is called his action; he must look to the consequences of it : and it is only in this way that the idea of pleasure, of pain, or of any other event, can give birth to it.   He must look, therefore, in every case, to some event posterior to the act in contemplation : an event which as yet exists not, but stands only in prospect. Now, as it is in all cases difficult, and in most cases unnecessary, to distinguish between objects so intimately connected, as the posterior possible object which is thus looked forward to, and the present existing object or event which takes place upon a man's looking forward to the other, they are both of them spoken of under the same appellation, *motive*.   To distinguish them, the one first mentioned may be termed a motive in *prospect*, the other a motive in *esse* : and under each of these denominations will come as well exterior as internal motives.   A fire breaks out in your neighbour's house : you are under apprehension of its extending to your own : you are apprehensive, that if you stay in it, you will be burnt : you accordingly run out of it.   This then is the act : the others are all motives to it.   The event of the fire's breaking out in your neighbour's house is an external motive, and that in *esse* : the idea or belief of the probability of the fire's extending to your own house, that of your being burnt if you continue, and the pain you feel at the thought of such a catastrophe, are all so many internal events, but still in *esse*: the event of the fire's actually extending to your own house, and that of your being actually burnt by it, external motives in prospect: the pain you would feel at seeing your house a burning, and the pain you would feel while you yourself were burning, internal motives in prospect: which events, according as the matter turns out, may come to be in *esse*: but then of course they will cease to act as motives.

402 VII. Of all these motives, which stand nearest to the act, to the production of which they all contribute, is that internal motive in *esse* which consists in the expectation of the internal motive in prospect: the pain or uneasiness you feel at the thoughts of being burnt [1]. All other motives are more or less remote: the motives in prospect, in proportion as the period at which they are expected to happen is more distant from the period at which the act takes place, and consequently later in point of time: the motives in *esse*, in proportion as they also are more distant from that period, and consequently earlier in point of time [2].

§ 2. *No motives either constantly good, or constantly bad.*

403 IX. In all this chain of motives, the principle or original link seems to be the last internal motive in prospect; it is to this that all the other motives in prospect owe their materiality:

[1] Whether it be the expectation of being burnt, or the pain that accompanies that expectation, that is the immediate internal motive spoken of, may be difficult to determine. It may even be questioned, perhaps, whether they are distinct entities. Both questions, however, seem to be mere questions of words, and the solution of them altogether immaterial. Even the other kinds of motives, though for some purposes they demand a separatè consideration, are, however, so intimately allied, that it will often be scarce practicable, and not always material, to avoid confounding them, as they have always hitherto been confounded.

[2] Under the term *esse* must be included as well *past* existence, with reference to a given period, as *present*. They are equally real, in comparison with what is as yet but future. Language is materially deficient, in not enabling us to distinguish with precision between *existence* as opposed to *unreality*, and present existence as opposed to past. The word existence in English, and *esse*, adopted by lawyers from the Latin, have the inconvenience of appearing to confine the existence in question to some single period considered as being present.

and the immediately acting motive its existence.   This motive in prospect, we see, is always some pleasure, or some pain ; some pleasure, which the act in question is expected to be a means of continuing or producing : some pain which it is expected to be a means of discontinuing or preventing. A motive is substantially nothing more than pleasure or pain, operating in a certain manner.

x. Now, pleasure is in *itself* a good : nay, even setting aside immunity from pain, the only good : pain is in itself an evil ; and, indeed, without exception, the only evil ; or else the words good and evil have no meaning.   And this is alike true of every sort of pain, and of every sort of pleasure.   It follows, therefore, immediately and incontestably, that *there is no such thing as any sort of motive that is in itself a bad one* [1].

404   xi. It is common, however, to speak of actions as proceeding from *good* or *bad* motives : in which case the motives meant are such as are internal.   The expression is far from being an accurate one ; and as it is apt to occur in the consideration of almost every kind of offence, it will be requisite to settle the precise meaning of it, and observe how far it quadrates with the truth of things.

xii. With respect to goodness and badness, as it is with every thing else that is not itself either pain or pleasure, so is it with motives.   If they are good or bad, it is only on account of their effects : good, on account of their tendency to produce pleasure, or avert pain : bad, on account of their tendency to produce pain, or avert pleasure.   Now the case is, that from one and the same motive, and from every kind of motive, may proceed actions that are good, others that are bad, and others that are indifferent.   This we shall proceed to

---

[1] Let a man's motive be ill-will ; call it even malice, envy, cruelty ; it is still a kind of pleasure that is his motive : the pleasure he takes at the thought of the pain which he sees, or expects to see, his adversary undergo. Now even this wretched pleasure, taken by itself, is good : it may be faint ; it may be short : it must at any rate be impure : yet while it lasts, and before any bad consequence arrive, it is as good as any other that is not more intense.   See ch. iv. [Value].

shew with respect to all the different kinds of motives, as
determined by the various kinds of pleasures and pains.

405   XIII. Such an analysis, useful as it is, will be found to be
a matter of no small difficulty; owing, in great measure, to
a certain perversity of structure which prevails more or less
throughout all languages.   To speak of motives, as of any thing
else, one must call them by their names.   But the misfortune is
that it is rare to meet with a motive of which the name expresses
that and nothing more.   Commonly along with the very name
of the motive, is tacitly involved a proposition imputing to it a
certain quality; a quality which, in many cases, will appear to
include that very goodness or badness, concerning which we
are here inquiring whether, properly speaking, it be or be not
imputable to motives.   To use the common phrase, in most
cases, the name of the motive is a word which is employed
either only in a *good sense*, or else only in a *bad sense*.   Now,
when a word is spoken of as being used in a good sense, all
that is necessarily meant is this: that in conjunction with the
idea of the object it is put to signify, it conveys an idea of
approbation: that is, of a pleasure or satisfaction, entertained
by the person who employs the term at the thoughts of such
object.   In like manner, when a word is spoken of as being
used in a bad sense, all that is necessarily meant is this: that,
in conjunction with the idea of the object it is put to signify, it
conveys an idea of *disapprobation*: that is, of a displeasure
entertained by the person who employs the term at the
thoughts of such object.   Now, the circumstance on which
such approbation is grounded will, as naturally as any other,
be the opinion of the *goodness* of the object in question, as
above explained: such, at least, it must be, upon the principle
of utility: so, on the other hand, the circumstance on which
any such disapprobation is grounded, will, as naturally as any
other, be the opinion of the *badness* of the object: such, at
least, it must be, in as far as the principle of utility is taken for
the standard.

Now there are certain motives which, unless in a few particular cases, have scarcely any other name to be expressed by
but such a word as is used only in a good sense.   This is the
case, for example, with the motives of piety and honour.   The
consequence of this is, that if, in speaking of such a motive,
a man should have occasion to apply the epithet bad to any
actions which he mentions as apt to result from it, he must
appear to be guilty of a contradiction in terms.   But the
names of motives which have scarcely any other name to be
expressed by, but such a word as is used only in a bad sense,
are many more[1].   This is the case, for example, with the
motives of lust and avarice.   And accordingly, if in speaking
of any such motive, a man should have occasion to apply the
epithets good or indifferent to any actions which he mentions
as apt to result from it, he must here also appear to be guilty
of a similar contradiction[2].

*   *   *   *   *   *   *

§ 3. *Catalogue of motives corresponding to that of Pleasures and Pains.*

*   *   *   *   *   *   *

406   xxv. To the pleasures of sympathy corresponds the motive
which, in a neutral sense, is termed good-will.   The word
sympathy may also be used on this occasion : though the sense
of it seems to be rather more extensive.   In a good sense it is
styled benevolence : and in certain cases, philanthropy ; and,
in a figurative way, brotherly love ; in others, humanity ; in

---

[1] For the reason, see chap. xi. [Dispositions] par. xvii. note.

[2] To this imperfection of language, and nothing more, are to be attributed, in great measure, the violent clamours that have from time to time
been raised against those ingenious moralists, who, travelling out of the
beaten tract of speculation, have found more or less difficulty in disen-
tangling themselves from the shackles of ordinary language : such as Roche-
foucault, Mandeville, and Helvetius.   To the unsoundness of their opinions,
and, with still greater injustice, to the corruption of their hearts, was often
imputed, what was most commonly owing either to a want of skill, in matters
of language on the part of the author, or a want of discernment, possibly
now and then in some instances a want of probity, on the part of the com-
mentator.

others, charity; in others, pity and compassion; in others, mercy; in others, gratitude; in others, tenderness; in others, patriotism;' in others, public spirit. Love is also employed in this as in so many other senses. In a bad sense, it has no name applicable to it in all cases : in particular cases it is styled partiality. The word zeal, with certain epithets prefixed to it, might also be employed sometimes on this occasion, though the sense of it be more extensive; applying sometimes to ill as well as to good will. It is thus we speak of party zeal, national zeal, and public zeal. The word attachment is also used with the like epithets : we also say family-attachment. The French expression, *esprit de corps*, for which as yet there seems to be scarcely any name in English, might be rendered, in some cases, though rather inadequately, by the terms corporation spirit, corporation attachment, or corporation zeal.

1. A man who has set a town on fire is apprehended and committed : out of regard or compassion for him, you help him to break prison. In this case the generality of people will probably scarcely know whether to condemn your motive or to applaud it : those who condemn your conduct, will be disposed rather to impute it to some other motive : if they style it benevolence or compassion, they will be for prefixing an epithet, and calling it false benevolence or false compassion[1]. 2. The man is taken again, and is put upon his trial: to save him you swear falsely in his favour. People, who would not call your motive a bad one before, will perhaps call it so now. 3. A man is at law with you about an estate : he has

---

[1] Among the Greeks, perhaps the motive, and the conduct it gave birth to, would, in such a case, have been rather approved than disapproved of. It seems to have been deemed an act of heroism on the part of Hercules, to have delivered his friend Theseus from hell : though divine justice, which held him there, should naturally have been regarded as being at least upon a footing with human justice. But to divine justice, even when acknowledged under that character, the respect paid at that time of day does not seem to have been very profound, or well-settled ; at present, the respect paid to it is profound and settled enough, though the name of it is but too often applied to dictates which could have had no other origin than the worst sort of human caprice.

no right to it : the judge knows this, yet, having an esteem or affection for your adversary, adjudges it to him.   In this case the motive is by every body deemed abominable, and is termed injustice and partiality.   4. You detect a statesman in receiving bribes : out of regard to the public interest, you give information of it, and prosecute him.   In this case, by all who acknowledge your conduct to have originated from this motive, your motive will be deemed a laudable one, and styled public spirit.   But his friends and adherents will not choose to account for your conduct in any such manner : they will rather attribute it to party enmity.   5. You find a man on the point of starving : you relieve him ; and save his life.   In this case your motive will by every body be accounted laudable, and it will be termed compassion, pity, charity, benevolence.   Yet in all these cases the motive is the same : it is neither more nor less than the motive of good-will.

407   XXVI. To the pleasures of malevolence, or antipathy, corresponds the motive which, in a neutral sense, is termed antipathy or displeasure : and, in particular cases, dislike, aversion, abhorrence, and indignation : in a neutral sense, or perhaps a sense leaning a little to the bad side, ill-will : and, in particular cases, anger, wrath, and enmity.   In a bad sense it is styled, in different cases, wrath, spleen, ill-humour, hatred, malice, rancour, rage, fury, cruelty, tyranny, envy, jealousy, revenge, misanthropy, and by other names, which it is hardly worth while to endeavour to collect[1].   Like good-will, it is used with epithets expressive of the persons who are the objects of the affection.   Hence we hear of party enmity,

[1] Here, as elsewhere, it may be observed, that the same words which are mentioned as names of motives, are also many of them names of passions, appetites, and affections : fictitious entities, which are framed only by considering pleasures or pains in some particular point of view.   Some of them are also names of moral qualities.   This branch of nomenclature is remarkably entangled : to unravel it completely would take up a whole volume ; not a syllable of which would belong properly to the present design.

party rage, and so forth. In a good sense there seems to be no single name for it. In compound expressions it may be spoken of in such a sense, by epithets, such as *just* and *laudable*, prefixed to words that are used in a neutral or nearly neutral sense.

1. You rob a man: he prosecutes you, and gets you punished: out of resentment you set upon him, and hang him with your own hands. In this case your motive will universally be deemed detestable, and will be called malice, cruelty, revenge, and so forth. 2. A man has stolen a little money from you: out of resentment you prosecute him, and get him hanged by course of law. In this case people will probably be a little divided in their opinions about your motive: your friends will deem it a laudable one, and call it a just or laudable resentment: your enemies will perhaps be disposed to deem it blameable, and call it cruelty, malice, revenge, and so forth: to obviate which, your friends will try perhaps to change the motive, and call it public spirit. 3. A man has murdered your father: out of resentment you prosecute him, and get him put to death in course of law. In this case your motive will be universally deemed a laudable one, and styled, as before, a just or laudable resentment: and your friends, in order to bring forward the more amiable principle from which the malevolent one, which was your immediate motive, took its rise, will be for keeping the latter out of sight, speaking of the former only, under some such name as filial piety. Yet in all these cases the motive is the same: it is neither more nor less than the motive of ill-will.

*   *   *   *   *   *   *

408   XXIX. It appears then that there is no such thing as any sort of motive which is a bad one in itself: nor, consequently, any such thing as a sort of motive, which in itself is exclusively a good one. And as to their effects, it appears too that these are sometimes bad, at other times either indifferent or good: and this appears to be the case with every sort of motive.

If any sort of motive then is either good or bad on the score of its effects, this is the case only on individual occasions, and with individual motives ; and this is the case with one sort of motive as well as with another. *If any sort of motive then can, in consideration of its effects, be termed with any propriety a bad one,* it can only be with reference to the balance of all the effects it may have had of both kinds within a given period, that is, of its most usual tendency.

409   xxx. What then? (it will be said) are not lust, cruelty, avarice, bad motives ? Is there so much as any one individual occasion, in which motives like these can be otherwise than bad ? No, certainly : and yet the proposition, that there is no one *sort* of motive but what will on many occasions be a good one, is nevertheless true. The fact is, that these are names which, if properly applied, are never applied but in the cases where the motives they signify happen to be bad. The names of these motives, considered apart from their effects, are sexual desire, displeasure, and pecuniary interest. To sexual desire, when the effects of it are looked upon as bad, is given the name of lust. Now lust is always a bad motive. Why ? Because if the case be such, that the effects of the motive are not bad, it does not go, or at least ought not to go, by the name of lust. The case is, then, that when I say, 'Lust is a bad motive,' it is a proposition that merely concerns the import of the word lust ; and which would be false if transferred to the other word used for the same motive, sexual desire. Hence we see the emptiness of all those rhapsodies of common-place morality, which consist in the taking of such names as lust, cruelty, and avarice, and branding them with marks of reprobation : applied to the *thing*, they are false ; applied to the *name*, they are true indeed, but nugatory. Would you do a real service to mankind, shew them the cases in which sexual desire *merits* the name of lust ; displeasure, that of cruelty ; and pecuniary interest, that of avarice.

410   XXXI. If it were necessary to apply such denominations as good, bad, and indifferent to motives, they might be classed in the following manner, in consideration of the most frequent complexion of their effects. In the class of good motives might be placed the articles of, 1. Good-will. 2. Love of reputation. 3. Desire of amity. And, 4. Religion. In the class of bad motives, 5. Displeasure. In the class of neutral or indifferent motives, 6. Physical desire. 7. Pecuniary interest. 8. Love of power. 9. Self-preservation ; as including the fear of the pains of the senses, the love of ease, and the love of life.

XXXII. This method of arrangement, however, cannot but be imperfect; and the nomenclature belonging to it is in danger of being fallacious. For by what method of investigation can a man be assured, that with regard to the motives ranked under the name of good, the good effects they have had, from the beginning of the world, have, in each of the four species comprised under this name, been superior to the bad? still more difficulty would a man find in assuring himself, that with regard to those which are ranked under the name of neutral or indifferent, the effects they have had have exactly balanced each other, the value of the good being neither greater nor less than that of the bad. It is to be considered, that the interests of the person himself can no more be left out of the estimate, than those of the rest of the community. For what would become of the species, if it were not for the motives of hunger and thirst, sexual desire, the fear of pain, and the love of life? Nor in the actual constitution of human nature is the motive of displeasure less necessary, perhaps, than any of the others : although a system, in which the business of life might be carried on without it, might possibly be conceived. It seems, therefore, that they could scarcely, without great danger of mistakes, be distinguished in this manner even with reference to each other.

411   XXXIII. The only way, it should seem, in which a motive can

with safety and propriety be styled good or bad, is with reference to its effects in each individual instance; and principally
from the intention it gives birth to: from which arise, as
will be shewn hereafter, the most material part of its effects.
A motive is good, when the intention it gives birth to is
a good one; bad, when the intention is a bad one: and
an intention is good or bad, according to the material consequences that are the objects of it. So far is it from the
goodness of the intention's being to be known only from the
species of the motive. But from one and the same motive,
as we have seen, may result intentions of every sort of
complexion whatsoever. This circumstance, therefore, can
afford no clue for the arrangement of the several sorts of
motives.

412   xxxiv. A more commodious method, therefore, it should
seem, would be to distribute them according to the influence
which they appear to have on the interests of the other members
of the community, laying those of the party himself out of the
question: to wit, according to the tendency which they appear
to have to unite, or disunite, his interests and theirs. On this
plan they may be distinguished into *social, dissocial,* and *self-
regarding.* In the social class may be reckoned, 1. Good-will.
2. Love of reputation. 3. Desire of amity. 4. Religion. In
the dissocial may be placed, 5. Displeasure. In the self-
regarding class, 6. Physical desire. 7. Pecuniary interest·
8. Love of power. 9. Self-preservation; as including the fear
of the pains of the senses, the love of ease, and the love
of life.

413   xxxv. With respect to the motives that have been termed
social, if any farther distinction should be of use, to that of
good-will alone may be applied the epithet of *purely-social*;
while the love of reputation, the desire of amity, and the
motive of religion, may together be comprised under the
division of *semi-social*: the social tendency being much more
constant and unequivocal in the former than in any of the three

latter.   Indeed these last, social as they may be termed, are
self-regarding at the same time [1].

§ 4. *Order of pre-eminence among motives.*

414   XXXVI. Of all these sorts of motives, good-will is that of
which the dictates [2], taken in a general view, are surest of coinciding with those of the principle of utility.   For the dictates of
utility are neither more nor less than the dictates of the most
extensive [3] and enlightened (that is *well-advised* [4]) benevolence.
The dictates of the other motives may be conformable to
those of utility, or repugnant, as it may happen.

XXXVII. In this, however, it is taken for granted, that in
the case in question the dictates of benevolence are not contradicted by those of a more extensive, that is enlarged,
benevolence.   Now when the dictates of benevolence, as
respecting the interests of a certain set of persons, are repugnant
to the dictates of the same motive, as respecting the more important [5] interests of another set of persons, the former dictates,
it is evident, are repealed, as it were, by the latter : and a man,
were he to be governed by the former, could scarcely, with propriety, be said to be governed by the dictates of benevolence.
On this account, were the motives on both sides sure to be
alike present to a man's mind, the case of such a repugnancy
would hardly be worth distinguishing, since the partial benevolence might be considered as swallowed up in the more
extensive : if the former prevailed, and governed the action, it
must be considered as not owing its birth to benevolence,
but to some other motive : if the latter prevailed, the former

---

[1] 'Religion,' says the pious Addison, somewhere in the Spectator, ' is
the highest species of self-love.'
[2] When a man is supposed to be prompted by any motive to engage, or
not to engage, in such or such an action, it may be of use, for the convenience of discourse, to speak of such motive as giving birth to an imaginary
kind of *law* or *dictate*, enjoining him to engage, or not to engage, in it.
[3] See ch. iv. [Value] and ch. vi. [Sensibility] xxi.
[4] See ch. ix. [Consciousness].
[5] Or valuable. See ch. iv. [Value].

might be considered as having no effect.   But the case is, that a partial benevolence may govern the action, without entering into any direct competition with the more extensive bene-volence, which would forbid it; because the interests of the less numerous assemblage of persons may be present to a man's mind, at a time when those of the more numerous are either not present, or, if present, make no impression.   It is in this way that the dictates of this motive may be repugnant to utility, yet still be the dictates of benevolence.   What makes those of private benevolence conformable upon the whole to the principle of utility, is, that in general they stand unopposed by those of public: if they are repugnant to them, it is only by accident.   What makes them the more conform-able, is, that in a civilized society, in most of the cases in which they would of themselves be apt to run counter to those of public benevolence, they find themselves opposed by stronger motives of the self-regarding class, which are played off against them by the laws; and that it is only in cases where they stand unopposed by the other more salutary dictates, that they are left free.   An act of injustice or cruelty, committed by a man for the sake of his father or his son, is punished, and with reason, as much as if it were committed for his own.

415   XXXVIII. After good-will, the motive of which the dictates seem to have the next best chance for coinciding with those of utility, is that of the love of reputation.   There is but one circumstance which prevents the dictates of this motive from coinciding in all cases with those of the former.   This is, that men in their likings and dislikings, in the dispositions they mani-fest to annex to any mode of conduct their approbation or their disapprobation, and in consequence to the person who ap-pears to practise it, their good or their ill will, do not govern themselves exclusively by the principle of utility.   Sometimes it is the principle of asceticism they are guided by: sometimes the principle of sympathy and antipathy.   There is another circumstance, which diminishes, not their conformity to the

principle of utility, but only their efficacy in comparison with
the dictates of the motive of benevolence.   The dictates of
this motive will operate as strongly in secret as in public :
whether it appears likely that the conduct which they recommend will be known or not : those of the love of reputation
will coincide with those of benevolence only in proportion as
a man's conduct seems likely to be known.   This circumstance, however, does not make so much difference as at first
sight might appear.   Acts, in proportion as they are material,
are apt to become known [1] : and in point of reputation, the
slightest suspicion often serves for proof.   Besides, if an act be
a disreputable one, it is not any assurance a man can have of
the secrecy of the particular act in question, that will of course
surmount the objections he may have against engaging in it.
Though the act in question should remain secret, it will go
towards forming a habit, which may give birth to other acts,
that may not meet with the same good fortune.   There is no
human being, perhaps, who is at years of discretion, on whom
considerations of this sort have not some weight : and they
have the more weight upon a man, in proportion to the strength
of his intellectual powers, and the firmness of his mind.   Add
to this, the influence which habit itself, when once formed, has
in restraining a man from acts towards which, from the view of
the disrepute annexed to them, as well as from any other cause,
he has contracted an aversion.   The influence of habit, in such
cases, is a matter of fact, which, though not readily accounted
for, is acknowledged and indubitable.

*   *   *   *   *   *   *

Chapter XI.—Of Human Dispositions in General.

416   1. In the foregoing chapter it has been shewn at large, that
goodness or badness cannot, with any propriety, be predicated
of motives.   Is there nothing then about a man that can

[1] See B. II. tit. [Evidence].

properly be termed good or bad, when, on such or such an occasion, he suffers himself to be governed by such or such a motive? Yes, certainly: his *disposition*. Now disposition is a kind of fictitious entity, feigned for the convenience of discourse, in order to express what there is supposed to be *permanent* in a man's frame of mind, where, on such or such an occasion, he has been influenced by such or such a motive, to engage in an act, which, as it appeared to him, was of such or such a tendency.

417   II. It is with disposition as with every thing else: it will be good or bad according to its effects: according to the effects it has in augmenting or diminishing the happiness of the community. A man's disposition may accordingly be considered in two points of view: according to the influence it has, either, 1. on his own happiness: or, 2. on the happiness of others. Viewed in both these lights together, or in either of them indiscriminately, it may be termed, on the one hand, good; on the other, bad; or, in flagrant cases, depraved [1]. Viewed in the former of these lights, it has scarcely any peculiar name, which has as yet been appropriated to it. It might be termed, though but inexpressively, frail or infirm, on the one hand: sound or firm, on the other. Viewed in the other light, it might be termed beneficent, or meritorious, on the one hand: pernicious or mischievous on the other. Now of that branch of a man's disposition, the effects of which regard in the first instance only himself, there needs not much to be said here. To reform it when bad, is the business rather

---

[1] It might also be termed virtuous, or vicious. The only objection to the use of those terms on the present occasion is, the great quantity of good and bad repute that respectively stand annexed to them. The inconvenience of this is, their being apt to annex an ill-proportioned measure of disrepute to dispositions which are ill-constituted only with respect to the party himself: involving them in such a degree of ignominy as should be appropriated to such dispositions only as are mischievous with regard to others. To exalt weaknesses to a level with crimes, is a way to diminish the abhorrence which ought to be reserved for crimes. To exalt small evils to a level with great ones, is the way to diminish the share of attention which ought to be paid to great ones.

of the moralist than the legislator: nor is it susceptible of
those various modifications which make so material a difference in the effects of the other. Again, with respect to that
part of it, the effects whereof regard others in the first instance,
it is only in as far as it is of a mischievous nature that the
penal branch of law has any immediate concern with it: in as
far as it may be of a beneficent nature, it belongs to a hitherto
but little cultivated, and as yet unnamed branch of law, which
might be styled the remuneratory.

418   III. A man then is said to be of a mischievous disposition,
when, by the influence of no matter what motives, he is
presumed to be more apt to engage, or form intentions of
engaging, in acts which are *apparently* of a pernicious tendency, than in such as are apparently of a beneficial tendency:
of a meritorious or beneficent disposition in the opposite
case.

IV. I say presumed: for, by the supposition, all that appears
is one single action, attended with one single train of circumstances: but from that degree of consistency and uniformity
which experience has shewn to be observable in the different
actions of the same person, the probable existence (past or
future) of a number of acts of a similar nature, is naturally and
justly inferred from the observation of one single one. Under
such circumstances, such as the motive proves to be in one
instance, such is the disposition to be presumed to be in
others.

V. I say *apparently* mischievous: that is, apparently with
regard to him: such as to him appear to possess that tendency: for from the mere event, independent of what to him
it appears beforehand likely to be, nothing can be inferred on
either side. If to him it appears likely to be mischievous, in
such case, though in the upshot it should prove innocent, or
even beneficial, it makes no difference; there is not the less
reason for presuming his disposition to be a bad one: if to
him it appears likely to be beneficial or innocent, in such case,

though in the upshot it should prove pernicious, there is not the more reason on that account for presuming his disposition to be a good one. And here we see the importance of the circumstances of intentionality [1], consciousness [2], unconsciousness [2], and mis-supposal [2].

419   VI. The truth of these positions depends upon two others, both of them sufficiently verified by experience : the one is, that in the ordinary course of things the consequences of actions commonly turn out conformable to intentions. A man who sets up a butcher's shop, and deals in beef, when he intends to knock down an ox, commonly does knock down an ox; though by some unlucky accident he may chance to miss his blow and knock down a man: he who sets up a grocer's shop, and deals in sugar, when he intends to sell sugar, commonly does sell sugar: though by some unlucky accident he may chance to sell arsenic in the room of it.

VII. The other is, that a man who entertains intentions of doing mischief at one time is apt to entertain the like intentions at another [3].

420   VIII. There are two circumstances upon which the nature of the disposition, as indicated by any act, is liable to depend : 1. The apparent tendency of the act: 2. The nature of the motive which gave birth to it. This dependency is subject to different rules, according to the nature of the motive. In stating them, I suppose all along the apparent tendency of the act to be, as it commonly is, the same as the real.

421   IX. 1. Where the tendency of the act is *good*, and the motive

---

[1] See ch. viii.   [2] See ch. ix.

[3] To suppose a man to be of a good disposition, and at the same time likely, in virtue of that very disposition, to engage in an habitual train of mischievous actions, is a contradiction in terms: nor could such a proposition ever be advanced, but from the giving, to the thing which the word disposition is put for, a reality which does *not* belong to it. If then, for example, a man of religious disposition should, in virtue of that very disposition, be in the habit of doing mischief, for instance, by persecuting his neighbours, the case must be, either that his disposition, though good in certain respects, is not good upon the whole: or that a religious disposition is not in general a good one.

is of the *self-regarding* kind. In this case the motive affords no inference on either side. It affords no indication of a good disposition : but neither does it afford any indication of a bad one.

A baker sells his bread to a hungry man who asks for it. This, we see, is one of those acts of which, in ordinary cases, the tendency is unquestionably good. The baker's motive is the ordinary commercial motive of pecuniary interest. It is plain, that there is nothing in the transaction, thus stated, that can afford the least ground for presuming that the baker is a better or a worse man than any of his neighbours.

422 x. 2. Where the tendency of the act is *bad*, and the motive, as before, is of the *self-regarding* kind. In this case the disposition indicated is a mischievous one.

A man steals bread out of a baker's shop : this is one of those acts of which the tendency will readily be acknowledged to be bad. Why, and in what respects it is so, will be stated farther on. His motive, we will say, is that of pecuniary interest ; the desire of getting the value of the bread for nothing. His disposition, accordingly, appears to be a bad one : for every one will allow a thievish disposition to be a bad one.

423 XI. 3. Where the tendency of the act is *good*, and the motive is the purely social one of *good-will*. In this case the disposition indicated is a beneficent one.

A baker gives a poor man a loaf of bread. His motive is compassion ; a name given to the motive of benevolence, in particular cases of its operation. The disposition indicated by the baker, in this case, is such as every man will be ready enough to acknowledge to be a good one.

424 XII. 4. Where the tendency of the act is *bad*, and the motive is the purely social one of good-will. Even in this case the disposition which the motive indicates is dubious : it may be a mischievous or a meritorious one, as it happens ; according as the mischievousness of the act is more or less apparent.

XIII. It may be thought, that a case of this sort cannot exist; and that to suppose it, is a contradiction in terms. For the act is one, which, by the supposition, the agent knows to be a mischievous one. How then can it be, that good-will, that is, the desire of doing good, could have been the motive that led him into it? To reconcile this, we must advert to the distinction between enlarged benevolence and confined[1]. The motive that led him into it, was that of confined benevolence. Had he followed the dictates of enlarged benevolence, he would not have done what he did. Now, although he followed the dictates of that branch of benevolence, which in any single instance of its exertion is mischievous, when opposed to the other, yet, as the cases which call for the exertion of the former are, beyond comparison, more numerous than those which call for the exertion of the latter, the disposition indicated by him, in following the impulse of the former, will often be such as in a man, of the common run of men, may be allowed to be a good one upon the whole.

XIV. A man with a numerous family of children, on the point of starving, goes into a baker's shop, steals a loaf, divides it all among the children, reserving none of it for himself. It will be hard to infer that that man's disposition is a mischievous one upon the whole. Alter the case, give him but one child, and that hungry perhaps, but in no imminent danger of starving: and now let the man set fire to a house full of people, for the sake of stealing money out of it to buy the bread with. The disposition here indicated will hardly be looked upon as a good one.

*   *   *   *   *   *   *

425   XVII. 5. Where the tendency of the act is *good*, and the motive is a semi-social one, the *love of reputation.* In this case the disposition indicated is a good one.

In a time of scarcity, a baker, for the sake of gaining the esteem of the neighbourhood, distributes bread *gratis* among

---

[1] See ch. x. [Motives].

the industrious poor. Let this be taken for granted : and let it be allowed to be a matter of uncertainty, whether he had any real feeling for the sufferings of those whom he has relieved, or no. His disposition, for all that, cannot, with any pretence of reason, be termed otherwise than a good and beneficent one. It can only be in consequence of some very idle prejudice, if it receives a different name [1].

426   XVIII. 6. Where the tendency of the act is *bad*, and the motive, as before, is a semi-social one, the love of reputation. In this case, the disposition which it indicates is more or less good or bad : in the first place, according as the tendency of the act is more or less mischievous : in the next place, according as the dictates of the moral sanction, in the society in question, approach more or less to a coincidence with those of utility. It does not seem probable, that in any nation, which is in a state of tolerable civilization, in short, in any nation in which such rules as these can come to be consulted, the dictates of the moral sanction will so far recede from a coincidence with

---

[1] The bulk of mankind, ever ready to depreciate the character of their neighbours, in order, indirectly, to exalt their own, will take occasion to refer a motive to the class of bad ones as often as they can find one still better, to which the act might have owed its birth. Conscious that his own motives are not of the best class, or persuaded that if they be, they will not be referred to that class by others ; afraid of being taken for a dupe, and anxious to show the reach of his penetration ; each man takes care, in the first place, to impute the conduct of every other man to the least laudable of the motives that can account for it : in the next place, when he has gone as far that way as he can, and cannot drive down the individual motive to any lower class, he changes his battery, and attacks the very class itself. To the love of reputation he will accordingly give a bad name upon every occasion, calling it ostentation, vanity, or vain-glory.

Partly to the same spirit of detraction, the natural consequence of the sensibility of men to the force of the moral sanction, partly to the influence of the principle of asceticism, may, perhaps, be imputed the great abundance of bad names of motives, in comparison of such as are good or neutral : and, in particular, the total want of neutral names for the motives of sexual desire, physical desire in general, and pecuniary interest. The superior abundance, even of good names, in comparison of neutral ones, would, if examined, be found rather to confirm than disprove the above remark. The language of a people on these points may, perhaps, serve in some measure as a key to their moral sentiments. But such speculative disquisitions are foreign to the purpose of the present work.

those of utility (that is, of enlightened benevolence) that the disposition indicated in this case can be otherwise than a good one upon the whole.

xix. An Indian receives an injury, real or imaginary, from an Indian of another tribe. He revenges it upon the person of his antagonist with the most excruciating torments: the case being, that cruelties inflicted on such an occasion, gain him reputation in his own tribe. The disposition manifested in such a case can never be deemed a good one, among a people ever so few degrees advanced, in point of civilization, above the Indians.

xx. A nobleman (to come back to Europe) contracts a debt with a poor tradesman. The same nobleman, presently afterwards, contracts a debt, to the same amount, to another nobleman, at play. He is unable to pay both: he pays the whole debt to the companion of his amusements, and no part of it to the tradesman. The disposition manifested in this case can scarcely be termed otherwise than a bad one. It is certainly, however, not so bad as if he had paid neither. The principle of love of reputation, or (as it is called in the case of this partial application of it) honour, is here opposed to the worthier principle of benevolence, and gets the better of it. But it gets the better also of the self-regarding principle of pecuniary interest. The disposition, therefore, which it indicates, although not so good a one as that in which the principle of benevolence predominates, is better than one in which the principle of self-interest predominates. He would be the better for having more benevolence: but would he be the better for having no honour? This seems to admit of great dispute[1].

427 xxi. 7. Where the tendency of the act is *good*, and the motive is the semi-social one of *religion*. In this case, the disposition indicated by it (considered with respect to the influence of it

---

[1] See the case of Duels discussed in B. I. tit. [Homicide].

on the man's conduct towards others) is manifestly a beneficent
and meritorious one.

A baker distributes bread *gratis* among the industrious poor.
It is not that he feels for their distresses : nor is it for the sake
of gaining reputation among his neighbours.   It is for the sake
of gaining the favour of the Deity : to whom, he takes for
granted, such conduct will be acceptable.   The disposition
manifested by such conduct is plainly what every man would
call a good one.

428   XXII. 8. Where the tendency of the act is *bad*, and the motive
is that of religion, as before.   In this case the disposition is
dubious.   It is good or bad, and more or less good or bad,
in the first place as the tendency of the act is more or less
mischievous ; in the next place, according as the religious
tenets of the person in question approach more or less to
a coincidence with the dictates of utility.

*   *   *   *   *   *   *

429   XXIV. 9. Where the tendency of the act is *good*, and the
motive (as before) is the dissocial one of ill-will.   In this case
the motive seems not to afford any indication on either side.
It is no indication of a good disposition ; but neither is it
any indication of a bad one.

You have detected a baker in selling short weight : you
prosecute him for the cheat.   It is not for the sake of gain
that you engaged in the prosecution ; for there is nothing to
be got by it : it is not from public spirit : it is not for the sake
of reputation ; for there is no reputation to be got by it : it is
not in the view of pleasing the Deity : it is merely on account
of a quarrel you have with the man you prosecute.   From the
transaction, as thus stated, there does not seem to be any
thing to be said either in favour of your disposition or against
it.   The tendency of the act is good : but you would not have
engaged in it, had it not been from a motive which there seems
no particular reason to conclude will ever prompt you to engage
in an act of the same kind again.   Your motive is of that

sort which may, with least impropriety, be termed a bad one : but the act is of that sort, which, were it engaged in ever so often, could never have any evil tendency ; nor indeed any other tendency than a good one. By the supposition, the motive it happened to be dictated by was that of ill-will : but the act itself is of such a nature as to have wanted nothing but sufficient discernment on your part in order to have been dictated by the most enlarged benevolence. Now, from a man's having suffered himself to be induced to gratify his resentment by means of an act of which the tendency is good, it by no means follows that he would be ready on another occasion, through the influence of the same sort of motive, to engage in any act of which the tendency is a bad one. The motive that impelled you was a dissocial one : but what social motive could there have been to restrain you? None, but what might have been outweighed by a more enlarged motive of the same kind. Now, because the dissocial motive prevailed when it stood alone, it by no means follows that it would prevail when it had a social one to combat it.

430   xxv. 10. Where the tendency of the act is *bad*, and the motive is the dissocial one of malevolence. In this case the disposition it indicates is of course a mischievous one.

The man who stole the bread from the baker, as before, did it with no other view than merely to impoverish and afflict him : accordingly, when he had got the bread, he did not eat, or sell it ; but destroyed it. That the disposition, evidenced by such a transaction, is a bad one, is what every body must perceive immediately.

   *   *   *   *   *   *   *

APPENDIX

---·---

HUTCHESON

I. An Essay on the Nature and Conduct of the Passions and Affections.

II. Illustrations upon the Moral Sense.

[First edition, 1728; reprinted here from the third edition, 1742.]

III. A System of Moral Philosophy.

[Reprinted here from the first edition, 1755.]

HUTCHESON

On the Nature and Conduct of the Passions and Affections

———•+•———

*　　*　　*　　*　　*　　*　　*　　*

431　SOME strange Love of Simplicity in the Structure of human Nature, or Attachment to some favourite Hypothesis, has engaged many Writers to pass over a great many simple Perceptions, which we may find in ourselves. We have got the number Five fixed for our external Senses, though a larger Number might perhaps as easily be defended. We have Multitudes of Perceptions which have no relation to any external Sensation; if by it we mean Perceptions immediately occasioned by Motions or Impressions made on our Bodies, such as the Ideas of Number, Duration, Proportion, Virtue, Vice, Pleasures of Honour, of Congratulation; the Pains of Remorse, Shame, Sympathy, and many others. It were to be wished, that those who are at such Pains to prove a beloved Maxim, that 'all Ideas arise from Sensation and Reflection,' had so explained themselves, that none should take their Meaning to be, that all our Ideas are either external Sensations, or reflex Acts upon external Sensations: Or if by Reflection they mean an inward Power of Perception, as Mr. Locke declares expressly, calling it internal Sensation, that they had as carefully examined into the several kinds of internal Perceptions, as they have done into the external Sensations: that we might have seen whether the former be not as natural and necessary and ultimate, without reference to any other, as the latter. Had they in like manner considered our Affections without a previous Notion, that they were all from Self-Love, they might have felt an ultimate Desire of the Happiness of others as easily conceivable, and as certainly implanted in the human Breast, though perhaps not so strong as Self-Love.

*   *   *   *   *   *   *   *

432   One may easily see from the great variety of Terms, and diversity of Schemes invented, that all Men feel something in their own Hearts recommending Virtue, which yet it is difficult to explain. This Difficulty probably arises from our previous Notions of a small Number of Senses, so that we are unwilling to have recourse in our Theories to any more; and rather strain out some Explication of moral Ideas, with relation to some of the natural Powers of Perception universally acknowledged. The like difficulty attends several other Perceptions, to the Reception of which Philosophers have not generally assigned their distinct Senses; such as natural Beauty, Harmony, the Perfection of Poetry, Architecture, Designing, and such like affairs of Genius, Taste, or Fancy; The Explications or Theories on these Subjects are in like manner full of Confusion and Metaphor.

*   *   *   *   *   *   *   *

SECTION I.—*A general Account of our several Senses and Desires, Selfish or Publick.*

*   *   *   *   *   *   *   *

433   I. If we may call 'every Determination of our Minds to receive Ideas independently of our Will, and to have Perceptions of Pleasure and Pain, a Sense' we shall find many other Senses beside those commonly explained. Though it is not easy to assign accurate Divisions on such Subjects, yet we may reduce them to the following Classes, leaving it to others to arrange them as they think convenient. A little Reflection will shew that there are such Natural Powers in the human Mind, in whatever Order we place them. In the 1st Class are the External Senses, universally known. In the 2nd, the Pleasant Perceptions arising from regular, harmonious, uniform Objects; as also from Grandeur and Novelty. These we may call, after Mr. Addison, the Pleasures of the Imagination; or we may call the Power of receiving them, an Internal Sense. Whoever dislikes this Name may substitute another. 3. The next Class of Perceptions we may call a

Publick Sense, viz. 'our Determination to be pleased with the Happiness of others, and to be uneasy at their Misery.' This is found in some degree in all Men, and was sometimes called Κοινονοημοσύνη, or *Sensus Communis* by some of the Antients. This inward Pain of Compassion cannot be called a Sensation of Sight. It solely arises from an Opinion of Misery felt by another, and not immediately from a visible Form. The same Form presented to the Eye by the exactest Painting, or the Action of a Player, gives no Pain to those who remember that there is no Misery felt. When Men by Imagination conceive real Pain felt by an Actor, without recollecting that it is merely feigned, or when they think of the real Story represented, then, as there is a confused Opinion of real Misery, there is also Pain in Compassion. 4. The fourth Class we may call the Moral Sense, by which 'we perceive Virtue or Vice, in ourselves, or others.' This is plainly distinct from the former Class of Perceptions, since many are strongly affected with the Fortunes of others, who seldom reflect upon Virtue or Vice, in themselves, or others, as an Object: as we may find in Natural Affection, Compassion, Friendship, or even general Benevolence to Mankind, which connect our Happiness or Pleasure with that of others, even when we are not reflecting upon our own Temper, nor delighted with the Perception of our own Virtue. 5. The fifth Class is a Sense of Honour, which makes the Approbation, or Gratitude of others, for any good Actions we have done, the necessary occasion of pleasure; and their Dislike, Condemnation, or Resentment of Injuries done by us, the occasion of that uneasy Sensation called Shame, even when we fear no further evil from them.

434   There are perhaps other Perceptions distinct from all these Classes, such as some Ideas 'of Decency, Dignity, Suitableness to human Nature in certain Actions and Circumstances; and of an Indecency, Meanness, and Unworthiness, in the contrary Actions or Circumstances, even without any conception of Moral Good, or Evil.' Thus the Pleasures of Sight, and Hearing, are more esteemed than those of Taste or Touch: The Pursuits of the Pleasures of the Imagination, are more approved than those of simple external Sensations.   Plato makes one of his Dialogists [1] account for this difference

---

[1] Hippias Major.   See also Treat. II. Sect. 5. Art. 7.

from a constant o nion of Innocence in this sort of Pleasures, which would reduce this Perception to the Moral Sense. Others may imagine that the difference is not owing to any such Reflection upon their Innocence, but that there is a different sort of Perceptions in these cases, to be reckoned another Class of Sensations.

435 II. Desires arise in our Mind, from the Frame of our Nature, upon Apprehension of Good or Evil in Objects, Actions, or Events, to obtain for ourselves or others the agreeable Sensation, when the Object or Event is good : or to prevent the uneasy Sensation, when it is evil. Our original Desires and Aversions may therefore be divided into five Classes, answering to the Classes of our Senses. 1. The Desire of sensual Pleasure, (by which we mean that of the external Senses, of Taste and Touch chiefly) ; and Aversion to the opposite Pains. 2. The Desires of the Pleasures of Imagination or Internal Sense [1], and Aversion to what is disagreeable to it. 3. Desires of the Pleasures arising from Public Happiness, and Aversion to the Pains arising from the Misery of others. 4. Desires of Virtue, and Aversion to Vice, according to the Notions we have of the Tendency of Actions to the Public Advantage or Detriment. 5. Desires of Honour, and Aversion to Shame [2].

436 And since we are capable of Reflection, Memory, Observation, and Reasoning about the distant Tendencies of Objects and Actions, and not confined to things present, there must arise, in consequence of our original Desires, ' secondary Desires of every thing imagined useful to gratify any of the primary Desires, and that with strength proportioned to the several original Desires, and the imagined Usefulness, or Necessity of the advantageous Object.' Thus as soon as we come to apprehend the Use of Wealth or Power to gratify any of our original Desires, we must also desire them. Hence arises the Universality of these Desires of Wealth and Power since they are the Means of gratifying all other Desires. How foolish then is the Inference, some would make, from the universal Prevalence of these Desires, that human Nature is wholly selfish, or that each one is only studious of his own Advantage ; since Wealth or Power are as naturally fit to gratify our Publick Desires, or to serve virtuous Purposes, as the selfish ones ? '

*   *   *   *   *   *   *   *

[1] See Treat. I.   [2] See Treat. II. Sect. 5. Art. 3–8.

437   Let it be premised, that there is a certain Pain or Uneasiness accompanying most of our violent Desires. Though the Object pursued be Good, or the Means of Pleasure, yet the Desire of it generally is attended with an uneasy Sensation. When an Object or Event appears Evil, we desire to shun or prevent it. This Desire is also attended with uneasy Sensation of Impatience : Now this Sensation immediately connected with the Desire, is a distinct Sensation from those which we dread, and endeavour to shun. It is plain then,

I. 'That no Desire of any Event is excited by any view of removing the uneasy Sensation attending this Desire itself.' Uneasy Sensations previously felt, will raise a Desire of whatever will remove them : and this Desire may have its concomitant Uneasiness. Pleasant Sensations expected from any Object may raise our Desire of it ; this Desire too may have its concomitant uneasy Sensations : But the uneasy Sensation, accompanying and connected with the Desire itself, cannot be a Motive to that Desire which it presupposes. The Sensation accompanying Desire is generally uneasy, and consequently our Desire is never raised with a view to obtain or continue it ; nor is the Desire raised with a view to remove this uneasy Sensation, for the Desire is raised previously to it. This holds concerning all Desire publick or private.

There is also a peculiar pleasant Sensation of Joy, attending the Gratification of any Desire, beside the Sensation received from the Object itself, which we directly intended. ' But Desire does never arise from a View of obtaining that Sensation of Joy, connected with the Success or Gratification of Desire ; otherwise the strongest Desires might arise toward any Trifle, or an Event in all respects indifferent : Since, if Desire arose from this View, the stronger the Desire were, the higher would be the Pleasure of Gratification ; and therefore we might desire the turning of a Straw as violently as we do Wealth or Power.' This Expectation of that Pleasure which merely arises from gratifying of Desire, would equally excite us to desire the Misery of others as their Happiness ; since this Pleasure of Gratification might be obtained from both Events alike.

438   2. It is certain that ' that Desire of the Happiness of others which we account virtuous, is not directly excited by prospects of any secular Advantage, Wealth, Power, Pleasure of the external Senses, Reward from the Deity, or future Pleasures of Self-Approbation.'

To prove this let us consider, 'That no Desire of any Event can arise immediately or directly from an Opinion in the Agent, that his having such a Desire will be the Means of private Good.' This Opinion would make us wish or desire to have that advantageous Desire or Affection ; and would incline us to use any means in our power to raise that Affection : but no Affection or Desire is raised in us, directly by our volition or desiring it. That alone which raises in us from Self-Love the Desire of any Event, is an Opinion that that Event is the Means of private Good. As soon as we form this Opinion, a Desire of the Event immediately arises : But if having the Desire, or the mere Affection, be imagined the Means of private Good, and not the Existence of the Event desired, then from Self-Love we should only desire or wish to have the Desire of that Event, and should not desire the Event itself, since the Event is not conceived as the Means of Good.

*   *   *   *   *   *   *   *

439 3. 'There are in Men Desires of the Happiness of others, when they do not conceive this Happiness as the Means of obtaining any sort of Happiness to themselves.' Self-Approbation, or Rewards from the Deity, might be the Ends, for obtaining which we might possibly desire or will from Self-Love, to raise in ourselves kind Affections ; but we could not from Self-Love desire the Happiness of others, except we imagined their Happiness to be the Means of our own. Now it is certain that sometimes we may have this subordinate Desire of the Happiness of others, conceived as the Means of our own ; as suppose one had laid a Wager upon the Happiness of a Person of such Veracity, that he would own sincerely whether he were happy or not; when Men are Partners in Stock, and share in Profit or Loss; when one hopes to succeed to, or some way to share in the Prosperity of another ; or if the Deity had given such Threatnings, as they tell us Telamon gave his Sons when they went to War, that he would reward or punish one according as others were happy or miserable : In such Cases one might have this subordinate Desire of another's Happiness from Self-Love. But as we are sure the Deity has not given such Comminations, so we often are conscious of the Desire of the Happiness of others, without any such Conception of it as the Means of our own; and are sensible that this subordinate Desire is not that virtuous Affection which we approve. The virtuous Benevolence must be an ultimate

Desire, which would subsist without view to private Good. Such ultimate publick Desires we often feel, without any subordinate Desire of the same Event, as the Means of private Good. The subordinate may sometimes, nay often does concur with the ultimate ; and then indeed the whole Moment of these conspiring Desires may be greater than that of either alone : But the subordinate alone is not that Affection which we approve as virtuous.

440   Art. IV. This will clear our Way to answer the chief Difficulty : ' May not our Benevolence be at least a Desire of the Happiness of others, as the Means of obtaining the Pleasure of the publick Sense, from the Contemplation of their Happiness ?' If it were so, it is very unaccountable, that we should approve this subordinate Desire as virtuous, and yet not approve the like Desire upon a Wager, or other Considerations of Interest. Both Desires proceed from Self-Love in the same manner : In the latter case the Desires might be extended to multitudes, if any one would wager so capriciously ; and, by increasing the Sum wagered, the Motive of Interest might, with many Tempers, be made stronger than that from the Pleasures of the publick Sense.

Do not we find that we often desire the Happiness of others without any such selfish Intention ? How few have thought upon this part of our Constitution which we call a Publick Sense ? Were it our only View, in Compassion to free ourselves from the Pain of the publick Sense ; should the Deity propose it to our Choice, either to obliterate all Ideas of the Person in Distress, or to harden our Hearts against all feelings of Compassion, on the one hand, while yet the Object continued in Misery ; or on the other hand to relieve him from it ; should we not upon this Scheme be perfectly indifferent, and chuse the former as soon as the latter ? Should the Deity assure us that we should be immediately annihilated, so that we should be incapable of either Pleasure or Pain, but that it should depend upon our Choice at our very Exit, whether our Children, our Friends, or our Country should be happy or miserable ; should we not upon this Scheme be entirely indifferent ? Or, if we should even desire the pleasant Thought of their Happiness, in our last Moment, would not this Desire be the faintest imaginable ?

It is true, our Publick Sense might be as acute at our Exit as ever ; as a Man's Taste of Meat or Drink and his Sensations of Hunger and Thirst might be as lively the instant before his

Dissolution as in any part of his Life. But would any Man have as strong Desires of the Means of obtaining these Pleasures, only with a view to himself, when he was to perish the next Moment? Is it supposable that any Desire of the Means of private Pleasure can be as strong when we only expect to enjoy it a Minute, as when we expect the Continuance of it for many Years? And yet, it is certain, any good Man would as strongly desire at his Exit the Happiness of others, as in any part of his Life, which must be the Case with those who voluntarily hazard their Lives, or resolve on Death for their Country or Friends. We do not therefore desire it as the Means of private Pleasure.

* * * * * * * *

441 The Occasion of the imagined Difficulty in conceiving distinterested Desires, has probably been from the attempting to define this simple Idea, Desire. It is called an uneasy Sensation in the absence of Good[1]. Whereas Desire is as distinct from any Sensation, as the Will is from the Understanding or Senses. This every one must acknowledge, who speaks of desiring to remove Uneasiness or Pain.

* * * * * * * *

SECTION II.—*Of the Affections and Passions: The natural Laws of pure Affection: The confused Sensations of the Passions with their final Causes.*

* * * * * * * *

442 There is a Distinction to be observed on this Subject, between 'the calm Desire of Good, and Aversion to Evil, either selfish or publick, as they appear to our Reason or Reflection; and the particular Passions towards Objects immediately presented to some Sense.' Thus nothing can be more distinct than the general calm Desire of private Good of any kind, which alone would incline us to pursue whatever Objects were apprehended as the Means of Good, and the particular selfish Passions, such as Ambition, Covetousness, Hunger, Lust, Revenge, Anger, as they arise upon particular Occasions. In like Manner our publick Desires may be distinguished into the general calm Desire of the Happiness of others, or Aversion to their Misery upon Reflection; and the

---

[1] See Mr. Locke's *Essay on Human Understanding* in the Chap. on the Passions.

particular Affections or Passions of Love, Congratulation, Compassion, natural Affection.

*   *   *   *   *   *   *   *

We obtain Command over the particular Passions, principally by strengthening the general Desires through frequent Reflection, and making them habitual, so as to obtain Strength superior to the particular Passions [1].

*   *   *   *   *   *   *   *

443   If it seems too rash to assert a Distinction between Affections and Passions, or that Desire may subsist without any uneasiness, since perhaps we are never conscious of any Desire absolutely free from all uneasiness ; 'let it be considered, that the simple Idea of Desire is different from that of Pain of any kind, or from any Sensation whatsoever : Nor is there any other Argument for their Identity than this, that they occur to us at once : But this Argument is inconclusive, otherwise it would prove Colour and Figure to be the same, or Incision and Pain.'

*   *   *   *   *   *   *   *

SECTION III.—*Particular Divisions of the Affections and Passions.*

*   *   *   *   *   *   *   *

444   Since our Moral Sense represents Virtue as the greatest Happiness to the Person possessed of it, our publick Affections will naturally make us desire the Virtue of others. When the Opportunity of a great Action occurs to any Person against whom we are no way prejudiced, we wish he would attempt it, and desire his good Success. If he succeeds we feel Joy ; if he is disappointed, or quits the

---

[1] The Schoolmen express this Distinction by the *Appetitus rationalis,* and the *Appetitus Sensitivus.* All Animals have in common the External Senses suggesting notions of things as pleasant or painful : and have also the *Appetitus Sensitivus,* or some instinctive Desires and Aversions. Rational Agents have, superadded to these, two higher analogous Powers : viz. the Understanding, or Reason, presenting farther notions, and attended with an higher sort of Sensations ; and the *Appetitus rationalis.* This latter is a ' constant natural Disposition of Soul to desire what the Understanding, or these sublimer Sensations, represent as Good, and to shun what they represent as Evil, and this either when it respects ourselves or others.' This many call the Will as distinct from the Passions. Some later Writers seem to have forgot it, by ascribing to the Understanding not only Ideas, Notions, Knowledge ; but Action, Inclinations, Desires, Prosecution, and their Contraries.

Attempt, we feel Sorrow. Upon like Opportunity of, or Temptation to a base Action, we have Aversion to the Event : If he resists the Temptation, we feel Joy ; if he yields to it, Sorrow. Our Affections toward the Person arise jointly with our Passions about this Event, according as he acquits himself virtuously or basely.

*   *   *   *   *   *   *   *

SECTION IV.—*How far our several Affections and Passions are in our Power, either to govern them when raised, or to prevent their arising : with some general Observations about their Objects.*

*   *   *   *   *   *   *   *

445   II. The Government of our Passions must then depend much upon our Opinions : But we must here observe an obvious Difference among our Desires, viz. that ' some of them have a previous, painful, or uneasy Sensation, antecedently to any Opinion of Good in the Object ; nay, the Object is often chiefly esteemed good, only for its allaying this Pain or Uneasiness ; or if the Object gives also positive Pleasure, yet the uneasy Sensation is previous to, and independent of this Opinion of Good in the Object.' ' These Desires we may call Appetites.' ' Other Desires and Aversions necessarily pre-suppose an Opinion of Good and Evil in their Objects ; and the Desires or Aversions, with their concomitant uneasy Sensations, are produced or occasioned by this Opinion or Apprehension.' Of the former kind are Hunger and Thirst, and the Desires between the Sexes ; to which Desires there is an uneasy Sensation previous, even in those who have little other Notion of Good in the Objects, than allaying this Pain or Uneasiness. There is something like to this in the Desire of Society, or the Company of our Fellow-creatures.

*   *   *   *   *   *   *   *

446   In other Desires the Case is different. No Man is distressed for want of fine Smells, harmonious Sounds, beautiful Objects, Wealth, Power, or Grandeur, previously to some Opinion formed of these things as good, or some prior Sensation of their Pleasures. In like manner, Virtue and Honour as necessarily give us Pleasure, when they occur to us, as Vice and Contempt give us Pain ; but, antecedently to some Experience or Opinion of this Pleasure, there is no previous uneasy Sensation in the Absence, as there is in the Absence of the Objects of Appetite. The Necessity of these

Sensations previous to our Appetites, has been considered already [1]. The Sensations accompanying or subsequent to our other Desires, by which they are denominated Passions, keep them in a just Ballance with our Appetites, as was before observed.

But this holds in general, concerning all our Desires or Aversions, that according to the Opinion or Apprehension of Good or Evil, the Desire or Aversion is increased or diminished : Every Gratification of any Desire gives at first Pleasure ; and Disappointment Pain, generally proportioned to the Violence of the Desire. In like manner, the escaping any Object of Aversion, tho' it makes no permanent Addition to our Happiness, gives at first a pleasant Sensation, and relieves us from Misery, proportioned to the Degree of Aversion or Fear. So when any Event, to which we had an Aversion, befals us, we have at first Misery proportioned to the Degree of Aversion. So that some Pain is subsequent upon all Frustration of Desire or Aversion, but it is previous to those Desires only, which are called Appetites.

     *   *   *   *   *   *   *   *

[1] Sect. 2. Art. 6.

Illustrations upon the Moral Sense

447   THE Words Election and Approbation seem to denote simple
Ideas known by Consciousness ; which can only be explained by
synonimous Words, or by concomitant or consequent Circumstances.
Election is purposing to do an Action rather than its contrary, or
than being inactive. Approbation of our own Action denotes, or is
attended with, a pleasure in the Contemplation of it, and in Reflection upon the Affections which inclined us to it. Approbation of
the Action of another has some little Pleasure attending it in the
Observer, and raises Love toward the Agent, in whom the Quality
approved is deemed to reside, and not in the Observer, who has
a Satisfaction in the Act of approving.

The Qualities moving to Election, or exciting to Action, are
different from those moving to Approbation : We often do Actions
which we do not approve, and approve Actions which we omit : We
often desire that an Agent had omitted an Action which we approve ;
and wish he would do an Action which we condemn. Approbation
is employed about the Actions of others, where there is no room for
our Election.

*   *   *   *   *   *   *   *

SECTION I.—*Concerning the Character of Virtue, agreeable to
Truth or Reason.*

448   Since Reason is understood to denote our Power of finding out
true Propositions, Reasonableness must denote the same thing, with
Conformity to true Propositions, or to Truth.

Reasonableness in an Action is a very common Expression, but
yet upon inquiry, it will appear very confused, whether we suppose
it the Motive to Election, or the Quality determining Approbation.

There is one sort of Conformity to Truth which neither determines to the one or the other; viz. that Conformity which is between every true Proposition and its Object. This sort of Conformity can never make us chuse or approve one Action more than its contrary, for it is found in all Actions alike : Whatever Attribute can be ascribed to a generous kind Action, the contrary Attribute may as truly be ascribed to a selfish cruel Action : Both Propositions are equally true, and the two contrary Actions, the Objects of the two Truths are equally conformable to their several Truths, with that sort of Conformity which is between a Truth and its Object. This Conformity then cannot make a Difference among Actions, or recommend one more than another either to Election or Approbation, since any Man may make as many Truths about Villany, as about Heroism, by ascribing to it contrary Attributes.

  *   *   *   *   *   *   *   *

449   But what is this Conformity of Actions to Reason ? When we ask the Reason of an Action, we sometimes mean, 'What Truth shews a Quality in the Action, exciting the Agent to do it ?' Thus, why does a Luxurious Man pursue Wealth ? The Reason is given by this Truth, 'Wealth is useful to purchase Pleasures.' Sometimes for a Reason of Actions we shew the Truth expressing a Quality, engaging our Approbation. Thus the Reason of hazarding Life in just War, is, that 'it tends to preserve our honest Countrymen, or evidences publick Spirit :' The Reason for Temperance, and against Luxury is given thus, 'Luxury evidences a selfish base Temper.' The former sort of Reasons we will call exciting, and the latter justifying[1]. Now we shall find that all exciting Reasons presuppose Instincts and Affections ; and the justifying pre-suppose a Moral Sense.

As to exciting Reasons, in every calm rational Action some end is desired or intended ; no end can be intended or desired previously to some one of these Classes of Affections, Self-Love, Self-Hatred, or desire of private Misery, (if this be possible) Benevolence toward others, or Malice : All Affections are included under these : no end can be previous to them all; there can therefore be no exciting Reason' previous to Affection.

We have indeed many confused Harangues on this Subject, telling

---

[1] Thus Grotius distinguishes the Reasons of War, into the *Justificæ*, and *Suasoriæ*, or these, *sub ratione utilis.*

us, 'We have two Principles of Action, Reason, and Affection or Passion : the former in common with Angels, the latter with Brutes : No Action is wise, or good, or reasonable, to which we are not excited by Reason, as distinct from all Affections ; or, if any such Actions as flow from Affections be good, it is only by chance, or materially and not formally.' As if indeed Reason, or the Knowledge of the Relations of things, could excite to Action when we proposed no End, or as if Ends could be intended without Desire or Affection.

450   Writers on these Subjects should remember the common Divisions of the Faculties of the Soul. That there is 1. Reason presenting the natures and relations of things, antecedently to any Act of Will or Desire : 2. The Will, or *Appetitus Rationalis*, or the disposition of Soul to pursue what is presented as good, and to shun Evil. Were there no other Power in the Soul, than that of mere contemplation, there would be no Affection, Volition, Desire, Action. Nay without some motion of Will no Man would voluntarily persevere in Contemplation. There must be a Desire of Knowledge, and of the Pleasure which attends it : this too is an Act of Willing. Both these Powers are by the Antients included under the Λόγος or λογικὸν μέρος. Below these they place two other powers dependent on the Body, the *Sensus*, and the *Appetitus Sensitivus*, in which they place the particular Passions : the former answers to the Understanding, and the latter to the Will. But the Will is forgot of late, and some ascribe to the Intellect, not only Contemplation or Knowledge, but Choice, Desire, Prosecuting, Loving. Nay some are grown so ingenious in uniting the Powers of the Soul, that contemplating with Pleasure, Symmetry and Proportion, an Act of the Intellect as they plead, is the same thing with Goodwill or the virtuous Desire of publick Happiness.

451   But are there not also exciting Reasons, even previous to any end, moving us to propose one end rather than another? To this Aristotle long ago answered, 'that there are ultimate Ends desired without a view to any thing else, and subordinate Ends or Objects desired with a view to something else.' To subordinate Ends those Reasons or Truths excite, which shew them to be conducive to the ultimate End, and shew one Object to be more effectual than another : thus subordinate Ends may be called reasonable. But as to the ultimate Ends, to suppose exciting Reasons for them, would

infer, that there is no ultimate End, but that we desire one thing for another in an infinite Series.

Thus ask a Being who desires private Happiness, or has Self-Love, ' what Reason excites him to desire Wealth ? ' He will give this Reason, that 'Wealth tends to procure Pleasure and Ease.' Ask his Reason for desiring Pleasure or Happiness : One cannot imagine what Proposition he could assign as his exciting Reason. This Proposition is indeed true, 'There is an Instinct or Desire fixed in his Nature, determining him to pursue his Happiness ;' but it is not this Reflection on his own Nature, or this Proposition which excites or determines him, but the Instinct itself. This is a Truth, 'Rhubarb strengthens the Stomach :' But it is not a Proposition which strengthens the Stomach, but the Quality in that Medicine. The Effect is not produced by Propositions shewing the Cause, but by the Cause itself.

*   *   *   *   *   *   *   *

452   We may transiently observe a Mistake some fall into; They suppose, because they have formed some Conception of an infinite Good, or greatest possible Aggregate, or Sum of Happiness, under which all particular Pleasures may be included; that there is also some one great ultimate End, with a view to which every particular Object is desired ; whereas, in truth, each particular Pleasure is desired without farther view, as an ultimate End in the selfish Desires. It is true, the Prospect of a greater inconsistent Pleasure may surmount or stop this Desire ; so may the Fear of a prepollent Evil. But this does not prove ' that all Men have formed Ideas of infinite Good, or greatest possible Aggregate, or that they have any Instinct or Desire, actually operating without an Idea of its Object. Just so in the benevolent Affections, the Happiness of any one Person is an ultimate End, desired with no farther view : and yet the observing its Inconsistency with the Happiness of another more beloved, or with the Happiness of many, though each one of them were but equally beloved, may overcome the former Desire. Yet this will not prove, that in each kind Action Men form the abstract Conception of all Mankind, or the System of Rationals. Such Conceptions are indeed useful, that so we may gratify either our Self-Love or kind Affections in the fullest manner, as far as our Power extends ; and may not content ourselves with smaller Degrees either of private or publick Good, while greater are in our power :

But when we have formed these Conceptions, we do not serve the Individual only from Love to the Species, no more than we desire Grapes with an Intention of the greatest Aggregate of Happiness, or from an Apprehension that they make a Part of the General Sum of our Happiness. These Conceptions only serve to suggest greater Ends than would occur to us without Reflection ; and by the Prepollency of one Desire toward the greater Good, to either private or publick, to stop the Desire toward the smaller Good, when it appears inconsistent with the greater.

* * * * * * * *

453 If any alledge as the Reason exciting us to pursue publick Good, this Truth, that the Happiness of a System, a Thousand, or a Million, is a greater Quantity of Happiness than that of one Person : and consequently, if Men desire Happiness, they must have stronger Desires toward the greater Sum, than toward the less.' This Reason still supposes an Instinct toward Happiness as previous to it : And again, To whom is the Happiness of a System a greater Happiness ? To one Individual, or to the System ? If to the Individual, then his Reason exciting his Desire of a happy System supposes Self-Love : If to the System, then what Reason can excite to desire the greater Happiness of a System, or any Happiness to be in the Possession of others ? None surely which does not presuppose publick Affections. Without such Affections this Truth, ' that an hundred Felicities is a greater Sum than one Felicity,' will no more excite to study the Happiness of the Hundred, than this Truth, ' an hundred Stones are greater than one,' will excite a Man, who has no desire of Heaps, to cast them together.

* * * * * * *

454 This leads to consider Approbation of Actions, whether it be for Conformity to any Truth, or Reasonableness, that Actions are ultimately approved, independently of any moral Sense ? Or if all justifying Reasons do not presuppose it ?

If Conformity to Truth, or Reasonableness, denote nothing else but that ' an Action is the Object of a true Proposition,' it is plain, that all Actions should be approved equally, since as many Truths may be made about the worst, as can be made about the best. See what was said above about exciting Reasons.

But let the Truths commonly assigned as justifying be examined.

Here it is plain, 'A Truth shewing an Action to be fit to attain an End,' does not justify it; nor do we approve a subordinate End for any Truth, which only shews it to be fit to promote the ultimate End; for the worst Actions may be conducive to their Ends, and reasonable in that Sense. The justifying Reasons then must be about the Ends themselves, especially the ultimate Ends. The Question then is, 'Does a Conformity to any Truth make us approve an ultimate End, previously to any moral Sense?' For example, we approve pursuing the publick Good. For what Reason? Or what is the Truth for Conformity to which we call it a reasonable End? I fancy we can find none in these Cases, more than we could give for our liking any pleasant Fruit[1].

*   *   *   *   *   *   *

455   When we say one is obliged to an Action, we either mean, 1. That the Action is necessary to obtain Happiness to the Agent, or to avoid Misery: Or, 2. That every Spectator, or he himself upon Reflection, must approve his Action, and disapprove his omitting it, if he considers fully all its Circumstances. The former Meaning of the Word Obligation presupposes selfish Affections, and the Senses of private Happiness: The latter Meaning includes the moral Sense. Mr. Barbeyrac, in his Annotations upon Grotius[2], makes Obligation denote an indispensable Necessity to act in a certain manner. Whoever observes his Explication of this Necessity, (which is not natural, otherwise no Man could act against his Obligation) will find that it denotes only 'such a Constitution of a powerful Superior, as will make it impossible for any Being to obtain Happiness, or avoid Misery, but by such a Course of Action.' This agrees with the former Meaning, though sometimes he also includes the latter.

Many other confused Definitions have been given of Obligation, by no obscure Names in the learned World. But let any one give a distinct Meaning, different from the two above-mentioned. To pursue them all would be endless; only let the Definitions be substituted in place of the Word Obligation, in other parts of each Writer, and let it be observed whether it makes good Sense or not.

*   *   *   *   *   *   *   *

---

[1] This is what Aristotle so often asserts that the Προαιρετόν or βουλευτόν is not the End, but the Means.

[2] Lib. I. chap. i. sect. 10.

456   We may transiently observe what has occasioned the Use of the Word reasonable, as an Epithet of only virtuous Actions. Tho' we have Instincts determining us to desire Ends, without supposing any previous Reasoning; yet it is by use of our Reason that we find out the Means of obtaining our Ends. When we do not use our Reason, we often are disappointed of our End. We therefore call those Actions which are effectual to their Ends, in one Sense reasonable of that Word.

Again, in all Men there is probably a moral Sense, making publickly useful Actions and kind Affections grateful to the Agent, and to every Observer: Most Men who have thought of human Actions, agree, that the publickly useful are in the whole also privately useful to the Agent, either in this Life or the next : We conclude, that all Men have the same Affections and Senses : We are convinced by our Reason, that it is by publickly useful Actions alone that we can promote all our Ends. Whoever then acts in a contrary manner, we presume is mistaken, ignorant of, or inadvertent to, these Truths which he might know ; and say he acts unreasonably. Hence some have been led to imagine, some Reasons either exciting or justifying previously to all Affections or a moral Sense.

457   Two Arguments are brought in defence of this Epithet, as antecedent to any Sense, viz. ' That we judge even of our Affections and Senses themselves, whether they are morally Good or Evil.'

The second Argument is, that ' if all moral Ideas depend upon the Constitution of our Sense, then all Constitutions would have been alike reasonable and good to the Deity, which is absurd.'

As to the first Argument, it is plain we judge of our own Affections, or those of others by our moral Sense, by which we approve kind Affections, and disapprove the contrary. But none can apply moral Attributes to the very Faculty of perceiving moral Qualities ; or call his moral Sense morally Good or Evil, any more than he calls the Power of Tasting, sweet or bitter ; or of Seeing, strait or crooked, white or black.

Every one judges the Affections of others by his own Sense ; so that it seems not impossible that in these Senses Men might differ as they do in Taste. A Sense approving Benevolence would disapprove that Temper, which a Sense approving Malice would delight in. The former would judge of the latter by his own

Sense, so would the latter of the former. Each one would at first
view think the Sense of the other perverted.   But then, is there no
difference ? Are both Senses equally good? No certainly, any Man
who observed them would think the Sense of the former more
desirable than of the latter : but this is, because the moral
Sense of every Man is constituted in the former manner.   But
were there any Nature with no moral Sense at all observing these
two Persons, would he not think the State of the former preferable
to that of the latter ? Yes, he might : but not from any Perception
of moral Goodness in the one Sense more than in the other.   Any
rational Nature observing two Men thus constituted, with opposite
Senses, might by reasoning see, not moral Goodness in one Sense
more than in the contrary, but a Tendency to the Happiness of the
Person himself, who had the former Sense in the one Constitution,
and a contrary Tendency in the opposite Constitution : nay, the
Persons themselves might observe this ; since the former Sense
would make these Actions grateful to the Agent which were useful
to others; who, if they had a like Sense, would love him, and
return good Offices ; whereas the latter Sense would make all such
Actions as are useful to others, and apt to engage their good
Offices, ungrateful to the Agent ; and would lead him into publickly
hurtful Actions, which would not only procure the Hatred of others,
if they had a contrary Sense, but engage them out of their Self-
Love, to study his Destruction, tho' their Senses agreed.   Thus
any Observer, or the Agent himself with this latter Sense, might
perceive that the Pains to be feared, as the Consequence of
malicious Actions, did over-ballance the Pleasures of this Sense ;
so that it would be to the Agent's Interest to counteract it.   Thus
one Constitution of the moral Sense might appear to be more
advantageous to those who had it, than the contrary ; as we may
call that Sense of Tasting healthful, which made wholsome Meat
pleasant ; and we would call a contrary Taste pernicious.   And
yet we should no more call the moral Sense morally good or evil,
than we call the Sense of Tasting savoury or unsavoury, sweet
or bitter.

458   But must we not own, that we judge of all our Senses by our
Reason, and often correct their Reports of the Magnitude, Figure,
Colour, Taste of Objects, and pronounce them right or wrong,
as they agree or disagree with Reason ? This is true.   But does it

then follow, that Extension, Figure, Colour, Taste, are not sensible Ideas, but only denote Reasonableness, or Agreement with Reason? Or that these Qualities are perceivable antecedently to any Sense, by our Power of finding out Truth? Just so a compassionate Temper may rashly imagine the Correction of a Child, or the Execution of a Criminal, to be cruel and inhuman: but by reasoning may discover the superior Good arising from them in the whole; and then the same moral Sense may determine the Observer to approve them. But we must not hence conclude, that it is any reasoning antecedent to a moral Sense, which determines us to approve the Study of publick Good, any more than we can in the former Case conclude, that we perceive Extension, Figure, Colour, Taste, antecedently to a Sense. All these Sensations are often corrected by Reasoning, as well as our Approbations of Actions as Good or Evil [1] : and yet no body ever placed the Original idea of Extension, Figure, Colour, or Taste, in Conformity to Reason.

*　　　*　　　*　　　*　　　*　　　*　　　*　　　*

459　As to the second Argument, What means [alike reasonable or good to the Deity?] Does it mean, 'that the Deity could have had no Reasons exciting him to make one Constitution rather than another?' 'Tis plain, if the Deity had nothing essential to his Nature, resembling or analogous to our sweetest and most kind Affections, we can scarce suppose he could have any Reason exciting him to any thing he has done: but grant such a Disposition in the Deity, and then the manifest Tendency of the present Constitution to the Happiness of his Creatures was an exciting Reason for chusing it before the contrary. Each sort of Constitution might have given Men an equal immediate Pleasure in present Self-Approbation for any sort of Action; but the Actions approved by the present Sense, procure all Pleasures of the other Senses; and the Actions which would have been approved by a contrary moral Sense, would have been productive of all Torments of the other Senses.

If it be meant, that 'upon this Supposition, that all our Approbation presupposes in us a moral Sense, the Deity could not have approved one Constitution more than another:' where is the

---

[1] See Sect. 4 of this Treatise.

Consequence? Why may not the Deity have something of a superior Kind, analogous to our moral Sense, essential to him? How does any Constitution of the Senses of Men hinder the Deity to reflect and judge of his own Actions? How does it affect the divine Apprehension, which way soever moral Ideas arise with Men?

If it means, 'that we cannot approve one Constitution more than another, or approve the Deity for making the present Constitution :' This Consequence is also false. The present Constitution of our moral Sense determines us to approve all kind Affections : This Constitution the Deity must have foreseen as tending to the Happiness of his Creatures ; it does therefore evidence kind Affection or Benevolence in the Deity, this therefore we must approve.

    *   *   *   *   *   *   *   *

460   Some farther perplex this Subject, by asserting, that 'the same Reasons determining Approbation, ought also to excite to Election.' Here, 1. We often see justifying Reasons where we can have no Election ; viz. when we observe the Actions of others, which were even prior to our Existence. 2. The Quality moving us to Election very often cannot excite Approbation ; viz. private usefulness, not publickly pernicious. This both does and ought to move Election, and yet I believe few will say, 'they approve as virtuous the eating a Bunch of Grapes, taking a Glass of Wine, or sitting down when one is tired. Approbation is not what we can voluntarily bring upon ourselves. When we are contemplating Actions, we do not chuse to approve, because Approbation is pleasant ; otherwise we would always approve, and never condemn any Action ; because this is some way uneasy. Approbation is plainly a Perception arising without previous Volition, or Choice of it, because of any concomitant Pleasure. The Occasion of it is the Perception of benevolent Affections in ourselves, or the discovering the like in others, even when we are incapable of any Action or Election. The Reasons determining Approbation are such as shew that an Action evidenced kind Affections, and that in others, as often as in ourselves. Whereas the Reasons moving to Election are such as shew the Tendency of an Action to gratify some Affection in the Agent.

The Prospect of the Pleasure of Self-Approbation, is indeed

often a Motive to chuse one Action rather than another; but this supposes the moral Sense, or Determination to approve, prior to the Election. Were Approbation voluntarily chosen, from the Prospect of its concomitant Pleasure, then there could be no Condemnation of our own Actions, for that is unpleasant.

As to that confused Word [ought] it is needless to apply to it again all that was said about Obligation.

*   *   *   *   *   *   *   *

SECTION IV.—*Shewing the Use of Reason concerning Virtue and Vice, upon Supposition that we receive these Ideas by a Moral Sense.*

*   *   *   *   *   *   *   *

461 Perhaps what has brought the Epithet Reasonable, or flowing from Reason, in opposition to what flows from Instinct, Affection, or Passion, so much into use, is this, 'That it is often observed, that the very best of our particular Affections or Desires, when they are grown violent and passionate, through the confused Sensations and Propensities which attend them, make us incapable of considering calmly the whole Tendency of our Actions, and lead us often into what is absolutely pernicious, under some Appearance of relative or particular Good.' This indeed may give some ground for distinguishing between passionate Actions, and those from calm Desire or Affection which employs our Reason freely : But can never set rational Actions in Opposition to those from Instinct, Desire or Affection. And it must be owned, that the most perfect Virtue consists in the calm, impassionate Benevolence, rather than in particular Affections.

462 If one asks 'how do we know that our Affections are right when they are kind?' What does the Word [right] mean? Does it mean what we approve? This we know by Consciousness of our Sense. Again, how do we know that our Sense is right, or that we approve our Approbation? This can only be answered by another Question, viz. How do we know we are pleased when we are pleased?'—Or does it mean, 'how do we know that we shall always approve what we now approve?' To answer this, we must first know that the same Constitution of our Sense shall always remain : And again, that we have applied ourselves carefully to consider the natural Tendency of our Actions. Of the

Continuance of the same Constitution of our Sense, we are as sure as of the Continuance of Gravitation, or any other Law of Nature: The Tendency of our own Actions we cannot always know; but we may know certainly that we heartily and sincerely study to act according to what, by all the Evidence now in our Power to obtain, appears as most probably tending to publick Good. When we are conscious of this sincere Endeavour, the evil Consequences which we could not have foreseen, never will make us condemn our Conduct. But without this sincere Endeavour, we may often approve at present what we shall afterwards condemn.

463 If the Question means, 'How are we sure that we approve, all others shall also approve?' Of this we can be sure upon no Scheme; but it is highly probable that the Senses of all Men are pretty uniform: That the Deity also approves kind Affections, otherwise he would not have implanted them in us, nor determined us by a moral Sense to approve them. Now since the Probability that Man shall judge truly, abstracting from any presupposed Prejudice, is greater than that they shall judge falsly; it is more probable, when our Actions are really kind and publickly useful, that all Observers shall judge truly of our Intentions, and of the Tendency of our Actions, and consequently approve what we approve ourselves, than that they shall judge falsly and condemn them.

464 If the Meaning of the Question be, 'Will the doing what our moral Sense approves tend to our Happiness, and to the avoiding Misery?' It is thus we call a Taste wrong, when it makes that Food at present grateful, which shall occasion future Pains, or Death. This Question concerning our Self-Interest must be answered by such Reasoning as was mentioned above, to be well managed by our Moralists both antient and modern.

Thus there seems no part of that Reasoning which was ever used by Moralists, to be superseded by supposing a moral Sense. And yet without a moral Sense there is no Explication can be given of our Ideas of Morality; nor of that Reasonableness supposed antecedent to all Instincts, Affections, or Sense.

465 'But may there not be a right or wrong State of our moral Sense, as there is in our other Senses, according as they represent their Objects to be as they really are, or represent them otherwise?' So may not our moral Sense approve that which is vicious, and disapprove Virtue, as a sickly Palate may dislike grateful Food, or

a vitiated Sight misrepresent Colours or Dimensions ?   Must we
not know therefore antecedently what is morally Good or Evil
by our Reason, before we can know that our moral Sense is right ?

To answer this, we must remember that of the sensible Ideas,
some are allowed to be only Perceptions in our Minds, and not
Images of any like external Quality, as Colours, Sounds, Tastes,
Smells, Pleasure, Pain.   Other Ideas are Images of something
external, as Duration, Number, Extension, Motion, Rest :   These
latter, for distinction, we may call concomitant Ideas of Sensation,
and the former purely sensible.   As to the purely sensible Ideas,
we know they are altered by any Disorder in our Organs, and
made different from what arise in us from the same Objects at
other times.   We do not denominate Objects from our Perceptions
during the Disorder, but according to our ordinary Perceptions, or
those of others in good Health : Yet nobody imagines that therefore Colours, Sounds, Tastes, are not sensible Ideas.   In like
manner many Circumstances diversify the concomitant Ideas :
But we denominate Objects from the Appearances they make to
us in an uniform Medium, when our Organs are in no disorder,
and the Object not very distant from them.   But none therefore
imagines that it is Reason and not Sense which discovers these
concomitant Ideas, or primary Qualities.

466   Just so in our Ideas of Actions. These three Things are to
be distinguished, 1. The Idea of the external Motion, known first
by Sense, and its Tendency to the Happiness or Misery of some
sensitive Nature, often inferred by Argument or Reason, which
on these Subjects, suggests as invariable eternal or necessary
Truths as any whatsoever. 2. Apprehension or Opinion of the
Affections in the Agent, inferred by our Reason : So far the Idea
of an Action represents something external to the Observer, really
existing whether he had perceived it or not, and having a real
Tendency to certain Ends. 3. The Perception of Approbation
or Disapprobation arising in the Observer, according as the
Affections of the Agent are apprehended kind in their just Degree,
or deficient, or malicious.   This Approbation cannot be supposed
an Image of any thing external, more than the Pleasures of
Harmony, of Taste, of Smell.   But let none imagine, that calling
the Ideas of Virtue and Vice Perceptions of a Sense, upon appre-
hending the Actions and Affections of another does diminish

their Reality, more than the like Assertions concerning all Pleasure and Pain, Happiness or Misery.   Our Reason often corrects the Report of our Senses, about the natural Tendency of the external Action, and corrects rash Conclusions about the Affections of the Agent.   But whether our moral Sense be subject to such a Disorder, as to have different Perceptions, from the same apprehended Affections in an Agent, at different times, as the Eye may have of the Colours of an unaltered Object, it is not easy to determine : Perhaps it will be hard to find any Instances of such a Change.   What Reason could correct, if it fell into such a Disorder, I know not ; except suggesting to its Remembrance its former Approbations, and representing the general Sense of Mankind.   But this does not prove Ideas of Virtue and Vice to be previous to a Sense, more than a like Correction of the Ideas of Colour in a Person under the Jaundice, proves that Colours are perceived by Reason, previously to Sense.

467   If any say, 'this moral Sense is not a Rule :' What means that Word ? It is not a strait rigid Body : It is not a general Proposition, shewing what Means are fit to obtain an end : It is not a Proposition, asserting, that a Superior will make those happy who act one way. and miserable who act the contrary way.   If these be the Meanings of Rule, it is no Rule ; yet by reflecting upon it our Understanding may find out a Rule.   But what Rule of Actions can be formed, without Relation to some End proposed ? Or what End can be proposed, without presupposing Instincts, Desires, Affections, or a moral Sense, it will not be easy to explain.

SECTION V.—*Shewing that Virtue may have whatever is meant by Merit ; and be rewardable upon the Supposition, that it is perceived by a Sense, and elected from Affection or Instinct.*

468   Some will not allow any Merit in Actions flowing from kind Instincts : 'Merit, say they, attends Actions to which we are excited by Reason alone, or to which we freely determine ourselves. The Operation of Instincts or Affections is necessary, and not voluntary ; nor is there more Merit in them than in the Shining of the Sun, the Fruitfulness of a Tree, or the Overflowing of a Stream, which are all publickly useful.'

But what does Merit mean ? or Praiseworthiness ? Do these Words denote the ' Quality Actions, which gains Approbation from the Observer, according to the present Constitution of the human Mind?' Or, 2dly, Are these Actions called meritorious, 'which, when any Observer does approve, all other Observers approve him for his Approbation of it; and would condemn any Observer who did not approve these Actions?' These are the only Meanings of meritorious, which I can conceive as distinct from rewardable, which is considered hereafter separately. Let those who are not satisfied with either of these Explications of Merit, endeavour to give a Definition of it reducing it to its simple Ideas: and not, as a late Author has done, quarrelling these Descriptions, tell us only that it is Deserving or being worthy of Approbation, which is defining by giving a synonimous Term.

  * * * * * * * *

469 But it may be said, that to make an Action meritorious, it is necessary not only that the Action be publickly useful, but that it be known or imagined to be such, before the Agent freely chuses it. But what does this add to the former Scheme? Only a Judgment or Opinion in the Understanding, concerning the natural Tendency of an Action to the publick Good: Few, it may be presumed, will place Virtue in Assent or Dissent, or Perceptions. And yet this is all that is superadded to the former Case. The Agent must not desire the publick Good, or have any kind Affections. This would spoil the Freedom of Choice, according to their Scheme, who insist on a Freedom opposite to Affections or Instincts: But he must barely know the Tendency to publick Good and without any Propensity to, or Desire of the Happiness of others, by an arbitrary Election, acquire his Merit. Let every man judge for himself, whether these are the qualities which he approves.

  What has probably engaged many into this way of speaking, 'that Virtue is the Effect of rational Choice, and not of Instincts or Affections,' is this; they find, that 'some Actions flowing from particular kind Affections, are sometimes condemned as evil,' because of their bad Influence upon the State of larger Societies; and that the Hurry and confused Sensation of any of our Passions, may divert the Mind from considering the whole Effect of its Actions: They require therefore to Virtue a calm and undisturbed Temper.

  * * * * * * * *

470 Some alledge, that Merit supposes, beside kind Affection, that the Agent has a moral Sense, reflects upon his own Virtue, delights in it, and chuses to adhere to it for the Pleasure which attends it[1]. We need not debate the Use of this Word Merit : it is plain, we approve a generous kind Action, tho' the Agent had not made this Reflection. This Reflection shews to him a Motive of Self-Love, the joint View to which does not increase our Approbation ; But then it must again be owned, that we cannot form a just Conclusion of a Character from one or two kind, generous Actions, especially where there has been no very strong Motives to the contrary. Some apparent Motives of Interest may afterwards overballance the kind Affections, and lead the Agent into vicious Actions. But the Reflection on Virtue, the being once charmed with the lovely Form, will discover an Interest on its side, which, if well attended to, no other Motive will overballance. This Reflection is a great Security to the Character ; and must be supposed in such creatures as Men are, before we can well depend upon a Constancy in Virtue.

*　　*　　*　　*　　*　　*　　*　　*

[1] See Lord Shaftesbury's Inquiry concerning Virtue, vol. i. pt. ii. § 3, p. 28.

A System of Moral Philosophy

* * * * * * *

471   II. The calm self-love, or the determination of each indiv dual toward his own happiness, is a motion of the will without any uneasy sensation attending it.   But the several selfish desires, terminating on particular objects, are generally attended with some uneasy turbulent sensations in very different degrees: yet these sensations are different from the act of the will to which they are conjoined; and different too from the motives of desire. The motive is some good apprehended in an object or event, toward which good the desire tends; and, in consequence of desire, some uneasiness arises, till the good is obtained.   To aversion, the motive is some evil apprehended or feared, and perhaps not yet felt.   Uneasiness too attends the aversion, untill the evil is repelled.   Prospects of the pleasures or powers attending opulence are the motives to the desire of wealth, and never the uneasy feelings attending the desire itself.   These feelings are, in nature, subsequent to the desire.

Again, when we obtain the thing desired; beside the pleasures to be obtained from this object, which were the motives of the desire, and often before we enjoy them, there is one pleasure immediatly arising from the success, at least in those cases where there was any difficulty in the pursuit, or fear of disappointment.   It would be absurd to say that this joy in the success was the motive to the desire.   We should have no joy in the success, nor could we have had any desire, unless the prospect of some other good had been the motive. This holds in all our desires, benevolent or selfish, that there is some motive, some end intended, distinct from the joy of success, or the removal of the pain of desire ; otherways all desires would be the most fantastick things imaginable, equally ardent toward any trifle, as toward the greatest good ; since the joy of success, and the removal of the uneasiness of desire, would be alike in both sorts of desires. 'Tis trifling therefore to say that all desires are selfish, because by gratifying them we obtain the joy of success, and free ourselves from the uneasy feelings of desire.

*   *   *   *   *   *   *   *

472 VI. This moral sense from its very nature appears to be designed for regulating and controlling all our powers. This dignity and commanding nature we are immediatly conscious of, as we are conscious of the power itself. Nor can such matters of immediate feeling be otherways proved but by appeals to our hearts. It does not estimate the good it recommends as merely differing in degree, tho' of the same kind with other advantages recommended by other senses, so as to allow us to practise smaller moral evils acknowledged to remain such, in order to obtain some great advantages of other sorts ; or to omit what we judge in the present case to be our duty or morally good, that we may decline great evils of another sort. But as we immediatly perceive the difference in kind, and that the dignity of enjoyment from fine poetry, painting, or from knowledge is superior to the pleasures of the palate, were they never so delicate ; so we immediatly discern moral good to be superior in kind and dignity to all others which are perceived by the other perceptive powers.

*   *   *   *   *   *   *   *

473 But of all such dispositions of our nature, different from all our kind affections, none is so nearly connected with them, none so natural an evidence of them, none so immediatly and necessarily subservient to them, as an acute moral sense itself, a strong desire of moral excellence, with an high relish of it wherever it is observed. We do not call the power or sense itself virtuous ; but the having this sense in a high degree naturally raises a strong desire of having all generous affections ; it surmounts all the little obstacles to them, and determines the mind to use all the natural means of raising them. Now, as the mind can make any of its own powers the object of its reflex contemplation, this high sense of moral excellence is approved above all other abilities.

*   *   *   *   *   *   *   *

474 That disposition therefore which is most excellent, and naturally gains the highest moral approbation, is the calm, stable, universal good-will to all, or the most extensive benevolence. And this seems the most distinct notion we can form of the moral excellency of the Deity.

Another disposition inseparable from this in men, and probably in all beings who are capable of such extensive affection, is the relish or approbation of this affection, and a naturally consequent desire of this moral excellence, and an esteem and good-will of an higher kind to all in whom it is found. This love of moral excellence is also an high object of approbation, when we find it in ourselves by reflection, or observe it in another. It is a pretty different affection from benevolence or the desire of communicating happiness; and is as it were in another order of affection; so that one cannot well determine whether it can be compared with the other. It seems co-ordinate, and the highest possible of that kind; never in opposition to benevolence, nay always conspiring with and assisting it. This desire of moral excellence, and love to the mind where it resides, with the consequent acts of esteem, veneration, trust, and resignation, are the essence of true piety toward God.

*   *   *   *   *   *   *   *

475 To discover wherein our true happiness consists we must compare the several enjoyments of life, and the several kinds of misery, that we may discern what enjoyments are to be parted with, or what uneasiness to be endured, in order to obtain the highest and most beatifick satisfactions, and to avoid the most distressing sufferings.

As to pleasures of the same kind, 'tis manifest their values are in a joint proportion of their intenseness and duration. In estimating the duration, we not only regard the constancy of the object, or its remaining in our power, and the duration of the sensations it affords, but the constancy of our fancy or relish: for when this changes it puts an end to the enjoyment.

476 In comparing pleasures of different kinds, the value is as the duration and dignity of the kind jointly. We have an immediate sense of a dignity[1], a perfection, or beatifick quality in some kinds, which no intenseness of the lower kinds can equal, were they also as lasting as we could wish. No intenseness or duration of any external sensation gives it a dignity or worth equal to that of the improvement of the soul by knowledge, or the ingenious arts ; and much less is it equal to that of virtuous affections and actions. We never hesitate in judging thus about the happiness or perfection of others, where the impetuous cravings of appetites and passions do not corrupt our judgments, as they do often in our case. By this intimate feeling of dignity, enjoyments and exercises of some kinds, tho' not of the highest degree of those kinds, are incomparably more excellent and beatifick than the most intense and lasting enjoyments of the lower kinds. Nor is duration of such importance to some higher kinds, as it is to the lower. The exercise of virtue for a short period, provided it be not succeeded by something vicious, is of incomparably greater value than the most lasting sensual pleasures. Nothing destroys the excellence and perfection of the state but a contrary quality of the same kind defacing the former character. The peculiar happiness of the virtuous man is not so much abated by pain, or an early death, as that of the sensualist ; tho' his complex state which is made up of all his enjoyments and sufferings of every kind is in some degree affected by them. Nor is it a view of private sublime pleasures in frequent future reflections which recommends virtue to the soul. We feel an impulse, an ardour toward perfection, toward affections and actions of dignity, and feel their immediate excellence, abstracting from such views of future pleasures of long duration. Tho' no doubt these pleasures, which are as sure as our existence, are to be regarded in our estimation of the importance of virtue to our happiness.

477   Now if we denote by intenseness, in a more general meaning, the degree in which any perceptions or enjoyments are beatifick, then their comparative values are in a compound proportion of their intenseness and duration. But to retain always in view the grand differences of the kinds, and to prevent any imaginations, that the intenser sensations of the lower kinds with sufficient duration may compleat our happiness ; it may be more convenient to estimate

[1] See above, chap. iv. § 10.

enjoyments by their dignity and duration : dignity denoting the excellence of the kind, when those of different kinds are compared ; and the intenseness of the sensations, when we compare those of the same kind.

*   *   *   *   *   *   *   *

478   Thus different men have different tastes. What one admires as the supreme enjoyments, another may despise. Must we not examine these tastes ? Are all persons, all orders of beings equally happy if each obtains the enjoyments respectively most relished ? At this rate the meanest brute or insect may be as happy as the wisest hero, patriot, or friend can be. What may make a brute as happy as that low order is capable of being, may be but despicable to an order endued with finer perceptive powers, and a nobler sort of desires. Beings of these higher orders are immediately conscious of the superior dignity and importance to happiness in their peculiar enjoyments, of which lower orders are incapable. Nature has thus distinguished the different orders by different perceptive powers, so that the same objects will not be sufficient for happiness to all ; nor have all equal happiness when each can gratify all the desires and senses he has.

The superior orders in this world probably experience all the sensations of the lower orders, and can judge of them. But the inferior do not experience the enjoyments of the superior. Nay in the several stages of life each one finds different tastes and desires. We are conscious in our state of mature years that the happiness of our friends, our families, or our country are incomparably nobler objects of our pursuit, and administer proportionably a nobler pleasure than the toys which once abundantly entertained us when we had experienced nothing better. God has assigned to each order, and to the several stages of life in the same person, their peculiar powers and tastes. Each one is as happy when its taste is gratified as it can then be. But we are immediately conscious that one gratification is more excellent than another, when we have experienced both. And then our reason and observation enables us to compare the effects, and consequences, and duration. One may be transitory, and the occasion of great subsequent misery, tho' for the present the enjoyment be intense : another may be lasting, safe, and succeeded by no satiety, shame, disgust, or remorse.

Superior beings by diviner faculties and fuller knowledge may, without experience of all sorts, immediately discern what are the noblest. They may have some intuitive knowledge of perfection and some standard of it, which may make the experience of some lower sorts useless to them. But of mankind these certainly are the best judges who have full experience, with their tastes or senses and appetites in a natural vigorous state. Now it never was alledged that social affections, the admiration of moral excellence, the desire of esteem, with their attendant and guardian temperance, the pursuits of knowledge, or a natural activity, impared any sense or appetite. This is often charged with great justice upon luxury, and surfeiting, and indolence. The highest sensual enjoyments may be experienced by those who employ both mind and body vigorously in social virtuous offices, and allow all the natural appetites to recur in their due seasons. Such certainly are the best judges of all enjoyments. Thus according to the maxim often inculcated by Aristotle, 'The good man is the true judge and standard of every thing.'

*   *   *   *   *   *   *   *

479   The most benign and wise constitution of a rational system is that in which the degree of selfish affection most useful to the individual is consistent with the interest of the system; and where the degree of generous affections most useful to the system is ordinarily consistent with or subservient to the greatest happiness of the individual. A mean low species may indeed be wholly subjected to the interests of a superior species, and have affections solely calculated for these higher interests. But in the more noble systems it would be a blemish if in fact there was an established inconsistence between the two grand ends to each rational being, personal enjoyment and publick happiness, and in consequence, an irreconcilable variance between the affections destined for the pursuit of them.

*   *   *   *   *   *   *   *

BOOK II.

*   *   *   *   *   *   *   *

480   II. The *righteousness* or goodness of actions is not indeed the same notion with *their tendency to universal happiness*, or flowing from the desire of it. This latter is the highest species of the former. Our *moral sense* has also other immediate objects of approbation, many narrower affections, which we must immediately approve without thinking of their tendency to the interest of a system.

*   *   *   *   *   *   *   *

481   VI. To each right there corresponds an *obligation,* perfect or imperfect, as the right is. The term obligation is both complex and ambiguous. We primarily say one is obliged to an action 'when he must find from the constitution of human nature that he and every attentive observer must disapprove the omission of it as morally evil.' The word is sometimes taken for 'a strong motive of interest constituted by the will of some potent *superior* to engage us to act as he requires.' In the former meaning, obligation is founded on our moral faculty ; in the latter, it seems to abstract from it. But in describing the *superior* who can constitute obligation, we not only include sufficient force or power, but also a just right to govern ; and this justice or right will lead us again to our *moral faculty.* Through this ambiguity[1] ingenious men have contradicted each other with keenness ; some asserting an obligation antecedent to all views of interest, or laws ; others deriving the original source of all obligation from the law or will of an omnipotent Being.

[1] See Leibnitz's censure on Puffendorf, and Barbeyaque's defence of him.

CATALOGUE OF DOVER BOOKS

Philosophy, Religion

GUIDE TO PHILOSOPHY, C. E. M. Joad. A modern classic which examines many crucial problems which man has pondered through the ages: Does free will exist? Is there plan in the universe? How do we know and validate our knowledge? Such opposed solutions as subjective idealism and realism, chance and teleology, vitalism and logical positivism, are evaluated and the contributions of the great philosophers from the Greeks to moderns like Russell, Whitehead, and others, are considered in the context of each problem. "The finest introduction," BOSTON TRANSCRIPT. Index. Classified bibliography. 592pp. 5⅜ x 8.
T297 Paperbound **$2.00**

HISTORY OF ANCIENT PHILOSOPHY, W. Windelband. One of the clearest, most accurate comprehensive surveys of Greek and Roman philosophy. Discusses ancient philosophy in general, intellectual life in Greece in the 7th and 6th centuries B.C., Thales, Anaximander, Anaximenes, Heraclitus, the Eleatics, Empedocles, Anaxagoras, Leucippus, the Pythagoreans, the Sophists, Socrates, Democritus (20 pages), Plato (50 pages), Aristotle (70 pages), the Peripatetics, Stoics, Epicureans, Sceptics, Neo-platonists, Christian Apologists, etc. 2nd German edition translated by H. E. Cushman. xv + 393pp. 5⅜ x 8.
T357 Paperbound **$1.85**

ILLUSTRATIONS OF THE HISTORY OF MEDIEVAL THOUGHT AND LEARNING, R. L. Poole. Basic analysis of the thought and lives of the leading philosophers and ecclesiastics from the 8th to the 14th century—Abailard, Ockham, Wycliffe, Marsiglio of Padua, and many other great thinkers who carried the torch of Western culture and learning through the "Dark Ages": political, religious, and metaphysical views. Long a standard work for scholars and one of the best introductions to medieval thought for beginners. Index. 10 Appendices. xiii + 327pp. 5⅜ x 8.
T674 Paperbound **$1.85**

PHILOSOPHY AND CIVILIZATION IN THE MIDDLE AGES, M. de Wulf. This semi-popular survey covers aspects of medieval intellectual life such as religion, philosophy, science, the arts, etc. It also covers feudalism vs. Catholicism, rise of the universities, mendicant orders, monastic centers, and similar topics. Unabridged. Bibliography. Index. viii + 320pp. 5⅜ x 8.
T284 Paperbound **$1.85**

AN INTRODUCTION TO SCHOLASTIC PHILOSOPHY, Prof. M. de Wulf. Formerly entitled SCHOLASTICISM OLD AND NEW, this volume examines the central scholastic tradition from St. Anselm, Albertus Magnus, Thomas Aquinas, up to Suarez in the 17th century. The relation of scholasticism to ancient and medieval philosophy and science in general is clear and easily followed. The second part of the book considers the modern revival of scholasticism, the Louvain position, relations with Kantianism and Positivism. Unabridged. xvi + 271pp. 5⅜ x 8.
T296 Clothbound **$3.50**
T283 Paperbound **$1.75**

A HISTORY OF MODERN PHILOSOPHY, H. Höffding. An exceptionally clear and detailed coverage of western philosophy from the Renaissance to the end of the 19th century. Major and minor men such as Pomponazzi, Bodin, Boehme, Telesius, Bruno, Copernicus, da Vinci, Kepler, Galileo, Bacon, Descartes, Hobbes, Spinoza, Leibniz, Wolff, Locke, Newton, Berkeley, Hume, Erasmus, Montesquieu, Voltaire, Diderot, Rousseau, Lessing, Kant, Herder, Fichte, Schelling, Hegel, Schopenhauer, Comte, Mill, Darwin, Spencer, Hartmann, Lange, and many others, are discussed in terms of theory of knowledge, logic, cosmology, and psychology. Index. 2 volumes, total of 1159pp. 5⅜ x 8.
T117 Vol. 1, Paperbound **$2.25**
T118 Vol. 2, Paperbound **$2.25**

ARISTOTLE, A. E. Taylor. A brilliant, searching non-technical account of Aristotle and his thought written by a foremost Platonist. It covers the life and works of Aristotle; classification of the sciences; logic; first philosophy; matter and form; causes; motion and eternity; God; physics; metaphysics; and similar topics. Bibliography. New Index compiled for this edition. 128pp. 5⅜ x 8.
T280 Paperbound **$1.00**

THE SYSTEM OF THOMAS AQUINAS, M. de Wulf. Leading Neo-Thomist, one of founders of University of Louvain, gives concise exposition to central doctrines of Aquinas, as a means toward determining his value to modern philosophy, religion. Formerly "Medieval Philosophy Illustrated from the System of Thomas Aquinas." Trans. by E. Messenger. Introduction. 151pp. 5⅜ x 8.
T568 Paperbound **$1.25**

LEIBNIZ, H. W. Carr. Most stimulating middle-level coverage of basic philosophical thought of Leibniz. Easily understood discussion, analysis of major works: "Theodicy," "Principles of Nature and Grace," "Monadology"; Leibniz's influence; intellectual growth; correspondence; disputes with Bayle, Malebranche, Newton; importance of his thought today, with reinterpretation in modern terminology. "Power and mastery," London Times. Bibliography. Index. 226pp. 5⅜ x 8.
T624 Paperbound **$1.35**

CATALOGUE OF DOVER BOOKS

THE SENSE OF BEAUTY, G. Santayana. A revelation of the beauty of language as well as an important philosophic treatise, this work studies the "why, when, and how beauty appears, what conditions an object must fulfill to be beautiful, what elements of our nature make us sensible of beauty, and what the relation is between the constitution of the object and the excitement of our susceptibility." "It is doubtful if a better treatment of the subject has since been published," PEABODY JOURNAL. Index. ix + 275pp. 5⅜ x 8.
T238 Paperbound **$1.00**

PROBLEMS OF ETHICS, Moritz Schlick. The renowned leader of the "Vienna Circle" applies the logical positivist approach to a wide variety of ethical problems: the source and means of attaining knowledge, the formal and material characteristics of the good, moral norms and principles, absolute vs. relative values, free will and responsibility, comparative importance of pleasure and suffering as ethical values, etc. Disarmingly simple and straightforward despite complexity of subject. First English translation, authorized by author before his death, of a thirty-year old classic. Translated and with an introduction by David Rynin. Index. Foreword by Prof. George P. Adams. xxi + 209pp. 5⅜ x 8.
T946 Paperbound **$1.45**

AN INTRODUCTION TO EXISTENTIALISM, Robert G. Olson. A new and indispensable guide to one of the major thought systems of our century, the movement that is central to the thinking of some of the most creative figures of the past hundred years. Stresses Heidegger and Sartre, with careful and objective examination of the existentialist position, values—freedom of choice, individual dignity, personal love, creative effort—and answers to the eternal questions of the human condition. Scholarly, unbiased, analytic, unlike most studies of this difficult subject, Prof. Olson's book is aimed at the student of philosophy as well as at the reader with no formal training who is looking for an absorbing, accessible, and thorough introduction to the basic texts. Index. xv + 221pp. 5⅜ x 8½.
T55 Paperbound **$1.50**

SYMBOLIC LOGIC, C. I. Lewis and C. H. Langford. Since first publication in 1932, this has been among most frequently cited works on symbolic logic. Still one of the best introductions both for beginners and for mathematicians, philosophers. First part covers basic topics which easily lend themselves to beginning study. Second part is rigorous, thorough development of logistic method, examination of some of most difficult and abstract aspects of symbolic logic, including modal logic, logical paradoxes, many-valued logic, with Prof. Lewis' own contributions. 2nd revised (corrected) edition. 3 appendixes, one new to this edition. 524pp. 5⅜ x 8.
S170 Paperbound **$2.00**

WHITEHEAD'S PHILOSOPHY OF CIVILIZATION, A. H. Johnson. A leading authority on Alfred North Whitehead synthesizes the great philosopher's thought on civilization, scattered throughout various writings, into unified whole. Analysis of Whitehead's general definition of civilization, his reflections on history and influences on its development, his religion, including his analysis of Christianity, concept of solitariness as first requirement of personal religion, and so on. Other chapters cover views on minority groups, society, civil liberties, education. Also critical comments on Whitehead's philosophy. Written with general reader in mind. A perceptive introduction to important area of the thought of a leading philosopher of our century. Revised index and bibliography. xii + 211pp. 5⅜ x 8½.
T996 Paperbound **$1.50**

WHITEHEAD'S THEORY OF REALITY, A. H. Johnson. Introductory outline of Whitehead's theory of actual entities, the heart of his philosophy of reality, followed by his views on nature of God, philosophy of mind, theory of value (truth, beauty, goodness and their opposites), analyses of other philosophers, attitude toward science. A perspicacious lucid introduction by author of dissertation on Whitehead, written under the subject's supervision at Harvard. Good basic view for beginning students of philosophy and for those who are simply interested in important contemporary ideas. Revised index and bibliography. xiii + 267pp. 5⅜ x 8½.
T989 Paperbound **$1.50**

MIND AND THE WORLD-ORDER, C. I. Lewis. Building upon the work of Peirce, James, and Dewey, Professor Lewis outlines a theory of knowledge in terms of "conceptual pragmatism." Dividing truth into abstract mathematical certainty and empirical truth, the author demonstrates that the traditional understanding of the a priori must be abandoned. Detailed analyses of philosophy, metaphysics, method, the "given" in experience, knowledge of objects, nature of the a priori, experience and order, and many others. Appendices. xiv + 446pp. 5⅜ x 8.
T359 Paperbound **$2.25**

SCEPTICISM AND ANIMAL FAITH, G. Santayana. To eliminate difficulties in the traditional theory of knowledge, Santayana distinguishes between the independent existence of objects and the essence our mind attributes to them. Scepticism is thereby established as a form of belief, and animal faith is shown to be a necessary condition of knowledge. Belief, classical idealism, intuition, memory, symbols, literary psychology, and much more, discussed with unusual clarity and depth. Index. xii + 314pp. 5⅜ x 8.
T235 Clothbound **$3.50**
T236 Paperbound **$1.50**

LANGUAGE AND MYTH, E. Cassirer. Analyzing the non-rational thought processes which go to make up culture, Cassirer demonstrates that beneath both language and myth there lies a dominant unconscious "grammar" of experience whose categories and canons are not those of logical thought. His analyses of seemingly diverse phenomena such as Indian metaphysics, the Melanesian "mana," the Naturphilosophie of Schelling, modern poetry, etc., are profound without being pedantic. Introduction and translation by Susanne Langer. Index. x + 103pp. 5⅜ x 8.
T51 Paperbound **$1.25**

Americana

THE EYES OF DISCOVERY, J. Bakeless. A vivid reconstruction of how unspoiled America appeared to the first white men. Authentic and enlightening accounts of Hudson's landing in New York, Coronado's trek through the Southwest; scores of explorers, settlers, trappers, soldiers. America's pristine flora, fauna, and Indians in every region and state in fresh and unusual new aspects. "A fascinating view of what the land was like before the first highway went through," Time. 68 contemporary illustrations, 39 newly added in this edition. Index. Bibliography. x + 500pp. 5⅜ x 8. T761 Paperbound **$2.00**

AUDUBON AND HIS JOURNALS, J. J. Audubon. A collection of fascinating accounts of Europe and America in the early 1800's through Audubon's own eyes. Includes the Missouri River Journals —an eventful trip through America's untouched heartland, the Labrador Journals, the European Journals, the famous "Episodes", and other rare Audubon material, including the descriptive chapters from the original letterpress edition of the "Ornithological Studies", omitted in all later editions. Indispensable for ornithologists, naturalists, and all lovers of Americana and adventure. 70-page biography by Audubon's granddaughter. 38 illustrations. Index. Total of 1106pp. 5⅜ x 8.

T675 Vol I Paperbound **$2.25**
T676 Vol II Paperbound **$2.25**
The set **$4.50**

TRAVELS OF WILLIAM BARTRAM, edited by Mark Van Doren. The first inexpensive illustrated edition of one of the 18th century's most delightful books is an excellent source of first-hand material on American geography, anthropology, and natural history. Many descriptions of early Indian tribes are our only source of information on them prior to the infiltration of the white man. "The mind of a scientist with the soul of a poet," John Livingston Lowes. 13 original illustrations and maps. Edited with an introduction by Mark Van Doren. 448pp. 5⅜ x 8.

T13 Paperbound **$2.00**

GARRETS AND PRETENDERS: A HISTORY OF BOHEMIANISM IN AMERICA, A. Parry. The colorful and fantastic history of American Bohemianism from Poe to Kerouac. This is the only complete record of hoboes, cranks, starving poets, and suicides. Here are Pfaff, Whitman, Crane, Bierce, Pound, and many others. New chapters by the author and by H. T. Moore bring this thorough and well-documented history down to the Beatniks. "An excellent account," N. Y. Times. Scores of cartoons, drawings, and caricatures. Bibliography. Index. xxviii + 421pp. 5⅝ x 8⅜.

T708 Paperbound **$1.95**

THE EXPLORATION OF THE COLORADO RIVER AND ITS CANYONS, J. W. Powell. The thrilling first-hand account of the expedition that filled in the last white space on the map of the United States. Rapids, famine, hostile Indians, and mutiny are among the perils encountered as the unknown Colorado Valley reveals its secrets. This is the only uncut version of Major Powell's classic of exploration that has been printed in the last 60 years. Includes later reflections and subsequent expedition. 250 illustrations, new map. 400pp. 5⅝ x 8⅜.

T94 Paperbound **$2.00**

THE JOURNAL OF HENRY D. THOREAU, Edited by Bradford Torrey and Francis H. Allen. Henry Thoreau is not only one of the most important figures in American literature and social thought; his voluminous journals (from which his books emerged as selections and crystallizations) constitute both the longest, most sensitive record of personal internal development and a most penetrating description of a historical moment in American culture. This present set, which was first issued in fourteen volumes, contains Thoreau's entire journals from 1837 to 1862, with the exception of the lost years which were found only recently. We are reissuing it, complete and unabridged, with a new introduction by Walter Harding, Secretary of the Thoreau Society. Fourteen volumes reissued in two volumes. Foreword by Henry Seidel Canby. Total of 1888pp. 8⅜ x 12¼. T312-3 Two volume set, Clothbound **$20.00**

GAMES AND SONGS OF AMERICAN CHILDREN, collected by William Wells Newell. A remarkable collection of 190 games with songs that accompany many of them; cross references to show similarities, differences among them; variations; musical notation for 38 songs. Textual discussions show relations with folk-drama and other aspects of folk tradition. Grouped into categories for ready comparative study: Love-games, histories, playing at work, human life, bird and beast, mythology, guessing-games, etc. New introduction covers relations of songs and dances to timeless heritage of folklore, biographical sketch of Newell, other pertinent data. A good source of inspiration for those in charge of groups of children and a valuable reference for anthropologists, sociologists, psychiatrists. Introduction by Carl Withers. New indexes of first lines, games. 5⅜ x 8½. xii + 242pp. T354 Paperbound **$1.75**

GARDNER'S PHOTOGRAPHIC SKETCH BOOK OF THE CIVIL WAR, Alexander Gardner. The first published collection of Civil War photographs, by one of the two or three most famous photographers of the era, outstandingly reproduced from the original positives. Scenes of crucial battles: Appomattox, Manassas, Mechanicsville, Bull Run, Yorktown, Fredericksburg, etc. Gettysburg immediately after retirement of forces. Battle ruins at Richmond, Petersburg, Gaines'Mill. Prisons, arsenals, a slave pen, fortifications, headquarters, pontoon bridges, soldiers, a field hospital. A unique glimpse into the realities of one of the bloodiest wars in history, with an introductory text to each picture by Gardner himself. Until this edition, there were only five known copies in libraries, and fewer in private hands, one of which sold at auction in 1952 for $425. Introduction by E. F. Bleiler. 100 full page 7 x 10 photographs (original size). 224pp. 8½ x 10¾.   T476 Clothbound **$6.00**

A BIBLIOGRAPHY OF NORTH AMERICAN FOLKLORE AND FOLKSONG, Charles Haywood, Ph.D. The only book that brings together bibliographic information on so wide a range of folklore material. Lists practically everything published about American folksongs, ballads, dances, folk beliefs and practices, popular music, tales, similar material—more than 35,000 titles of books, articles, periodicals, monographs, music publications, phonograph records. Each entry complete with author, title, date and place of publication, arranger and performer of particular examples of folk music, many with Dr. Haywood's valuable criticism, evaluation. Volume I, "The American People," is complete listing of general and regional studies, titles of tales and songs of Negro and non-English speaking groups and where to find them, Occupational Bibliography including sections listing sources of information, folk material on cowboys, riverboat men, 49ers, American characters like Mike Fink, Frankie and Johnnie, John Henry, many more. Volume II, "The American Indian," tells where to find information on dances, myths, songs, ritual of more than 250 tribes in U.S., Canada. A monumental product of 10 years' labor, carefully classified for easy use. "All students of this subject . . . will find themselves in debt to Professor Haywood," Stith Thompson, in American Anthropologist. ". . . a most useful and excellent work," Duncan Emrich, Chief Folklore Section, Library of Congress, in "Notes." Corrected, enlarged republication of 1951 edition. New Preface. New index of composers, arrangers, performers. General index of more than 15,000 items. Two volumes. Total of 1301pp. 6⅛ x 9¼.   T797-798 Clothbound **$12.50**

INCIDENTS OF TRAVEL IN YUCATAN, John L. Stephens. One of first white men to penetrate interior of Yucatan tells the thrilling story of his discoveries of 44 cities, remains of once-powerful Maya civilization. Compelling text combines narrative power with historical significance as it takes you through heat, dust, storms of Yucatan; native festivals with brutal bull fights; great ruined temples atop man-made mounds. Countless idols, sculptures, tombs, examples of Mayan taste for rich ornamentation, from gateways to personal trinkets, accurately illustrated, discussed in text. Will appeal to those interested in ancient civilizations, and those who like stories of exploration, discovery, adventure. Republication of last (1843) edition. 124 illustrations by English artist, F. Catherwood. Appendix on Mayan architecture, chronology. Two volume set. Total of xxviii + 927pp.

Vol I T926 Paperbound **$2.00**
Vol II T927 Paperbound **$2.00**
The set **$4.00**

A GENIUS IN THE FAMILY, Hiram Percy Maxim. Sir Hiram Stevens Maxim was known to the public as the inventive genius who created the Maxim gun, automatic sprinkler, and a heavier-than-air plane that got off the ground in 1894. Here, his son reminisces—this is by no means a formal biography—about the exciting and often downright scandalous private life of his brilliant, eccentric father. A warm and winning portrait of a prankish, mischievous, impious personality, a genuine character. The style is fresh and direct, the effect is unadulterated pleasure. "A book of charm and lasting humor . . . belongs on the 'must read' list of all fathers," New York Times. "A truly gorgeous affair," New Statesman and Nation. 17 illustrations, 16 specially for this edition. viii + 108pp. 5⅜ x 8½.
                                                                            T948 Paperbound **$1.00**

HORSELESS CARRIAGE DAYS, Hiram P. Maxim. The best account of an important technological revolution by one of its leading figures. The delightful and rewarding story of the author's experiments with the exact combustibility of gasoline, stopping and starting mechanisms, carriage design, and engines. Captures remarkably well the flavor of an age of scoffers and rival inventors not above sabotage; of noisy, uncontrollable gasoline vehicles and incredible mobile steam kettles. ". . . historic information and light humor are combined to furnish highly entertaining reading," New York Times. 56 photographs, 12 specially for this edition. xi + 175pp. 5⅜ x 8½.   T964 Paperbound **$1.35**

BODY, BOOTS AND BRITCHES: FOLKTALES, BALLADS AND SPEECH FROM COUNTRY NEW YORK, Harold W. Thompson. A unique collection, discussion of songs, stories, anecdotes, proverbs handed down orally from Scotch-Irish grandfathers, German nurse-maids, Negro workmen, gathered from all over Upper New York State. Tall tales by and about lumbermen and pirates, canalers and injun-fighters, tragic and comic ballads, scores of sayings and proverbs all tied together by an informative, delightful narrative by former president of New York Historical Society. ". . . a sparkling homespun tapestry that every lover of Americana will want to have around the house," Carl Carmer, New York Times. Republication of 1939 edition. 20 line-drawings. Index. Appendix (Sources of material, bibliography). 530pp. 5⅜ x 8½.   T411 Paperbound **$2.00**

Teach Yourself

These British books are the most effective series of home study books on the market! With no outside help they will teach you as much as is necessary to have a good background in each subject, in many cases offering as much material as a similar high school or college course. They are carefully planned, written by foremost British educators, and amply provided with test questions and problems for you to check your progress; the mathematics books are especially rich in examples and problems. Do not confuse them with skimpy outlines or ordinary school texts or vague generalized popularizations; each book is complete in itself, full without being overdetailed, and designed to give you an easily-acquired branch of knowledge.

TEACH YOURSELF ALGEBRA, P. Abbott. The equivalent of a thorough high school course, up through logarithms. 52 illus. 307pp. 4¼ x 7. T680 Clothbound **$2.00**

TEACH YOURSELF GEOMETRY, P. Abbott. Plane and solid geometry, covering about a year of plane and six months of solid. 268 illus. 344pp. 4½ x 7. T681 Clothbound **$2.00**

TEACH YOURSELF TRIGONOMETRY, P. Abbott. Background of algebra and geometry will enable you to get equivalent of elementary college course. Tables. 102 illus. 204pp. 4½ x 7. T682 Clothbound **$2.00**

TEACH YOURSELF THE CALCULUS, P. Abbott. With algebra and trigonometry you will be able to acquire a good working knowledge of elementary integral calculus and differential calculus. Excellent supplement to any course textbook. 380pp. 4¼ x 7. T683 Clothbound **$2.00**

TEACH YOURSELF THE SLIDE RULE, B. Snodgrass. Basic principles clearly explained, with many applications in engineering, business, general figuring, will enable you to pick up very useful skill. 10 illus. 207pp. 4¼ x 7. T684 Clothbound **$2.00**

TEACH YOURSELF MECHANICS, P. Abbott. Equivalent of part course on elementary college level, with lever, parallelogram of force, friction, laws of motion, gases, etc. Fine introduction before more advanced course. 163 illus. 271pp. 4½ x 7. T685 Clothbound **$2.00**

TEACH YOURSELF ELECTRICITY, C. W. Wilman. Current, resistance, voltage, Ohm's law, circuits, generators, motors, transformers, etc. Non-mathematical as much as possible. 115 illus. 184pp. 4¼ x 7. T230 Clothbound **$2.00**

TEACH YOURSELF HEAT ENGINES E. DeVille. Steam and internal combustion engines; non-mathematical introduction for student, for layman wishing background, refresher for advanced student. 76 illus. 217pp. 4¼ x 7. T237 Clothbound **$2.00**

TEACH YOURSELF TO PLAY THE PIANO, King Palmer. Companion and supplement to lessons or self study. Handy reference, too. Nature of instrument, elementary musical theory, technique of playing, interpretation, etc. 60 illus. 144pp. 4¼ x 7. T959 Clothbound **$2.00**

TEACH YOURSELF HERALDRY AND GENEALOGY, L. G. Pine. Modern work, avoiding romantic and overpopular misconceptions. Editor of new Burke presents detailed information and commentary down to present. Best general survey. 50 illus. glossary; 129pp. 4¼ x 7. T962 Clothbound **$2.00**

TEACH YOURSELF HANDWRITING, John L. Dumpleton. Basic Chancery cursive style is popular and easy to learn. Many diagrams. 114 illus. 192pp. 4¼ x 7. T960 Clothbound **$2.00**

TEACH YOURSELF CARD GAMES FOR TWO, Kenneth Konstam. Many first-rate games, including old favorites like cribbage and gin and canasta as well as new lesser-known games. Extremely interesting for cards enthusiast. 60 illus. 150pp. 4¼ x 7. T963 Clothbound **$2.00**

TEACH YOURSELF GUIDEBOOK TO THE DRAMA, Luis Vargas. Clear, rapid survey of changing fashions and forms from Aeschylus to Tennessee Williams, in all major European traditions. Plot summaries, critical comments, etc. Equivalent of a college drama course; fine cultural background 224pp. 4¼ x 7. T961 Clothbound **$2.00**

TEACH YOURSELF THE ORGAN, Francis Routh. Excellent compendium of background material for everyone interested in organ music, whether as listener or player. 27 musical illus. 158pp. 4¼ x 7. T977 Clothbound **$2.00**

TEACH YOURSELF TO STUDY SCULPTURE, William Gaunt. Noted British cultural historian surveys culture from Greeks, primitive world, to moderns. Equivalent of college survey course. 23 figures, 40 photos. 158pp. 4¼ x 7. T976 Clothbound **$2.00**

Miscellaneous

THE COMPLETE KANO JIU-JITSU (JUDO), H. I. Hancock and K. Higashi. Most comprehensive guide to judo, referred to as outstanding work by Encyclopaedia Britannica. Complete authentic Japanese system of 160 holds and throws, including the most spectacular, fully illustrated with 487 photos. Full text explains leverage, weight centers, pressure points, special tricks, etc.; shows how to protect yourself from almost any manner of attack though your attacker may have the initial advantage of strength and surprise. This authentic Kano system should not be confused with the many American imitations. xii + 500pp. 5⅜ x 8.
T639 Paperbound **$2.00**

THE MEMOIRS OF JACQUES CASANOVA. Splendid self-revelation by history's most engaging scoundrel—utterly dishonest with women and money, yet highly intelligent and observant. Here are all the famous duels, scandals, amours, banishments, thefts, treacheries, and imprisonments all over Europe: a life lived to the fullest and recounted with gusto in one of the greatest autobiographies of all time. What is more, these Memoirs are also one of the most trustworthy and valuable documents we have on the society and culture of the extravagant 18th century. Here are Voltaire, Louis XV, Catherine the Great, cardinals, castrati, pimps, and pawnbrokers—an entire glittering civilization unfolding before you with an unparalleled sense of actuality. Translated by Arthur Machen. Edited by F. A. Blossom. Introduction by Arthur Symons. Illustrated by Rockwell Kent. Total of xlviii + 2216pp. 5⅜ x 8.
T338 Vol I   Paperbound **$2.00**
T339 Vol II   Paperbound **$2.00**
T340 Vol III Paperbound **$2.00**
The set **$6.00**

BARNUM'S OWN STORY, P. T. Barnum. The astonishingly frank and gratifyingly well-written autobiography of the master showman and pioneer publicity man reveals the truth about his early career, his famous hoaxes (such as the Fejee Mermaid and the Woolly Horse), his amazing commercial ventures, his filing in politics, his feuds and friendships, his failures and surprising comebacks. A vast panorama of 19th century America's mores, amusements, and vitality. 66 new illustrations in this edition. xii + 500pp. 5⅜ x 8.
T764 Paperbound **$1.65**

THE STORY OF THE TITANIC AS TOLD BY ITS SURVIVORS, ed. by Jack Winocour. Most significant accounts of most overpowering naval disaster of modern times: all 4 authors were survivors. Includes 2 full-length, unabridged books: "The Loss of the S.S. Titanic," by Laurence Beesley, "The Truth about the Titanic," by Col. Archibald Gracie; 6 pertinent chapters from "Titanic and Other Ships," autobiography of only officer to survive, Second Officer Charles Lightoller; and a short, dramatic account by the Titanic's wireless operator, Harold Bride. 26 illus. 368pp. 5⅜ x 8.
T610 Paperbound **$1.50**

THE PHYSIOLOGY OF TASTE, Jean Anthelme Brillat-Savarin. Humorous, satirical, witty, and personal classic on joys of food and drink by 18th century French politician, litterateur. Treats the science of gastronomy, erotic value of truffles, Parisian restaurants, drinking contests; gives recipes for tunny omelette, pheasant, Swiss fondue, etc. Only modern translation of original French edition. Introduction. 41 illus. 346pp. 5⅝ x 8⅜.
T591 Paperbound **$1.50**

THE ART OF THE STORY-TELLER, M. L. Shedlock. This classic in the field of effective storytelling is regarded by librarians, story-tellers, and educators as the finest and most lucid book on the subject. The author considers the nature of the story, the difficulties of communicating stories to children, the artifices used in story-telling, how to obtain and maintain the effect of the story, and, of extreme importance, the elements to seek and those to avoid in selecting material. A 99-page selection of Miss Shedlock's most effective stories and an extensive bibliography of further material by Eulalie Steinmetz enhance the book's usefulness. xxi + 320pp. 5⅜ x 8.
T635 Paperbound **$1.50**

CREATIVE POWER: THE EDUCATION OF YOUTH IN THE CREATIVE ARTS, Hughes Mearns. In first printing considered revolutionary in its dynamic, progressive approach to teaching the creative arts; now accepted as one of the most effective and valuable approaches yet formulated. Based on the belief that every child has something to contribute, it provides in a stimulating manner invaluable and inspired teaching insights, to stimulate children's latent powers of creative expression in drama, poetry, music, writing, etc. Mearns's methods were developed in his famous experimental classes in creative education at the Lincoln School of Teachers College, Columbia Univ. Named one of the 20 foremost books on education in recent times by National Education Association. New enlarged revised 2nd edition. Introduction. 272pp. 5⅜ x 8.
T490 Paperbound **$1.75**

FREE AND INEXPENSIVE EDUCATIONAL AIDS, T. J. Pepe, Superintendent of Schools, Southbury, Connecticut. An up-to-date listing of over 1500 booklets, films, charts, etc. 5% costs less than 25¢; 1% costs more; 94% is yours for the asking. Use this material privately, or in schools from elementary to college, for discussion, vocational guidance, projects. 59 categories include health, trucking, textiles, language, weather, the blood, office practice, wild life, atomic energy, other important topics. Each item described according to contents, number of pages or running time, level. All material is educationally sound, and without political or company bias. 1st publication. Second, revised edition. Index. 244pp. 5⅜ x 8.
T663 Paperbound **$1.50**

New Books

101 PATCHWORK PATTERNS, Ruby Short McKim. With no more ability than the fundamentals of ordinary sewing, you will learn to make over 100 beautiful quilts: flowers, rainbows, Irish chains, fish and bird designs, leaf designs, unusual geometric patterns, many others. Cutting designs carefully diagrammed and described, suggestions for materials, yardage estimates, step-by-step instructions, plus entertaining stories of origins of quilt names, other folklore. Revised 1962. 101 full-sized patterns. 140 illustrations. Index. 128pp. 7⅞ x 10¾.
T773 Paperbound **$1.85**

ESSENTIAL GRAMMAR SERIES
By concentrating on the essential core of material that constitutes the semantically most important forms and areas of a language and by stressing explanation (often bringing parallel English forms into the discussion) rather than rote memory, this new series of grammar books is among the handiest language aids ever devised. Designed by linguists and teachers for adults with limited learning objectives and learning time, these books omit nothing important, yet they teach more usable language material and do it more quickly and permanently than any other self-study material. Clear and rigidly economical, they concentrate upon immediately usable language material, logically organized so that related material is always presented together. Any reader of typical capability can use them to refresh his grasp of language, to supplement self-study language records or conventional grammars used in schools, or to begin language study on his own. Now available:

ESSENTIAL GERMAN GRAMMAR, Dr. Guy Stern & E. F. Bleiler. Index. Glossary of terms. 128pp. 5⅜ x 8.
T422 Paperbound **$1.00**

ESSENTIAL FRENCH GRAMMAR, Dr. Seymour Resnick. Index. Cognate list. Glossary. 159pp. 5⅜ x 8.
T419 Paperbound **$1.00**

ESSENTIAL ITALIAN GRAMMAR, Dr. Olga Ragusa. Index. Glossary. 111pp. 5⅜ x 8.
T779 Paperbound **$1.00**

ESSENTIAL SPANISH GRAMMAR, Dr. Seymour Resnick. Index. 50-page cognate list. Glossary. 138pp. 5⅜ x 8.
T780 Paperbound **$1.00**

PHILOSOPHIES OF MUSIC HISTORY: A Study of General Histories of Music, 1600-1960, Warren D. Allen. Unquestionably one of the most significant documents yet to appear in musicology, this thorough survey covers the entire field of historical research in music. An influential masterpiece of scholarship, it includes early music histories; theories on the ethos of music; lexicons, dictionaries and encyclopedias of music; musical historiography through the centuries; philosophies of music history; scores of related topics. Copiously documented. New preface brings work up to 1960. Index. 317-item bibliography. 9 illustrations; 3 full-page plates. 5⅜ x 8½. xxxiv + 382pp.
T282 Paperbound **$2.00**

MR. DOOLEY ON IVRYTHING AND IVRYBODY, Finley Peter Dunne. The largest collection in print of hilarious utterances by the irrepressible Irishman of Archey Street, one of the most vital characters in American fiction. Gathered from the half dozen books that appeared during the height of Mr. Dooley's popularity, these 102 pieces are all unaltered and uncut, and they are all remarkably fresh and pertinent even today. Selected and edited by Robert Hutchinson. 5⅜ x 8½. xii + 244p.
T626 Paperbound **$1.00**

TREATISE ON PHYSIOLOGICAL OPTICS, Hermann von Helmholtz. Despite new investigations, this important work will probably remain preeminent. Contains everything known about physiological optics up to 1925, covering scores of topics under the general headings of dioptrics of the eye, sensations of vision, and perecptions of vision. Von Helmholtz's voluminous data are all included, as are extensive supplementary matter incorporated into the third German edition, new material prepared for 1925 English edition, and copious textual annotations by J. P. C. Southall. The most exhaustive treatise ever prepared on the subject, it has behind it a list of contributors that will never again be duplicated. Translated and edited by J. P. C. Southall. Bibliography. Indexes. 312 illustrations. 3 volumes bound as 2. Total of 1749pp. 5⅜ x 8.
S15-16 Two volume set, Clothbound **$15.00**

THE ARTISTIC ANATOMY OF TREES, Rex Vicat Cole. Even the novice with but an elementary knowledge of drawing and none of the structure of trees can learn to draw, paint trees from this systematic, lucid instruction book. Copiously illustrated with the author's own sketches, diagrams, and 50 paintings from the early Renaissance to today, it covers composition; structure of twigs, boughs, buds, branch systems; outline forms of major species; how leaf is set on twig; flowers and fruit and their arrangement; etc. 500 illustrations. Bibliography. Indexes. 347pp. 5⅜ x 8.
T1016 Clothbound **$4.50**

CATALOGUE OF DOVER BOOKS

HOW PLANTS GET THEIR NAMES, L. H. Bailey. In this basic introduction to botanical nomenclature, a famed expert on plants and plant life reveals the confusion that can result from misleading common names of plants and points out the fun and advantage of using a sound, scientific approach. Covers every aspect of the subject, including an historical survey beginning before Linnaeus systematized nomenclature, the literal meaning of scores of Latin names, their English equivalents, etc. Enthusiastically written and easy to follow, this handbook for gardeners, amateur horticulturalists, and beginning botany students is knowledgeable, accurate and useful. 11 illustrations. Lists of Latin, English botanical names. 192pp. 5⅜ x 8½.   T796 Paperbound **$1.15**

PIERRE CURIE, Marie Curie. Nobel Prize winner creates a memorable portrait of her equally famous husband in a fine scientific biography. Recounting his childhood, his haphazard education, and his experimental research (with his brother) in the physics of crystals, Mme. Curie brings to life the strong, determined personality of a great scientist at work and discusses, in clear, straightforward terms, her husband's and her own work with radium and radioactivity. A great book about two very great founders of modern science. Includes Mme. Curie's autobiographical notes. Translated by Charlotte and Vernon Kellogg. viii + 120pp. 5⅜ x 8½.   T199 Paperbound **$1.00**

STYLES IN PAINTING: A Comparative Study, Paul Zucker. Professor of Art History at Cooper Union presents an important work of art-understanding that will guide you to a fuller, deeper appreciation of masterpieces of art and at the same time add to your understanding of how they fit into the evolution of style from the earliest times to this century. Discusses general principles of historical method and aesthetics, history of styles, then illustrates with more than 230 great paintings organized by subject matter so you can see at a glance how styles have changed through the centuries. 236 beautiful halftones. xiv + 338pp. 5⅝ x 8½.
                                                                        T760 Paperbound **$2.00**

NEW VARIORUM EDITION OF SHAKESPEARE

One of the monumental feats of Shakespeare scholarship is the famous New Variorum edition, containing full texts of the plays together with an entire reference library worth of historical and critical information: all the variant readings that appear in the quartos and folios; annotations by leading scholars from the earliest days of Shakespeare criticism to the date of publication; essays on meaning, background, productions by Johnson, Addison, Fielding, Lessing, Hazlitt, Coleridge, Ulrici, Swinburne, and other major Shakespeare critics; original sources of Shakespeare's inspiration. For the first time, this definitive edition of Shakespeare's plays, each printed in a separate volume, will be available in inexpensive editions to scholars, to teachers and students, and to every lover of Shakespeare and fine literature. Now ready:

KING LEAR, edited by Horace Howard Furness. Bibliography. List of editions collated in notes. viii + 503pp. 5⅜ x 8½.   T1000 Paperbound **$2.25**

MACBETH, edited by Horace Howard Furness Jr. Bibliography. List of editions collated in notes. xvi + 562pp. 5⅜ x 8½.   T1001 Paperbound **$2.25**

ROMEO AND JULIET, edited by Horace Howard Furness. Bibliography. List of editions collated in notes. xxvi + 480pp. 5⅜ x 8½.   T1002 Paperbound **$2.25**

OTTHELLO, edited by Horace Howard Furness. Bibliography. List of editions collated in notes. x + 471pp. 5⅜ x 8½.   T1003 Paperbound **$2.25**

HAMLET, edited by Horace Howard Furness. Bibliography. List of editions collated in notes. Total of 926pp. 5⅜ x 8½.   T1004-1005 Two volume set, Paperbound **$4.50**

THE GARDENER'S YEAR, Karel Capek. The author of this refreshingly funny book is probably best known in U. S. as the author of "R. U. R.," a biting satire on the machine age. Here, his satiric genius finds expression in a wholly different vein: a warm, witty chronicle of the joys and trials of the amateur gardener as he watches over his plants, his soil and the weather from January to December. 59 drawings by Joseph Capek add an important second dimension to the fun. "Mr. Capek writes with sympathy, understanding and humor," NEW YORK TIMES. "Will delight the amateur gardener, and indeed everyone else," SATURDAY REVIEW. Translated by M. and R. Weatherall. 59 illustrations. 159pp. 4½ x 6½.
                                                                        T1014 Paperbound **$1.00**

THE ADVANCE OF THE FUNGI, E. C. Large. The dramatic story of the battle against fungi, from the year the potato blight hit Europe (1845) to 1940, and of men who fought and won it: Pasteur, Anton de Bary, Tulasne, Berkeley, Woronin, Jensen, many others. Combines remarkable grasp of facts and their significance with skill to write dramatic, exciting prose. "Philosophically witty, fundamentally thoughtful, always mature," NEW YORK HERALD TRIBUNE. "Highly entertaining, intelligent, penetrating," NEW YORKER. Bibliography. 64 illustrations. 6 full-page plates. 488pp. 5⅜ x 8½.   T437 Paperbound **$2.25**

THE PAINTER'S METHODS AND MATERIALS, A. P. Laurie. Adviser to the British Royal Academy discusses the ills that paint is heir to and the methods most likely to counteract them. Examining 48 masterpieces by Fra Lippo Lippi, Millais, Boucher, Rembrandt, Romney, Van Eyck, Velazquez, Michaelangelo, Botticelli, Frans Hals, Turner, and others, he tries to discover how special and unique effects were achieved. Not conjectural information, but certain and authoritative. Beautiful, sharp reproductions, plus textual illustrations of apparatus and the results of experiments with pigments and media. 63 illustrations and diagrams. Index. 250pp. 5⅜ x 8.   T1019 Clothbound **$3.75**

CATALOGUE OF DOVER BOOKS

CHANCE, LUCK AND STATISTICS, H. C. Levinson. The theory of chance, or probability, and the science of statistics presented in simple, non-technical language. Covers fundamentals by analyzing games of chance, then applies those fundamentals to immigration and birth rates, operations research, stock speculation, insurance rates, advertising, and other fields. Excellent course supplement and a delightful introduction for non-mathematicians. Formerly "The Science of Chance." Index. xiv + 356pp. 5⅜ x 8. **T1007 Paperbound $1.85**

THROUGH THE ALIMENTARY CANAL WITH GUN AND CAMERA: A Fascinating Trip to the Interior, George S. Chappell. An intrepid explorer, better known as a major American humorist, accompanied by imaginary camera-man and botanist, conducts this unforgettably hilarious journey to the human interior. Wildly imaginative, his account satirizes academic pomposity, parodies cliché-ridden travel literature, and cleverly uses facts of physiology for comic purposes. All the original line drawings by Otto Soglow are included to add to the merriment. Preface by Robert Benchley. 17 illustrations. xii + 116pp. 5⅜ x 8½. **T376 Paperbound $1.00**

TALKS TO TEACHERS ON PSYCHOLOGY and to Students on Some of Life's Ideals, William James. America's greatest psychologist invests these lectures with immense personal charm, invaluable insights, and superb literary style. 15 Harvard lectures, 3 lectures delivered to students in New England touch upon psychology and the teaching of art, stream of consciousness, the child as a behaving organism, education and behavior, association of ideas, the gospel of relaxation, what makes life significant, and other related topics. Interesting, and still vital pedagogy. x + 146pp. 5⅜ x 8½. **T261 Paperbound $1.00**

A WHIMSEY ANTHOLOGY, collected by Carolyn Wells. Delightful verse on the lighter side: logical whimsies, poems shaped like decanters and flagons, lipograms and acrostics, alliterative verse, enigmas and charades, anagrams, linguistic and dialectic verse, tongue twisters, limericks, travesties, and just about very other kind of whimsical poetry ever written. Works by Edward Lear, Gelett Burgess, Poe, Lewis Carroll, Henley, Robert Herrick, Christina Rossetti, scores of other poets will entertain and amuse you for hours. Index. xiv + 221pp. 5⅜ x 8½. **T1020 Paperbound $1.25**

LANDSCAPE PAINTING, R. O. Dunlop. A distinguished modern artist is a perfect guide to the aspiring landscape painter. This practical book imparts to even the uninitiated valuable methods and techniques. Useful advice is interwoven throughout a fascinating illustrated history of landscape painting, from Ma Yüan to Picasso. 60 half-tone reproductions of works by Giotto, Giovanni Bellini, Piero della Francesca, Tintoretto, Giorgione, Raphael, Van Ruisdael, Poussin, Gainsborough, Monet, Cezanne, Seurat, Picasso, many others. Total of 71 illustrations, 4 in color. Index. 192pp. 7⅜ x 10. **T1018 Clothbound $6.00**

PRACTICAL LANDSCAPE PAINTING, Adrian Stokes. A complete course in landscape painting that trains the senses to perceive as well as the hand to apply the principles underlying the pictorial aspect of nature. Author fully explains tools, value and nature of various colors, and instructs beginners in clear, simple terms how to apply them. Places strong emphasis on drawing and composition, foundations often neglected in painting texts. Includes pictorial-textual survey of the art from Ancient China to the present, with helpful critical comments and numerous diagrams illustrating every stage. 93 illustrations. Index. 256pp. 5⅜ x 8. **T1017 Clothbound $3.75**

PELLUCIDAR, THREE NOVELS: AT THE EARTH'S CORE, PELLUCIDAR, TANAR OF PELLUCIDAR, Edgar Rice Burroughs. The first three novels of adventure in the thrill-filled world within the hollow interior of the earth. David Innes's mechanical mole drills through the outer crust and precipitates him into an astonishing world. Among Burroughs's most popular work. Illustrations by J. Allan St. John. 5⅜ x 8½. **T1051 Paperbound $2.00**
T1050 Clothbound $3.75

JOE MILLER'S JESTS OR, THE WITS VADE-MECUM. Facsimile of the first edition of famous 18th century collection of repartees, bons mots, puns and jokes, the father of the humor anthology. A first-hand look at the taste of fashionable London in the Age of Pope. 247 entertaining anecdotes, many involving well-known personages such as Colley Cibber, Sir Thomas More, Rabelais, rich in humor, historic interest. New introduction contains biographical information on Joe Miller, fascinating history of his enduring collection, bibliographical information on collections of comic material. Introduction by Robert Hutchinson. 96pp. 5⅜ x 8½. **Paperbound $1.00**

THE HUMOROUS WORLD OF JEROME K. JEROME. Complete essays and extensive passages from nine out-of-print books ("Three Men on Wheels," "Novel Notes," "Told After Supper," "Sketches in Lavender, Blue and Green," "American Wives and Others," 4 more) by a highly original humorist, author of the novel "Three Men in a Boat." Human nature is JKJ's subject: the problems of husbands, of wives, of tourists, of the human animal trapped in the drawing room. His sympathetic acceptance of the shortcomings of his race and his ability to see humor in almost any situation make this a treasure for those who know his work and a pleasant surprise for those who don't. Edited and with an introduction by Robert Hutchinson. xii + 260pp. 5⅜ x 8½. **T58 Paperbound $1.00**

CATALOGUE OF DOVER BOOKS

GEOMETRY OF FOUR DIMENSIONS, H. P. Manning. Unique in English as a clear, concise intro-duction to this fascinating subject. Treatment is primarily synthetic and Euclidean, although hyperplanes and hyperspheres at infinity are considered by non-Euclidean forms. Historical introduction and foundations of 4-dimensional geometry; perpendicularity; simple angles; angles of planes; higher order; symmetry; order, motion; hyperpyramids, hypercones, hyper-spheres; figures with parallel elements; volume, hypervolume in space; regular polyhedroids. Glossary of terms. 74 illustrations. ix + 348pp. 5⅜ x 8. S182 Paperbound **$2.00**

PAPER FOLDING FOR BEGINNERS, W. D. Murray and F. J. Rigney. A delightful introduction to the varied and entertaining Japanese art of origami (paper folding), with a full, crystal-clear text that anticipates every difficulty; over 275 clearly labeled diagrams of all important stages in creation. You get results at each stage, since complex figures are logically developed from simpler ones. 43 different pieces are explained: sailboats, frogs, roosters, etc. 6 photographic plates. 279 diagrams. 95pp. 5⅝ x 8⅜. T713 Paperbound **$1.00**

SATELLITES AND SCIENTIFIC RESEARCH, D. King-Hele. An up-to-the-minute non-technical ac-count of the man-made satellites and the discoveries they have yielded up to September of 1961. Brings together information hitherto published only in hard-to-get scientific journals. In-cludes the life history of a typical satellite, methods of tracking, new information on the shape of the earth, zones of radiation, etc. Over 60 diagrams and 6 photographs. Mathemati-cal appendix. Bibliography of over 100 items. Index. xii + 180pp. 5⅜ x 8½. T703 Paperbound **$2.00**

LOUIS PASTEUR, S. J. Holmes. A brief, very clear, and warmly understanding biography of the great French scientist by a former Professor of Zoology in the University of California. Traces his home life, the fortunate effects of his education, his early researches and first theses, and his constant struggle with superstition and institutionalism in his work on microorganisms, fermentation, anthrax, rabies, etc. New preface by the author. 159pp. 5⅜ x 8. T197 Paperbound **$1.00**

THE ENJOYMENT OF CHESS PROBLEMS, K. S. Howard. A classic treatise on this minor art by an internationally recognized authority that gives a basic knowledge of terms and themes for the everyday chess player as well as the problem fan: 7 chapters on the two-mover; 7 more on 3- and 4-move problems; a chapter on selfmates; and much more. "The most important one-volume contribution originating solely in the U.S.A.," Alain White. 200 diagrams. Index. Solutions, viii + 212pp. 5⅜ x 8. T742 Paperbound **$1.25**

SAM LOYD AND HIS CHESS PROBLEMS, Alain C. White. Loyd was (for all practical purposes) the father of the American chess problem and his protégé and successor presents here the diamonds of his production, chess problems embodying a whimsy and bizarre fancy entirely unique. More than 725 in all, ranging from two-move to extremely elaborate five-movers, including Loyd's contributions to chess oddities—problems in which pieces are arranged to form initials, figures, other by-paths of chess problem found nowhere else. Classified accord-ing to major concept, with full text analyzing problems, containing selections from Loyd's own writings. A classic to challenge your ingenuity, increase your skill. Corrected republica-tion of 1913 edition. Over 750 diagrams and illustrations. 744 problems with solutions. 471pp. 5⅜ x 8½. T928 Paperbound **$2.25**

FABLES IN SLANG & MORE FABLES IN SLANG, George Ade. 2 complete books of major American humorist in pungent colloquial tradition of Twain, Billings. 1st reprinting in over 30 years includes "The Two Mandolin Players and the Willing Performer," "The Base Ball Fan Who Took the Only Known Cure," "The Slim Girl Who Tried to Keep a Date that was Never Made," 42 other tales of eccentric, perverse, but always funny characters. "Touch of genius," H. L. Mencken. New introduction by E. F. Bleiler. 86 illus. 208pp. 5⅜ x 8. T533 Paperbound **$1.00**

Prices subject to change without notice.

Dover publishes books on art, music, philosophy, literature, languages, history, social sciences, psychology, handcrafts, orientalia, puzzles and entertainments, chess, pets and gardens, books explaining science, intermediate and higher mathematics, math-ematical physics, engineering, biological sciences, earth sciences; classics of science, etc. Write to:

Dept. catrr.
Dover Publications, Inc.
180 Varick Street, N. Y. 14, N. Y.